THE AMERICAN
PLAY-PARTY SONG

THE AMERICAN PLAY-PARTY SONG

B. A. BOTKIN

FREDERICK UNGAR PUBLISHING CO.
NEW YORK

First published 1937
in the University Studies of the University of Nebraska,
Vol. XXXVIII, Nos. 1-4

Printed in the United States of America

Library of Congress Catalog Card No. 63-22456

TO THE MEMORY OF

LOUISE POUND

(1872-1958)

TEACHER, MENTOR, FRIEND

PREFACE — 1963

Looking back on the quarter-century that has elapsed since this book was first published, I can report that, although the play-party has vanished as a social institution, it has not been sunk without a trace. As part of our folk music heritage, the play-party has had an estimable place in the present folklore and folksong revival. Play-party games serve as mixers at square dances and folk and country dance sessions. In school, camp, and playground circles, the games are taught to youngsters as rhythmic play. Texts, tunes, and directions for playing are published in the literature of recreation, physical education, school music, singing games, and folk dance as well as in scholarly collections and studies. Play-party songs are also being made available on records.

For these reasons, and in response to some demand, it seemed that the time was ripe to bring *The American Play-Party Song* back into print. At one time I had thought of revising the book and bringing it up to date. But since I have not changed my conclusions and since no important body of new material or theory has appeared, I have decided to let the book stand in its original form, except for a few minor corrections. To omit or abridge any of the documentation and analysis would, it seemed, impair the usefulness of the study for reference or teaching.

A word may be in order here as to how I came to write this book, as the first of my folklore studies to be undertaken though not the first to be published. In 1926, five years after I began teaching English at the University of Oklahoma, I went in quest of a dissertation subject. I was unhappy with the general run of Ph.D. subjects in English literature and was removed from good research libraries. I looked about me for a field of investigation in which I could make a collection of new material and a fresh interpretation. Fortunately, I had come to Oklahoma at a time when physical pioneering had given way to cultural pioneering in the form of the Southwest folk and regional movement, with which I became identified in 1926. Among pioneer customs the play-party was still alive in the usage of young people as well as in the memories of old-timers, and the moment was favorable for a study of the folk process of survival and revival.

In the late Twenties, at rural and small-town birthday and high school parties, ice cream and watermelon socials, "swinging plays"

1

still found favor as an occasional change from more sophisticated games. At the University play-party games were taught in women's physical education and playground-leaders' training classes. State folklore societies and publications stimulated research in the songs of frontier folk. The genesis of my book was an article on "The Play-Party in Oklahoma," published in the Texas Folklore Society's *Foller de Drinkin' Gou'd* in 1928. This was based on a paper read at the 1928 meeting of the Oklahoma Folklore Society, after which I coined the word "Folk-Say" as the title of the Society's first publication by the newly founded University of Oklahoma Press in 1929.

It was in connection with another revival, the poetry and ballad revival on the University of Oklahoma campus, that I became interested in the play-party as part of a projected study of American folk poetry in ballads, folk songs, singing games, and square dance jingles. This larger field of interest was gradually narrowed to traditional play and dance songs and rhymes, and, finally, to the play-party song.

While my interest was primarily literary and folkloristic, it was at the same time functional. I was interested in the play-party as a rural and pioneer amusement which flourished on a make-it-yourself-or-do-without level of culture and which tended to disappear when cultural isolation was broken and religious objections against dancing were relaxed.

For much of my theoretical background I am indebted to the late Louise Pound. By coincidence, unaware that I was ultimately to complete my dissertation under her at the University of Nebraska in 1931, in 1926 I first read in her *Poetic Origins and the Ballad* (1921) that, far from originating in the "ballad dance," narrative folk songs deteriorate under the wearing usage of the dance. In studying the threefold relationship of the play-party to the game, the dance, and the song I had an opportunity to test her conclusions and also to carry them a step further.

In dedicating this new edition to Louise Pound's memory I want to pay tribute to her stimulating guidance of the book through its later stages as acknowledged in my original preface, as well as to her continued, unstinting encouragement and assistance over three decades and the constant inspiration of her interdisciplinary, humanistic scholarship in the fields of literature, dialect, and folklore.

More than cultural data for her theory of poetic origins, the play-party was part of Louise Pound's Midwest pioneer heritage, which she never forgot. In a paper on "Old Nebraska Folk Customs" in 1946 she wrote prophetically: "The present revival of folksong and folk dance in general, especially of the square dance, has brought with it the revival of many dances of the old circle and line type, and it may bring the renewal to some extent of the play-party. But if so, it will be conducted in more sophisticated surroundings than in pioneer days. . . ."

Yet for all our sophistication and self-consciousness the revival and study of play-party games may well make us more appreciative of and eager to recover, in an age of mass entertainment, the unselfconscious "togetherness" of old-time amusements involving the participation of the whole group. As Lewis Gannett wrote in his 1937 review of the book: "One of the great problems before America is the rediscovery of that spontaneity which was ours before we began reading about ourselves in books."

B. A. BOTKIN

Croton-on-Hudson, N.Y.
August, 1963

PREFACE

I

THE American play-party song is unique in the history of folk-song. *Danser aux chansons* is well-nigh instinctive in man, and dance-songs have existed in virtually all times, places, and languages. The fact that such songs have not always come down to us is not to be taken as evidence that they did not exist, but is to be attributed to the ephemeral nature of rude improvisations which were not thought worthy of preservation. And yet, in spite of the universality of dance-songs, there is nothing quite like the play-party to be found outside of America. The very name is American; and distinctively American are the form and content of the songs.

The peculiar nature of the play-party and the peculiar importance and interest attaching to it arise largely from the influence of the square dance, which in its tunes and calls is another typically American offshoot of an Old-World stock—an influence so strong that in many cases the play-party song consists of little or nothing more than dance calls affixed to jingles and formulae borrowed or adapted from traditional games, nursery rhymes, ballads and other folk-songs, and popular songs. This anomalous, hybrid, eclectic character of the play-party, which is thus game, dance, and song all in one and yet no one of them in particular, complicated by all the accidents of oral transmission and the whims of local and temporal adaptation and improvisation, provides an unusual opportunity for the study of the problems and processes of folk-song.

In addition to their literary and folkloristic interest, play-party songs possess a certain value for the social historian. For in spite of the preponderance of rigmarole, repetition, and refrain (which make up the framework of movement songs), they contain a good deal of authentic and dramatic portrayal of the background and interests of the players, the objects, activities, and characters of rural and pioneer America. Their wild, rude medley of realism and nonsense — childish, humorous, picturesque, and satirically sentimental — is a creation of the American frontier.

For a brief while, before its ultimate disappearance, the shifting frontier has paused in the Southwest, where, in Oklahoma, with its successive land-openings and waves of migration from neighboring states and the East, the play-party may be studied in cross-section. Here the songs first entered with the cattlemen on the trail and continued to drift in with the settlers in the course of a series of openings beginning in 1889. In these migrations Kentucky, Tennessee, Iowa, Nebraska, Missouri, Kansas, Arkansas, and Texas have contributed the largest share of play-party material.

Against this rich and varied background, a survey made among teachers and students at the State University and in high schools through the state in 1926-1927—before the play-party's destined extinction in the death-struggle of pioneering and civilization—has yielded over a thousand variants of one hundred and twenty-eight play-party songs—two or three times as many as have appeared in any one printing, including versions of almost all the songs recovered in other states and many never before published. This material, sifted from a large body of ballads, folk-songs, counting-out rhymes, children's games, and dance calls, was obtained through the combined efforts of seventeen university and high-school teachers of English and some six hundred students of English, besides other interested individuals ranging from newspaper editors to square dance musicians and callers. Sixty-three of the seventy-seven counties in the state are known to be represented, and since in many cases the provenience was not given the chances are that nearly all counties have been heard from.[1]

Since the bulk of the songs were taken down by students from their own singing as well as from that of relatives and friends (principally during the Christmas and Easter holidays), they are offered as representative of the play-party usage of both the younger and older generations. Of the tendency on the part of young folk of today to apologize for and come to the defense of an outworn custom, half-ashamed, half-defiant, the following statement is typical:

> Although I am acquainted with various folk-songs and the manner in which they are carried out and played, that does not necessarily mean that I am an inhabitant of a district remote from civilization; neither does it mean that I was reared under conditions fifty years behind time. It is true that my father and mother while young played the games which appear odd to most people at the present time, but they took as much interest in their games as we do in the modernized party games. And I might say that the old party games are very beautiful and afford much fun to those who engage in them.

II

The working apparatus of the collection of Oklahoma play-party songs printed in Part Two is explained in detail in the introductory note thereto.

---

[1] The Oklahoma counties represented are as follows: Alfalfa, Atoka, Beaver, Beckham, Blaine, Caddo, Canadian, Carter (the Choctaw Nation), Cleveland, Coal, Comanche, Cotton, Craig, Creek, Custer, Dewey, Ellis, Garfield, Garvin, Grady, Grant, Jackson, Jefferson, Kay, Kingfisher, Kiowa, Latimer, LeFlore, Lincoln, Logan, Love, Major, Mayes, McClain, McCurtain, McIntosh, Murray, Muskogee, Noble, Nowata, Okfuskee, Oklahoma, Okmulgee, Osage, Ottawa, Payne, Pittsburg, Pontotoc, Pottawatomie, Pushmataha, Roger Mills, Rogers, Seminole, Sequoyah, Stephens, Texas, Tillman, Tulsa, Wagoner, Washington, Washita, Woods, Woodward.

But at this point certain considerations of terminology and procedure are in order.

First, as to the term "Oklahoma play-party song"—short for "play-party song found in Oklahoma"—, this is meant to include all songs recovered in Oklahoma, irrespective of their source, on the analogy of the term "ballad found in America," which is taken to mean all "ballads derived from singers and reciters living in the United States, no matter what the original nationality of the reciters or singers." [2] In Part One an attempt has been made to distinguish between the troublesome terms "version" and "variant"—the former to denote texts recovered from different states (or, in the case of Great Britain, different countries), on the basis of their possessing marked differences, and the latter to denote a copy of a song recovered within the state, generally one with minor variations; but in the headnotes in Part Two this distinction has been abandoned as needlessly awkward, and the term "text" generally preferred. To distinguish songs collected in Oklahoma but not known to have been played there, a hyphenated term—e.g., Oklahoma-Missouri—is sometimes employed, signifying that the song has been communicated by some one living in Oklahoma who heard or played it in Missouri.

In selecting the texts printed in Part Two, in each case the most representative have been used; that is, those containing the largest numbers of typical stanzas belonging to the song or the stanzas occurring most frequently in the present collection. In most cases, where they are of sufficient interest, variants are printed either in full (under a distinguishing letter) or in part (under the head of "Variants" or "Variant and Additional Stanzas"). As a matter of record, the names of all informants who have communicated other variants are listed following the texts.

In connection with their respective contributions specific acknowledgments are made to the many friends and informants who have assisted in the task of collection. To the following among them I am indebted for valuable suggestions and other aid: Dr. Josiah H. Combs, of Texas Christian University, for placing at my disposal his manuscript collections of Kentucky and West Virginia play- and dance-songs, as well as some publications not generally accessible; Dr. Lawrence M. Levin, of Columbia University, for reading this material in an earlier form; Dr. Alexander Haggerty Krappe, for suggestions as to method; and Professor Kenneth C. Kaufman, of the University of Oklahoma, for making many of the songs live for me.

---

[2] Compare Reed Smith, "The Traditional Ballad in the South," *JAFL*, 27:55. Dr. Smith here makes a plea for the uniform usage of "version" and "variant" in the senses established by Child—*version* for "a copy with distinguishing characteristics in plot, style, age, atmosphere, or the like" and *variant* for a mere copy without such characteristics.

The following members of the Department of English in the University of Oklahoma, in 1926-1927, were instrumental in putting me in touch with material in the possession of their students: Mr. Roy Lee Atkins, Miss Goldia D. Cooksey, Professor Paul Eldridge, the late Minnie M. Forbes, Mrs. Neva R. Gahring, Miss Winifred Johnston, Professor Elizabeth Jordan, Mrs. Phoebe W. Lowry, Professor Lawrence N. Morgan, the late Annie Laurie Robey, Miss Thelma Wild Rose, and Dr. Jewel Wurtzbaugh.

The following teachers in other institutions rendered invaluable service: Miss Dorothy Long, of Billings High School; Miss Florette McNeese, of Classen High School, Oklahoma City, who kindly placed at my disposal her master's essay on Oklahoma play-party songs; Professor Lena Misener, of Oklahoma City University; Mrs. Edna Muldrow, of Norman High School; and Miss Doris G. Waters, of Ponca City High School.

The following students were especially helpful: Mrs. Marjorie Allen, Lexington; Miss Hattie Bell Bethea, Marion, South Carolina; Clifford Chandler, Crescent; Miss Sarah K. Davis, Oklahoma City; Miss Tephia Folsom, Atoka; Mr. Frank Allan Hanna, Drumright; Paul Howard, Headrick. Professor John Alley, of the University of Oklahoma; Mr. O. B. Campbell, of the *Medford Patriot-Star*; Mr. Alec Gilbreath, dance-caller, of Atoka; the late Ben Hennessy, of Oklahoma City; Mrs. Anne D. McClure, of Oklahoma City; Mrs. L. T. Monnett, of Norman; Mr. Walter Morrow, of Oklahoma City; and Mrs. Della I. Young, of Cheyenne, Oklahoma—all have been generous in their assistance.

To the late Maurice G. Smith, of the Department of Anthropology, University of Oklahoma, I owe the initial suggestion that led to the completion of this study at the University of Nebraska in 1931 under the stimulating guidance of Dr. Louise Pound. To the libraries of Harvard and Columbia Universities and the Universities of Oklahoma and Nebraska, and to J. Frank Dobie, editor of the *Publications of the Texas Folk-Lore Society,* in whose pages, in 1928, my findings first appeared in print, thanks are due.

The collection of sixty-two play-party tunes printed in Part Two was made possible by a faculty research grant of the University of Oklahoma in the spring of 1932. The tunes were recorded in the field by my assistant, Gerald Whitney, now of the music department of Hobart High School and Junior College.

To my wife, finally, for sharing and lightening my labors at every step of the way, I am more than grateful.

Norman, Oklahoma
May, 1936

B. A. BOTKIN

CONTENTS

9

PART ONE
THE AMERICAN PLAY-PARTY

"These amusements came into existence because they were adapted to the conditions of early life; they pass away because those conditions are altered. The taste of other days sustained them; the taste of our day abandons them."

—W. W. NEWELL

CHAPTER I

ORIGINS AND BACKGROUNDS

1. The Game-Song and the Ballad

"The history of the game-rhyme," wrote W. W. Newell in 1903,[1] "is included in that of the ballad." By the term "history" he understands age, transmission (from higher to lower), and common origin in the dance. In the first two of these respects no one would question his claims. The fact, however, that we no longer accept dance origin or any single origin for either ballad or game-song, although both appear in dance usage, is simply an indication of the advance in ballad study made since Newell's day. The fact also indicates that the treatment of the English game-song as a species of folk-song, especially the identification and analysis of the origin of the game-song in other types, is an aspect of the subject that has been comparatively neglected by students of both the ballad and the game.[2]

In her two volumes of *The Traditional Games of England, Scotland, and Ireland,* which appeared in 1894 and 1898, respectively, Lady Alice Bertha Gomme (the wife of the eminent British folklorist, George Laurence Gomme), while making the first exhaustive collection and study of dramatic games and of their methods of play, was still interested in them almost exclusively as evidence of the customs and beliefs of primitive man which exist as survivals in the form and content of games. In his *Games and Songs of American Children,* published in 1883 and in a new and enlarged edition twenty years later, William Wells Newell (1839-1907), the leading organizer of the American Folk-Lore Society, which he helped found in 1888, and its permanent secretary and editor of its *Journal* for the last nineteen years of his life, exhibited stronger interest in the comparative literary and historical side. As a poet and a student of philosophy and European languages and literatures, with a broad historical and human viewpoint, he revivified the whole subject of folklore and of games in particular in this country.[3] And as a result of his literary as well as folkloristic interest, Newell's "selection," as he modestly termed it, although

---

[1] *Games and Songs of American Children,* p. vi.

[2] Newell was, of course, familiar with his friend Child's researches (published in a first edition from 1857 to 1859), as indicated in a foot-note written in the 1883 edition (p. 11), but at that time the work was only in its beginning stage; and though it was completed five years before the appearance of the second edition of *Games and Songs of American Children,* it left little mark even on the latter.

[3] See the memorial notice by F. N. Robinson, *JAFL,* 20:59-60, and the account of the Memorial Meeting in Newell's honor, *ibid.,* pp. 61-66, including the tribute of Franz Boas. In her introduction to *American Ballads and Songs* (pp. xxix and xxxi) Louise Pound acknowledges the importance of Newell as a pioneer among folk-song collectors and scholars in America.

13

it contains a mere handful of texts beside Lady Gomme's encyclopedic "Dictionary" (a model in method as well as a monument in the materials made available), is far more fruitful for the student who approaches the traditional game as a form of folk-song and popular poetry.

As ballad researches have taught us much about the game-song, so, in return, the study of the game-song throws valuable light on the ballad and the folk-song. To the clearing up of the vexed problem of folk-song origins Newell made two contributions, which, if only confirmations rather than discoveries, were much needed and have done much to forward the study in this country. One was the recognition of the significant truth that, without necessarily going all the way back to a bygone age of culture on the ceremonial level, many of the games of children originated or were once popular as rounds, reels, and carols among men and women on the social plane.[4] Newell also perceived the corollary that, far from originating with peasants or describing the life of peasants, "The tradition, on the contrary, invariably came from above, from the intelligent class" and "If these usages seem rustic, it is only because the country retained what the city forgot, in consequence of the change of manners to which it was sooner exposed. Such customs were, at no remote date, the pleasures of courts and palaces."[5] In the same way, he observes, ballads were once "favored in the castle even more than in the cottage," some of

---

[4] This was the view of German scholarship in Newell's day. Compare Franz Magnus Böhme: "Als endlich die Erwachsenen ganz und gar den Reigen aufgaben und mit ihm auch das Tanzlied erstarb, waren es die Kinder welche in ihrem Ringelreihen ihn bis heute fortpflegen." (*Geschichte des Tanzes in Deutschland*, 1886, pp. 149-150.) Compare also H. Morf (cited by Miller, p. 26): "Im Mittelalter kannten die Erwachsenen keinen anderen Tanz als den Reigen, den man zum Rhythmus von *Liedern* tanzte. Dieses *danser aux chansons* ist heute aus den sitten des Volkes geschwunden und zum blossen Spiel der Kinder herabgesunken. Damit ist auch so manches Lied, in das vor Jahrunderten erwachsene Menschen ihre Freude und ihr Leid gegossen, zum Kinderreim geworden und hat im Kindermund ein letztes Asyl gefunden." (*Archiv für das Studium der neueren Sprachen und Literaturen*, September, 1903, p. 153.)

[5] P. 7. Lady Gomme also admits that many of the games in her collection "were played as amusements by young men and women up to a few years ago" and that "Some are still so played, and some years further back it was a general practice for men and women in country districts to play these or similar games at fairs and festivals," adding that "it is unlikely that adults would play seriously at children's games, but children having seen their elders playing at these amusements would adopt them and use them in their turn, until these amusements become in turn too frivolous and childish for them" (II, p. 518). She also sees a connection between the dramatic games of children and the dramatic dances of the savage and folk-drama. But, with her anthropological interest in the survivals of ceremonial and ritual dances and of the "more serious avocations of adults" she does not make sufficient allowance for the survival in games of the social dances and pastimes of adults. At the same time Newell makes the necessary reservation that "Many games . . . , on the other hand, have, it is true, always belonged to children" (p. 7), nor does he entirely neglect the mythology in children's games.

14

them being translated (and others, we infer, written) by minstrels, and as "Superior minds came to entertain for the old type of song a distaste which was enforced by the advent of printing; ballads in the ancient manner were composed only in rural districts, or left to the lips of 'the vulgar,' on which they acquired a rustic accent. With game-songs . . . owing to the absence of print such change was postponed." [6]

It is surprising that, in spite of this enlightened and advanced view of the literary and aristocratic origin of ballads held by Newell in 1903, he should have left unrevised a statement made in 1883:

> All this [any feature of nature or life which excited interest] was expressed in song shared by the whole company, which was once the invariable attendant of the dance, so that the two made up but one idea, and to "sing a dance" and "dance a song" were identical expressions. [7]

If Newell had carried to their logical conclusion the implications of the evidence furnished by the game-songs in his own collection, he would have been forced to reject the theory of dance origin, as he abandoned the theory of illiterate origin, for ballads. This, however, was left to other scholars to accomplish. Chief among them in America is Louise Pound, who in her epoch-making work, *Poetic Origins and the Ballad,* has given full and vigorous expression and application to the theory of multiplicity of origin, style, and methods of diffusion and recovery of ballad and folk-song. In her chapter on "Ballads and the Illiterate" she has established conclusively the "high descent" and "gradual deterioration" instead of "humble origin and gradual improvement" of the English and Scottish ballads. [8] And in her chapter on "The Medieval Ballad and the Dance" she has brought to bear on the question of the relations of the ballad and the dance the evidence of play-party songs among other ring-games and dance-songs.

After Newell the time was ripe, not only for ballad scholars to tie up game- and dance-songs with the ballad, but for collectors to scour his field (New England and the East) more thoroughly and to extend the search to regions which he had only barely touched.

---

[6] P. vi.

[7] P. 10. It is not clear from the phrase "shared by the whole company" whether Newell believed in actual group composition or only in group performance of dance-songs, though one would infer the latter from what he says of ballads being *"composed . . . in rural districts"* and *translated* by minstrels.

[8] P. 107. Miss Pound was the first ballad scholar in this country to bridge the gap between literature and anthropology. Thus in her chapter on "The Beginnings of Poetry," by drawing upon the latest findings of ethnology as to the actual song and dance usage of living primitive peoples, she explodes the "crowd psychology" and "folk soul" fallacies of earlier theorists.

This has been the task carried on (chiefly in the pages of *The Journal of American Folk-Lore* and partly under Newell's own editorial inspiration and guidance) by collectors of song-games and ring-games in the East and South and of play-party songs proper in the Southwest and Middle-West.

It is the purpose of the present work to carry further the quest of the play-party song and the correlation of game-songs and folk-songs, setting forth the results of a collection made for Oklahoma and the Southwest, and, in its light, reëxamining previous evidence and conclusions with a view to verifying or revising present theory on the subject. The point of view represented is the only one possible in the light of, and the only one confirmed by, actual existing song and dance usage in the play-party; namely, that the theory of the inseparableness of the dance and the ballad is untenable; that narrative songs did not originate as dance accompaniments or by group composition; and that, far from originating in the dance, ballads and folk-songs used as dance accompaniments tend to break down under the wearing usage of the dance.

2. THE PLAY-PARTY: THE NAME, THE FORM, AND THE INSTITUTION

The play-party (at its height a generation or two ago) was a rural American social gathering for playing games, distinguished by the manner in which it was "got up," by the age of its participants, and by the character of the games played. In its typical form it was not an "invitation affair" but was open to the whole countryside. Attended by the entire family for the same reason that they attended the singing school and the literary society, because they had no other place to go, it had for its active participants the young people of high school and marriageable age and young married couples, with the old folk and the children present chiefly as spectators, although the former might serve as leaders or have their square dances (if they were not conscientious objectors) and the latter might play their own games off at one side or before the regular party began. The most important differentia, however, was the character of the games played. Play-party or party games (to give them their generic name) were, with few exceptions, singing-games, including both dramatic choosing or marching games (which may conveniently be known as "party *plays*") and dancing games, in which the dancers swung each other by the hands or, if permitted, by the waist, with no music save their own singing ("swinging plays"). Synonyms for the play-party include "party," which meant a play-party as distinguished from a "dance," and "bounce-around" or "frolic" to distinguish the more boisterous and rollicking fun

16

of the play-party from the milder diversions of the social or evening party, "social," or "sociable," which was for invited guests and, although it might include swinging plays, was largely restricted to parlor and school games.[9]

Although loose usage has tended to confuse the play-party with any kind of party at which games are played and play-party games with ring-games and singing-games in general, these must be regarded as unwarranted extensions of the terms. And although one might conceivably apply the name "play-party" to picnics and birthday parties at which party games were an incidental feature and from which any or all of the three conditions laid down above might be absent, and although many play-party

---

[9] "Bounce-around" occurs in Missouri, from the game of that name often used to open a party (Ames, p. 297); also in the Nebraska Sandhills, according to Melvin Van den Bark, of the University of Nebraska, who also reports the variant "bounce-about." "Social" is the term used by Hogue (p. 86) for the Ozark play-party. "Flang party" has been reported to me from Texas.

"Frolic" is reported from the Ozarks of Missouri and Arkansas (Randolph, pp. 201, 232). A "frolic" (now generally a lively "spree"), as early as 1817, also meant a "bee" (Thornton, p. 347); e.g., "reaping frolic" (*idem*, p. 348), "husking-frolic" (*idem*, p. 466), "quilting frolic" (*idem*, p. 715; Schele De Vere, p. 527). The term "frolicking" is used by Shearin and Combs (p. 35) together with "folk-dances" and "movement-games" to head a list of twenty-one Kentucky play-party and singing games. Curiously enough, the word "play-party" does not appear anywhere in the Kentucky *Syllabus* of 1911, the year of the publication of the first regular collection of play-party texts and tunes (Ames, "The Missouri Play-Party"), after which the term became standard in the literature on the subject.

The earliest treatment of "swinging plays" that has come to my attention is that of "J. B. S." in *Godey's Lady's Book and Magazine* for July and September, 1874. She refers to the games simply as "games" or "plays" (p. 268), the players as "ginners" (p. 62), and the occasion as a "gin-around" (from the fact that the players "marched around and around, like horses in a gin, about as slow and monotonous, singing something . . . ") or a "party." The locality is "Piny Woods," which, though no state is named, is possibly the Piney Woods of Mississippi. I am indebted to Miss Mamie Meredith, of the University of Nebraska, for bringing the article to my notice.

The first printed use of the term "play-party" that I have been able to locate is that of Emma Bell Miles, writing of the Southern Mountains in *Harper's Magazine*, 1904. In 1905 G. M. Miller, in connection with *The Dramatic Element in the Popular Ballad*, writes of "dancing games" at "parties" of "young folks" in Indiana (pp. 30-32) but does not employ the term "play-party." The term "playing games," as a euphemism for dancing to one's own singing, is to be found in Miller (p. 31), before him in Newell (pp. 5, 17, 56), and after him in Wolford (p. 12). For such gatherings in New England towns in the last century Newell and Backus employ the general term, "evening party." According to Paul Howard, of Headrick, Jackson County, Oklahoma, the term "play-party" was unknown there, but any game with words and tune was called a "swinging game." "Swinging play" is reported from Western Texas by Dudley and Payne, p. 8, and would seem to be of Texas origin, inasmuch as Jackson County, prior to the settling of the state boundary, was part of Texas and there, as in Texas, the farmer's pond is still his "tank" and a hurdle or a low place in the fence, or an opening for a gate, is a "gap." Randolph, p. 201, speaks of "party-games" in the Ozarks and Jacobs of "party plays," "plays," "jig plays," and "jig tunes" in Kentucky.

games have passed into the tradition of the schoolroom and playground,[10] strict usage requires that the term be limited to country or country town gatherings of young people from the teens on up, for the sole purpose of playing games with words, tune, dance figures, and dramatic action.

With respect to origins, the play-party game was the natural outgrowth or extension of the traditional game among those who sought a more convenient, well-balanced, and self-sufficient form of rhythmic group movement than either the game or the square dance afforded, one that would combine the best features of both for those who were past the age for the one and yet not wholly content with the other, and one that could be "jumped up" on short notice without the complicated organization that the square dance required, including a good floor, a floor manager, a caller, and musicians.[11] It must not be thought, however, that the play-party arose by any such process of rationalization. Rather, in the nature of things, with the precedent of the singing game before them and the lack of instruments and other facilities for dancing as a motive, the young people hit upon the idea, and once tried and approved, it gained headway, and in competition with the dance had to take over more and more of the features of the dance, being kept alive as an independent form and prevented from passing over entirely into the square dance as much by the definite advantages it developed as by church restrictions on dancing.

The evidence in favor of this natural development of the play-party out of the traditional game, quite apart from questions of religious conscience on the part of the dancers, may be summarized as follows:

1. That the play-party game was not truly a substitute for the dance but a parallel and supplementary form is borne out by the fact that play-party games frequently made use of instrumental accompaniment; that dances had in themselves the seeds of vocal accompaniment in the words that went with many dance tunes (especially those derived from popular songs), which were often sung in the absence of fiddle or to reinforce it; [12] and that play-parties sometimes came under the ban of the church along with dances.

---

[10] "Skip to My Lou" is a favorite school game. A bulletin issued by the Office of Indian Affairs in 1911, *Social Plays, Games, Marches, Old Folk Dances and Rhythmic Movements for Use in Indian Schools,* includes "Old Dan Tucker" and "Shoot the Buffalo."

[11] Compare Piper, pp. 262-263; Wedgwood, pp. 268-269; Wolford, p. 12.

[12] An interesting example of this process is afforded by the following note on "Ozark Milling Days": "Two or three generations ago, the mill was a vigorous community center, the popular meeting place for all classes and conditions of men. It was no uncommon thing to ride fifty miles to mill and camp two or three days while waiting a turn. The burrs ground slowly and quite often the output did not exceed two or three bushels an hour. This gave opportunity for amusement and social contacts. It was a great place to play marbles, pitch horseshoes, to play rustic pranks, swap news,

18

2. That the play-party satisfied a larger need than mere dancing is seen from the fact that the swinging plays were only one form of play-party game, and dramatic plays, such as choosing and marching games, since they were not intended for dancing, could not possibly have come within the church edict against dancing and so could not have arisen as a result of it; and that party games were played at other gatherings than the play-party proper, including Fourth of July picnics.[13] ice-cream parties,[14] literary societies,[15] weddings,[16] and even church socials.[17]

3. That cultural isolation was the primary, positive, and underlying determining factor in the growth of the play-party and church repression simply a secondary, negative conditioning factor is proved by the fact that even persons without religious objections to dancing attended play-parties and that the play-party proper was unknown in more urban and sophisticated communities where evangelical Protestantism was nevertheless a powerful enemy of dancing, and has all but disappeared in modern times when fundamentalism is still a force to be reckoned with.

In other words, in the days before railroads, highways, automobiles, mail-order houses, and rural free delivery had brought the town and the city to the crossroads and the farm, and the moving-pictures, the phonograph, and the radio had brought the nation and the world to the provinces, the play-party would naturally arise as one solution of the amusement problem on a "make-it-yourself-or-do-without" and "hand-me-down" level of culture. Although illiteracy is not a prerequisite of the play-party any more than it is of the traditional game or folk-song, the play-party flourished best where the oral tradition was a strong one and where folk-songs and folklore were living vital forces.[18] Accordingly, the history of the play-party in America has been one of growth and decay through the successive stages of Western migration, its tendency being to spring up in new and sparse settlements and persist there as long as cultural isolation

---

stories, and jack knives. Sometimes there were fights, for hill blood is fighting blood, but, for the most part, the men fought fair. . . . Sometimes the mill floor was used for the dance when the day's work was done. Or if no fiddlers were present, the young folks stepped to the tune of 'Buffalo Girls' or 'Old Dan Tucker,' singing as they played." (*Arcadian Magazine*, February, 1931, p. 11.)

13 Compare Hogue, *Scribner's*, 89:510-511. Here the games were a substitute for the dance among those who had joined the church.

14 Compare Hudson, p. 125: " 'Ice-cream' parties were about the same thing as the play-parties, except that they were free to all who had the price of ten cents a 'saucer.' " In Oklahoma the ice-cream is often made coöperatively.

15 Compare Piper, p. 262.

16 Compare "J. B. S.", pp. 266-268. For the play-party at the infare-wedding, see Thomas, *Devil's Ditties*, pp. 1-8, 46 ff.

17 "Jump Jim Crow" and "Rig-a-Jig" are reported by Danny Kay, Manford, Creek County, Oklahoma, as in use at church socials at Stillwater, Payne County.

18 Compare the Southern Highlands and Southern mountain songs as a source of play-party songs.

prevails, only to be crowded out and be dispersed once more, until the spread of standardized living and commercialized vicarious or canned amusement has pushed it to the wall.

3. Social Status and Customs of the Play-Party

The place of the play-party and dancing in the social life of the community is indicated in the following statement of Mr. W. L. Wilkerson, of Norman, Cleveland County, Oklahoma, obtained in an interview on November 30, 1929. Mr. Wilkerson, who is employed as a cabinet-maker by the University of Oklahoma, was born at Osage Iron Works in the Ozark Hills of Missouri, December 4, 1878. Coming of a family of musicians, his father and his uncle having played at dances before him, he has since the age of twelve been playing the old five-stringed banjo (also the fiddle and the guitar) at entertainments and square dances in Southern Oklahoma and in Norman and vicinity, in an old-time combination with his three brothers.

> In my boyhood days the play-party, the dance, and the literary society were the three modes of entertainment for the young people—besides the singing school and the church, though we went to church with a feeling and spirit of reverence, whereas we went to the dance with the full intention of enjoying ourselves to the limit.
>
> At that time a man who came to a dance with liquor on his breath was ostracized, cast out as undesirable. This was in Oklahoma and Indian Territory. And a girl with a doubtful reputation was the cause of the dance being dismissed if she insisted on staying. The young ladies of the neighborhood, if they felt that a young lady in the crowd didn't have a good reputation, went to their escorts and to their hosts with the ultimatum that the girl leave or they would leave. That was not always the case. That was the case in the dances that were considered respectable, that the parents of good boys and girls would let them go to.
>
> My boyhood was spent in the country up until twenty-three years ago. The principal dances were around the Denver neighborhood, east of Norman, in Eastern Cleveland County. We lived right on Little River, and we played all over the county, especially in the eastern part. The people as a rule were landowners. Some of the best citizens we had were tenant farmers. There were no class distinctions; everyone was on an equal basis in the community there if considered respectable.
>
> We don't mean by that that drinking was absolutely taboo—what I mean is not that every one totally abstained but that every one must be temperate and keep themselves above the liquor. If you drank, you either brought your liquor or drank with some friend. A householder that supplied the liquor couldn't get a crowd, though he might get too many men. The parents wouldn't allow their children to go. Of course the boys the parents didn't have much control over—but the girls. It wasn't condoned. He'd have something to kill his breath with, usually sensen—they bought it at the store. And he'd have to stand

20

straight. Instead of people trying to show it, they tried to conceal the fact that they were drinking.

The church's attitude was against dancing. The church at present is much more lenient than it was at that time. How could a man reconcile religious scruples and dancing? He didn't. The active church members didn't go to dances. If a boy or a girl belonging to any church danced, the saying went round that they had danced themselves out of the church, and that was made a moment of history. The reference was made that at such and such a dance a boy or a girl danced themselves out of the church. For there seemed no ground of justification from the church standpoint for a boy to dance.

Some of the plays were taboo the same as the dances. But there were other plays that we were allowed to go to. Or we could go to a party with certain restrictions that we didn't dance a certain swinging play. One time it would be one, and one time another. A swinging play was one where you'd sing—the same as the dance except for the music. The ordinary plays were games. We played very often plays like "Drop the Handkerchief," "Snap," "Pleased or Displeased." Those were strictly games. The play-party was the same as the dance with the exception that you sang the words and exchanged partners according to the song and words instead of the music and prompting.

I can't understand why it was but in my boyhood days—I don't know how to express it—but the fiddle was the instrument of Satan. The Devil was in the fiddle—that's the saying exactly. It's only been of recent years that the fiddle or violin is allowed in church. The organ is still forbidden in the Non-Progressive Christian Church. The people I mixed with were Christians—they were called Campbellites then—, Methodists, and Baptists. At that time, as far as dancing was concerned, I think they were all of about the same mind. I don't believe there was any connection between church prejudice and the popularity of the dance. I think the circumstances under which we lived caused the dance to flourish, and the conditions under which we lived caused the degeneration.

We were all farmers and we had to make our own entertainment. We couldn't get canned entertainment like now. It was not only self-made but vigorous.

From this and other testimony it is clear that the church was divided on the question of the play-party. On the one hand—and this was the more general attitude—it might tolerate and even encourage the play-party as the lesser of two evils; on the other hand, fanaticism might proceed to the point where the play-party was outlawed along with the dance. Accordingly, in some communities we find that the play-party was most popular after religious revivals, which invariably struck at dancing, and that ministers even gave their tacit assent by presence at, though not participation in, parties. In other communities both dance and parties were kept alive by stealth or open defiance and, like drinking, were referred to under the breath and in a jesting manner.

A typical expression of the latter state of affairs, as it existed some fifteen years ago in a Southwestern Oklahoma community of about one hundred and fifty persons, was obtained from one of the younger generation in Headrick, Jackson County, near the North Fork of the Red River.[19]

> Those who have "got religion" look on them [play-parties] with horror as devices of the Devil to lure the young folk into sin and everlasting torment. This attitude tends to lend an element of mystery and adventure to them, and the children of the religious folk dare not let their parents know that they sang "Old Joe Clark" or that they were at the dance last Friday night.

According to the same informant, these games, when taught in physical education work, take on an entirely different aspect and are immune to criticism. Thus a May festival at Headrick with swinging games attracted people for miles around. The convictions or prejudices of the community may further be gauged by the incident of the Sunday school superintendent who one Sunday got up and actually wept because he had heard that his daughter had gone to a dance. He offered to resign because he didn't feel fit for the place, but the people wouldn't hear of it. His daughter, a graduate of Oklahoma Agricultural and Mechanical College, was teaching school and had accidentally mentioned the dance in a letter. Headrick is not a backward community, but one that supports its schools very well, and one in which the young folk growing up and going to school do not allow themselves to be dictated to. Thus my informant's parents do not object to his dancing away from home—for instance, at the University—but he must not dance in Headrick. ("This is just a superstition that hangs on.") There are no public dances in Headrick. Sometimes the young people of the better families will get up a dance and church folk will find out, by gossip, who the ringleaders are— usually the "younger married set." Then the offenders will be regarded as "sinners" until the next revival when they have to be "saved" again by repenting and "giving testimony"—only to have the same thing happen again with the return of the dancing season. Here, unlike the community described by Mr. Wilkerson in his boyhood, there were class distinctions. Since people who went to dances were social outcasts, dances came to be restricted largely to the homes of the lower classes—that is, the "tenants" as distinct from the "settlers"—who had no caste to lose.[20] The social line was likewise drawn at revivals, which each church held during the summer and at which the better-educated folk did not go in for the extremes of shouting and singing whereby the vulgar worked off surplus energy and emotion.

The license of the lower classes, among whom drunkenness, fighting, love-making, and card-playing followed in the wake of dancing—spreading

---

[19] Paul Howard. Similar condemnation of the play-party by the church in Indiana is described by Wolford, pp. 17-18.

[20] Compare Ames, p. 295.

even to the play-party—sometimes, among the rougher element, extended to the lawlessness of breaking up the parties and socials of the better families.[21] Thus, from Lexington, a central Oklahoma community some fifteen miles from the State University (formerly infested with "last chance" saloons—some of them in the middle of the South Canadian River—which supplied Indian Territory traffic on the other bank), came this complaint in 1926:

> Within the last fifteen years, the "moonshine" element has had its effect. Social parties have almost become extinct because the uninvited guests of the lower class seemed to grow more numerous and troublesome with every party.[22]

From the point of view of the church, the cardinal sins of dancing were the music and the waist swing. If the Devil had his picture-book in playing-cards and his ditties (in the Southern Mountains) in ballads,[23] he had his music-box in the fiddle. Testimonies are rife to the effect that the absence of fiddles at play-parties constituted their saving grace.[24] Thus in Oklahoma:

> Many of the girls of the pre-Statehood days believed it a sin to dance but not to go to a play-party. Consequently they would do the regulation square dances as long as the accompaniment was sung, but if the fiddle was sounded they would stop immediately.[25]

That the waist or two-hand swing was regarded as a daring liberty (sought or invited by some, frowned upon by others) even at dances is indicated by the abundant jesting references to it in dance calls.

> Paw says swing them, Maw says no.
> Sis says the waist swing or it don't go.[26]

The following couplets (of which there are many variants) have been interpreted to mean: If you can't swing her waist, take her by the hand [27] (out of deference to the wishes of mothers who often admonished their daughters: "Don't let those boys swing you round the waist."):

---

21 Compare Hudson, p. 125.

22 Mrs. Marjorie K. Allen, Lexington, Cleveland County.

23 Compare William Aspenwall Bradley, "Song-Ballets and Devil's Ditties," *Harper's,* 130:910-914; J. H. Combs, *Folk-Songs du Midi des États-Unis,* pp. 62-63, 114-116 ("those old things must be the very works of the devil"; "as thick as fiddlers in hell"); E. C. Perrow, *JAFL,* 25:143, and note.

24 Compare all the play-party references for expressions of opinion on the sinfulness of fiddling and the sinlessness of no-fiddling.

25 Cora Frances Starritt, Ada, Pontotoc County.

26 Mrs. Marjorie K. Allen, Lexington, Cleveland County.

27 My informant was the late Ben Hennessy of Oklahoma City, Oklahoma County, formerly of Kansas. A significant commentary on the waist swing in the play-party is to be found in Lynn Riggs' Oklahoma play, *Big Lake,* pp. 60-61, where Miss

Meet your honey, slap her on the back,
If she don't like biscuits, feed her a flap-jack.[28]

Meet your lady, pat her on the head,
If she don't like biscuits, feed her cornbread.[29]

The fact that "cornbread" signifies the one-hand swing instead of the opposite, as might conceivably be the case, is borne out by two other variants:

Swing them around, pat them on the head,
If you can't get biscuit, take cornbread.[30]

Meet your pardner, pat her on the head,
If she wants to eat hoke cake [hoecake], feed her cornbread.[31]

The entire blamelessness of the no-hand, back-to-back dancing of the do-ce-do, on the other hand, may be intended in the following:

Four ladies domineck, four gents shanghai,
Then build your hopes on the sweet bye and bye.
Do-ce, ladies, ain't you old enough to know,
That you'll never get to heaven till you do-ce-do? [32]

The picture of the play-party is not complete without some account of the customs connected with it.[33] Play-parties were either "jumped up" on

Meredith, the straight-laced teacher, interrupts a play-party in righteous horror and indignation:

> Stop it, Bud Bickel! (*She crosses over right, angrily.*) We won't play any more.
> Bud (*following her over*): Whut is it, whut've I done?
> Miss Meredith: You're swinging the Waist Swing, Bud Bickel!
> Bud: Well, o' course.
> Miss Meredith: It's wrong, it's wicked. I'm ashamed of you. I'm surprised at you. . . . Don't you ever do it again, you hear me? And don't you girls ever let me catch you letting a boy swing you by the waist instead of by the arms. . . .

[28] William E. Chisholm, Ardmore, Carter County; John Rinehart, Guthrie, Logan County, from Carl Courtney, Wynnewood, Garvin County; Byron Williams, Norman, Cleveland County.

[29] Freeda Hines, Sallisaw, Sequoyah County, from Spiro, Le Flore County; Alice Lucile Jackson, Supply, Woodward County, from Neil Mason, Supply; Mary Elizabeth Maloy, Norman, Cleveland County.

[30] Ruth Johnson, Erick, Beckham County.

[31] Warren Barnhill, Yukon, Canadian County.

[32] Mary E. Vaughn, Tulsa County (printed in *Whiz Bang,* November, 1926, p. 53).

[33] The customs given here are found in, but by no means restricted to, Oklahoma, as most of them may be paralleled in any of the play-party references. On account of the general resemblances of dance and party setting and procedure, it is impossible to keep the two entirely distinct, though differences are pointed out wherever they exist. The time is the past. For accounts of square dances compare John R. Craddock, "The Cowboy Dance," *PTFS,* 2:31-37; Mary Elizabeth Osborn, "Country Dance Calls from

24

short notice or announced as much as a month ahead, the play-party, as
has been pointed out, having the advantage over the dance in lending
itself more readily to extemporaneous getting-up. The invitation, as has
been said, included the neighborhood or the countryside for miles around,
barring not even the undesirable (whom one might wish absent but could
not very well exclude), especially since a slight of this kind might pro-
voke retaliation in the way of "busting up" the party.[34] When and where
the telephone had come in, those who were on the same party line might
be informed by a general call, and thence the word was passed to neighbors. Otherwise the news was relayed from house to house or carried by
messengers on horseback. Ten miles were as nothing as a prelude to the
evening's entertainment, regardless of the condition of the roads or the
means of conveyance. Buggies, wagons, saddle-horses, even balky mules
(carrying as many as three astride), and later the ubiquitous Ford were
pressed into service. Those who could not ride went afoot.

The setting for the party was generally the front room or yard of the
farm or ranch house. though sometimes the school-house or school-yard
was used. In at least one case that has come to my notice it was the
custom for the young people to occupy the front-room and the older folk
the dining-room and kitchen, an arrangement that favored kissing games
behind closed doors when the young folk went in for that sort of thing.
In preparation, all the furniture (at times even to the stoves) was removed
to another room or out-of-doors, with the exception of the chairs and
benches, which were placed around the walls. Often an impromptu bench
was made of a long board placed on two chairs and covered with quilts.

The time set was after dark, as soon as the chores could conveniently
be done, an unusual activity and alacrity being inspired by the occasion.
People began to arrive between seven and eight, with late-comers drifting
in until ten. But it was not until the children had been taken into a
separate room and put to bed that the fun really began.

Sometimes the party would open with a non-compromising game without a song or dance, like "Snap" or "Spin the Pan" as an ice-breaker, to
overcome bashfulness or religious scruples. To guide the players through
the swinging plays every party had its leader, who combined the functions

---

the Catskill Mountains," *American Speech*, 3:142-145; Edwin Ford Piper, "Quadrille
Calls," *ibid.*, 1:391-395; Roy S. Scott, "The Cowboy Dance of the Northwest," *PTFS*,
4:53-58; Della I. Young, "The Pioneer Dance," *Folk-Say, A Regional Miscellany: 1930*,
pp. 253-265. The present description of play-party customs is reprinted with a few
changes from the author's "The Play-Party in Oklahoma," *PTFS*, 7:7-24.

For additional material on the "Social Status and Customs of the Play-Party," see
Appendix.

[34] Compare Hudson, p. 125.

of the floor-manager and the caller at dances.[35] Like the caller he was qualified for the place by a strong voice, unlimited energy and ability to keep the others stimulated or amused, an inexhaustible store of songs, and skill in improvising new stanzas to fill gaps in his memory or introduce variety and humor at the expense of individuals. Old-timers, on account of the superiority of their knowledge, in quality and quantity, were often in demand as leaders and thus took an active part.

Music at play-parties, as has been indicated, was the exception, if for no other reason than that instruments and musicians were scarce; but it might—especially when square dances were to be introduced in the course of the evening—be furnished by any of the time-honored dance instruments—fiddle, banjo, guitar, French harp (the harmonica), with often a piano or organ for chording. The musicians were usually old-timers, self-taught, and like the leaders and callers, picturesque characters—frontier survivals of the old minstrel type—who played with more vigor and endurance than art and who required the inevitable stimulus of perpetual chewing and an occasional drink.

Refreshments were more common at dances than at parties. They included cakes and pies, roasted apples and roasted shelled corn in the winter, watermelon or ice-cream (often made coöperatively) in the summer. Black coffee, cider, lemonade, and grape-juice might also be served, while strong men who required stronger drink brought their own—in a jug (in the days before the hip-flask).

The dress varied with the social status of the participants. Dandies sported red flannel and black sateen shirts, fancy neckwear in the form of a bandana handkerchief (sometimes slipped through a ring) or stiff collar and loud tie. Those were the days when the clicking of cuff-buttons in celluloid cuffs sounded "like a dozen typewriters or the undertone of surf," according to one informant. Then, too, high boots were very much in favor, high-heeled, with straps, costing ten or twelve dollars a pair in contrast to store shoes, which could be had for a dollar or two. The man who tucked his trousers into his boots roughly was a regular guy, while the one who put them in evenly was a dude. Spurs were removed, though it was not necessary to "park the artillery." In the gestures and move-

---

[35] For the function of the leader as an arbiter of play-party songs compare Piper, p. 265. The leader, like the caller, was apt to be a local wit or "smart aleck," who as borrower or lender played an important part in the diffusion of songs and games from one neighborhood or region to another.

Adds Professor Kenneth C. Kaufman, of the University of Oklahoma, in an interview on June 4, 1932: "There must have been a bunch of poets as well as singers in that outfit. And the wit—just think of the wit you're resurrecting and giving back to the world. If you study the wit in these, you'll see what appealed to primitive people."

ments of the dancers, affectation vied with awkwardness, the characteristic attitude of the bashful maiden being arms akimbo and that of the dude being the hand raised high with exaggerated effeminate grace. The more hardened players frequently crossed the line and threw in square dances for variety, just as dances (which might include Virginia reels and even two-steps and draggy waltzes) often closed with a party game like "Needle's Eye" or "Wink 'Em." The gathering broke up after midnight, sometimes lasting into the early hours of the morning, so that the men often got back just in time to do the chores. During a siege of parties and hoe-downs, one would think nothing of going without a wink of sleep for several nights in a row. But occasionally the tired guest, ashamed to confess to his lack of endurance, would break away with some such excuse as, "It's a long drive, and the team will have to take it slow over the south ridge."

CHAPTER II

THE PLAY-PARTY AND THE GAME

1. THE DRAMATIC ELEMENT

THE game element in the play-party is the dramatic element—the essential feature of all games with words and action, whether of the singing type (with tune) or the dialogue type (without tune), which distinguishes them from games of skill, chance, guessing, forfeit, ball, and the like.[1] The dramatic element takes several varied forms, from the simplest *"pleasures of motion"* [2] contained in rhythmic group movements like

---

[1] For a complete classification of traditional games on these principles see Lady Gomme's "Memoir on the Study of Children's Games," II, pp. 458-531.

[2] These categories are Newell's, though only those games are included which survive in Oklahoma (listed by their Oklahoma titles). Since these games are not strictly play-party games, they are, with few exceptions, excluded from the present collection, but bibliographical notes are given in this chapter. The following games, which in all but four cases, are not found in Newell, complete the Oklahoma record of dramatic games:

"The Bear Went over the Mountain": 2 Oklahoma variants. Compare Gardner, pp. 91-92.

"Carrousel": 3 Oklahoma variants. A Swedish singing-game. Compare Crampton, p. 44; Elsom and Trilling (2 versions), pp. 228-234.

"Did You Ever See a Lassie?": 6 Oklahoma variants. Compare Dearmer and Shaw, p. 66; Elsom and Trilling, pp. 220-221; Gomme, "When I Was a Young Girl," II, pp. 362-374, 457 (14 versions); Newell, "When I Was a Shoemaker," pp. 88-89; Newton, pp. 3-4; *Social Plays, Games,* etc., pp. 19-20.

"Frog in the Middle": 2 Oklahoma variants. Compare Brand (who traces it back to 1343), *Popular Antiquities,* pp. 526-527; Heck, p. 34; Newell, p. 171; Shearin and Combs (listed), p. 38; *Social Plays, Games,* etc., p. 50.

"Good Morning to You": 1 Oklahoma version. A school song.

"How Do You Do, My Partner": 4 Oklahoma variants. A Swedish singing-game. Compare Elsom and Trilling, pp. 226-227.

"I See You": 7 Oklahoma variants. A Swedish singing-game. Compare Crampton, pp. 42-43.

"Lazy Mary": 1 Oklahoma version. Compare Heck, pp. 18-19; Newell, p. 96; Pound, *American Ballads and Songs,* pp. 225-226; *Syllabus,* pp. 44, 74; Piper, pp. 273-274; Wier, p. 13.

"Let the Feet Go Tramp": 2 Oklahoma variants. Compare *Social Plays, Games,* etc., p. 13; Wier, p. 22.

"The Muffin Man": 5 Oklahoma variants. Compare Dearmer and Shaw, p. 78; Gardner, p. 113; Gomme (5 versions), I, pp. 402-404; Kidson and Moffat, pp. 8-9; Newton, pp. 11-12; *Social Plays, Games,* etc., pp. 22-23; Walter, p. 8.

"New York": 3 Oklahoma variants. Compare Grahame, pp. 70-71; Gomme, "Trades" (5 versions), II, pp. 305-306; Heck, p. 30; Newell, "Jamestown, Virginia," pp. 249-250; Northall, "Tradesmen," p. 402.

"The Old Gray Goose is Dead": 5 Oklahoma variants. Compare Scarborough, pp. 195-196; Sharp, *Nursery Songs from the Appalachian Mountains,* No. 11; Sullivan, *Our Times,* 2:78 (where it is given as a parody of a hymn).

"Old Grumbler's Song": 3 Oklahoma variants. Compare Babcock, p. 245; Broadwood and Maitland, pp. 94-95; Douglas, pp. 76-77; Gomme (12 versions), II, pp. 16-24; Heck, p. 20; Kittredge, *JAFL,* 35:407; Newell, pp. 100-101; *JAFL,* 12:74;

"Farmer in the Dell," [3] "Lubin," [4] "Marching round the Levy," [5] and "Ring around a Rosie," [6] through the *imitative action* (already glimpsed in the pantomime of "Lubin") involved in the "playing at work" of "Draw a Bucket of Water," [7] "Mulberry Bush," [8] "Needle's Eye," [9] and "Oats,

---

Pound, *American Ballads and Songs*, p. 232; *Syllabus*, pp. 57, 74-75; Scarborough, p. 136; Spenney, pp. 112-113; Tolman and Eddy, p. 407; Walter, p. 32.

"Oranges and Lemons": 1 Oklahoma version. This does not seem to be well known in America, perhaps because of the remoteness of its local names and allusions. Compare Dearmer and Shaw, pp. 84-85; Gomme (16 versions), II, pp. 25-35; Graham, p. 31; Halliwell, pp. 111-112; Northall (3 versions), pp. 399-400; Walter, pp. 4-5.

"Pop Goes the Weasel": 11 Oklahoma variants. Compare Burchenal, *American Country-Dances*, pp. 22-23; Elsom and Trilling, pp. 160-163; Gardner, p. 119; Gomme, II, pp. 63-64; *"Good Morning,"* pp. 108-109; Pound, *Syllabus*, p. 71; Wier, p. 247; Wolford, p. 83.

"Roman and English Soldiers": 1 Oklahoma version. Compare Babcock, pp. 261-262; Dudley and Payne, pp. 26-27; Gomme (19 versions), II, pp. 343-360, 456; Heck, p. 40; Kidson and Moffat, p. 13; Newell, pp. 248-249; Udal, p. 361.

"The Shoemaker's Dance": 1 Oklahoma version. A school game. Compare *Social Plays, Games*, etc., p. 34.

"William Trembletoe" (Newell, p. 203, gives this merely as a counting-out rhyme): 42 Oklahoma variants. Compare Hoke, p. 119; Hudson, p. 113; Johnson, p. 162; Parsons, "Notes on Folk-Lore of Guilford County, North Carolina," *JAFL*, 30:207; Shearin and Combs, p. 38 (listed); Smiley, p. 377.

"Wind the Ball": 2 Oklahoma variants.

[3] 46 Oklahoma variants. Compare Babcock, pp. 254-255; Dudley and Payne, p. 26; Gardner, p. 97; Gomme, II, p. 420; Heck, p. 25; Hofer, p. 20; Hornby, p. 64; Newell, pp. 129-130; Newton, pp. 9-10; Pound, *Syllabus*, p. 74; *Social Plays, Games*, etc., p. 27; Wier, p. 10; Wolford, p. 42.

[4] 8 Oklahoma variants. Compare Ames, pp. 312-313; Champlin, p. 753; Dearmer and Shaw, p. 68; Douglas, p. 74; Gardner, pp. 110-111; Gomme (14 versions), I, pp. 352-361; Heck, p. 25; Kidson and Moffat, pp. 29, 56; Mason, p. 12; Newell. p. 131; Newton, pp. 10-11; Northall, p. 361; Van Doren, p. 496; Walter, p. 20; Wier, p. 21.

[5] 61 Oklahoma variants. Compare Ames, pp. 306-307; Babcock, pp. 255-256; Dearmer and Shaw, p. 81; Douglas, p. 74; Gardner, pp. 120-121; Gomme (19 versions), II, pp. 122-143; Grahame, pp. 64-66; Heck, p. 26; Hudson, pp. 119-120; Newell, pp. 128-129, 229-231; Newton, pp. 39-40; Pound, *Syllabus*, p. 73; Shearin and Combs (described), pp. 36, 38; *Social Plays, Games*, etc., pp. 18-19, 24; Udal, pp. 345-346; Wier, p. 18.

[6] 10 Oklahoma variants. Compare Dearmer and Shaw, p. 82; Gardner, pp. 119-120; Gomme (11 versions), II, pp. 108-111; Heck, p. 25; Kidson and Moffat, p. 68; Newell, pp. 127-128; Northall, p. 360; Parsons, "Folk-Lore from Aiken, S. C.," *JAFL*, 34:38; *Social Plays, Games*, etc., p. 16; Walter, p. 13; Wier, p. 14.

[7] 6 Oklahoma variants. Compare Dearmer and Shaw, p. 66; Gomme (15 versions), I, pp. 100-108; Halliwell, p. 116; Heck, pp. 15-16; Newell (2 versions), pp. 90-91; Northall (3 versions), pp. 395-396, 400; *Social Plays, Games*, etc., p. 20.

[8] 11 Oklahoma variants. Compare Chambers, pp. 134-135; Champlin, p. 52; Dearmer and Shaw, p. 79; Gardner, pp. 113-114; Gomme, I, pp. 404-407; Graham, p. 11; Grahame, pp. 66-67; Halliwell, *Popular Rhymes and Nursery Tales*, p. 224; Heck, p. 15; Hofer, p. 18; Kidson and Moffat, pp. 10, 75; Newell, pp. 86-87; Newton, pp. 21-22; Pound, *Syllabus*, p. 74; Scarborough, p. 138; Udal, pp. 344-345; Walter, p. 19; Wier, p. 9; Wolford, pp. 56-57.

[9] 62 Oklahoma variants. Compare Champlin, p. 723; Clarke, p. 289; Dudley and Payne, p. 23; Gardner, pp. 115-116; Gomme (15 versions), II, pp. 228-232, 289-290;

Peas, Beans, and Barley Grows," [10] to the truly *dramatic situation* (seen in the choosing and kissing of a lover in "Marching round the Levy" and "Oats, Peas, Beans, and Barley Grows") acted out in the "histories" (chiefly love tales) of "Doctor, Doctor," [11] "Down She Comes as White as Milk," [12] "Green Gravel," [13] "Jennie Jones," [14] "King William Was King James' Son," [15] "Sally Walker," [16] and "Uncle Johnny's Sick Abed," [17] or the *struggle* (reflected in the tug-of-war of "Needle's Eye") of "games of chase" such as "Chick-a-me, Chick-a-me, Craney Crow," [18] "Itiskit, Itaskit," [19] and "Molly, Molly Bright." [20]

Grahame, pp. 51-52; Hamilton, p. 297; Heck, p. 18; Hofer, p. 17; Hudson (2 versions), pp. 122-123; Newell, pp. 91, 212, 241; Northall (7 versions), pp. 397-398; Partridge (7 versions), *FL*, 23:196-203, 446; Piper, pp. 262-263; Pound, *Syllabus*, p. 73; Randolph, pp. 228-229; Shearin and Combs (described), p. 37; *Social Plays, Games*, etc., pp. 25-26; Wolford, pp. 72-73.

[10] See Part Two.

[11] 1 Oklahoma version. Compare Babcock, p. 251; Newell, pp. 99-100.

[12] 2 Oklahoma variants. Compare Gardner, pp. 132-133, and note; Newell (3 versions), pp. 67-70; Northall, p. 378.

[13] 13 Oklahoma variants. Compare Babcock, pp. 244-245; Broadwood and Maitland (2 versions), pp. 26-27; Dearmer and Shaw, p. 78; Douglas, p. 58; Gardner, p. 100; Gomme (17 versions), I, pp. 170-183; Halliwell, p. 148; Heck, p. 13; Newell, pp. 71, 242; Pound, *Syllabus*, p. 74; Randolph, pp. 220-221; Shearin and Combs, p. 37; *Social Plays, Games*, etc., p. 15; Udal, pp. 348-349; Walter, p. 12.

[14] 2 Oklahoma variants. Compare Champlin, p. 492; Gardner, p. 104; Gilchrist, *Journal of the Folk-Song Society*, 6:80-90; Gomme (21 versions), I, pp. 260-283; II, pp. 432-435; Heck, pp. 11-12; Newell (3 versions), pp. 63-66, 243-245; Pound, *Syllabus*, p. 73; Walter, pp. 16-17; Wier, pp. 19-20.

[15] See Part Two.

[16] 4 Oklahoma variants. Compare Babcock, pp. 248-249; Dearmer and Shaw, pp. 80-81; Douglas, p. 89; Gomme (50 versions), II, pp. 149-179; 453-454; Gardner, pp. 122-123; Heck, pp. 12-13; Hornby, p. 23; Hudson, pp. 121-122; Kidson and Moffat, p. 30; Newell, p. 70; Northall (11 versions), pp. 375-378; Udal (4 versions), pp. 339-342; Wier, pp. 22-23; Wolford, p. 86.

[17] 3 Oklahoma variants. Compare Champlin, p. 753; Gomme (2 versions), II, pp. 321-322; Heck, p. 13; Newell, p. 72; Northall, p. 380; Wier, p. 15; Wolford, p. 97.

[18] 4 Oklahoma variants. Compare Babcock, pp. 283-284; Gomme (3 versions), I, pp. 67, 201-202; Heck, pp. 30-31; Hoke, p. 119; Hudson, p. 112; Isham, p. 116; Kidson and Moffat, p. 49; Newell, pp. 155-156, 215-221, 259-263; *JAFL*, 3:139-148, 12:75; Northall, p. 388; Parsons, "Folk-Lore from Aiken, South Carolina," *JAFL*, 34:38-39; Shearin and Combs (listed), p. 38; *Social Plays, Games*, etc., pp. 38-39; Scarborough, pp. 138-139; Talley, p. 74; Udal, p. 351.

[19] 4 Oklahoma variants. Compare Babcock, p. 257; Champlin, pp. 272-273; Gardner, pp. 96-97; Gomme (28 versions), I, pp. 109-112, 144, 305-310; II, pp. 407-408, 418; Grahame, pp. 37-38; Heck, p. 33; Hudson, p. 118; Kidson and Moffat, p. 23; Newell (3 versions), pp. 168-169; Northall (7 versions), pp. 364-365; Pound, *Syllabus*, p. 74; Udal (3 versions), pp. 346-348; Wier, p. 13; Wolford, pp. 59-60. According to Wolford, "This has recently lost the song and at the play-party it is merely a game of chase."

[20] 10 Oklahoma variants. Compare Babcock, pp. 280-281; Gomme (19 versions), I, pp. 231-238; Halliwell, p. 157; Hoke, p. 120; Hudson, p. 114; Kidson and Moffat, p. 28; Newell, pp. 153-154; Northall (8 versions), pp. 396-398; *Social Plays, Games*, etc., p. 67; Talley, p. 74; Udal, p. 364.

Inasmuch as play-party games are singing-games, with words, tune, and action, they are dramatic games; and their dramatic elements arise in response to the same fundamental need of rhythmic group movement and imitative and histrionic action. But the particular expression of these dramatic elements is necessarily different on account of differences in the age, interests, and tastes of the participants and differences in their environment, affecting both the form and the content of their play.

Considering first the histrionic element in the play-party, we find that the players, having with adolescence naturally passed beyond the stage of mere playing at work and at love (as in kissing rounds), still preserve a lively interest in human life and in their environment and reflect in their games and dances the familiar objects and experiences of rural and especially pioneer America. In identifying themselves with this life and its surroundings the players assume or assign to each other imaginatively the characters of flora and fauna and inanimate objects with which they come in daily contact. With compliments for the girls and satire for the boys,[21] the players are pretty little pinks, apples, peaches, bird in the cage, redbird, bluebird, sugar and tea, candy, sugar lump, cinnamon, hogs in the cornfield, cows in the clover, pig in the parlor, cat in the cream jug, cow in the kitchen, big-footed nigger, hobo, soapstick, old bums, and so forth. Or, introducing native scenes and place-names, at first or second hand, into their imaginary journeys and adventures, they are marching down to Old Quebec where the drums are loudly beating, coming through the wilderness, the canebrake, the bushes, the timber, down in or bound for Alabama, Mississippi River . . . bound to cross, rallying round the canebrake to shoot the buffalo, going to Texas two by two, raisin' sweet taters in a sandy land, going back to Tennessee, wishing they were in Arkansas, going down to Rowser's to get some lager beer, leading her up and down the valley on that good old cider wine, losing her on that raging canal. In most of these cases the action is narrated rather than represented, but in other cases the action may be suited to the words as in "Three Crows," or a bit of dumbshow introduced as in "Poor Old Joe" [22] (in which Joe stays behind the girl acting as if he were old and crippled), or the actual formation is dramatized, as in "Miller Boy," in which the circling double ring represents the turning of the mill wheel.[23]

---

21 Compare Piper, pp. 274-275. In "Little Red Rose" appear in turn the little red rose, the whiskey jug, the lily so fair, the old plough horse, the violet blue, the old stick-in-the-mud. Dudley and Payne in "Ground Hog" (p. 28) give ground hog, buzzard, lizard, crow for the boys, and a pretty white rose, a sweet little pink for the girls.
22 See below, p. 62 ff., for these and other dramatizations of songs.
23 For other examples compare Wolford, pp. 111-112.

2. GAME BORROWINGS AND ADAPTATIONS

Turning to the factor of rhythmic movement (which in the play-party
tends to take precedence over dramatic action), we find that again the
play-party departs from the traditional game in that it passes beyond the
choral or ring dance into the reel and the quadrille. As long as ring-games
and singing-games were confined to such simple movements and actions
as walking, running, skipping, advancing and retiring, marching or dancing round and round, turning round, turning one's back, bowing, kneeling,
stooping, crouching, squatting, falling down, clapping hands, stamping
feet, clasping and unclasping hands, performing grotesque antics or imitative motions—in a group with linked hands in circle or line form, or
singly, or in couples in, inside, or outside a ring, or back and forth in
front of a row, or up and down the aisle, or passing under an arch formed
by raised hands—they remained, with few exceptions, outside the scope of
the play-party. The exceptions are the cases in which a children's game
was taken over because it lent itself to dance adaptation.[24] Such is the
case with "Walking on the Green Grass," [25] which was originally played
with one or two children advancing and retiring in front of a row from
which each girl is led out in turn to dance around. Newell, however,
describes this as a dance "belonging to young men and women as well as
to children," similar to a reel, with a stanza of dance directions added to
the original song:

> Oh, swing the king and swing the queen,
> Oh, swing the king and swing the queen,
> Oh, swing 'em round and round the green,
> Oh, swing 'em round the green.[26]

[24] The play-party retained, as resting-games between dances or partner-choosing
games for the bashful or non-compromising games for the puritanical, a number of
parlor games involving a chase, guessing, forfeits, and the like. These include "Brother,
I'm Bobbed" (Ames, p. 313; Hudson, p. 114), "Cat and Mouse" (Melvin Van den
Bark, Lincoln, Nebraska, from the Sandhills), "Clap-in, Clap-out" (Ames, p. 313),
"Drop the Handkerchief" (W. L. Wilkerson, Norman, Cleveland County, Oklahoma;
Wolford, pp. 16, 60; compare "Itiskit, Itaskit," Note 19); "Fishing for Love" (Hudson,
p. 125); "Late for Supper" (Dr. Howard P. Doole, Adams, Gage County, Nebraska);
"Pleased or Displeased" (W. L. Wilkerson, Norman, Cleveland County, Oklahoma);
"Promenade" (Hudson, p. 125); "Ruth and Jacob" (Melvin Van den Bark, Lincoln,
Nebraska, from the Sandhills); "See, Laugh, and Say Nothing" (Ames, p. 313);
"Shadow" (Hudson, p. 125); "Simon Says Wigwag" (Ames, p. 313; compare "Grand
Mufti," Champlin, p. 377; "Obadiah," Gomme, II, pp. 13-14; "Quaker," *ibid.*, pp.
89-90); "Snap" (Dudley and Payne, p. 8; Paul Howard, Headrick, Jackson County,
Oklahoma; W. L. Wilkerson, Norman, Cleveland County, Oklahoma); "Spin the Pan"
(Grahame, p. 72; *Social Plays, Games,* etc., pp. 45, 66); "Three Deep" (Grahame, p.
75; Gomme, II, pp. 144-145; Wolford, p. 60); "Wink 'Em" (Grahame, pp. 71-72; Paul
Howard, Headrick, Jackson County, Oklahoma).
[25] See Part Two.
[26] Pp. 227-228. Compare pp. 50-51, 226-227.

In Texas this is danced with a grand right and left, with the addition of lines reminiscent of "Weevily Wheat" and of familiar dance call couplets borrowed from "Chase the Squirrel":

> Walking on the green grass, dus, dus, dus,
> Come all ye pretty fair maids and take a walk with us,
> If you are as fair as I take you to be
> I take you by the right hand and walk along with ye.
> (*Swinging*) Grandma she likes butter and cheese,
> Grandpa he loves brandy,
> Grandma she loves butter and cheese.
> And the girls are sweeter than candy.

> Over the hills and chase the squirrel,
> My true love is the beauty of the world,
> Grandma she loves, etc.

> Over the hills and chase the possum,
> My true love is sweeter than a blossom,
> Grandma she loves, etc.[27]

In Texas also "London Bridge" is danced in the same way, with dance directions added:

> Sticks and clay will wash away, O girls, remember me,
> Build it up with iron and steel,
> To my hop light, ladies turn,
> Turn, turn, turn, to my hop light, ladies, turn,
> Hop light, ladies, turn, etc.
> (*Repeat till partners come together again.*)

> Iron will break and steel will bend, O girls, remember me,
> Build it up with sticks and clay,
> To my hop light, ladies turn, etc.

> Sticks and clay will wash away, O girls, remember me.
> We'll build it up with pretty little girls,
> To my hop light, ladies, turn, etc.[28]

---

[27] Dudley and Payne, p. 20. For "London Bridge," of which 18 Oklahoma variants have been reported, compare Babcock, pp. 262-264; Dearmer and Shaw, pp. 70-71; Gardner, p. 110; Gomme (13 versions), I, pp. 333-350; II, pp. 441-442; Hamilton, p. 303; Kidson and Moffat, pp. 44-45, 58; Newell (6 versions), pp. 204-211, 253-254; Newton, pp. 24-25; Northall, pp. 365-366; Parsons, "Folk-Lore from Aiken, S. C.," *JAFL*, 34:38; Pound, *Syllabus*, p. 74; Udal, pp. 366-367; Walter, pp. 10-11; Wier, p. 14; Wolford, pp. 64-65.

[28] Dudley and Payne, pp 20-21. For "hop light, ladies" see the stanzas reported from Virginia and Mississippi by Perrow, *JAFL*, 28:184. For the dance adaptation and refrain

A striking instance of the grafting of a swinging-play upon a ring-game is seen in "Marching round the Levy," which in one Oklahoma version has been crossed with "Coffee Grows on a White Oak Tree":

> We're marching around the levy,
> We're marching around the levy,
> We're marching around the levy,
>   For the night has gained the day.

> Go forth and choose your lover, etc.

> Silver star and you can't catch Josie,
> Silver star and you can't catch Josie,
> Silver star and you can't catch Josie,
> All down the cellar and you can't catch Josie.

> Hold my mule while I catch Josie, etc.[29]

In Iowa and Michigan "Bingo" is danced with a grand right and left, with a second stanza containing dance directions as follows:

> Right hand to your partner;
> Left hand to your neighbor.
> B-i-n-g-o go
> B-i-n-g-o go
> B-i-n-g-o go
> Bingo was his name, sir.[30]

---

compare the Virginia reel reported by Spenney, from Raleigh, North Carolina, pp. 111-112.
    London Bridge is burning down, Oh, how it troubles me!
    The mortar and the clay will wash away, 'til the first go, ladies, turn.
    Heist, go, ladies, turn, turn!
    Heist, go, ladies, turn!
    Heist, go, ladies, turn, turn!
    Heist, go, ladies, turn!
    Heist, go, ladies, turn!
    Heist, go, ladies, turn, turn!
    Heist, go, ladies, turn!
    Take your lady home. Take—(unfinished).
Related to "Hop light, ladies, turn" and "Heist, go, ladies, turn" is "Moscow ladies, turn," in an Oklahoma-Tennessee version of "Chase the Squirrel," in which the line "So say remember me" also occurs (Walter L. Payne, Hobart, Kiowa County, from Mrs. Jesse Fields, who played it at a rural school near Nashville, Tennessee, some thirty-five years ago). "Heist, go" and "Moscow" are apparently corruptions of "hop light." Compare also "Rock-a-by, ladies, turn" in "Have Two Prisoners Here in Jail" (Kathryn C. Nicolett, Bache, Pittsburg County).

[29] Doris G. Waters, Ponca City, Kay County.

[30] Gardner, pp. 93-94; Grahame, pp 60-61. For the ordinary children's version of which there are 5 Oklahoma variants, compare Dearmer and Shaw, pp. 66-67; Gomme (8 versions), I, pp. 29-33; Sharp (*Folk-Songs from Somerset*), Set I, pp. 14-16; Walter, p. 9.

In Oklahoma "John Brown Had a Little Indian," originally a finger-play, a counting-out rhyme, and an additive-subtractive game, is danced like a Virginia reel. One version includes directions similar to "Do-Se-Do":

> Doce doe and don't you touch her,
> Doce doe and don't you touch her,
> Doce doe and don't you touch her,
>> One little Indian boy.

> *Chorus:*
> One little Indian, two little Indian,
> Three little Indian, four little Indian,
> Five little Indian, six little Indian,
> Seven little Indian boys.

> Doce doe to your best likings, etc.
>> Two little Indian boys.

> Fall of the year comes in October, etc.
>> Three little Indian boys.[31]

"Jim Along Josie" is a dance adaptation of the game of tag.[32] "Pig in the Parlor" and "Skip to My Lou" are "Bull in the Park" with a swinging feature added.[33] "Miller Boy" has taken to itself dance figures and a dance call.[34]

In the class of courtship and marriage games, which would seem to appeal to the play-party by reason of their love interest, those which involve simply the choosing of a partner, with or without kissing[35] (e.g., "Green Gravel," "King William Was King James' Son," "Oats, Peas, Beans, and Barley Grows," "Sally Walker") are usually relegated to the school and playground as too static or childish. From the traditional game, however, the play-party has taken over a partner-choosing game such as

---

[31] Walter Myers Gable, Norman, Cleveland County.
[32] Compare "Fire on the Mountains," Gomme, II, p. 421, which contains the words, "Fire on the mountain, run, boys, run!" and is suggested as an origin for "Round Tag."
[33] Compare "Bull in the Park," Gomme, I, pp. 50-51, which is similar in method of playing and in some of the words:
> Cat's i' t' cream-pot up t' knees,
> Hen's i' t' hurdle crowing for day,
> Cock's i' t' barn threshing corn . . . .

> Pig in the middle and can't get out.
[34] See below, p. 47.
[35] Public sentiment on the question of kissing games, like the religious attitude toward play-parties, varied. In general, however, kissing games belong to younger children when they first become boy- and girl-conscious and are not characteristic of the play-party.

"Jolly Sailor Girls" [36] and a chasing game such as "Chase the Squirrel" because of a certain humor and vigorous movement. For similar reasons "Three Dukes" and even "King William Was King James' Son" and "Oats, Peas, Beans, and Barley Grows" may be retained, although these are surpassed in appeal by such courtship and marriage games as "All Down to Sleep," "Hog Drovers," and "Sister Phoebe," in which there is greater opportunity for flirtatious fooling and satire.

Other play-party games with retained choosing and kissing features include "Chimney Sweeper," "Come, My Love," "Consolation Flowing Free," "Green Leaf," "I've Been to the East," and "Kila Ma Cranky." But more characteristic of the play-party are longways games in which a boy and a girl march between the lines, separate, and "cast off," or go round the outside of their respective lines, to rejoin each other ("Yonder She Comes"); or the boys and girls line up, pair off, separate, and meet again ("Baltimore"); or the line of girls marches around the line of boys and *vice versa* ("Boston"); or the leader and his partner go up and down the lines, swinging first each other, next each player in turn, then each other again, in the most strenuous and exhausting of all these varieties ("Lead through That Sugar and Tea").[37]

Also related to the game, finally, in the use of dramatic devices for stealing partners, is a number of marching and swinging plays—chiefly of American origin, though in general modeled after "Jolly Miller" [38]—including "Come, All Ye Young Men in Your Wicked Ways," "Down in Alabama," [39] "It Rains and It Hails," "Little Fight in Mexico," [40] "Miller Boy," "Old Dan Tucker," "Pig in the Parlor," "Sandy, He Belonged to the Mill," "Skip to My Lou," and "Stole My Partner."

---

[36] Dr. S. R. Hadsell, of the University of Oklahoma, notes: "This was a good game to start a party and get acquainted—an ice-breaker. Three girls choose three boys, and when you got a circle you could go on to play 'Ugly Mug.'"

[37] "'Sugar and Tea' is awful. Just like a square dance."—Katherine Harris, Norman, Cleveland County.

[38] Played like it in Great Britain are "Green Grow the Leaves" (Gomme, I, pp. 183-185) and "Joggle Along" (*ibid.*, pp. 285-286).

[39] In Indiana this is a longways game of the casting-off type (Wolford, pp. 92-93) and in Illinois a chasing and kissing game like "Chase the Squirrel" (Van Doren, pp. 492-493).

[40] Cora Frances Starritt, Ada, Pontotoc County. From Texas Dudley and Payne (p. 14) report this as played like "Marching Down to Old Quebec," with simple marching and choosing.

CHAPTER III

THE PLAY-PARTY AND THE DANCE

1. SQUARE DANCE AND RING-DANCE

STRICTLY the term "square dance" should be limited to the quadrille,[1] which is a dance in the form of a hollow square with one couple (in the single quadrille) or two couples (in the double quadrille) on each side. The quadrille is thus to be distinguished from the contra-dance, which is a dance in longways formation (that is, in two parallel lines facing each other), as in the Virginia reel, or in a circle or wheel formation, as in "Old Dan Tucker." Herein the terms "quadrille" and "contra-dance" are used as defined, and "square dance" is used as a generic term for group dancing of either the quadrille or the contra-dance type, as distinguished from the round dance, or for a special gathering where such dances are danced.

The two essential features of the square dance, which set it apart from and, according to old-timers and modern enthusiasts, above the "one and one" quality of the round dance,[2] are its group character and its progressive character. By the one is meant simply that the group of couples, or the set, is the unit instead of the individual linked couple; and by the other, that the continuous sequence or routine of figures permits the dancers to progress to new places so that by the end of the dance "every one will have danced with every one else." "After you danced a figure," one old-timer put it, "you changed partners. You wouldn't dance all night with the same person. You'd have two sweethearts there, or three."

According to another old-timer, the present revival of square dancing is due largely to the fact that "All good people are tired of that jazz lovey dovey dope" and "our good girls of old U. S. A. are getting tired of going to a dance so called and walking backward all night long, with forehead to forehead, with just the dear one she came with."[3] In the same way one may conceive of the young people of rural America several generations

---

[1] In the United States a quadrille is also known as a cotillion. According to the *New English Dictionary*, "contra-dance" and the French *contre-danse* are corruptions or folk-etymological forms of "country dance" (the confusion of *contra* with *country* arising from the longways form of many country dances) and not, as erroneously believed, *vice versa*. In the same way the English country dance is not of French origin, though it has undergone French influence, as evidenced by French terms employed. Square dances, in common parlance, are known as "old-time" and "old-fashion" dances.

[2] To some religious-minded folk, round dancing was more reprehensible than square dancing, on account of the intimacy of the waist swing. "The sin of the deepest dye is dancing . . . and the round dancing has perhaps a shade deeper tinge." (Paul Howard, Headrick, Jackson County.)

[3] L. L. Smith, "Old-Time Dance Calls," p. 4.

ago as wearying of the old circle or line games of their childhood. The typical traditional game, as has been pointed out, is one in which the players clasp hands in a ring and circle round and round, or in a line with one player advancing and retiring in front, repeating over and over some simple formula to which they suit simple actions. Such a perform- ance, involving identical repetition, is inherently monotonous and bound to be uninteresting to young folk of play-party age. The players, it is true, may take turn about as one after another is called into the center of the ring or in front of the line to join or replace the one before, but the change is a successive rather than a progressive one in view of the fact that there is no change of position through a series of steps or stages or sequence of figures. To use an arithmetical analogy, the movement is additive or subtractive but not multiplicative. In the typical party game, on the other hand, which is a swinging play, each player is a multiplier for a whole series of multiplicands, as neatly expressed in the multiplica- tion stanza of "Twistification," often used to accompany the movements of the Virginia reel in "Weevily Wheat":

> Five times five is twenty-five,
>> And five times six is thirty,
> Five times seven is thirty-five,
>> And five times eight is forty.
> Five times nine is forty-five,
>> Five times ten is fifty,
> Five times eleven is fifty-five,
>> And five times twelve is sixty.[4]

The weaving figures which these words accompany are as follows: The boys and girls stand facing each other in two parallel rows, with partners opposite each other. The boy at the top meets half-way the girl at the bottom, they swing, and return to their places. Then the boy swings his partner and the girl her partner, then they swing each other again, then each swings the person next to his or her partner, and so on down the line. They then take their places at the foot of their lines and the process is repeated by the next boy and girl until all have swung. The movements may be further complicated by introducing between the first figures and the repetitions of the second figure the variations of the Vir- ginia reel (e.g., dancing face to face, with right hands crossed, left hands crossed, left shoulder to shoulder, right shoulder to shoulder, back to back, etc.).

In the grand right and left (another favorite party figure) we have another form of weaving movement in which two lines weave in and out

---

[4] Lacie Huff, Norman, Cleveland County, from W. T. Huff.

38

as the boys and girls go in opposite directions, each boy swinging his partner by and with the right hand, then the next girl with her left hand in his left, and so on until he gets back to his partner, when the couples promenade (that is, walk or skip round in a circle or round the room, arm in arm or with joined hands crossed in front).

In both of these forms of swinging play the simple choosing or relieving of players has been replaced by the progressive changing of partners, with continuous change in position; and the accompanying song, in its typical form, consists not in the identical repetition of a stanza but in the incremental or accretionary iteration of a line containing some new element with each repetition.

The question may be asked whether traditional games do not contain or resemble country dances. Among Lady Gomme's classifications is a group of "dance games." [5] But on examination the title proves misleading, for only a few of them are even rounds or ring-dances. Here "dance game" is simply a convenient label to distinguish a game with words and singing from a dramatic game of the singing type—with words, tune, *and action*—or dialogue type—with words and action *but no tune*. Only two games in the list approach or are under the influence of the country dance and so may be said to resemble the swinging play of the play-party. One of these, which has not been recovered in this country, is "Push the Business On" (said to be "of kin to the old-fashioned country dances"):

> I hired a horse and borrowed a gig,
> And all the world shall have a jig;
> And I'll do all 'at ever I can
> To push the business on.
>> To push the business on,
>> To push the business on;
>> And I'll do all 'at ever I can
>> To push the business on.[6]

The method of playing is described as follows:

> The players stand in a circle, boy and girl alternately, and sing the lines. At the fourth line they all clap their hands, keeping time with the song. When singing the seventh line each boy takes the girl on his left hand—dances round with her and places her on his right hand. This is done till each girl has been all round the circle and has been turned or danced with by each boy.[7]

Another of the "dance games," "Green Grow the Leaves," is described as being "more like a country dance"; [8] and a third, "Babbity Bowster,"

---

[5] II, pp. 465-466.
[6] II, pp. 86-88.
[7] II, pp. 87-88.
[8] I, pp. 185-186.

which is described as "taking place at the end of a country ball" and "danced somewhat like the country dance of Sir Roger" (i.e., the Virginia reel), is not included among the "dance games" because the words are sung only to the pairing-off that precedes the dance proper.[9]

2. Dance Calls as Dance-Songs

But the real interest of our subject, from the point of view of the study of folk-song, is in the song that accompanies the swinging play and the process by which it comes into being. There are all kinds of dance-songs, from those that simply accompany movement, without any connection between the words and the movements, to those that direct, suggest, and stimulate movement. For dance accompaniments of the first type, which usually accompany a stately dance, even ballads have been used.[10] Songs of the second type have a direct relation to the movements and so may originate in a dance call rhymed, versified, set to music, and sung by the dancers instead of chanted by the caller or prompter.

Simple directions, of course, occur even in traditional games. But here the typical directions consist of a choosing or kissing formula, which, after all, is a formula and so remains more or less fixed, resisting change or variation. The typical dance directions of the play-party song, on the other hand, take the form of a loose accretionary catalogue or rigmarole, which is highly elastic and may be shortened or lengthened at will. And as the movements of the dance are more flexible than those of the game and may be altered to suit the occasion, so the words may vary accordingly.

A dance song develops from a dance call somewhat as follows: Conscientious objections to dancing to music on the part of church members or the scarcity of the supply of music in isolated or pioneer communities might keep music and musicians out of the play-party, but they could hardly keep the play-party from appropriating dance tunes and dance calls. The borrowing process was facilitated by the fact that many dance tunes already had songs to go with them, which were often sung in lieu of fiddling or to supplement it—minstrel songs like "Buffalo Gals" and "Old Dan Tucker" and Southern mountain songs like "Cotton-Eyed Joe," "Cripple Creek," "Shady Grove," and "Sourwood Mountain." [11]   And

---

[9] I, pp. 9-11.

[10] See below, p. 58.

[11] Compare Hudson, pp. 123-124, who cites some fragments employed for the same purpose and notes that such songs were often sung by the "non-dancing part of the party . . . to mark the rhythms"—much, it might be added, after the fashion of patting out the rhythm in Negro dances. Sandburg notes with regard to "One Morning in May" (pp. 136-138): "Such a song was particularly useful when the fiddler failed to show up or went out of commission with a heavy cargo of 'corn'."

many of the rhymed calls were rhythmical and even metrical enough to be sung as they were.

The musical dance call, then, would be the simplest and probably the earliest kind of dance-song, though it would be hazardous to go beyond classification and attempt to reconstruct historical or evolutionary stages. An example of such a song which is little more than a dance call set to music is "Gents to the Centre," which in Oklahoma is sung to the tune of "The Irish Washerwoman":

> Gents to the centre and back to the bar,
> Ladies to the centre and form in a star.
> Gents to the centre and form in a ring,
> Oh, when you do form, oh, then you do swing.
> When you do swing, remember my call,
> Bow to your partner and promenade all.
> Promenade all, promenade all,
> Bow to your partner and promenade all.[12]

Although this is merely a fragment, it indicates the tendency of the dance call, in its transition to the dance-song, to take on extra verses to fill out the time. Here the closing couplet forms a sort of refrain obviously intended to fill the interval required for the execution of the direction, "promenade all." Instead of repeating the call, however, the bars may be filled with nonsense syllables—

> Tra, la, la, la, la, la, la, la, la, la, la. (*Three times.*)[13]

---

[12] Professor Kenneth C. Kaufman, Norman, Cleveland County, who played it in Eastern Custer County.

[13] William Plaster, Meeker, Lincoln County. "Gents to the Centre" also appears as a part of other songs, e.g., "Coffee Grows on a White Oak Tree":
> Gents to the centre
>   With a ding, dong, ding,
> Ladies to the centre
>   And form a little ring.
> Tra, la, la, la, la, la, la. (*Twice.*)
>   (Bertha Matthews, Norman, Cleveland County, from Chickasha, Grady County.)
And in "Skip to My Lou":
> Ladies to the centre with a ding, ling, ling,
> Gents to the centre and form a ring.
> Twice round the circle, once round the ring,
> Grab a partner and everybody swing.
>   (A. J. Strange, Clinton, Custer County.)
Also in "Captain Jinks" (Carl West, Perico, Texas, from Raymond Kiser, Perico). See below, p. 52. The same call is reported by Piper in "Heel and Toe Polka" (p. 286) with these nonsense lines reminiscent of folk-song refrains:
> Sing whack ti O li, ti O lo, ti ling daddy O,
> Whack ti O li, ti O lo, ti ling day.
Randolph reports a refrain, "la-de-da-de-da-da," in a dance song composed of a call ("Across the Hall," p. 224).

41

In either case the refrain serves a definitely rhythmic purpose.

To make clear the exact relation of the dance-song to the dance call from which it evolved, the complete version of "Gents to the Centre" reported by Mrs. Goldy M. Hamilton from Missouri is set beside the call for "Ladies to the Centre and Back to the Bar," as reported from Iowa. In the Missouri play-party song a nonsense line creeps into two stanzas which are unrhymed and thus serves a melodic as well as a rhythmic purpose.

> All gents to centre with right hand cross,
> Ha! da di diddle a dum,
> Form a star with left hand back,
> Take your partner as you go round.
>
> *Chorus:*
> Gents swing·out, and ladies swing in,
> Hold your "holts" and circle again,
> Break the swing and promenade,
> Promenade with a waltzing swing.
>
> All gents to the centre with right hand cross,
> Ha da diddle do dum,
> Form a star with left hand back,
> Skip your partner and take the next.
>
> All gents to the centre and form in a ring,
> And when you have formed, go balance and swing,
> And when you have swung, remember your call,
> Swing the next lady and run away all.
>
> Up and down the railroad-track,
> Half a swing around,
> Back to the centre with the same old swing
> And swing four hands round, and swing four hands round.[14]

The Iowa dance call together with explanations, minus several figures that are not matched in the play-party song, is as follows:

> *Ladies to the Center and Back to the Bar*—(All four ladies walk, facing each other, until they meet in the center of the set, then walk backward to their own station. While the ladies are passing to the center and back, the gents remain at their station.)
>
> *Gents to the Center and Form a Star, with the Right Hands Crossed*—(All four gents pass to the center of the set. The first and third gent clasp right hands and at the same time, the second and fourth gent clasp right hands, the four hands being crossed, thus forming a star in the center of the set. While this is being done the ladies remain in their station. The gents turn in a circle to the left until they are near their own station.)

---

[14] Hamilton, p. 299. The last stanza is an interpolation from "Up and Down," *idem*, pp. 302-303.

The Left Hand Back—(The gents let loose right hands and turn around. Take hold left hands forming the star and continue to circle in the opposite direction.)

Skip Your Partner and Take the Next—(The gents pass their own partners and hold fast left hands, lock their right arm with the next ladies' left arm and continue to circle with all four ladies in the same direction. Gents remember this lady is now your partner until told to skip her.)

Gents Swing Out and the Ladies Swing in. Join Their Right Hands and Circle Again.—(The gents let go hands in the center and walk backward, holding fast to the lady's left arm with their right arm and swinging her forward, half way around. The ladies join their right hands and continue to circle as before, but in the opposite direction, when the gents come near their own station.)[15] . . .

With line division this gives us the following stanza:

Ladies to the center and back to the bar,
Gents to the center and form a star
With the right hands crossed, the left hand back,
Skip your partner and take the next.
Gents swing out and the ladies swing in,
Join their right hands and circle again.

In dance games with complicated figures requiring detailed and explicit directions, accordingly, the quadrille call assumes first place. And the song arises simply by grouping the calls into stanzas, one of which may serve as chorus. The result is so close to the dance call as to be almost indistinguishable from it except as it is known to have been sung by the players instead of chanted by the caller.

This type of song may be called a *dance direction song,* to distinguish it from the mere *dance call,* on the one hand, and the true *dance-song,* on the other, which has fewer directions and more song. On account of its complicated pattern, the dance direction song is not very common among play-party songs and is open to several objections. In the first place, it did not satisfy the requirement of simplicity which the players demanded in addition to the variety that traditional games failed to give. It lacked simplicity both in execution (in the absence of the square dance organization of floor manager, caller, and musicians) and in words. The latter are not easy to remember or sing. They lack memorableness because, in the second place, being directions and so purely mechanical and informative, they lack the human interest and imaginative appeal of the usual play-party song with its frequently poetic imagery, its dramatic characters and situations, and its humorous quips and sallies.[16] Finally, these dance

---

[15] L. L. Smith, pp. 28-29.
[16] In common with all folk rhymes dance-songs must stand the test of memory. And the same condition holds good for them that Talley postulates for Negro Folk

direction songs, being so close to the borderline between play-party and square dance, are always in danger of reverting to type and being absorbed by the square dance; that is, as soon as the vigilance of the church is relaxed or music happens to be furnished, it would be natural and simpler for the directions to be taken over by the caller or to disappear altogether.[17] In other words, this type of dance-song, more than any other, has little justification for existence except as a substitute for instrumental music.

3. ACCRETIONARY DANCE-SONGS

Far more satisfactory and characteristic is a second type of dance-song derived from the dance call. The difference between the two types is evinced clearly in form. In the dance direction song there is little if any repetition. Each line adds a new detail to the directions and carries us a step further in the figure. The result is highly concentrated and involved. If, on the other hand, by repetition and refrain a single direction may be elaborated into a stanza, the result is more leisurely, puts far less strain on the memory and attention, and enables the dancers to concentrate on the movements, which, after all, are the main thing. Especially when one considers two other advantages is the superiority of this type of song apparent. The repetition provides a loose elastic structure which may be shortened or lengthened at will. And with the compression removed, the directions may be suggested instead of mechanically stated, and alternated and varied with patter, involving, usually, a dramatic action, character, or situation to make the play vivid and concrete and permitting adaptation and improvisation *ad lib.* Finally, the elements of repetition and refrain add the charm of music and rhythm as well as the value of a mnemonic device.

A simple example of the type is "Jutang." This takes the form of couplets ringing the changes on a delightful nonsense word [18] (whatever

---

Rhymes: " . . . and since Memory works largely through Association; one readily sees that the putting of the Rhymes into a story, descriptive, or striking thought form, was the only thing that could cause their being kept alive. It was through their being composed thus that Association was able to assist Memory in recalling them. Those carrying another form carried their death warrant" (pp. 273-274).

[17] Compare Dudley and Payne, p. 9: "Indeed, where they have violins . . . the weary singer, or caller, as he is often termed, sings only the first line of the verse, and the figure is continued to the music."

[18] The use of an additive or subtractive formula, as successive couples are taken in or dropped out, heightens the appeal of the mystifying jargon and its resemblance to the counting-out rhyme's "combination of numerals with senseless words" which has been taken as evidence of their "connection with sortilege" (Bolton, p. 47)—a consideration which, it need hardly be added, affects these dance songs only as an atavistic memory of ancient magical charms and prayers, lurking in the background of the mind, may help to explain the taste for queer enumerative jingles. Compare "John Brown Had a Little Indian" and Leland, *JAFL,* 2:113-114.

else it may have been in the beginning) which works the spell of an incantation.

> Circle four in Ju Tang a Ju Tang Ju.
> Circle four in Ju Tang a Ju Tang Ju.
> Work right and left in Ju Tang a Ju Tang Ju.
> Work right and left in Ju Tang a Ju Tang Ju.
> Once in a half in Ju Tang a Ju Tang Ju.
> Once in a half in Ju Tang a Ju Tang Ju.
> On down the line to the next pretty girl a Ju Tang Ju.
> On down the line to the next pretty girl a Ju Tang Ju.
> Next young lady to your right a Ju Tang Ju.
> Next young lady to your right a Ju Tang Ju.
> On down the line in Ju Tang a Ju Tang Ju.
> On down the line in Ju Tang a Ju Tang Ju.
> Meet your partner in Ju Tang a Ju Tang Ju.
> Meet your partner in Ju Tang a Ju Tang Ju.
> All night long in Ju Tang a Ju Tang Ju.
> All night long in Ju Tang a Ju Tang Ju.

(Repeat for "Circle six," "Circle eight," etc.)[19]

In "London" the nonsense word gives way to a place-name denoting location or destination—a common enough device in accretionary dance-songs suggesting progression by means of a journey—and the couplets tend to break up into quatrains, with the first line repeated in the third and a refrain in the second and fourth lines.

> Round up four in London,
>   So I heard them say.
> Round up four in London,
>   So I heard them say.
>
> Do-ce-do in London, etc.
>
> Break and swing in London, etc.
>
> Treat 'em all alike in London, etc.
>
> Lots of pretty girls in London, etc.
>
> One more time in London, etc.
>
> Promenade home in London, etc.

(Repeat for "Round up six," "Round up eight.")[20]

---

[19] Melvin Culbertson, Amber, Grady County.

[20] Mary Haxel, McClain County, who played it near Noble, Cleveland County, and Washington, McClain County. In another version, after the picking up in twos, there follows the dropping out of two by two, in additive and subtractive fashion (Leonard C. Dresser, Lahoma, Garfield County).

The secret of the success and the basis of the appeal of this type of dance-song lie in the skillful varying of the directions with cajoling patter which suggests the movements indirectly and allusively rather than directly and literally. (Lines made up or borrowed from popular songs may be designated as "verses" and lines made up of calls, as "directions.") The combination is happiest in "The Irish Trot," "On to Galilee," "The Old Brass Wagon," and "Sandy Land," all of which contain a dramatic element and concrete allusions related to the personalities and incidents of the dance and their background in rural or frontier life. In all of these, moreover, as the directions become simpler and the patter grows livelier, we get further away from the square dance and closer to the swinging play—the typical form of combination game-and-dance developed by the play-party (for which, incidentally, "swinging play" is an apt name, the first part of the term denoting the dance and the second the game).

In "On to Galilee," in which the enumeration is combined with a journey, we have a call as chorus, and variety is secured and interest sustained further by the emulation of nicknames for the players who go down the wilderness in turn. Usually, as stated in the preceding chapter, there are complimentary names for the girls and uncomplimentary names for the boys, but the practice is not consistent here.

> First young lady, go down the wilderness,
>> Down the wilderness, down the wilderness,
> First young lady, go down the wilderness,
>> On to Galilee.

> *Chorus:*
> Hands up around the lady,
>> Around the lady, around the lady,
> Hands up around the lady,
>> On to Galilee.[21]

Then: Swing that lady out of the wilderness, Next old married lady go down the wilderness, Next old maid (or fair lady) go down the wilderness, Swing all the ladies out of the wilderness, while the boys become old hobo, old soapstick, old bachelor.

With the swinging play in circle form, we return to the game, involving not choosing but capture, so to speak, in the form of stealing a partner. This is the case with "Skip to My Lou" and "Pig in the Parlor," in which the rivalry of satiric nonsense, permitting unlimited improvisation and accretion, keeps the play from lapsing into the monotony of the mere game, while the directions are relegated entirely to the chorus.

---

[21] Mary Haxel, Purcell, McClain County.

Oh, my father and mother were Irish, (*Three times.*)
And I am Irish too.

Chorus:
Oh, your right hand to your partner,
Your left hand to your neighbor,
Your right hand to your partner,
And all promenade. (*Three times.*)
Your right hand to your partner
And all promenade.

We kept the pig in the parlor, etc.

We kept the cat in the cream jug, etc.

We kept the cow in the kitchen, etc.[22]

In "Miller Boy," the prototype of "Pig in the Parlor," the presence of the game formula hampers variation, though a dance call is introduced into many play-party versions and, in the American form of the game, the simple injunction to "grab" [23] is replaced by a dance direction which is varied through two or more stanzas, with limited accretion.

Miller boy, miller boy, living by the mill.
The mill turned around with a free good will.
Hand on the hopper and the other on the sack,
Gents step forward and ladies step back.

Chorus:
Sailing east, sailing west,
Sailing over the ocean.
All you boys who want a good cook
Had better be quick in the motion.

---

[22] Florette McNeese, Oklahoma City, Oklahoma County.

[23] Gomme reports one version in which "the 'grab' appears to be lost, and the 'hunting' put in before the rush for the vacant place is made" (II, pp. 436-437). The "hunting" thus corresponds to the "sailing" of the American chorus.
A hunting we will go,
A hunting we will go,
We'll catch a little fox, and we'll put him in a box,
And a hunting we will go.
This stanza is borrowed from "Hunting" (Gomme, I, pp. 243-245), recovered in this country as "Have You Seen the Sha?" (Gardner, p. 102). For variations in the words of "Miller Boy," see Chapter V.

Happy was the miller boy that lived by the mill.
If he hadn't moved away, he'd be living there still.
Hand on the hopper and the other on the ground,
Ladies stand still and the gents go round.

Happy was the miller boy that lived by the mill.
The mill turned around with a free good will.
Hand on the hopper and the other on the sack,
Turn right around and go right back.[24]

The call added may be short—

All got a partner, all in ring,
Stomp that foot and everybody swing.
Hands exchange, feet on ground,
Right and left all way round.[25]

or long—

First gent out, swing that lady
With a right hand about,
Partner by the left as you come around,
Lady in the centre and you'll all run around.
Such a kitten upstairs, well, I never did see,
Such a kitten upstairs, well, she don't suit me.

First couple down the centre and divide the ring,
Lady go right and gent go left.
When they meet, everybody swing,
Alemond a left, go round the ring.
Down the centre as you uster do,
Down the centre and a cast off two.
When you meet, everybody swing,
Alemond a left, go round the ring.

First couple out to the right of the ring.
Honor that lady with a howdy do do,
Swing your honey, go round and through,
Swing your honey, go through and around.
When you meet, four hands up
And around you go,
Two little ladies, come dosey do.
One more change and on you go.[26]

---

[24] Nieto Looney, El Reno, Canadian County, who played it at Hennepin, Garvin County.
[25] Cora Huddleston, Norman, Cleveland County.
[26] Evelyn Roach, Shamrock, Texas.

The Play-Party and the Dance

4. POPULAR SONGS AS DANCE-SONGS

Coming finally to a third type of dance-song, that based on a popular song, we find that the existence of the contra-dance and play-party versions of the same song affords an opportunity for studying the reciprocal relationship and influence of the square dance and the play-party. In "Old Dan Tucker," another game of the partner-stealing type, the verses of the original minstrel song contain so much entertainment in their comic portraiture of Tucker that the play-party was loth to give them up entirely for dance directions, and when it did the result was colorless and flat in the extreme, as in

: Swing three ladies, Old Dan Tucker,: 3 times
Down in the valley.

: Promenade round Old Dan Tucker,: 3 times
Down in the valley.

: Circle to the left, Old Dan Tucker,: 3 times
Down in the valley.

: Swing, oh swing, Old Dan Tucker,: 3 times
Down in the valley.

: Promenade home, Old Dan Tucker,: 3 times
Down in the valley.[27]

In other cases the original song may survive only in a stanza or two, in a line serving to introduce or conclude a stanza of dance directions, or in a refrain composed of the title of the song or its original refrain.

Thus, in "The Girl I Left Behind Me," the refrain line is taken over to fit the movement in which each boy swings the girl *behind* him, with or without additional lines describing the girl and her effect on the singer. The dance figure is expressed in some form of the following stanza:

Same old boy and brand new girl,
Swing her by the right hand.
Now your partner by the left,
And promenade the girl behind you.[28]

[27] Wolford, pp. 78-79. Piper (p. 287) is of the opinion that the intricacy of the quadrille figures of "Old Dan Tucker" kept them from passing over into the play-party since they would have caused confusion without a caller. It must not be overlooked, however, that the colorlessness of a version like that cited above would also be a deterrent.
[28] Gerald Bond, Bonnie Mae Close, and Glenn A. Roe, Oklahoma City, Oklahoma County; Thelma Wild Rose, Chickasha, Grady County. Compare Dudley and Payne, pp. 28-29; Hamilton, p. 297; Wolford, p. 46. For the contra-dance, see *"Good Morning,"* p. 103, and for the Morris dance, Sharp, *Sword Dancers,* p. 40.

49

Words are also used as an accompaniment in the contra-dance:

> I take that girl, that pretty little girl,
>   The girl I left behind me,
> And pass right through, and balance too,
>   And swing that girl behind me.[29]

> Swing that girl, that pretty little girl,
>   Th' girl I left behind me.
> Oh! she's pretty in th' face
> And slim around th' waist,
>   Th' girl I left behind me.[30]

In "Buffalo Girls" and "Captain Jinks" references to dancing in the original songs are mainly taken over to suit the dance movement, with or without additional directions, while the other stanzas drop out.

> Buffalo boys are coming out to-night,
>   Coming out to-night, coming out to-night,
> Buffalo boys are coming out to-night,
>   To dance by the light of the moon.

> They dance all night till broad daylight,
>   Till broad daylight, till broad daylight,
> They dance all night till broad daylight
>   And go home with the girls in the morning.[31]

> Captain Jenks is out to-night.
> The lady dances to the right.
> The gentleman dances to the left,
>   And we'll all promenade.

> Captain Jenks got tight one night.
> The gentleman changes to the right
> And swings the lady with all his might,
>   And we'll all promenade.

> My ma she cried when I left home,
>   When I left home, when I left home,
> My ma she cried when I left home,
>   For that's the style of the army.[32]

In one Oklahoma version of "Buffalo Girls" the song and the directions are evenly divided:

---

[29] *"Good Morning,"* p. 26.
[30] Young, p. 257.
[31] Mrs. Bertha Downing, Norman, Cleveland County, who played it in Southern Noble, Northeastern Logan, and Northern Payne Counties.
[32] Frances T. Henderson, Fort Cobb, Caddo County.

Form a star the right hands crossed,
  The right hands crossed, the right hands crossed,
Form a star the right hands crossed,
  The left hand back again.

Eight hands up and round we go,
  Round we go, round we go,
Eight hands up and round we go,
  Ladies don't see any gents they know.

Buffalo girls a-coming by night,
  Coming by night, coming by night,
Buffalo girls a-coming by night,
  To dance my the light of the moon.

Dance all night till broad daylight,
  Till broad daylight, till broad daylight,
Dance all night till broad daylight,
  Go home with the girls in the morning.[33]

In another version the directions predominate:

Buffalo girls all around the outside,
  All around the outside, all around the outside,
Buffalo girls all around the outside,
  And balance unto your partner.

Swing them around with a waltz and a swing,
With a waltz and a swing, with a waltz and a swing.
Swing them around with a waltz and a swing.
  And balance unto your places.[34]

In most versions of "Captain Jinks" the refrain "For that's the style of the army" and the line introducing Captain Jinks are the only carryover from the song.

Captain Jenks, of the horse marinks,
Claps his hands with all his minks,
And swing your partner if you're not too green,
  For that's the style of the army.

We'll all join hands and circle left,
  And circle left, and circle left.
We'll all join hands and circle left,
  For that's the style of the army.

---

[33] Lela L. Conrad, Perry, Noble County.

[34] Wallas M. McCown, Emporia, Kansas, from Earl Denton, Norman, Cleveland County. In other versions it is "One Buffalo girl, all around inside" (Fanny W. Kelly, Jefferson, Grant County; Evelyn Roach. Shamrock, Texas). Compare Piper (pp. 285-286), "First young gent all around inside."

51

Ladies to the centre and back again,
Gents to the centre and form in a ring,
And when you've formed, then you may swing,
And when you've swung, remember my call,
Skip one partner and promenade all.[35]

In " 'Tain't Goin' to Rain No More" the original may survive with some integrity—

My old mistress she told me,
It ain'ta gonna rain no more,
When she died she'd set me free,
It ain'ta gonna rain no more,
It ain'ta gonna rain no more.
She lived so long her head got bald,
It ain'ta gonna rain no more.
She give it up not dyin' at all,
It ain'ta gonna rain no more,
It ain'ta gonna rain no more.

She had an ol' bonnet all ruffled round the brim,
It ain'ta gonna rain no more.
Looked like a crow's nest hangin' on a limb,
It ain'ta gonna rain no more,
It ain'ta gonna rain no more.
She had another bonnet all ruffled round the crown,
It ain'ta gonna rain no more.
Looked like poor folks livin' in town,
It ain'ta gonna rain no more,
It ain'ta gonna rain no more.[36]

or only in the refrain—

Down the centre and divide the ring,
'Tain't goin' to rain no more,
Meet in the hall and bow and swing.
'Tain't, etc.
Promenade your corner girl, etc.
Meet on the corner and do the whirl, etc.

Chorus:
Rainin' on the hillside, fare you well,
'Tain't, etc.
Rained all yesterday and day before,
'Tain't, etc.[37]

---

[35] Carl West, Perico, Texas, from Raymond Kiser, Perico.
[36] Bertha Matthews, Norman, Cleveland County, from Chickasha, Grady County. These lines have been transferred from "Promises of Freedom" (Talley, pp. 25-26), otherwise known as "Pore Mournah" (Scarborough, p. 194).
[37] Florette McNeese, Oklahoma City, Oklahoma County.

5. SUMMARY

To sum up the case for the influence of the square dance on play-party songs, we find that the following processes may be distinguished:

1. The dance accompaniments sung by the dancers in the prohibition or absence of instrumental music may consist of little or nothing more than dance calls set to music, as in "Gents to the Centre."

2. Play-party songs made up entirely of calls for complicated changes rhymed and versified (so-called *dance direction songs*) are less frequent and less characteristic because of the difficulty of executing them without square dance organization and because of the lack of narrative and descriptive associations to assist the memory and to prevent the songs from being taken over by the square dance.

3. The most characteristic form of play-party song under square dance influence is that in which actual calls give way to allusive directions varied with patter in an elastic accretionary rigmarole, the call sometimes being retained as a chorus.

4. When the verses are borrowed from popular songs which have given rise to rival play-party and square dance versions, the dance and the song vie with each other for preëminence, resulting in four types, depending upon the relative vitality of the dance and the song: one in which the song has been practically displaced by the calls; a second in which the calls are in the ascendency; a third in which the song is in the ascendency; and a fourth in which the calls have been almost entirely displaced by the song.

5. These considerations prompt the conclusion that what instigated and fostered the play-party as a separate and independent form and institution and prevented it from going over to the square dance was not religious prejudice alone but the possibilities the play-party afforded for a combination of game and dance which possessed distinct advantages over either type singly.[38] These advantages appear best in the accretionary song like "Skip to My Lou," which has here been designated as the typical form of dance-song developed by the play-party and which justified its existence by eliminating the complications of the square dance and by developing to the utmost the opportunity for human, humorous, and dramatic by-play.

---

[38] See above, p. 18.

CHAPTER IV

THE PLAY-PARTY AND THE SONG

In drawing upon folk-songs and popular songs for tunes to dance to and words to accompany them, the play-party was simply following the tendency of conservative folk tradition to take over what is already at hand rather than invent anew. In so doing it had a precedent in the game and dance usage of the past, which has adapted and usually mutilated songs of all types to accompany, suggest, or stimulate movement. And in the results of this borrowing, adjusting, and degrading process the play-party illustrates not only the law of levelling oral transmission, which implies descent from higher to lower and resultant deterioration, but also the decay of song material under the wearing usage of the dance.

Two types of games derived from songs may be distinguished: those apparently preserving the remains of ancient songs which have not survived separately—games of hypothetical song origin; and those which may be traced definitely to existing songs—games with established song originals. One may distinguish also between game-songs of the ballad and dramatic type—derived from narrative and dialogue pieces—and game-songs of the lyric type. The second classification points to a twofold division according to source. On the one hand the play-party drew upon a heritage of the older traditional pieces—English and Scottish ballads and imported folk-songs and nursery songs: and on the other hand it called into play the newer indigenous pieces—American folk-songs and popular songs, including war songs, western pioneer songs, stage and street songs (especially minstrel songs), Negro songs, and Southern Mountain songs.

1. Song Survivals in Traditional Games

Both Lady Gomme and Newell have (though for different reasons) postulated ballad origins for game-songs or reported game and dance utilization of ballads. In her "Memoir on the Study of Children's Games" the former states that in the class of circle games "a few examples have evidently been derived from love ballads, drinking songs, and toasts," adding that "some of the dance games are of this origin." This she accounts for on the basis of a love and courtship motive in the ballad, inasmuch as "children, knowing the general form of marriage games, would naturally dance in circle form to any ballad verses in which marriage or love and courtship occurs, and in this manner the ballad would become apparently a fresh game, though it would only be putting new words to an old formula of action." [1]

---

[1] II, p. 497.

54

One would have wished her to be more explicit as to the methods of utilizing songs for dance or game accompaniment and as to the titles in her collection coming under this head. But beyond a quotation from Dr. Jacob Jacobsen on the use of ballads for ring-dances in Shetland and mere mention of Newell's account of "Barbara Allen" as "sung and danced in New England at children's parties at a period when dancing was forbidden to be taught in schools" and of "Auld Lang Syne" as a "further instance," she gives us no basis for inference. In her elaborate classification of games according to form and content, a grouping of games according to song source obviously finds no place; and since her interest is mainly in cultural survivals she can hardly be taken to task for a deficiency on the literary side.

The collection itself yields a handful of examples which substantiate her claim for love and marriage interest in games derived from ballads. "Oats and Beans and Barley" [2] she believes probably to "have preserved the tradition of a formula sung at the sowing of grain" or at harvest, adding that "As soon as it has become a child's game, however, the process of decadence sets in" until in one version the lines relating to farming have dropped out entirely and all that we have left is the marriage formula. "Isabella" [3] likewise "has probably had its origin in a ballad," a likelihood strengthened, she adds, "by the fact that only one version [from London] has the marriage formula sung at the end, and this is probably an arbitrary addition." (It should be added that both "Oats and Beans and Barley" and "Isabella" have choosing or kissing formulae in addition to the marriage formula—the most obvious game features.) In "Isabella" the lines apparently surviving from the "ballad" are reminiscent of a sentimental lyric, somewhat garbled:

> Isabella, Isabella, Isabella, Farewell!
> Last night when we parted
> I left you broken-hearted,
> And on a green mountain
> There stands a young man.
>
> .   .   .
>
> The trees are uncovered, uncovered, uncovered,
> The trees are uncovered, Isabella, for me!

The rest of the game-song consists of added lines calling for imitative action.

So much for her games of hypothetical song origin. Four other love and marriage games in Lady Gomme's collection may be assigned to well-known ballads or folk-songs: "Lady on the Mountain" and "Lady on

---

[2] II, pp. 1-13.
[3] I, pp. 247-256.

Yonder Hill," [4] game versions of the comic song "No, Sir," consisting of one song stanza followed by choosing and marriage formulae; and "Paper of Pins" [5] and "Keys of Heaven," [6] fragments of a folk-song related to "No, Sir." Three other song survivals fall outside the love and marriage class. One is "Dinah," in which a blindfolded player inside the ring takes the place of any one whose name he succeeds in guessing. The song consists of one stanza, which, curiously enough, is from "Dinah," a Christy minstrel song of the Fifties (the only instance of minstrel origin in her collection, though it is one of the most fertile sources of play-party songs):

> No one in the house but Dinah, Dinah,
> No one in the house I know, I know;
> No one in the house but Dinah, Dinah,
> Playing on the old banjo.[7]

A second is "Three Little Ships," a fairly good version of the Christmas carol, "I saw a ship come sailing in," in which the players dance in turn between parallel rows.[8] A debased version of the same carol turns up in "Duck Dance," [9] which, in one variant, ends with little girls quacking like ducks in a string and, in another, is simply a "nursery paradox" to be sung. Finally, the only ballad is represented by a single stanza—the last of "The Mermaid" (Child, No. 289) in "Round and Round Went the Gallant Ship," in which the original third line, "For the want of a life-boat they all went down," is displaced by a mere repetition:

> Three times round goes our gallant ship,
> And three times round went she;
> Three times round went our gallant ship,
> Then she sank to the bottom of the sea.[10]

This ballad, obviously, is chosen not for its love and marriage interest but because it suggests movement, all the dancers bobbing down on the last line.

---

[4] I, pp. 320-324. See below, p. 61.
[5] II, pp. 450-451.
[6] II, pp. 437-438.
[7] I, p. 97.
[8] II, pp. 279-282.
[9] I, pp. 113-114.
[10] II, p. 143. Also *Social Plays, Games,* etc., p. 40. Hudson (p. 23) reports the stanza in practically the same form in a ballad version from Mississippi. Another ballad text is printed by Pound (*American Ballads and Songs*, pp. 26-27) from Wyoming. Compare the intrusion of this stanza in a version of "Merry-Ma-Tansa" entitled "Gala Ship" ("Three times round goes the gala, gala ship," I, p. 375), which combines choosing with the head-duck, and in "Galley, Galley Ship" ("Three times round goes the galley, galley ship," II, pp. 422-424). A larger fragment of the ballad appears as "Gallant Ship" (II, p. 422).

With Newell we are on a little surer ground as regards song survivals. Defining the ballad as a "dramatic poem sung and acted in the dance," he sees it passing into the children's game on account of its dramatic element and the natural tendency of children to "act out the stories they hear." [11] As a result of this process, however, the history is reduced to a *historiette,* which omits the narrative and retains only a strong situation, as in "Here Sits the Queen of England":

> Here sits the Queen of England in her chair,
> She has lost her true love that she had last year;
> So rise upon your feet, and kiss the first you meet,
> For there's many around your chair.[12]

Here, Newell observes, is "the tragedy told in a line; and what more is needed since an excuse is already provided for the kiss or the romp?" [13] In this class belong the games which Newell classifies as "Histories," [14] all of them love-tales save "Miss Jennia Jones": "Down She Comes as White as Milk," "Little Sally Waters," "Green Gravel," "Uncle John," "King Arthur Was King William's Son," and the fragment cited above, to which might be added many of the games entitled "Love-Games," [15] most of which are in dialogue form. In addition to the ballad situation Newell also applies the test of style to establish the ballad affiliations of nursery rhymes as a whole—by such phrases as "red rose," a "pretty fair maid," the "finest flower," the "flower of May." [16]

2. GAME AND DANCE USAGE OF NARRATIVE AND DIALOGUE SONGS

Turning from these general considerations of song sources to the types of songs adapted, let us consider first what happens when narrative and dialogue songs are utilized for game or dance purposes. There are four possibilities. The song may serve as an accompaniment to a stately dance; it may be sung or spoken as a mere dialogue without dancing; it may be acted out in the form of a drama or a dramatic game; or it may serve as the starting-point of a choosing or swinging game.

---

[11] Pp. 8, 9.

[12] P. 70.

[13] P. 9.

[14] Pp. 63-79. In his second edition Newell changed his mind about the ballad origin of "Green Gravel" and "King William Was King James's Son" (pp. 242, 247-248).

[15] Pp. 39-62. These include "I'll Give to You a Paper of Pins" and "There She Stands, a Lovely Creature" (Gomme's "Lady on Yonder Hill").

[16] Compare Miller (p. 29) who, following Newell, points out that "Besides the ballad situations, the game songs have many reminiscences of ballad style and diction," including stock-epithets like "lily-white hand," stock motives such as the sympathetic entwining plants, and ballad stanza forms (though ballad stanza forms are also found in game-songs with no ballad connections).

For usage of the first type, which would seem to be the most obvious and most common, the evidence is meagerest. The chief instance is "Barbara Allen," in Newell's oft-cited account of its use as a "game or dance at evening parties" at Keene, New Hampshire, in the first quarter of the nineteenth century. This account is of especial interest from the point of view of the play-party since it is one of the few instances given by Newell of a dance-game intended to allay religious prejudice against dancing to music.[17] "It is noteworthy," he observes, "that while, in the town of which we speak, the establishment, at the period alluded to, of a children's dancing-school was bitterly opposed, and the children of 'church members' were hardly permitted to attend, no such prohibition applied to amusements like this, which were shared in irrespective of sectarian prejudice, by boys as well as by girls." He describes the "performers as standing in couples, consisting each of a boy and a girl, facing each other. An elderly lady, who was in particular request at children's parties on account of her extensive stock of lore of the sort, sang the ballad, to which the dancers kept time with a slow metrical movement, balancing without any considerable change of place. At the final words, 'Barbara Allen,' which end every stanza, a courtesy took the place of the usual refrain. The whole performance is described as exceedingly pretty, stately, and decorous. It cannot be doubted that the version of the ballad sung was traditional, but we have not been able to secure it." [18]

This description of the method of dancing "Barbara Allen" has been reproduced in full for the reason that in references to it (which are frequent because it is the only case of dance utilization of the song on record) it is not made clear that the ballad was sung by an onlooker instead of by the dancers themselves.[19] To give the latter impression, as most of the commentators do by implication, is misleading, since the real issue involved is one of *participants in the dance singing while dancing,* not *dancing to the singing of a non-participant,* who under the circumstances serves merely as orchestra. The latter procedure would hardly be a fair test of dance usage of a song inasmuch as the song could scarcely be exposed to the wearing influence of the dance unless it were actually made a part of the performance. Only then do dancers feel the need of adapting the words to suit the movements, and this especially when the movements are vigorous and varied instead of merely "pretty, stately, and decorous," and

---

[17] Other games of this type described by Newell are "The Baptist Game" ("Come, all ye young men in your evil ways"), pp. 101-102, and "Swine-Herders," pp. 232-234.
[18] Pp. 78-79.
[19] Compare Gomme, II, p. 497; Miller, p. 28; Pound (*Poetic Origins and the Ballad*), pp. 53-54.

involve *considerable* change of place. In such cases, of course, the song really ceases to be an accompaniment and becomes a game.[20]

"The Two Sisters" is a ballad which seems to have had widespread use as a dance-song in the South and the Middle West, being reported to the writer from Oklahoma, Arkansas, and Missouri as well as by Louise Pound from Nebraska, Jean Thomas from Kentucky, and A. P. Hudson from Mississippi.[21] The Oklahoma-Arkansas version is described as an "old dance-song, the leader singing alone, all except the last two lines of each stanza. All joined in the chorus on the last two lines." This text, like the Oklahoma-Missouri text, is incomplete, and again shows no effects of dance usage except in the occurrence of the words "bow" and "balance" (apparently dance directions). Thus, in the Oklahoma-Arkansas version, entitled "Bow-ee down (Bow Ye Down)":

> There lived an old lady by the northern sea,
> > Bow-ee down!
> There lived an old lady by the northern sea,
> > Bow and balance to me!
> There lived an old lady by the northern sea,
> And she had daughters, one, two, three.
> > I'll be true to my love,
> > If my love'll be true to me.[22]

And in the Oklahoma-Missouri version:

> The miller he courted the eldest one,
> > Bow down, bow down.
> The miller he courted the eldest one,
> > For the bow was bent to me.

---

[20] An example of the use of a folk-song for simple ring-dance accompaniment is furnished by the nursery song "The Cuckoo" (*Mother Goose,* p. 78; Sharp, *One Hundred English Folksongs,* pp. 82-83), reported from Oklahoma by Kenneth Mc-Afee, Seminole, Seminole County: "Any number would catch hands and dance around in a circle singing this."

For the complete identification and understanding of the game or dance usage of a song one must have both full text and full directions. As in the case of "Barbara Allen" Newell gives the general method of dance usage without the text, so in the case of "Little Harry Hughes and the Duke's Daughter" (pp. 75-78) he gives the text with only the general comment that it is a "song of negro children in New York." As such the song obviously has no value as evidence of anything save the singing of the ballad by children at play, since there is nothing in the text itself to indicate game or dance usage.

[21] For the Pound text and comment, see *Poetic Origins and the Ballad,* pp. 53-54. For the Thomas text and its dance usage, see *Devil's Ditties,* pp. 70-73, 3-5. For the Hudson note, see *Culture in the South,* pp. 524, 540. Although in *Specimens* (p. 4) Dr. Hudson cites no dance usage for his text, he has referred me to his *Folk-Songs of Mississippi and Their Background* (in MS.) for a report of such usage by Mrs. R. C. Jones, Oxford, Mississippi.

[22] Mrs. Demma Ray Oldham, Oklahoma City, Oklahoma County, who played it in Arkansas.

> The miller he courted the eldest one
> Although he loved the youngest one.
> Bow down, tiddle tum tee.[23]

"Bow down" and "The bow (bough) is (was) bent to me" are found in the Child versions R and U (Long Island) and U, Y, and Z, respectively; but of the British refrains "With a hie down, down a down-a" is more typical. Whether "bow down" is in itself conclusive evidence of dance usage for all the American versions in which it occurs is doubtful, but it is at least reasonable to assume that the refrain came in through the dance. The variations and corruptions of the fourth line are interesting as showing loss of meaning when the song loses its dance usage. In the Nebraska dance version reported by Pound it appears as "Balance true to me." [24] In Virginia (where there is no record of dance usage) it becomes: "Bow down you bittern to me," "Bow it's been to me," "The bough has been to me," "The boughs they bend to me," "The bow has been to me," "For the bows bent to me," "The bough were given to me," [25] and in West Virginia likewise, "Bow and bend to me," "The bough has been to me." [26] And what appear to be corruptions of corruptions are the lines in three Oklahoma versions: "Sing bow your bends to me" [27] and "The boys are (all) bound for you," [28] and "Boys all bound to me," reported by Hudson from Mississippi.

The evidence becomes so contradictory that one is at a loss to state which is the corruption and which is the original and, without additional corroborative evidence in the form of narrative decay,[29] or explicit descriptions of the movements, one hesitates to ascribe dance usage to the piece. An exception might be made in the case of the following Oklahoma version, for which, however, the definitive evidence of directions has not been obtained. On purely internal evidence, the words would accompany a swinging play in which each of two girls, side by side, is chosen and swung by each of the boys—a usage to which the mutilation of the text combined with the repetition, if not the actual tenor of the words, points indubitably.

---

[23] Mrs. L. T. Monnett, Norman, Cleveland County, who played in in Missouri.

[24] *Poetic Origins and the Ballad*, p. 53. Compare her Missouri-Kentucky version (*American Ballads and Songs*, pp. 12-13), where "Bow down" is retained in the second line and the fourth becomes "And a bow 'twas unto me."

[25] Davis, pp. 93-104.

[26] Cox, pp. 21-22.

[27] Mrs. Ethel Perry Moore, Prague, Lincoln County.

[28] Audra A. Plumlee, Norman, Cleveland County.

[29] This is the condition laid down for dance usage by Miss Pound in commenting on "The Maid Freed from the Gallows" and "The Two Sisters," as follows: "For dance songs proper, preserved in tradition, one expects a strong refrain formula and a fading or utterly absent narrative element" (p. 54).

Two little sisters side by side,
Saying I do, saying I do.

Two little sisters side by side
The boys are bound for you,
The boys are bound for you.

Two little sisters side by side
One of them promised to be my bride.
I'll be kind to my true love
If she'll be true to me.[30]

In the next type of usage, that in which there is mere dialogue without dancing or game movements, the original song has also, as in the case of the song used as an accompaniment for a stately dance, a good chance of surviving intact. This is the case (allowing for Americanization and modernization) with "Billy Boy." In Indiana it is played simply with "the woman or girl questioning and the boy answering the questions." [31] In Michigan, after choosing sides, "two rings stand, one inside the other, the inside ring facing out and taking the part of 'Billy Boy' by answering the questions put to him in the song" and "Each side accompanies its part with appropriate gestures." [32] In Oklahoma the children in a circle ask the questions of a chosen player in the center.[33]

In another song of the same type (the comic song in dialogue) there is adaptation to suit the need of the game—in this case the addition of an opening stanza to indicate the approach of the central player and of a closing stanza to indicate the choice of a partner. In an Oklahoma version reported as a ballad [34] the inclusion of these stanzas would seem to indi-

---

[30] Audra A. Plumlee, Norman, Cleveland County; Ethel Perry Moore, Prague, Lincoln County. The "two sisters" become "two little sisters" under the influence of the square dance of that name.

[31] Wolford, pp. 24-25.

[32] Gardner, pp. 92-93.

[33] John V. Early, Oklahoma City, Oklahoma County.

[34] "Yonder Comes a Heavenly Creature," O. B. Campbell, Medford, Grant County. The stanzas referred to are:

Yonder comes a heavenly creature,
    Who she be I do not know.
I'll go and court her for her beauty,
    Whether she says yes or no.

"What do I care for your gold and silver?
    What do I care for your house and land?
What do I care for your world of pleasure?
    All I want is a handsome man."

Newell notes (p. 55): "It is an old English song, which has been fitted for a ring-game by the composition of an additional verse, to allow the selection of a partner."

cate a curious combination of the original song, "No, Sir," and the game based on it, which has been referred to above as "Lady on Yonder Hill," inasmuch as the stanzas in question are not a part of the original song, whereas the dialogue preserved in the Oklahoma version has dropped out of most game versions.[35]

Among ballads that have passed into children's games on account of their dramatic element, to turn to the third type of usage, none is more dramatic than "The Maid Freed from the Gallows," recovered in Oklahoma as a party game under the name of "Hangman, Hangman, Slack Your Rope." [36] With its simple yet strong emotional situation and its vivid, climactic sequence of relatives this has lent itself to dramatization not only as a game but also as a play, especially among Negroes of the South, with whom it is the most popular of the traditional ballads.[37] In view of the strictly dramatic dialogue form of the original, this has been taken over essentially unchanged.

Another ballad recovered as a game in Oklahoma (the only instance of game usage of this ballad that has come to the writer's attention) is

---

[35] This is the case in the versions reported in Great Britain by Douglas, p. 85; Gomme, I, pp. 320-324; and Northall, p. 376. Some of the dialogue survives in the American versions recorded by Babcock, p. 247, and Newell, pp. 55-56. On the other hand, the game stanzas are not a part of the dialogue versions recorded by Gardner and Wolford. The reference to the "lady on the mountain" is explained by Northall to mean that "presumably, the central player mounts a hillock or other elevation." In view of the fact that Northall records this game as a kissing game similar to "Sally Water," it is interesting to note that the first stanza forms the opening of "King William Was King James' Son" as reported to the writer from Gilmer County, West Virginia, by Dr. J. H. Combs of Texas Christian University.

In "Billy Boy" and "No, Sir" the appeal is doubtless based on the guessing or riddling element. Thus my Oklahoma informant recalls that "The fun of the game was to give Billy a 'hot one' in the way of a question, and Billy in return was supposed to ably give back an answer funny and thrilling, to the merriment of our gang" (John V. Early, Oklahoma City, Oklahoma County). In this connection it is worth noting that Child (4:439b) records a game use of another riddle ballad, "The Elfin Knight," communicated by the Rev. S. Baring-Gould from the North of Cornwall. For other game uses of ballads noted by Child, see 1:33 n., 2:346, 3:516b, and 4:441b.

[36] Mrs. Ethel Perry Moore, Prague, Lincoln County.

[37] Compare Child, No. 95, Ha, Hb, Hc, for prose and verse versions related to the *cante-fable* (for which see Martha W. Beckwith, "The English Ballad in Jamaica," *PMLA*, 39:475, 476; Joseph Jacobs, *More English Fairy Tales*, pp. 12-15; Walter Jekyll, *Jamaican Song and Story*, p. 58 ff.; Parsons, *Folk-Tales of Andros Island, Bahamas*, pp. 152-154). Kittredge (*JAFL*, 30:119) reports it as sung (with a prose dialogue acted out as a prelude) by children in the slums of New York. For these mutations of the ballad and other references see Reed Smith, "Five Hundred Years of 'The Maid Freed from the Gallows'," in *South Carolina Ballads*, pp. 80-94. See also Davis, pp. 360-362 (including several instances of its dramatic or game use); and Scarborough (especially for accounts of dramatization by Negroes), pp. 35-43, 283-284. The *cante-fable* forms are discussed by Barry, Eckstorm, and Smyth, pp. 210-213. Game use is noted by A. P. Hudson, and Negro dramatization by Guy B. Johnson in *Culture in the South*, pp. 540, 567.

"The Three Ravens" (Child, No. 26). Here the players form a circle and move around three in the center who are the crows and sit flapping their wings and cawing, to the singing of the lines:

> There were three crows sat in a tree,
>   Billy McGee McGar!
> There were three crows sat on a tree,
> And they were as black as black could be.
> They all flapped their wings and cried:
>   "Caw! caw! caw!"
>   Billy McGee McGar! [38]

---

[38] Mrs. Ethel Perry Moore, Prague, Lincoln County, who played it during recess at school, taught by the teacher. Having entered into American tradition as a comic animal song, this has also become a college song and given rise to parodies. Compare "In Eighteen Hundred and Sixty-Four," Part Two, and the two Civil War parodies given by Davis (Virginia), p. 145. This has also been communicated to me as a children's song in Indiana by Florence Whitelock. For American versions of "The Three Ravens," "The Three Crows," "The Three Black Crows," etc., based on "The Twa Corbies," a comic version of "The Three Ravens" (Child, No. 26), see Barry, Eckstorm, and Smyth (*British Ballads from Maine*), pp. 435-437; Cox (West Virginia), pp. 31-32 (two texts); Davis (Virginia), pp. 137-144 (seventeen texts); Henry (Indiana, North Carolina), *JAFL*, 45:8-12 (three texts); Hudson (Mississippi, *Specimens*), No. 6.

A

THERE WERE THREE CROWS *

(Mrs. Ethel Perry Moore, Prague, Lincoln County.)

1 There were three crows sat on a tree,
    Billy McGee McGar!
  There were three crows sat on a tree,
  And they were as black as black could be.
  They all flapped their wings and cried:
    "Caw! Caw! Caw!"
    Billy McGee McGar!

2 Said one old crow unto his mates,
  "What shall we do for grub to eat?"

3 "There lies a horse on yonder plains,
  Who was by some butcher slain."

4 "We'll perch upon his bare back bones,
  And pick his eyes out one by one."

B

THERE WERE THREE CROWS

(Florence Whitelock, Norman, Cleveland County, from Indiana.)

1 There were three crows sat on a tree
  They were as black as crows could be.
  One old crow said unto his mate,
  Where shall we go for grub to eat?

* "An Experiment in Collecting and Classifying the Folk-Songs Sung in Oklahoma" (in MS.), No. 4.

The fourth type of usage—that of the choosing or swinging game—involves the adaptation, and results in the mutilation, demanded by the needs of the movement song proper—that is, a song whose words direct, suggest, and stimulate movement. "Three Old Maids" is a case in point. As printed by Halliwell,[39] the nursery rhyme, "Three Children Sliding on the Ice," contains two stanzas; and the *Mother Goose* version, three:

> Three children sliding on the ice,
>   Upon a summer's day;
> As it fell out, they all fell in,
>   The rest they ran away.
>
> Now had these children been at home,
>   Or sliding on dry ground,
> Ten thousand pounds to one penny
>   They had not all been drowned.
>
> You parents all that children have,
>   And you that have got none,
> If you would have them safe abroad,
>   Pray keep them safe at home.[40]

In the play-party version the delightful paradox has largely been sacrificed [41] to the play for which the song seems made. The swinging game retains the basic situation of girls (or boys) skating and falling in and the boys (or girls) coming to help them out. In Oklahoma and Michigan [42] three girls, joining hands, skip round inside a circle while the rest sing, and at the line "Ask some one to help them out," they choose partners who swing them round and take their place in the center. In Indiana the girls in an inner circle facing an outer circle of boys circle to the left and at the lines "The ice was thin, and they broke in, and they broke in, and they broke in," break line, and each swings the first boy she comes to. Then at the lines "The ice was thin, and they broke in, The rest all ran

---

> 2 They flew away, across the bay
>   To where an old dead horse lay,
>   They perched upon his old dry bones
>   And picked them off, one by one.

[39] P. 19.

[40] P. 72.

[41] Save for "Upon a summer's day," which is retained in Michigan and in the following Oklahoma variants: "(So) Early in the month of May" (Mary Esther Coffman, Geary, Blaine County; Ruby Home, Calumet, Canadian County); "Right in the month of May" (Alvin C. Meixner, Alva, Woods County); "On a summerish day" (Viola Harris, Porter, Wagoner County).

[42] Gardner, pp. 128-129.

away," all form for a new game.[43] In form the song shows the influence of the dance in the use of repetition and refrain as well as the results of Americanization and modernization:

> Three old maids at a skating rink,
>   At a skating rink, at a skating rink,
> Three old maids at a skating rink,
>   So early in the morning.
>
> The ice was thin, and they fell in,
>   And they fell in, and they fell in,
> The ice was thin, and they fell in,
>   So early in the morning.
>
> Three old bums come to help them out,
>   Come to help them out, come to help them out,
> Three old bums come to help them out,
>   So early in the morning.[44]

Intrusion of dance directions also occurs:

> Three old maids a-skating went,
>   A-skating went, a-skating went
> Three old maids a-skating went
>   Right in the month of May.
> Swing your partners once and a half
>   And play it over again.[45]

Or:

> Choose your partner and swing him in, swing him in,
> Upon one Sunday morn.
>
> Change again and they all fell in, they all fell in, etc.
>
> Change again and they all fell out, they all fell out, etc.[46]

In another swinging play based on a nursery song, "Oh! Dear! What Can the Matter Be?", we have a situation acted out and followed by swinging, according to added dance directions. In the Oklahoma-Missouri version communicated to the writer (the only occurrence of the game recorded), the girl marches round the circle followed by the boy acting old and crippled, singing:

---

[43] Wolford, p. 88.

[44] Gerald Whitlaw, Waynoka, Woods County.

[45] Alvin C. Meixner, Alva, Woods County. Compare the chorus reported from Missouri by Hamilton (p. 301): "Swing them all around as you bring them in."

[46] Bonnie Mae Close, Oklahoma City, Oklahoma County; Viola Harris, Porter, Wagoner County.

> Poor old Joe, what is the matter,
> Poor old Joe, what is the matter,
> Poor old Joe, what is the matter,
>   You stay so far behind?

in which the first line appropriately adapts "Oh! dear! what can the matter be?" and the last line, "Johnny's so long at the fair." Then follows a stanza of the original song:

> You promised you'd buy me a ring and gold locket
> And lots of fine [things] to go in my pocket,
> An old straw hat and a bunch of blue ribbon
> To tie up my bonnie brown hair.

With the last stanza the players in the circle start swinging:

> Swing them ladies, tu du la, (*Four times.*)
> Swing them ladies, tu du la de.
> Swing them if you love them, tu du la. (*Four times.*)[47]

Two nursery songs have been adapted to game use with a choosing formula. Under the title "Froggie Would a-Courting Go" three stanzas of "The Frog and the Mouse" survive in a Michigan ring-game, stating first the facts of the courtship and the place and nature of the wedding supper, after which follows the first choosing formula:

> The Ring Ring's eye, the Ring Ring's eye,
> The rain is falling from the sky.
> Some one says —— [*name*] will die,
> If she doesn't get married in the Ring Ring's eye.

While the players in the ring sing the first four stanzas, "Froggie" in the center makes his choice and claims his kiss; then "the girl chosen selects another young man to be 'Froggie'" to the singing of

> She is handsome, she is pretty,
> She's the girl of —— [*name*] city.
> Let them say what they will,
> She will love —— [*name*] still.[48]

In an Oklahoma-Missouri ring-game version of "Polly, Put the Kettle On" a choosing and kissing formula borrowed from "Come, Philanders" is added to the nursery rhyme. While the odd player in the center chooses, the players dance round in a circle singing:

---

[47] Ruby Pfautsch, Norman, Cleveland County, from near Springfield, Douglas County, Missouri.
[48] Gardner, pp. 98-99. For a complete account of the song see Payne, *PTFS*, 5:5-48; Tolman and Eddy, pp. 394-399 (Note by Kittredge).

Polly, put the kettle on,
    Kettle on, kettle on.
Polly, put the kettle on,
    We'll all take tea.

Slice your bread and butter thin,
    Thin enough for you and me.
Choose the one you love the best
    And call her in the ring.

Oh, you dearest dear,
    You don't know how I love you.
There is no one in this world
    That I adore above you.

My heart you have gained,
    My right hand I give you.
One sweet kiss
    And then I'll have to leave you.[49]

In the swinging play proper dance directions occupy an increasing place. The nursery rhyme "Over the Water to Charley" [50] (a remnant or derivative of the Jacobite song "O'er the Water to Charlie" [51]) has been adapted to the weaving figures of the Virginia reel, as best indicated in one Oklahoma and one Indiana version. In the former, at 1 the two rows stand facing each other and the end players lead out crisscross; at 2 the rows step out and back; at 3 they vigorously shake their heads; at 4 the couples walk around each other with backs turned; at 5 the couples in turn join hands and sing up and back.

1. Over the river to feed my sheep,
    Over the river to Charlie.
Over the river to feed my sheep
    And gather in some barley.

2. Step or two with your weevily wheat.
    Step or two with your barley.
Step or two with your weevily wheat,
    And gather in some barley.

3. I don't want none of your weevily wheat,
    Don't want none of your barley;
Don't want none of your weevily wheat
    To make a cake for Charlie.

---

[49] Mrs. L. T. Monnett, Norman, Cleveland County, who played it in Missouri. The stanzas from "Come, Philanders" are in reverse order.

[50] Halliwell, p. 11; *Mother Goose*, p. 76.

[51] Gummere, II, p. 399; Macquoid, p. 148.

4. Scorn-a-man round with your weevily wheat,
   Scorn-a-man round with your barley.
   Scorn-a-man round with your weevily wheat
   To make a cake for Charlie.

5. Up and down with your weevily wheat,
   Up and down with your barley.
   Up and down with your nice clean wheat
   To make a cake for Charlie.[52]

Another Jacobite song, "Killicrankie," has been preserved in a swinging play crossed with a fragment of a hymn, "Consolation Flowing Free." The original stanza of the Jacobite song is as follows:

Where ha'e ye been sae braw, lad?
   Where ha'e ye been sae brankie, O?
Where ha'e ye been sae braw, lad?
   Came ye by Killicrankie, O?
      An' ye had been where I ha'e been
      Ye wadna been sae cantie, O;
      An' ye had seen what I ha'e seen,
         I' the braes o' Killicrankie, O.[53]

And the play-party derivative:

If you had been where I have been
And seen the sights that I have seen,
Four-and-twenty Irish girls
Dancing on a sheepskin.[54]

The stanza of the hymn—

Come and taste along with me
Consolation flowing free,
All that come with a free good will
Make the banquet sweeter still.[55]

---

[52] Mrs. Jennie Harris Oliver, Fallis, Lincoln County. Similar words and directions are reported from Indiana by Wolford (pp. 102-106 and note). The weaving idea (perhaps implied in the word "weevily") is carried out in an Oklahoma variant, "Twistification," by means of a multiplication stanza. See above, p. 38, and Dudley and Payne, p. 18. Compare the additive and subtractive stanzas of "John Brown Had a Little Indian" in its Oklahoma reel form, which embodies a stanza from the chantey "What Shall We Do with the Drunken Sailor?"

[53] Macquoid, pp. 40-41, Second Set.

[54] Florette McNeese, Oklahoma City, Oklahoma County. Also "Four-and-twenty Irishmen" (Beatrice Jennings McMullin, Norman, Cleveland County, brought from Kentucky to Missouri, then to Kay and Grant Counties on the Oklahoma-Kansas border).

[55] Chester Harley Anderson, Guthrie, Logan County; Louise James, Norman, Cleveland County; Dorothy H. Smith, Oklahoma City, Oklahoma County, who also report a second stanza:

Now I go rejoicing home
From the banquet of perfume,
Gleaning manna all the way
Falling from the mouth of God.

68

gives the play-party stanza—

> Consolation rolling free, (*Three times.*)
> Come and go along with me.[56]

Another stanza of "Kila Ma Cranky" is related to a stanza in "Cushion Dance," the former being—

> Fiddle-ma-cranky is my song.
> Now we'll dance and promenade along,
> From the elbow to the wrist,
> And now is the time to make the twist.[57]

and the latter—

> Frinkum, frankum is a fine song,
> An' we will dance it all along;
> All along and round about,
> Till we find the pretty maid out.[58]

The tendency of the play-party to burlesque as well as mutilate the original is seen in a Texas version of "Weevily Wheat," in which the following stanzas of the English folk-song, "I'm Seventeen Come Sunday"—

> As I walked out one May morning,
> One May morning so early,
> I overtook a handsome maid,
> Just as the sun was rising.
> > With my rue dum day, fol the diddle dol,
> > Fol the dol, the diddle-dum the day.
>
> . . .
>
> How old are you, my fair pretty maid,
> How old are you, my honey?
> She answer'd me quite cheerfully:
> I am seventeen come Sunday.
> > With my rue dum day, etc.
>
> Will you marry me, my fair pretty maid?
> Will you marry me, my honey?
> She answer'd me right cheerfully:
> I dare not for my mammy.
> > With my rue dum day, etc.[59]

---

[56] Florette McNeese, Oklahoma City, Oklahoma County. A similar stanza appears in 11 Oklahoma variants of the related play-party song, "Consolation Flowing Free."
[57] Beatrice Jennings McMullin, Norman, Cleveland County.
[58] Gomme, I, p. 88.
[59] Sharp, *English Folk-Songs,* Vol. I, No. XLV. Compare the lines in "Consolation Flowing Free":

turn up with travesty of both setting and situation:

> Way down yonder in the maple swamp, the water's deep and muddy,
> There I spied my pretty little miss, O there I spied my honey.
> How old are you, my little miss, how old are you, my honey?
> She answered with a ha-ha laugh, "I'll be sixteen next Sunday." [60]

3. NATIVE SONG MATERIAL

In American folk-songs and popular songs the play-party had a source of material closer to home and to the knowledge and tastes of the players. A catchy tune, a familiar refrain, a bit of extravagant burlesque or satiric nonsense, a touch of graceful sentiment or soothing pathos, a well-known historical or topical allusion—any or all of these sufficed to recommend a song for play-party use. Here the lyric had the obvious advantage over the ballad, in spite of the dramatic possibilities of the latter—not only because an emotional situation or attitude replaces the narrative plot but also because of the freer lyrical rhythms conducing to movement.

Closer to the ballad are historic songs preserving memories of national conflicts. The theme of the separation of lovers by war and their reunion by peace has the dramatic utility of suggesting marching games, in which a player or a couple in the center chooses another to enter the center, and joins the marching ring or ranks, or a boy and a girl march down the aisle, separate and go round the outside of the lines, and meet again to go down the aisle under raised arms. Played according to the former method is "We're Marching Down to Old Quebec," based on a war ballad which has variously been assigned Revolutionary [61] and War of 1812 [62] origin:

> We're marching down to old Quebec,
>> Where the drums are loudly beating.

> I am too young, I cannot go (*Three times.*)
> For my mamma (mother) told me so.

(Lela L. Conrad, Perry, Noble County; Mrs. Bertha Downing, Norman, Cleveland County, who played it in Southern Noble, Northeastern Logan, and Northern Payne Counties.)

> Oh, I'm too young, I cannot go, (*Three times.*)
> Because I love my mamma so.
>> (Audra A. Plumlee, Norman, Cleveland County.)

> I'm too young, I cannot go, (*Three times.*)
> Cannot leave my mamma (mammy) O.

(Alec Gilbreath, Atoka, Atoka County, who played it at Lehigh, Coal County; Logan Earl Hysmith, Wilburton, Latimer County, from Sebastian County, Arkansas; Sue Marguerite Patterson, Erick, Beckham County, from Jackson County.)

[60] Dudley and Payne, p. 18.
[61] Newell, p. 125. Compare Belden, p. 14.
[62] Pound, *Cambridge History*, p. 505; *Poetic Origins and the Ballad*, p. 204.

The American boys are gaining on the day
  And the British are retreating.

The war's all over, and we'll turn back
  To the place where we first started.
We'll open up the ranks and choose a couple in
  To relieve the broken-hearted.[63]

In North Carolina the ballad is further adapted to game usage by the addition of a kissing formula belonging to "Sister Phoebe"—

Put a hat on her head to keep her head warm,
And a loving sweet kiss will do her no harm.[64]

or to "Come, Philanders"—

Oh, you're the one that I love best,
  I praise you high and dearly;
My heart you'll get, my hand I'll give,
  The kiss is most sincerely.[65]

Other possible remnants of historic songs relating to war may be seen in "Little Fight in Mexico," [66] "Jim Lane," [67] and "Pretty Little Pink," [68] whose method of playing resembles that of "Marching Down to Old Quebec." The war theme, without the specific ballad setting, is carried over to the marching game of the longways casting-off type represented by "Yonder She Comes." [69] In "Jersey Boys" is a suggestion of a recruiting song and in "Virginia," a reminiscence of a song sung by Sherman's men as the natives fled before them.[70] Another Civil War song, "John Brown's

---

[63] Chester Harley Anderson, Guthrie, Logan County. The game is a very popular one, being reported from ten states. In the Missouri version reported by Randolph (pp. 206-207) it is played very much like "Miller Boy."

[64] Hoke, p. 118; Newell, p. 246.

[65] Newell, p. 125.

[66] In Oklahoma this is played more or less like "Miller Boy," with an odd player in the center stealing a partner as "The boys slowed up and the girls went ahead" (Cora Frances Starritt, Ada, Pontotoc County).

[67] Dr. J. H. Combs reports the following method of playing from Gilmer County, West Virginia: The girl who during the singing of the first slow movements has "sat down in her sad station, Mourning the loss of her true love," jumps up at the beginning of the fast movement and joins the players, singing, first alone and then accompanied by the others while skipping:
  Now I know it is not so,
  He'll come back and be my beau,
  If I go seek and find him.

[68] This presents a curious example of a dance song which has been converted into a soldiers' marching song, with Mexican War references, and then taken back into dance usage, war references and all. Compare Sandburg, p. 166.

[69] Dr. S. R. Hadsell, Norman, Cleveland County.

[70] Walter Morrow, Oklahoma City, Oklahoma County.

Body," is sung as an accompaniment for a Virginia reel in Oklahoma and Nebraska.[71]

A second and larger class of native songs drawn upon by the play-party is made up of stage songs, especially minstrel songs. Three reasons may be assigned for their popularity: first, most of them were gay banjo or fiddle tunes, whose airs were used for dancing; secondly, their jesting and clowning had an irresistible appeal for the play-party in its mood of rambling nonsense, with its double taste for silly jingle and burlesque banter; and thirdly, they had the advantage of wide diffusion by travelling minstrel-troupes, medicine shows, circus concerts, and the song-sheets of patent medicine companies. Foremost among minstrel songs in play-party usage is "Old Dan Tucker," which, though not of Negro origin, was sung by slaves before the war and "fiddled" for Negro dances.[72] Other minstrel and stage songs, representing various stages of decay, are, in the order of the number of Oklahoma play-party variants collected, "Buffalo Gals," "Dem Golden Slippers," "Brown Jug," "Captain Jinks," "Shoo Fly," "Get Along, Josie," "Down the River," "Old Virginny Neber Tire," "Getting Upstairs," "Jim Crow," "Turkey in the Straw," and "Lucy Long." Negro folk-songs proper are represented by the following slave, plantation, and dance songs: " 'Tain't Goin' to Rain No More," "Run, Nigger, Run," "Pore Mourner," "Jawbone," "Marsa's Yaller Gal" ("When de Band Begins to Play"), "Hawkie is a Schemin' Bird," "I Wouldn't Marry a Yellow [Black, White, Negro] Girl," and even a shine reel, "Black the Boots." Most of these survive in the play-party only in fragments of verses and refrain (already discussed in connection with the influence of the dance),[73] or crossed and amalgamated with one another and with other songs (to be discussed in the next chapter under style).[74]

Many of these Negro songs have influenced and been influenced by mountain white songs, another fertile source of lyric stanzas in play-party songs, including "Shady Grove," "Laura Lee," and "Liza Jane," which have also been crossed back and forth with one another.

Two remaining types of native song entering into play-party tradition are the western song, including "Shoot the Buffalo," originally an emigrant's song,[75] and "The Girl I Left Behind Me," [76] which the cowboys

---

[71] Florette McNeese, Oklahoma City, Oklahoma County; Piper, p. 270.

[72] Scarborough, p. 199. This appears in practically every play-party collection and in 50 Oklahoma variants.

[73] See above, p. 49 ff. Gardner (pp. 109-110) and Hamilton (p. 301) report versions of "Brown Jug" close to the original song in contrast to the usual dance derivative.

[74] See below, p. 89 ff.

[75] "The Hunting of the Buffalo." Compare Belden, p. 16.

[76] Compare Lomax, pp. 342-343.

made over from a British march of the eighteenth century, and the religious song, including "Consolation Flowing Free" and "I Want to Be an Angel" [77] (the latter having passed into the play-party by way of the granger movement). Finally, popular songs have been drawn upon—sentimental songs like "Nellie Gray" (used in its original form as an accompaniment for a Virginia reel [78]) and "Wait for the Wagon," college and comic songs like "We Won't Go Home Till Morning," "The Old Gray Mare," and "Chewing Gum," [79] and even a bawdy song echoed in "Baltimore."

4. CONCLUSIONS

1. Narrative and dialogue songs appeal to the play-party for one of three reasons: a dramatic situation; love and marriage interest; riddles or guessing.

2. Perhaps because of the starkness of the English and Scottish ballads, the play-party prefers comic versions, such as "Billy Boy" and "The Three Ravens."

3. Stage and street songs have been appropriated for play-party use generally for one of two reasons: a catchy tune that has entered into dance tradition; or a flavor of satiric nonsense or vulgar buffoonery.

4. A popular song may be utilized as a dance accompaniment for no other reason than that the dancers have run out of material or can think of nothing else on the spur of the moment.

5. Stanzas and fragments of songs, often amalgamated, are more common in play-party usage than complete or nearly complete songs, as a result of mutilation and shifting.

[77] Compare Pound, *Syllabus*, p. 54.
[78] Florette McNeese, Oklahoma City, Oklahoma County; Piper, p. 265.
[79] See "Old Joe Clark." Compare Pound, *Syllabus*, p. 59.

CHAPTER V

LANGUAGE AND STYLE

1. VARIATIONS

WHEN one considers that even in the instance of ballads, which are held together by a framework of narrative or dramatic plot, "There are *texts,* but there is no *text,*" [1] and that this constant process of variation and modification is inevitably one of decay,[2] one is not surprised to find that the more structureless and ephemeral play-party songs fare even worse at the hands of mutilating and distorting oral tradition. In this respect the play-party differs from the traditional game, which is held together by a game formula, by the conservatism of children (e. g., the "necessity of general currency, and the difficulty of obtaining it" [3]) and (recently) by preservation in print (whereby they are often taught to children in school-rooms and on playgrounds).[4]

Play-party songs, on the other hand, are essentially dance-songs, in which the interest is in the movements rather than in the words and the appeal is to the feet rather than to the heart or the head. The result is a minimum of meaning and a maximum of movement, with only the barest rudiments of sentiment, situation, and character to provide a basis for repetition and refrain, which here become the most stable elements instead of, as in the ballad, the most fluctuating. Moreover, in play-party songs derived from the square dance, the bulk of the words consists of dance directions and, since movements in the dance are more variable than in the game, the directions and so the words may vary accordingly. Again, since the same tune may do duty for more than one song or, conversely, the same song be sung to several airs,[5] transference of stanzas or adaptation to suit the melody may take place accordingly. Finally, on account of the progressive character of the square dance and the large amount of repetition required to enable every one to dance with every one else, a large amount of variation is necessary to keep the repetitions from becoming monotonous. And since the need of keeping the players enter-

---

[1] Kittredge, Introduction to *English and Scottish Popular Ballads,* p. xvii. Compare Pound, *American Ballads and Songs,* p. xii.

[2] Compare Pound, "The Term Communal," p. 451.

[3] Newell, p. 27.

[4] Collections of play-party songs in scholarly journals and in works of research would hardly come under this head since they are rarely used as teaching material. A recent instance of the diffusion of play-party songs in print is furnished by Cornell Junior Extension Bulletin 55, *Program of Songs, Games, and Folk Dances for 4-H Clubs,* by Mary Eva Duthie (New York State College of Agriculture, Ithaca, November, 1935), containing "Brass Wagon," "Captain Jinks," and "Wait for the Wagon."

[5] On the whole the presence of several tunes for the same song is less common in play-party songs than in other types of folk-song, though variations in tune are frequent.

tained is almost as great as the need of keeping them moving, the variations are seldom standardized but tend to adjust themselves constantly to the time, the place, and the participants, with all manner of local, temporal, and personal allusions. In other words, if a ballad is defined as a "theme" on which variations are played,[6] play-party songs may be described as variations looking for a theme.

The most characteristic of play-party variations are those belonging to the accretionary type of dance-song, which, as has been seen, consists of an elastic catalogue of directions for changes with interpolated comments on whatever interests the players in the immediate occasion or their environment, the whole being loosely knit together by a refrain word, line, or stanza. Because of this double function of the play-party song in suggesting and stimulating movement, on the one hand, and in expressing and entertaining the dancers, on the other, the variations are interesting not only in themselves but for the shifting light they throw on the customs, characters, objects, activities, and background of rural and frontier America.

The process may best be illustrated by the 67 variants of "Skip to My Lou" and the 33 variants of "Coffee Grows on a White Oak Tree" recovered in Oklahoma—the two most popular games in the accretionary class. The method of playing "Skip to My Lou" exhibits some variation, but generally, in Oklahoma, a ring is formed with an extra boy in the center who tries to steal another boy's partner and swing her across to his place, while the boy left without a partner tries to steal another. In Indiana, the deserted boy may recover his partner if he succeeds in overtaking the couple before they get back to her former position after swinging round the circle.[7] The stealing of a partner has given rise to innumerable verses, 157 of which, recovered in Oklahoma, are given below, grouped according to formulae, with the number of variants for each line and for each formula. In each case the line is the basis of a stanza constructed by singing the line three times and adding the refrain, "Skip to my Lou, my darling."

First in popularity is the natural history formula (which has 74 variants), comparing the successful or unsuccessful "skippers" to various insects, pests, pets, and livestock, playing their pranks or haunting their favorite habitations. Here almost any creature might be conceived as doing almost anything, provided, for the sake of rhyme, it be "two by two" or "shoo, shoo, shoo"—and even a hair will do.

> Fly in the buttermilk, skip to my Lou.   (2)
> Fly in the buttermilk, what'll I do?

---

[6] Compare Pound, "A Recent Theory of Ballad-Making," p. 625.
[7] Wolford, p. 90.

Drink that fly and the buttermilk too.   (2)
Fly (Fly's) in the buttermilk, shoo, shoo, shoo.   (2)
Fly in the buttermilk, left for you.
Flies in the buttermilk, two by two.   (4)
Flies in the buttermilk, shoo, fly, shoo.
Flies in the buttermilk, big as a mule.
Flies in the buttermilk, shoo, shoo, shoo.   (2)
Flies in the biscuits, bite them in two.   (2)
Fly in the biscuit, I bit it into (*sic*).
Fly in the biscuit, bit him ('im) in two.   (2)
Fly in the biscuit, bit him into (*sic*).
Flies in the sugar bowl, two by two.   (5)
Flies in the gravy, two by two.

Mice in the buttermilk, two by two.
Mice in the sugar bowl, two by two (three by three).   (2)
Mice in the cream jar, two by two.

Rats in the flour bin, kickin' like a mule.
Rat's in the sugar bowl—chew-chew-chew.
Rats in the sugar bowl, skip to my Lou.
Rats in the buttermilk, shoo, shoo, shoo (two by two)   (2)
Rats in (the) sugar bowl, two by two.   (2)
Rats in the buttermilk, kickin' out cream.
Rats in the rail pile, two by two.

Cat in the buttermilk, lapping up two (too?).

Hair in the biscuit, three inches long.
Hair in the biscuit, two feet long.
Hair in the biscuit, six feet long.
Hairs in the biscuit, three feet long.
Hairs in the biscuit, ten feet long.
Hairs in the buttermilk, two by two.
Hairs in the sugar bowl, two feet long.
Hair in the butter, three feet long.

Bugs in the biscuit, two by two.

Ants in the sugar bowl, two by two.

Chicken in the dough pan, shoo, shoo, shoo.
Chicken on (in) a (the) haystack, shoo, shoo, shoo.   (3)
 Chickens in the haystack, shoo, shoo, shoo.   (2)
Chickens in the garden, shoo, shoo, shoo.
Chickens in the pea patch, shoo, shoo, shoo.
Hen on a strawstack, rooster too.

76

Skeeter on a gate post, skip to my Lou.

Hogs in the tater patch, two by two.
Hogs in the cornfield, skip to my Lou (shoo, fly, shoo).   (2)
Pigs in the parlor, what'll I do? [8]   (3)
Brand new pig in the parlor and he is Irish too.
Pig in the yard fence and he can't get through.

Rabbit in the pea patch, bigger than a mule.
Rabbits in the cornfield, big as a mule.

Here comes a mule on a telegraph wire.
My beau rides an old gray mule.

Next in popularity is the "little . . . wagon" formula (39 variants), the wagon perhaps symbolizing the skipper and his feints and failures, for the wagon is usually of one color but "painted" another.

(A) (The) Little red wagon painted blue.   (32)
Little red wagon, painted green.
Little red wagon, painted red.
Little red wagon, faded brown.   (2)
Little red wagon and harness too.
Lead her up and down, little brass wagon.
Three wheels off and the axle dragging.[9]

"Shoes" (26 variants).

My Beau wears a number ten shoe.   (4)
My wife wears a number ten shoe.
My wife wears a number 'leven shoe.
My old lady wears a number ten shoe.
My old wife wears a number ten shoe.
My girl wears a number ten shoe.
My Grandpa wears a number ten shoe.
Dad's old hat and Ma's (Mam's) old shoe.   (2)
Dad's old boot and a man's old shoe.
Ma's old (ole) hat an' (and) Dad's (Pa's) old (ole) shoe.   (2)
Ma's old bonnet and Pa's old shoes.
An old rubber boot and (a) rundown shoe.   (2)
Ma makes buttermilk in Pa's old shoe.
Ma made buttermilk in Dad's (Pa's) old shoe.   (2)
My Ma churns in Pa's old shoe.
Ma churns butter in Pa's old shoe.
Ma made gravy in Dad's old shoe.   (2)
Sitting on the bedpost, tying up a shoe.

---

[8] This and the next line belong to "Pig in the Parlor."
[9] The last two lines belong to "Old Brass Wagon."

"If you can't . . . will do" (23 variants).

 If you can't get a red bird, a blue bird will do.   (9)
 If you can't get a red bird, a blue one will do.
 If you can't get a blue bird, a red bird will do.
 If you can't get a hawk, a crow will do.
 If I can't get a red bird, a blue bird will do.   (2)
 (If I) Can't get a red bird, a jay bird will do.
 Can't get a red bird, blackbird will do.
 Can't get a red bird, take a blue.
 If you can't get a white one, a black one will do.
 If I can't get a white girl, a negro'll do.
 If I can't get you, another will do.
 If I can't get you, your sister'll do.   (2)
 Can't get a pretty girl, ugly one will do.

"Gone again" (20 variants).

 Gone again, skip to my Lou (Lu) (Milieu).   (4)
 Gone again, and skip to maloo.
 Gone again, skip the maloo (malu).   (2)
 Gone again, (oh) what shall I do?   (3)
 (She's) Gone again, (so) what'll I do?   (3)
 Come again, what'll I do?
 My girl's gone, what shall I do?
 My wife's gone, I'm going too.
 My old wife's gone, what'll I do.
 Lost my pardner, skip to my Lou.
 Lost my partner, I don't care.
 Sweetheart's left and I don't care.

"I'll get another" (18 variants).

 I'll get another one better than (better 'n) you.   (5)
 I get another one better than you.
 I can get another better than you.
 I can get another (one) as pretty as you.   (2)
 I'll get another one (girl) prettier than (prettier 'n) you. (4)
 I'll get another one prettier too.   (2)
 I'll get one prettier than you.
 I'll get another as good as you.
 I kin get another one just as fair.

"Stand there" (14 variants).

 Stand there, big foot, don't know what to do.   (2)
 Stand there, big foot, stand there, fool.
 Stand there, big foot, skip to my Lou.   (2)
 Stand there, big foot, what you goin' to do?
 Stand there, club foot, don't know what to do.

Stand there, dumbbell, don't know what to do.
Stand there, blockhead, what's you gonna do?
Stand there, blockhead, stand there, fool.
Stand there, stand there, you big fool you.
Stand there and gawk, you old (big) fool you.[10]   (2)
Where you goin', you big fool you?

Miscellaneous (65 variants).

My wife skip(s) and I'll skip too.   (6)
My wife skipped and I skipped you.
Skip, skip, skip to my Lou.   (5)
Skip a little faster, this'll (will) never do.   (3)
Skip a little faster, this is too slow.
Catch that red bird, skip to my Lula.
Round and round here we go.
All promenade with hands on shoulder.[11]
First couple come down, skip to my Lula.
Four hands round and skip to my Lula.
Four hands round and skip to my Lou.
Swing your partner, two by two.
Bounce around, cinnamon, skip to my Lou.
Hilo shilo, skip to my Lou.   (2)
All go to market, two by two.
All go to market, swinging hands.
Going (All go) (Let's all go) (Gone) (We'll all go) (We will go)
   to Texas, two by two.   (12)
(We're) Back from Texas, two by two (how-do-you-do) (howda do).   (3)
If ——— [*name*] goes to Texas, I'll go too.
We have all fallen in love, two by two.
Going to get married, two by two.
You stole from me, and I'll steal from you.
Went to church and saw a friend.
Went to church and lost a friend.
I was mad, but so was you.
If I had a rock, I'd throw it at you.   (4)
If I had a six-shooter (shotgun), I'd shoot you.   (2)
Can't bake biscuits, cornbread will do.
Only one oyster in the stew.
Sweet as buttermilk, sweeter too.
My father and mother were Irish, and I am Irish too.[12]
Little white house and nobody livin' in it.
We'll get married and we'll go to livin' in it.[13]

---

[10] "Of course, some of the boys were bashful. Hence the first verse of 'skipping part': 'Stand there and gawk, you old fool you.'" (A. J. Strange, Clinton, Custer County). Compare Piper (p. 277), who points out that these verses are commonly accepted as being directed against the slow-witted leader.
[11] Compare "Down in Alabama."
[12] Compare "Pig in the Parlor."
[13] Compare "Virginia."

Negro on the haystack, he fell through.
Nigger in the woodshed, he fell through.
Needle in haystack, can't be found.

In "Coffee Grows on a White Oak Tree" choosing takes the place of stealing a partner, and in the lines sung as the two couples in the middle dance about (before the first couple leaves the second to choose another in) the changes are rung on the same rustic or homely allusions. The stanza pattern is as follows:

Flies in the buttermilk, and I can't jump Josey.
    Flies in the buttermilk, and I can't get around.
Flies in the buttermilk, and I can't jump Josey.
    Hello, Susan Brown.

Flies in the buttermilk, and I can't jump Josey.
Rats in the buttermilk, and I can't get 'm out, Ma.
Rat's in the boots and the boots turned over.
Hog's in the tater patch, rutting (rooting) up corn.
Teeter up and down in your little brass wagon.
Hind wheel off, and the axle draggin'.
Hold my mule (mules) while (till) I jump (dance) Josie.   (6)
Hold my mule till I get on him.
Hold Old Gray while I jump Josey.
Old Gray's tied and don't need holding.   (2)
Tie my mule while I jump Josie.   (2)
Hold my dog till I tree a possum.
Your (My) shoe's untied, and you (I) can't jump Josie.   (3)
Hold my hat while I dance Josie.
Tie my tie while I jump Josie.   (2)
Chew my gum while I dance Josie.
Big wad of gum, and everybody chewing it.
Big old shoe, and nobody wearing it.
Goin' to pick it up, then I'll be wearing it.
House on the hill, nobody livin' in it.
Big white house, and nobody livin' in it.   (4)
We'll get married, we'll live in it.
(I'm) Going to get married, (and) then go to living in it.   (2)
Briar in my heel, and I can't jump Joseph.
Frog in the pond, and the pond runs over.
Frog in the pond, pond froze over.
Cat is in the well, and can't dance Josie.
Pig is in the pen, and I can't dance Josie.
Had a glass of buttermilk, and I danced Josey.   (2)
Big foot guy and can't jump Josie.   (2)
Big-footed nigger and can't jump Josey.
Fiddler's drunk, and we can't dance Josie.
I wouldn't give a nickel if I couldn't dance Josie.   (3)

The plasticity and profuseness of variation resulting from accretion and improvisation in a song of the loose, elastic catalogue type like "Skip to My Lou" may best be appreciated by comparison with a game like "Miller Boy," in which the presence of a game formula limits the number of themes which may be varied and restricts the kinds of variation to the form and arrangement of words within the line. In comparison with British versions play-party versions of "Miller Boy" possess the further interest of dance influence and Americanism in style. The single stanza of the traditional game, as has been pointed out, may be expanded to two, three, and four stanzas to introduce complications in the movements, directions for which are substituted for the original "grab," and a chorus is sung while the change is taking place, with or without an added call.

A line-for-line and word-for-word comparison of British and Oklahoma versions yields the following results, indicating the nature and extent of these changes.

In the first line, 7 Gomme versions [14] and the single Douglas [15] and Northall [16] versions read "There was a jolly miller, and he lived by himself," the eighth Gomme version being: "He was a jolly miller, He lived by himself." [17] In 82 Oklahoma variants of this line "miller boy" occurs 70 times: "miller," 10 times, and "farmer boy," twice. "Happy" occurs 60 times; "jolly," 6; and in 16 cases there is no epithet. "Lives (lived) by the mill" occurs 76 times; "lives (lived) by himself," 5 times; and "tends to the mill," once. "Living," "at," "on," "a," and "his," occur once each, and "in," twice. "Happy as the (a) miller boy that (who) lives (lived) by the mill" occurs 4 times; "There was," 9 times; "Once there was," 4 times; "(A) Miller boy, miller boy," 3 times; the remaining variants begin with "happy" or "jolly."

In the second line 5 Gomme versions have "As the wheel (mill) went (goes) round he made (gained) (makes) his wealth"; the following occur once each: "As the wheel went round he made his pelf," "As the wheel went round he made his grab," "The sails went round, he made his ground." [18] In the 80 Oklahoma variants containing this line "made his pelf" occurs but once; "gaining on (in) his wealth" occurs 3 times; "The wheel turns and never stands still," "He's been living forty years and 's living there still," occur once each; and the remaining variants contain some form of the phrase "with its own free will" ("by" occurring once;

---

[14] I, pp. 289-293.
[15] P. 73.
[16] P. 366.
[17] II, pp. 436-437.
[18] Douglas: "As the mill went round he made his wealth." Northall: "As the wheel went round he made his wealth (pelf?)."

"on," twice; and "of," 4 times).[19] "Free good will" occurs 37 times; "own free will," 14 times; "right good will," 6 times; "good free will," 3 times; "own good will," twice; "frequent will," "free and good will," once each.

In the third line 4 Gomme versions have "One hand in the (his) hopper, and the other (another) in the (his) bag"; "One hand in his pocket, the other in his bag," "One hand in his pocket, the other at his back," "One hand in the upper and the other in the bank" (a curious corruption), occur once each.[20] Of the 90 Oklahoma variants containing this line 77 have "sack" and 4 have "bag," while "on the pole," "on the ground," "on the slab," "on the string," "on the rack," "on the jug," "on ring" occur once each.

In the fourth line the accepted British version is "As the wheel went round, he made his grab," while Newell gives "The wheel (mill) turns (goes) around, and he cries out, Grab!" Here the Oklahoma variants, being freest on account of the introduction of dance directions, display most variation. The British line occurs once; Newell's, 3 times (including "and all cry, Grab," once); and the rest employ some form of "The ladies step forward, and the gents turn back," of which the following variants are characteristic:

(Just) Hold your holts and turn (whirl) right back.	(4)
Straight across the hall and turn right back.	
Grab your girl (partner) and turn right back.	(2)
Keep your pardner and don't run back.	
Go straight on and keep the right track.	
Jump right up and turn right back.	
Turn right around and go right back.	(2)
Mill fell down on the old cow's back.	
The boy in the center (middle) says, "Smack, boys, smack."	(2)
The boy in the center (middle) says, "Hug, boys, hug."	(2)
The mill turned round and didn't do a thing.	
Hold your oats and turn right back.	
Keep on going in the same old track.	
The boys in the center yells, "Hold, boys, hold."	
Hold your holts, come a-raggin' right back.	(4)
Turn right around and don't lose track.	

The Oklahoma changes, apparently in the interest of informality and simplification (as in the substitution of "miller boy" for "miller" and "happy" for "jolly"), also illustrate various types of alteration. Thus the substitution of "will" for "wealth" may be due to folk-etymology, and of

---

[19] Newell (p. 102) has "While the mill goes round, he works with a will"; "All the bread and cheese he piles upon the shelf."

[20] Douglas: "One hand in his pocket and the other in his bag." Northall: "One hand in the hopper and one in the bag."

"sack" (which is the preferred American term) for "bag," to the exigencies of rhyming with "back," in the fourth line, which in itself is fixed by the movement.[21] For the rest, variations in the fourth line are characterized chiefly by colloquialism and Americanism.

2. ADAPTATION

Next to variations by accretion or improvisation, adaptation is the most considerable form of change. Adaptation may be local or temporal. Local adaptation commonly consists in the substitution of familiar for unfamiliar names.

The substitution of place-names is the most obvious form of local adaptation. In an Oklahoma-Arkansas version of "Buffalo Girls" occurs "Choctaw girls, ain't you coming out to-night?" [22] In an Oklahoma variant of "Going Down to Rowser" from the neighborhood of Lexington the opening stanza becomes:

> We'll all go down to Lexington,
>   To Lexington, to Lexington,
> We'll all go down to Lexington
>   To measure up some barley.[23]

Two Cleveland County variants of "Old Joe Clark" likewise incorporate a reference to Lexington:

> Went down to Lexington,
>   Didn't know the route,
> Put me in the coffee pot
>   And poured me out the spout.[24]

---

21 The chorus—
> We're sailing east, we're sailing west,
>   We're sailing over the ocean.
> All the boys that want a good wife
>   Had better be quick in the motion.

shows only slight changes: "Notion" for "motion," "cook" for "wife," and "If you don't want a scolding wife, You had better change your motion" (the last from Harry Deupree, Oklahoma City, Oklahoma County, from Nebraska, Iowa, and Missouri).

22 Other interesting variants of "Buffalo Girls" (which probably had its origin in "Charleston Gals" in *Slave Songs of the United States,* p. 88) include "Jim Town Girls" (Dr. J. H. Combs, Gilmer County, West Virginia); "The Lushbaugh Girls" (Shoemaker, Pennsylvania, pp. 129-130); "Louisiana Gal" (Scarborough, p. 112); "Cincinnati Girls" (Wolford, Indiana, p. 32).

23 Mary Haxel, Purcell, McClain County, who played it at Noble, Cleveland County, and Washington, McClain County, and who also reports "Summerset" as a variant. The last line is a reminiscence of "Weevily Wheat," and the whole may be a facetious reference to the activities of Lexington saloons in the days before statehood. See above, p. 12.

24 Marguerite M. Durkee, Norman, Cleveland County; Zelma Oliver, from Eugene Nolen, Norman, Cleveland County. The last two lines may also involve reference to Lexington saloons.

In "Coffee Grows on a White Oak Tree" the chorus—

> We're going down the river,
>> We're going down below.
>
> We're going down the river
>> To old Shiloh.

becomes, in Eastern Custer County, on Deer Creek, near Hydro:

> We're going down old Deer Creek,
>> We're going down below.
>
> We're going down old Deer Creek,
>> To old Hydro.[25]

In "Liza Jane" "As I went down the Newport road" [26] is substituted for "As I went down the Norfolk road." [27]

An instance of the substitution of local personal names is afforded by "Skip to My Lou," in which the familiar line "If you can't get a red bird, a blue bird will do" gave rise to "If you can't get a hawk, a crow will do" in the following manner: According to my informant,[28] the line originated at Ames, Major County, where there were two families who had considerable representation among the females. These families were named Hawk and Crow respectively. But by analogy with the many other species and colors of birds, like the jaybird and the blackbird, which appear in the song, "Hawk" and "Crow" became common nouns and passed into general currency with complete loss of their original significance.

Local speech usage also results in adaptation. The dance use of the verb "round up," meaning to take additional couples into a circle, is obviously of Western origin, being found, to the writer's knowledge, only in Oklahoma and Texas.[29] In "Coffee Grows on a White Oak Tree" "black-jack trees" [30] and "black-jack stump" [31] are Oklahoma substitutions, the black-jack or scrub oak being better known to the players. In the line from "Old Joe Clark," "He chased the big hogs through the fence," "fence," at Headrick, Jackson County, Oklahoma, becomes "gap,"

---

[25] Professor Kenneth Kaufman, Norman, Cleveland County.

[26] Winnifred Spencer, Walters, Cotton County, from Jefferson, Marion County, Texas. See below, p. 102.

[27] Dudley and Payne, p. 31. Scarborough (p. 109) gives "Three Chop Road."

[28] Leon Kidd, Billings, Noble County.

[29] Compare "London" (Mary Haxel, Purcell, McClain County, who played it near Noble, Cleveland County, and Washington, McClain County) and " 'Tain't Goin' to Rain No More," "The Irish Trot," and "Rouser" (Dudley and Payne, pp. 10, 11, 12).

[30] Joseph Edward Terral, Oklahoma City, Oklahoma County.

[31] Walter Myers Gable, Norman, Cleveland County.

the local word for a hurdle or low place in a fence or an opening for a gate.[32]

In "Hog Drovers" [33] (the common Southern form of "Swine-Herders") a variety of local adaptations is seen. The line "I'll bet you five dollars we better ourselves" [34] becomes, in one Oklahoma variant, "We've been through Arkansas and bettered ourselves." [35] In the same variant is reflected the local attitude toward various occupations (some of them local), illustrating the place of local customs in adaptations. Rich merchants, school teachers, and gold miners are accepted; farmers are sometimes accepted and sometimes rejected; and oil-drillers and cowboys are rejected. In other Oklahoma variants "sheep herders" and "pig drivers" may be substituted for "hog drovers," [36] and the latter also becomes "hog drivers" [37] and is shortened to "rovers." [38]

Temporal adaptations are chiefly modernizations. Thus "Marching Down to Old Quebec" has been given Mexican War reference by the substitution of "New Orleans," [39] Civil War reference in the Yankee paraphrase, "The Yankee boys have gained the day, and the Rebels are retreating," [40] and World War reference:

> We're marching down to Old Berlin,
> Where the drums are loudly beating.

---

[32] Paul Howard, Headrick, Jackson County. Formerly, before the adjustment of the state boundary, Jackson County was part of Texas, and many Texas localisms survive among the large Texas contingent in the population. See above, p. 17n.

[33] In Kentucky, Oklahoma, and Texas. Also "Hog Drovers" in Texas (Dudley and Payne, pp. 15-16). Gardner (Michigan, p. 131) gives "wagoners." Newell in "Swine-Herders" (pp. 232-234) gives "hog-drivers." In "Three Kings" (Newell, pp. 46-47) soldiers, sailors, tinkers, and kings are represented; also (Babcock, pp. 259-260; Newell, pp. 234-236), sweeps and bakers. In British versions ("Three Sailors," Gomme, II, pp. 282-289) the occupations rejected in favor of kings are sailors, soldiers, tinkers, sweeps, bakers, tailors, and blacksmiths.

[34] Dudley and Payne, pp. 15-16. Compare "For three-halfpence more I'd get a far better wife" (Duncan, *Folklore,* 5:190).

[35] Florette McNeese, Oklahoma City, Oklahoma County, from Pearl Mobley, Rubottom, Love County, who also gives: "We'll go on a piece farther and better ourselves." Also "I'll travel on farther and better myself" (Atta LeGate, Muskogee, Muskogee County; Cora Frances Starritt, Ada, Pontotoc County); "We'll bet you five dollars we'll better ourself" (Boyce Billingsley, Wayne, McClain County, from North Arkansas).

[36] Cora Frances Starritt, Ada, Pontotoc County.

[37] Boyce Billingsley, Wayne, McClain County, from Northern Arkansas.

[38] Martin Odom, Checotah, McIntosh County. The title is given, by confusion, as "Jolly Rovers."

[39] Florette McNeese, Oklahoma City, Oklahoma County, who considers this a local substitution.

[40] Wolford, p. 65. Compare Mooney (*JAFL,* 2:104), who reports the substitution of "Quebec Town" for "New Orleans" in "Pretty Little Pink," as possibly indicating French and Indian War origin for that variant.

The American boys have gained the day
And the Germans are retreating.[41]

In "Jim Lane" "Some say she was taken in the wars of Germany" [42] takes the place of "It has been said that he was slain All in the wars of General Lee (Lane, Wayne, Rose [43])."

Modernization often takes the special form of a democratic change, which, being American as well as modern, represents a combination of local and temporal adaptations. Such is the substitution of "The farmer's daughter" [44] for "My lady's daughter" in "Draw a Bucket of Water."

Modernization or Americanization is also seen in the naming of gold automobile and gold aeroplane as the objects chosen as emblems of opposing sides in "London Bridge"; [45] gold watch and Ford car, in "Needle's Eye"; [46] and makes of motor-cars,[47] mule, and train [48] in the choice of transportation offered to the player who has been "called out" in "William Trembletoe"; and in the substitution of "levy" for "valley" or "village" [49] in "Marching round the Levy."

A third form of adaptation takes place for the sake of rhyme. In "It Rains and It Hails"

It rains, it hails, it's cold stormy weather,
In comes the farmer drinking all the cider; [50]

---

[41] Doris G. Waters, Ponca City, Kay County.

[42] Dr. J. H. Combs, of Texas Christian University, from Knott County, Kentucky.

[43] The same, from Gilmer County, West Virginia.

[44] Louise Aldridge, Quinton, Pittsburg County; Julia Howell, Muskogee, Muskogee County; Mrs. Edna Muldrow, Norman, Cleveland County; Marjorie Nice, Norman, Cleveland County.

Modernization and Americanization may be considered forms of folk-etymology in that they consist in substituting the nearest familiar or intelligible equivalent for an obscure or meaningless expression. In "Pop Goes the Weasel" Wolford (p. 84) notes that "All around the American flag" may have originated in the association of the original British line "In and out the Eagle" (in which the Eagle, according to Alfred Nutt, was a "well-known tavern and dancing saloon") with the national emblem.

Democratization is a familiar process in the imported ballad in America, where it is an aspect of the deterioration or "downward process" resulting from adjustment "to the social class of those who sing" the ballad. Compare the examples cited by Pound in *Poetic Origins and the Ballad* as evidence of high origin for ballads (pp. 93-94) and the vulgarization of Old-World pieces in America (p. 197).

[45] Pearl Bessie Corn, Taloga, Dewey County.

[46] Walter Myers Gable, Norman, Cleveland County.

[47] Ruth Johnson, Erick, Beckham County, from Tennessee.

[48] C. L. Cowan, Okemah, Okfuskee County.

[49] This (Gomme, II, pp. 122-143), according to Newell (p. 230), is a corruption of "valley," which he gives.

[50] Newell, p. 84.

becomes

> It rains and it hails and it's cold stormy weather,
> Me and my true love is marching on together.[51]

> It rains and it hails and it's cold stormy weather.
> The old cow died and we got lots o' leather.[52]

Or internal rhyme is introduced:

> It rains and it hails and it's cold stormy weather.
> Along comes old Jack *Snyder* and drinks all our *cider*.[53]

A change in the usual order of the line, throwing a new rhyme word at the end, may result in adaptation of this type. In "King William Was King James' Son" the inversion of the line "Upon his breast he wore a star" gives

> He wore a star upon his breast,
> As big as any hornet's nest.[54]

> He wore a star upon his breast,
> Pointing to the east and west.[55]

In "Needle's Eye" the change of "The thread that runs so true" to (for grammatical correctness?) "The thread that runs so truly" produces

> Needle's eye, thou dost supply
>   The thread that runs so truly.
> Many a beau have I left go
>   Because I wanted youly.[56]

—a case of out of the frying-pan into the fire, as it were. Less violent, in this line, are "Because I love(d) you truly," [57] "Because I wanted July," [58] "Because he was unruly," [59] and, with imperfect rhyme, "But now I've caught my jewel," [60] "Because I loved you dearly." [61]

Similarly a change in the rhyme scheme, such as a shift from the four-line stanza, with third and fourth lines rhyming, to couplets, produces

[51] Winnifred Spencer, Walters, Cotton County, from Jefferson, Marion County, Texas.
[52] Mary Virginia Maloy, Norman, Cleveland County.
[53] Alice Flora Hare, Norman, Cleveland County, from Bernice Taylor, Norman.
[54] Florette McNeese, Oklahoma City, Oklahoma County.
[55] Ada M. Scheirman, Kingfisher, Kingfisher County.
[56] Mildred Brown, Norman, Cleveland County, and 17 other Oklahoma variants. Compare Gardner, pp. 115-116.
[57] Vaughan Daniel, Norman, Cleveland County, and 6 other Oklahoma variants.
[58] Lucy I. Pitts, Oklahoma City, Oklahoma County. Compare Hamilton, p. 297.
[59] Elizabeth A. Cate, Muskogee, Muskogee County.
[60] Doris G. Waters, Ponca City, Kay County.
[61] Milton West, McAlester, Pittsburg County.

interesting and often unexpected results. Thus, in "Coffee Grows on a White Oak Tree," the usual

> Coffee grows on a white oak tree,
>> The river flows with brandy-O,
> Come choose your one to roam with you
>> As sweet as 'lasses candy-O.

may give way to

> Coffee grows on a high oak tree,
> And the river flows with brandy free.
> The streets are lined with dollar bills
> And the girls are sweet as sugar pills.
> Go choose your lover to roam with you
> Over the dreary ocean blue.[62]

Or:

> Coffee grows on white oak trees,
> Brandy flows from here to the sea.[63]

Or, it may be simply a change in the rhyme word; e.g., when "Coffee grows on a white oak tree" has been changed to "Coffee grows on a white oak stump," the next line becomes "The river flows with sugar lumps." [64] Thus the substitution of "toot" for the usual "blow" in the second line of the following produces

> Went upon the mountain top,
>> Give my horn a toot,
> Thought I heard my Liza say
>> "Yonder comes my Newt." [65]

Even more commonly this type of adaptation for the sake of rhyme results from the freedom rather than the exigencies of the latter. Thus, in "King William Was King James' Son," "Upon his breast he wore a star" is followed by "Pointing to the ocean far," [66] a picturesque departure from the usual "That's a sign there's going to be a war." [67] In "Shoo Fly" the original

> I feel, I feel, I feel, I feel like a morning star, (*Four times.*)

---

[62] Doris G. Waters, Ponca City, Kay County.

[63] Walter Myers Gable, Norman, Cleveland County.

[64] Mrs. Della I. Young, Cheyenne, Roger Mills County, from J. R. Weatherly, Elk City, Beckham County.

[65] Mrs. Pearl Yates Kaufman, Norman, Cleveland County, who played it in Greenwood, Sebastian County, Arkansas, and notes that the stanza may be varied to fit the boy's name.

[66] Beatrice Jennings McMullin, Norman, Cleveland County, brought from Kentucky to Missouri, then to Kay and Grant Counties on the Oklahoma-Kansas border. Compare Newell (p. 74), "Point your way across the sea," in the following (the fifth) line.

[67] Mrs. L. T. Monnett, Norman, Cleveland County, who played it in Missouri.

prompts the humor of

> I feel, I feel, I feel,
>> I feel like a morning star.
> I feel, I feel, I feel,
>> I feel like a big (an old) box-car.[68]

> I feel, etc.
> I shine, I shine, I shine,
>> I shine like a railroad car.[69]

> I feel, etc.
> I feel, I feel, I feel,
>> I feel like a big cigar.[70]

> I feel, etc.
> I feel, I feel, I feel,
>> Just like a smoked cigar
> And I wonder where
>> In this wide world you are.[71]

3. Crossing and Shifting

Shifting of stanzas may take place chiefly for one of two reasons. The more obvious process is a confusion that arises in the texts themselves, due to faulty memory or accidental association in the words. Less obvious is the shifting of stanzas, or of the chorus, that accompanies the shifting of the tune.[72]

A simple example of the latter process is offered by the tune of "We Won't Go Home Till Morning" (a play-party song in its own right [73] as well as a popular song), to which are sung both "Going Down to Rowser" and "Pig in the Parlor." The identity of the tune has resulted in the

---

[68] Elsie Montgomery, Sunset, Beaver County, from New Home in the Panhandle of Texas; Harold Roberts, Blackwell, Kay County; Emma Vilhauer, Norman, Cleveland County.

[69] Leon Kidd, Billings, Noble County.

[70] Professor Kenneth Kaufman, Norman, Cleveland County, who played it in Eastern Custer County.

[71] Naomi Maye Porter, Ringling, Jefferson County.

[72] Compare Pound, *American Ballads and Songs,* p. xxvii. That this mixing and crossing of songs is often due to the scarcity of tunes as compared with the abundance of songs is brought out by Perrow (*JAFL,* 28:182n.). The opposite process, that of adaptation to the melody, when the same song is sung to a different tune, is discussed by Phillips Barry (*JAFL,* 27:76), who states the following as an axiom of oral transmission of folk-song: "If the melody did not happen to fit the text exactly, the text adapted itself to the melody."

[73] Atlee Margaret Garrett, Loco, Stephens County; Florette McNeese, Oklahoma City, Oklahoma County.

crossing of the first two songs in one Oklahoma variant [74] and in a Missouri text of "We'll All Go Down to Rowser," [75] and of the latter two in an Iowa text of the same song.[76]

In another Oklahoma variant of "Going Down to Rowser" occurs an adaptation of the first stanza of "The Bear Went over the Mountain," sung to the same tune as "We Won't Go Home Till Morning":

> Oh, the duck flew over the ocean,
> The ocean, the ocean,
> Oh, the duck flew over the ocean
> To see what he could see.[77]

In "Old Joe Clark" the tune of the minstrel song, "Lucy Long," has been taken over, and with it the chorus—

> So take your time, Miss Lucy,
> Take your time, Miss Lucy Long;
> Take your time, Miss Lucy,
> O Lucy, Lucy Long!

which gives—

> Round and round, old Joe Clark,
> Round and round, I'm gone.
> Round and round, old Joe Clark,
> And good-by, Lucy Long.[78]

> Fly around, Old Joe Clark,
> Fly around, I'm gone.
> Round and round, old Joe Clark,
> Good-by, Lucy Long.[79]

---

[74] William Plaster, Meeker, Lincoln County. The sentiment is echoed in "And stay away all night," "For staying away all night" in Ames' version (pp. 297-298).

[75] Randolph, pp. 217-218.

[76] Pound, *American Ballads and Songs,* pp. 237-238.

[77] Audra A. Plumlee, Norman, Cleveland County, from Northwestern Arkansas. "Skip to My Lou" is often sung to the tune of "Brown Jug," and "Old Brass Wagon" and "Boston" are sung to the same tune or similar tunes, but in these cases there has been no transference of stanzas.

[78] Mabel Harryman, Lexington, Cleveland County.

[79] Helen Jacobs, Tulsa, Tulsa County; Lucy I. Pitts, Oklahoma City, Oklahoma County (played in Indian Territory). Another "Lucy Long" chorus (communicated by Mrs. L. T. Monnett, Norman, Cleveland County, from Missouri)—
> Oh, rock that cradle, Miss Lucy,
> Miss Lucy, Lucy Long.
> Oh, rock that cradle, Miss Lucy,
> And keep the children warm.
may find an echo in another form of the chorus of "Old Joe Clark" from Oklahoma

The famous "scolding wife" stanza of "Lucy Long" also appears in the Nebraska song of "Ain't I Goin'," [80] sung to the tune and containing many of the stanzas of "Old Joe Clark," other variants of which are reported from Missouri as "Oh, Ain't I Gone" [81] (in which "Lucy Long" becomes "Susan Jane") and "Up and Down" [82] and from Oklahoma as "Oh, Ain't I Sweet." [83] With "Old Joe Clark" have also been crossed stanzas of two mountain songs, "Shady Grove" (often sung to the same tune [84] and in turn crossed with "O My Laura Lee!") and "Liza Jane," which has several tunes, one of which is close to that of "Old Joe Clark." [85]

Two stanzas of "Liza Jane" in particular have been taken over by "Old Joe Clark," with many variants:

> Went on top of a mountain (Goin' up the mountain)
> To sow a patch of cane
> To raise a barrel of 'lasses
> To sweeten Liza Jane.

> You go down the new-cut road,
> And I'll go down the lane.
> You can hug the old gatepost,
> While I'll hug Liza Jane.[86]

Sometimes the reference to Liza Jane is eliminated from "Old Joe Clark" as follows:

> I went upon the mountain top
> To give my horn a blow.
> I thought I heard my true love say,
> "Yonder comes your beau." [87]

(Mrs. Della I. Young, Cheyenne, Roger Mills County, from J. R. Weatherly, Elk City, Beckham County):
> Rock, rock, old Joe Clark,
>   Rock, rock, I say.
> Rock, rock, old Joe Clark,
>   You'd better be getting away.
Compare the Texas version (Dudley and Payne, p. 34) containing "Rockity rock."

[80] Piper, pp. 271-272.

[81] Ames, pp. 299-300.

[82] Hamilton, pp. 302-303.

[83] Florette McNeese, Oklahoma City, Oklahoma County.

[84] Perrow, *JAFL*, 28:182-183. Combs (*Folk-Say, 1930,* pp. 241-244) gives a different tune but several similar stanzas.

[85] Douthitt (pp. 35-36) gives "Liza Jane" and "High Low Jack an' the Game" (a variant of "Old Joe Clark") as sung to the same tune. Sandburg (who prints four "Liza Jane" texts and tunes, pp. 51, 132-133, 308-309) notes: "There are as many Liza songs in the Appalachian mountains as there are species of trees on the slopes of that range" (p. 132).

[86] Florette McNeese, Oklahoma City, Oklahoma County.

[87] Ruby Pfautsch, Norman, Cleveland County.

And the latter has been taken into "Liza Jane":

> I went up on the mountain
>> To give my horn a blow,
> I thought I heard my Liza say,
> "There comes my Joe." [88]

One Oklahoma-Arkansas variant of "Liza Jane" contains the following chorus:

> Get along home, home, Cinda,
>> Get along home, I say.
> Get along home, home, Cinda,
>> Get along home, I say.[89]

a rendering of which appears as the chorus of "Garber Town" and "Got a Little Home to Go to"—two fragments which have stanzas in common with both "Liza Jane" and "Old Joe Clark":

> Run away home, run away home,
>> Run away home, I say;
> Run away home, my little blue eyes,
>> And don't forget the way.[90]

> Home an' a home,
> Home an' a home,
>> I've got a little home to go to.[91]

Because of its utter formlessness and the ease with which almost any stanza of four short lines may be fitted to its tune, "Old Joe Clark" has attracted to itself stanzas from more songs than has any other game, and it has without a doubt the largest number of stanzas among play-party songs.[92] Among the sources drawn upon are many songs of Negro or minstrel origin or influence, such as " 'Tain't Goin' to Rain No More," "Oh! Dem Golden Slippers," "Oh, Mourner!" "Bile dem Cabbage Down," "Raccoon Up in de 'Simmon Tree" ("Karo Song"), "Masser Had a Yaller

---

[88] Catherine Harris, Antlers, Pushmataha County, from S. B. Hackett, Norman, who played it in Arkansas.

[89] The same. The chorus of "Liza Jane" is usually some form of
> Oh, how I love her!
> Ain't that a shame!
> Oh, how I love her!
> Good-by, Liza Jane.

[90] Pauline Goodson, Blackwell, Kay County, from Northern Oklahoma and Southern Kansas.

[91] Audra A. Plumlee, Norman, Cleveland County.

[92] Paul Howard, Headrick, Jackson County, quotes from a friend to this effect: "There's thousands of 'em. Every one has his own version." Dudley and Payne (p. 32) set the number more modestly at 144.

For details of crossing and shifting see the headnote to "Old Joe Clark" below.

Gal" ("When de Band Begins to Play"), "Oh, Susan, Quit Your Fooling," "Susan Jane," "Sally Ann," and "Allie Bell," many of which have crossed with one another.

Shifting also takes place, it has been pointed out, as a result of confusion of, or association with, words, idea, or method of playing. In this way stanzas of "Old Joe Clark" and "Liza Jane" find their way into other songs: "You may ride the ol' gray hoss" is found in "In Somebody's Garden"; [93] and "Going up on a mountain" and "And O how I love her" occur in "Shoo Fly." [94] "There is somebody waiting for me" passes from "Bird in the Cage" into "Pig in the Parlor"; [95] "Pig in the Parlor" and "Old Brass Wagon" stray into "Skip to My Lou"; [96] "Skip to My Lou" passes into "Coffee Grows on a White Oak Tree"; [97] "Big white house and nobody living in it" passes from "Virginia" into "Coffee Grows on a White Oak Tree" [98] and "Shoo Fly." [99] A good example of association is presented by "Needle's Eye," which, through the association of needle and "The thread that runs so true," often appends a stanza from "Pop Goes the Weasel"—

> Mother taught me how to sew
> And how to thread the needle.
> Evertime I take a stitch (Every time my finger slipped),
> Pop goes the weasel!

adapted from

> A nickel for a spool of thread,
> A penny for a needle.
> That's the way the money goes,
> Pop goes the weasel!

A good example of confusion is seen in a Missouri version of "We're Marching to Quebec," [100] which appends to that song two stanzas of "Pretty Little Pink," with the result that "We're marchin' down to ol' Quebec" at the opening gives way to "An' I'll march away to New Orleans" at the close. The confusion is perhaps to be explained not only by the similarity of the war themes but also by the fact that both songs often have the following stanza in common (to judge from one Oklahoma variant of "Pretty Little Pink): [101]

---

[93] Clifford Chandler, Crescent, Logan County.
[94] Leon Kidd, Billings, Noble County.
[95] Mary Esther Coffman, Geary, Blaine County.
[96] See above, p. 77.
[97] See above, p. 80.
[98] Joseph Edward Terral, Oklahoma City, Oklahoma County.
[99] Fanny W. Kelly, Jefferson, Grant County.
[100] Randolph, pp. 206-207.
[101] O. B. Campbell, Medford, Grant County.

> Now the war's over and we'll turn back
>> To the place where we first started,
> So open the ring and choose another
>> To relieve the broken-hearted.

One or more stanzas of a song may become detached as a fragment, as in the case of "Garber Town" and "Got a Little Home to Go to" discussed above; "Going Down the River," [102] which is generally found as part of "Coffee Grows on a White Oak Tree"; and "Railroad, Steamboat," which also appears as a chorus of "Brown Jug," "Coffee Grows on a White Oak Tree," and "Going Down to Rowser." As in the last case, in which a stanza of "Going Down to Rowser"—"Oh, never mind the old folks"— is reported in a variant of "Railroad, Steamboat," [103] it is sometimes difficult to tell whether the fragment is entitled to separate existence or should be included under the more familiar song. There is no question, however, that many fragments are played as fragments and not merely recorded as such. [104]

Sometimes one song arises out of another by division, as in "Coffee Grows on a White Oak Tree," which derives from "Pretty Little Pink." Sometimes the same song, with slight variations, is known by different titles, e. g., "Marriage" in Massachusetts, [105] "Getting Married" in Indiana [106] and Oklahoma, [107] "Yonder She Comes" in Missouri, [108] "Loving Couple" in Nebraska, [109] and "Lordy, What a Man" in Texas. [110]

Sometimes, not only the title, but the text may change under the influence of another song, but not enough to destroy the integrity of the former. Thus, in the last of the variants mentioned above, which is sometimes sung to the tune of "Shoot the Buffalo," the influence of the latter is seen on the first stanza, the opening lines of which are those of the other song:

> Rise you up, my true love,
>> Present to me your hand,
> I know you are a pretty girl
>> But Lordy, what a man.

---

[102] Clarence W. Anthony, Norman, Cleveland County.

[103] Mrs. T. H. Maness, Oswalt, Love County.

[104] Dudley and Payne (p. 9) report "Railroad, Steamboat" as a separate song.

[105] Newell, pp. 59-62. A similar case of a song with several titles and minor variations is presented by "Come, My Love," "Consolation Flowing Free," and "Kila Ma Cranky."

[106] Wolford, p. 43.

[107] Chester Harley Anderson, Guthrie, Logan County.

[108] Ames, p. 310.

[109] Piper, pp. 275-276.

[110] Dudley and Payne, pp. 29-30.

Here the last two lines in turn seem to have influenced "Shoot the Buffalo" in the following Oklahoma variant:

> Rise up to me, my dearest dear,
>   And present to me your hand,
> For I know you want to marry
>   And I want to be your man.[111]

Two versions of "Marriage," essentially the same but with stanzas attracted from other songs, are "Roving Bachelor," [112] which opens with choosing stanzas under the influence of "Three Dukes"; and "I'll Be the Reaper," [113] which opens with a stanza of the game of that name dealing with the loss of a true love ("I've lost my true-love, and I don't know where to find her"), no doubt suggested by the finding of her in the "Marriage" stanza that follows ("Here comes your true-love, and how do you do?").

Sometimes a snatch or reminiscence of another song is introduced into a game for the sheer incongruity of it or for padding, as in "Shoo Fly":

> Mary had a little lamb,
>   A little lamb, a little lamb,
> Mary had a little lamb,
>   Its fleece was white as snow.
>
> I feel, I feel, religion in my soul,
> I feel, I feel, religion in my soul,
> There'll be a hot time in the old town to-night, my baby.[114]

And in "Boston":

> Here we go round the mulberry bush, (*Three times.*)
>   So early in the morning.
>
> John Brown's dead and his wife's a widow, etc.
>
> Maybe she'll die and she'll be with him, etc.[115]

Sometimes a game derived from a folk-song which has given rise to popular imitation or parody takes in stanzas from the latter, as in "Buffalo Girls," one Oklahoma variant of which has absorbed the chorus and one stanza of the comic derivative "Ain't-cha, Ain't-cha, Ain't-cha, Ain't-cha Comin' Out To-night?"—

---

[111] Wallace N. McCown, Emporia, Kansas, from Earl Denton, Norman, Cleveland County.

[112] Tolman and Eddy, pp. 431-432.

[113] Ethel Rose Baird, Bixby, Tulsa County, from Logan Summers, Bixby, who played it in Vernon County, Missouri; Gardner, pp. 103-104.

[114] Emma Vilhauer, Norman, Cleveland County.

[115] Glenn A. Roe, Oklahoma City, Oklahoma County, who played it at Frederick, Tillman County.

I got a girl, freckles on her chin,
Wart on her nose and her eyes turned in,
Darn good girl for the shape she's in,
    Tell me ain't you comin' out to-night?

Chorus:

Ain't you, ain't-you, ain't-you, ain't you comin' out tonight,
    Comin' out to-night, comin' out to-night?
Ain't you, ain't you, ain't you, ain't you comin' out to-night
    To dance by the light of the moon? [116]

And in one Oklahoma variant of " 'Tain't Goin' to Rain No More," sand-wiched between *bona fide* folk stanzas beginning "Had an old hat and it had no crown" and "Some folks say that niggers won't steal" is a Whiz-Bang-up parody of one of the stanzas in Wendell Hall's parody-popular-song:

The night was dark and dreary,
    The air was full of sound,
The old man stole the last clean sheet,
    And joined the Ku Klux Klan.[117]

4. Corruption and Analogy

Aside from the instability of text revealed by play-party songs in the processes of variation (by accretion or improvisation), adaptation (by local or temporal substitutions or adaptation to rhyme), and transference, individual words are subject to the distortions of oral transmission in the form' of corruption and analogy. Although the line between the two is sometimes purely arbitrary, corruptions may be distinguished as changes that result in loss of meaning, usually nonsense, whereas analogical or folk-etymological changes are distinguished by an attempt to restore meaning to the unfamiliar or unintelligible. The way in which these processes operate in the play-party is clear enough. Corruption is due to imperfect hearing or reproduction of sounds. Some one in a group, playing a game for the first time perhaps, may not catch accurately what is said or sung but, restrained by bashfulness or good manners or misled by overconfidence or ignorance, goes on reproducing the word incorrectly until it becomes habitual with him and others to whom he passes it on, until it gradually finds acceptance as the only way of saying or singing it. Thus the unknown becomes the unintelligible—until some one else comes along who tries to restore meaning to it, undoing the damage wrought by corruption or trying to prevent its recurrence, and by analogy translates the unknown into the known—a different "known," however, from the original.

---

[116] Lois Ferguson Beckham, Norman, Cleveland County, from Memphis, Tennessee.
[117] Cora Frances Starritt, Ada, Pontotoc County.

Corruptions illustrate various phonological changes. Unintelligible or nonsense refrains, having little or no meaning to enforce consistency, are especially subject to vowel and consonant substitution. In the refrain of "Farmer in the Dell,"[118] which is more commonly "Heigh-ho the dairy-O," [119] "dairy-O (Oh, ho)" becomes "derry-O (derrio, derio)," "dearie-O (deary-O)," "cherry," "cherry-O (cherio)," "ferry-O (ferrie-O)," "merry-O (merrio, merri-O")"; and "Heigh- (high, hi) ho (O, Oh)" becomes "I, O" (in "I, O, a cherry") and (with a diphthongal glide) "high-e-oh (higheo)." "Hey-O ma derry-O" shows vowel substitution in both words and the use of the dialectal "ma" for "my."

In "Jutang" the refrain "Jutang, Jutang, Ju" gives rise to "Jew Tong, Jew Tong, Jew," "Jue tain jue," "Shoo Tang, Shoo Tang," and "U-tang, U-tang-U."

Assimilation is seen in "rassamatassamatee"[120] and "rismal, tasmal, tee"[121] for "ransom a tansom a tee," in "Three Dukes."

An intrusive initial *n* due to wrong group subdivision is seen in "form a no"[122] for "form an O" in "Captain Jinks." An intrusive consonant also produces "Irish stew"[123] for "Irish too" in "Pig in the Parlor." Other examples of wrong subdivision are:

"Many a beau, a violet go"[124] for "Many a beau have I let go" in "Needle's Eye" (with glide).

"To get a log of beer"[125] for "To get some lager beer" in "Going Down to Rowser" (partly by analogy with "keg of beer," "bottle of beer").

"Captain Jinks with a horse my ring"[126] for "Captain Jinks of the horse marines."

"Sweetest land I ever knew."[127] for "Sweet as 'lasses candy O" in "Coffee Grows on a White Oak Tree" (with dropping out).

---

[118] Also "The Farmer's in the Dell." Six out of 46 Oklahoma variants have "Farmer in the Dale" (one of these being "Farmer's in the Dale"). Gomme's title is "The Farmer's Den" (II, p. 420); Wolford's, "Farmer in the Well" (p. 42); Babcock's "The Man in the Cell" (pp. 254-255).

[119] Compare "Hio, manerio" (Dr. J. H. Combs, Texas Christian University, from Gilmer County, West Virginia; "He I Hedy Ho" (Douglas, London, p. 68), "Hi-O, Ki-O" (Dudley and Payne, Texas, p. 26); "Highery O Valerio" (Toronto, *JAFL*, 8:254); "High-O-Maderio" (Wolford, Louisiana, p. 43).

[120] Hazel Black, Higgins, Texas. Compare "Th' raz-ma-taz-a-ma-tee," Randolph, p. 229.

[121] Helen A. Cook, Norman, Cleveland County, from Texas County in the Panhandle of Oklahoma.

[122] Emma Vilhauer, Norman, Cleveland County.

[123] William Cunningham, Watonga, Blaine County.

[124] Mildred L. Nicholson, Shattuck, Ellis County.

[125] Lillian A. Jasper, Roosevelt, Kiowa County.

[126] Emma Vilhauer, Norman, Cleveland County.

[127] Leonard C. Dresser, Lahoma, Garfield County.

"Rufus Santa Jackson Payne" [128] for "Rufus Andrew Jackson Payne" in "Susan Jane."

"Oh down the river Oh!-hi!-Oh!" [129] for "O down the Ohio" in "Down the River" (partly by analogy).

In "Skip to My Lou" the dialectal "ma" (as in "skip to ma Lou" and "skip-ta-ma-Lou (loo)" produces "Skip to Milieu," "skip the maloo (malu)," and, by syncopation, "skip to m' loo" and "skip tum lue." [130] The last, by analogy, gives "skip come a Lou." [131]

In "Liza Jane" "Oh how I love her" becomes "O how lovers." [132]

In "Old Joe Clark" "Massa had an old coon dog" becomes "Mushy had an old coon dog." [133]

In "Shoot the Buffalo" "Rise you up my dearest dear" becomes "Round me up you dears deer." [134]

In "Do-Se-Do" "Right hand around to your best liking" becomes "Right hand around to your best like-em." [135]

In "Going Down to Rowser" "Lost my true lover on that raging canal" becomes "I lost my true lover in the waving canal." [136]

In "Shoo Fly" "To see what I could see" becomes "Something to deceive." [137]

In "Getting Upstairs" "Such a getting upstairs" becomes (by unvoicing of *g* in the dialectal "gittin") "Such a kitten upstairs." [138]

"Kila Ma Cranky" (itself a corruption of "Killicrankie") becomes "Fiddle-ma-cranky." [139]

---

[128] Beatrice Jennings McMullin, Norman, Cleveland County, brought from Kentucky to Missouri, then to Kay and Grant Counties on the Oklahoma-Kansas border.

[129] Verla Summers, Snyder, Pottawatomie County.

[130] Sixty-two Oklahoma variants of "Skip to my Lou" are distributed as follows: skip-to-my-Lou (29), skip to ma Lou (2), skip the maloo (2), skip to mayloo, skip to my lue (2), skip to me Lou (3), skip-to-Maloo (2), skip to my Loo (3), skip to a maloo, skip-ta-ma-Lou (2), skip come a Lou, skip-to-ma-loo, skip to my Lulu, skip to my lu, skip to the lu, skip to m' loo, skip the malu, skip tum lue (2), skip to Mileu, skip-to-me-lu, skip-ta-ma-loo, skip the mi Lou, skip to Lou (2).

[131] Also reported from Michigan by Gardner, p. 123.

[132] Emma Vilhauer, Norman, Cleveland County.

[133] Lillie O. Heaton, Watonga, Blaine County.

[134] Tephia Folsom, Atoka, Atoka County, from Pat Lowry, Atoka County.

[135] Verla Summers, Snyder, Pottawatomie County.

[136] Sam West, Duke, Jackson County.

[137] Elsie Montgomery, Sunset, Beaver County, from New Home district in the Panhandle of Texas.

[138] Fanny Kelly, Jefferson, Grant County. Cf. "Di-dee-o" for "Tideo," Scarborough, p. 115.

[139] Beatrice J. McMullin, Norman, Cleveland County, brought from Kentucky to Missouri, then to Kay and Grant Counties on the Oklahoma-Kansas border. Compare "Kilmacrankie," Piper, p. 272; "Kilamakrankie," Wolford, p. 61; "Creel-My-crankie," Van Doren, p. 489; "Crinny My Cranky," Hamilton, p. 297; "Crinkely, Cronkely," Gardner, p. 95.

"Old Betty Larkin" becomes "Sold Betsy Larkin." [140]

"Rowser (Rouser)," probably originally "Rauser," [141] becomes "Rowsey," [142] "Rosea," [143] and "Russell." [144]

"Molly Bright," in the game of that name, is a corruption of "Marley Bright" [145] and "Marlow bright," the latter of which Newell gives as a corruption of "Barley Break" in the old English game of that name.[146]

"In "William Trembletoe" "Wire, briar, limber lock" become "Yiar, briar, limber lock" [147] and "Riar, briar, limber lock." [148]

"Pop goes the weasel" becomes "Pop goes the easel." [149]

In "Green Gravel" "free mason" becomes "free mashion." [150]

"Needle's Eye" gives the following corruptions (partly by wrong sub-division) of "does (doth) supply" in the line "The needle's eye that does (doth) supply": "the desso ply," "dess so ply," "des o' ply," "the desi ply," "the de's' ply," "the dest supply," "dost o ply," "the dessel fly," "the dis supply," "the disreply," "the disapply," "dis-o-ply."

"On to Galilee" becomes (partly by wrong subdivision) "On the galla of Lee" [151] and "On the galla-lee." [152]

"Captain Jinks" becomes "Captain Jenks" in several variants, and, partly for the sake of rhyme, "Captain Jinks, the horse marinks" [153] and gives

Captain Jenks, of the horse merinks
Claps his hands with all his minks.[154]

"Terrapin" becomes "peddler" in the following fragment:

As I went down the new-cut road,
I met a peddler and a toad.
Every time the toad would jump,
The peddler would dodge behind a stump.[155]

140 Florette McNeese, Oklahoma City, Oklahoma County.
141 Compare Miller, p. 31.
142 Tephia Folsom, Atoka, Atoka County, from Pat Lowry, Atoka County.
143 Lucy I. Pitts, Oklahoma City, Oklahoma County, from Middle Tennessee.
144 Florette McNeese, Oklahoma City, Oklahoma County.
145 Hoke, p. 120.
146 Newell, p. 153.
147 Walter L. Payne, Hobart, Kiowa County.
148 Lacie Huff, Norman, Cleveland County; Fern Tuttle, Norman, Cleveland County, from Indiana.
149 Atta LeGate, Muskogee, Muskogee County.
150 Anita D. Shaw, Thomas, Custer County, from Beatrice Joy.
151 Alma Dixon, Norman, Cleveland County.
152 William Plaster, Meeker, Lincoln County.
153 Doris G. Waters, Ponca City, Kay County.
154 Carl West, Perico, Texas, from Raymond Kiser, Perico.
155 Audra A. Plumlee, Norman, Cleveland County.

Terms employed in dance calls exhibit a large number of phonetic and orthographic variations. "Do-se-do" (from the French *dos-à-dos*) appears as "do-si-do," "do-ce-do," "do c do," "dosey do," "dough-so-dough," "dolsee do," "dosey you do"; is clipped to "do see," "do c," "do" ("Ladies do and gents do-so") and "doe" ("Ladies doe, gents you know"); and suggests a pun, "Do-se-do and a little more dough?" [156]

In their attempts to inject meaning into that which, from remoteness in time or space, has lost meaning, or to make the less familiar more familiar, the analogical changes of folk-etymology are no less surprising and ludicrous than the phonological changes of corruptions. "Dreary Lane" [157] for "Drury Lane" in "The Muffin Man"; "Wild-brier, limber lock" [158] for "Wire, brier, limber lock" in "William Trembletoe"; "Around the royal race he run," [159] "Around the royal course he run," [160] "In the royal race he run," [161] "Upon the Rio Race he run," [162] for "And from the royal race he sprung" in "King William Was King James' Son"; "And marched away to the convict war" [163] for "And marched away to the con-script war" in the same: "ennamon cinnamon tea" [164] for "ennamon, cen-namon tea" in "Three Dukes," "Miss Jenny Ann Jones" [165] for "Miss Jennia Jones"; "Old Grumbler" [166] for "Old Crompty;" "Oh high o'er the dairy" [167] for "Hi-O, the dairy-O"; "many a beau that violets grow" [168] and "Many are gold and violets bold" [169] for "Many a beau have I let go"

---

[156] Other terms belonging to dance calls and in some cases entering into the play-party, with their corruptions, are as follows: "Allemande (*à la main*)," which becomes "alm and," "alamand," "Adam and," "alamond," "alemond," "alamon," "aliman," "elimant," "elemate," "elemen," "elem and," and, by folk-etymology, "Alamo," "all men," "element," "elementary," "emigrate;" *dos à balinet*, which becomes "do see bobinette;" "simmer down," which becomes "semi down;" *chassée,* which becomes, by metathesis, "sashay," "sashaway," "sachet;" "re-sashay," which becomes "resasha-way" and "re-sash;" "promenade," which becomes "pro made" and "pomade."

[157] Mary Esther Coffman, Geary, Blaine County.

[158] Lois F. Beckham, Norman, Cleveland County, from Texas.

[159] Florette McNeese, Oklahoma City, Oklahoma County.

[160] Mrs. L. T. Monnett, Norman, Cleveland County, who played it in Missouri.

[161] Beatrice Jennings McMullin, Norman, Cleveland County, brought from Kentucky to Missouri, then to Kay and Grant Counties on the Oklahoma-Kansas border.

[162] Ada M. Scheirman, Kingfisher, Kingfisher County.

[163] Mrs. Anne McClure, Oklahoma City, Oklahoma County, who played it in Benton County, Arkansas.

[164] Bertha Matthews, Norman, Cleveland County. Compare "team" for "tea" and "drowsy" for "blowsy" in the same (Van Doren, pp. 486-487).

[165] Mrs. L. T. Monnett, Norman, Cleveland County, who played it in Missouri.

[166] Mrs. Louise D. Sayres, Norman, Cleveland County, from Texas. Compare Kittredge, *JAFL,* 35:407.

[167] T. Lloyd Osborne, Carter, Beckham County. Compare "High on the merry-O," Mary Coffman, Geary, Blaine County.

[168] Mrs. Edna Muldrow, Norman, Cleveland County.

[169] A. J. Strange, Clinton, Custer County.

in "Needle's Eye"; "We just reply," "does (doth) so fly (ply)," "the dust so fly," "that dust supply," "the best supply," "the dress so ply," "thy dress I ply," "the best I ply," "this I spy," in the same; "Johnny was a miller boy" [170] for "Jolly was the miller boy who lived by the mill"; "How many miles to Boston Town" [171] for "How many miles to Babylon"; "For night has gained the day" [172] for "For we have gained the day" in "Marching Round the Levy"; "all over creation a sight to be seen" (or "I'm ashamed to be seen") [173] and "free mason, free mason, I'm ashamed to be seen" for "Grieved maiden, grieved maiden, you're ashamed to be seen" in "Green Gravel"; "frequent will" for "free good will" in "Miller Boy"; "round the level," [174] "o'er the lea," [175] "round the mill-wheel" [176] for "round the levy" in "Marching Round the Levy"—these are examples of analogy gleaned from traditional games.

The following occur in native songs: "The river flows in Borneo," [177] "The river flows to the Grande Rio," [178] "River flows in Brandy, Ore.," [179] for "The river flows with brandy-O" in "Coffee Grows on a White Oak Tree"; "As sweet as lassie's candy-O" [180] for "As sweet as 'lasses candy-O" in the same; "Coffee grows on a high oak tree" [181] and "Coffee grows on high trees" [182] for "(Green) Coffee grows on a white oak tree" in the same; "The corners off the ceiling" [183] for "Break corners off Cecila" in "Old Doc Collins"; "Let her go to that land, fare-ye-well" [184] for "I remember that last fare-you-well" in "Going Down to Rowser"; "Oh, down the river we go, Oh, Oh, Oh!" [185] for "Oh down the Ohio"; "Rowser" as verb in "Two round two to rouse her" and "Round the gent to rouse him"; [186] "Aunt Jermima" [187] for "Angelina"; "He preached all over Spain" [188] for "He preached all over the plain" in "Old Joe Clark"; "My

---

[170] Lois Ferguson Beckham, Norman, Cleveland County, from Western Oklahoma.
[171] Mrs. Louise D. Sayres, Norman, Cleveland County.
[172] Doris G. Waters, Ponca City, Kay County.
[173] Five out of 13 Oklahoma variants.
[174] Hattie Bell Bethea, Marion, South Carolina; Gardner, p. 120.
[175] Leon Kidd, Billings, Noble County.
[176] Alice Lucile Jackson, Supply, Woodward County.
[177] Boyce Billingsley, Wayne, McClain County.
[178] For "Rio Grande," Lela L. Conrad, Perry, Noble County.
[179] Leonard C. Dresser, Lahoma, Garfield County.
[180] Lillian A. Jasper, Roosevelt, Kiowa County.
[181] Doris G. Waters, Ponca City, Kay County.
[182] Bonnie Mae Close, Oklahoma City, Oklahoma County. Compare "Coffee Grows on White Folks' Trees," Talley, p. 107.
[183] Leora Austin, Foss, Washita County.
[184] William Plaster, Meeker, Lincoln County.
[185] Florette McNeese, Oklahoma City, Oklahoma County.
[186] The same.
[187] Walter L. Payne, Hobart, Kiowa County.
[188] Mabel Harryman, Lexington, Cleveland County.

ma she cried" [189] for "Mamma she cried" in "Captain Jinks"; "newcut road" [190] for "Newport road" and "Norfolk road," or vice versa, in "Old Joe Clark"; "She sat down in her sad way station," [191] "As she sits down in hesitation," [192] "She sat down in meditation," [193] for "She sat down in her sad station," [194] which is in turn substituted for "She sat down in a sad condition" [195] in "Jim Lane"; "Rosa Becky Diner" [196] for "Rosy-Betsy-Lina"; "June apple tree" [197] and "John Jones' peach tree" [198] for "Juniper tree" in "Sister Phoebe"; "Way down in the poppy bed" [199] for "Way down in the paw-paw patch" in "John Brown"; "Breaking the trail in sandy land" [200] for "Break and trail"; "Patch one window, Tideo" [201] for "Pass one window, Tideo"; "cane brick" [202] and "cane break" [203] for "cane-brake"; "Down the narrow lane" [204] for "Down in Alabama"; "Injun pony" [205] for "Indian boy" in "John Brown Had a Little Indian"; "hold your oats" [206] for "hold your holts" in "Miller Boy"; "ridge of the canal" [207] for "raging canal" in "Railroad, Steamboat."

5. Word List

The following list of words and phrases drawn from Oklahoma play-party songs illustrates the lexical and grammatical peculiarities and irreg-

---

[189] Ruby Home, Calumet, Canadian County.

[190] Florette McNeese, Oklahoma City, Oklahoma County. Also "rocky road" ("Liza Jane," Frank Henry Dearden, Britton, Oklahoma County). "New-cut" is given in *Slave Songs of the United States* ("Charleston Gals," p. 88), and by Talley ("Rejected by Liza Jane," p. 134), Scarborough (the same, p. 106; also p. 164), Perrow ("Liza Jane," *JAFL*, 28:179, 180), Edmands (the same, p. 131). In the event that "new-cut" was the original epithet, "Newport" and "Norfolk" would be local substitutions.

[191] J. Kyle McIntyre, Ardmore, Carter County.

[192] Martin Odom, Checotah, McIntosh County.

[193] Marguerite M. Durkee, Norman, Cleveland County.

[194] Dr. J. H. Combs, Texas Christian University, from Gilmer County, West Virginia. In *Dialect Notes,* 4:317, he defines "station" as "condition."

[195] The same, from Knott County, Kentucky.

[196] Mrs. Ora Morris, Oklahoma City, Oklahoma County, who played it in Tennessee.

[197] O. B. Campbell, Medford, Grant County.

[198] Delmar Denton, Blackwell, Kay County.

[199] Mrs. Bertha Downing, Norman, Cleveland County, who played it in Southern Noble, Northeastern Logan, and Northern Payne Counties. Combs (*Dialect Notes,* 4:312) records "bouquet patch."

[200] Fanny W. Kelly, Jefferson, Grant County.

[201] Audra A. Plumlee, Norman, Cleveland County.

[202] Hattie Bell Bethea, Marion, South Carolina, in "Down the River."

[203] Tephia Folsom, Atoka, Atoka County, from Pat Lowry, Atoka County, in "Shoot the Buffalo."

[204] Doris G. Waters, Ponca City, Kay County.

[205] Mrs. L. T. Monnett, Norman, Cleveland County, who played it in Missouri.

[206] J. O. Conner, Shawnee, Pottawatomie County.

[207] Emma Vilhauer, Norman, Cleveland County. Other examples in print: "Sweetheart a-hunting" becomes "We're a true love-a-honey" (Heck, Cincinnati, *JAFL*, 40:28); "Tideo" becomes "Toddy, O' " (Douthitt, p. 31).

ularities of the genre. It is a hodge-podge of colloquialism, slang, Americanism, dialect and localism, (including Southern Mountain and Southwestern expressions, negroisms, and Westernisms), facetious, figurative, and allusive expressions, dance jargon (technical or slangy), archaisms, solecisms, ellipses, interjections, corruptions, folk-etymological terms, and what not. Many of the usages are not at all unusual but are included simply as representative of the colloquial level of play-party speech.

a by-by, a good-by, int. (For meter.) "And a by (good)-by Liza Jane."

a hippety hop, adv. (For meter.) "He went off a hippety hop."— "'Tain't Goin' to Rain No More."

ain'ta, v. (For meter.) "It ain'ta gonna rain no more."

aisle, n. (Dance term.) Space between rows. See center.

Alabam. Alabama. "Way down in Alabam."—"Virginia."

alemond, Allemande (Fr. *à la main*). "Alemond left, go round the ring."—"Miller Boy." A dance figure here performed as follows: "each gentleman turns the lady on his left with his left hand (lady also gives left hand), . . . and immediately after gives right hand to partner and executes grand right and left. . . . " (*"Good Morning,"* p. 21.)

all around. Elliptical for "Circle all around." "All around those pretty little pinks."

all hands up. Elliptical for "All join hands and circle round." "All hands up in the Irish trot."

allow, v. (Dance term.) Swing. "Allow your partner by the left."— "The Girl I Left Behind Me."

a many. Many. "They spent their days in a many foolish ways."— "Jolly Sailor Girls."

Arkansaw. Arkansas. "An' I'm from Arkansaw."—"You're from Virginny." "I wish I was in Arkansaw."—"Old Joe Clark." "And to Arkansaw I'd go."—*ibid.*

arter, prep. (Negroism.) After. "And arter dat we form a ring."— "Old Virginny Never Tire."

arternoon, n. (Negroism.) Afternoon. "In old Kentuck, in de arternoon."—"Old Virginny Never Tire."

ask your Maw for Saturday night, phr. Ask you mother for an appointment for me Saturday night. "Consolation Flowing Free."

a-tall, adv. At all. "Didn't get to see his Lawd a-tall."—"Old Dan Tucker."

a-trinklin' down, phr. Trickling down (?). "Love come a-trinklin' down."—"Old Virginny Never Tire."

a-zig-zag, adv. (For meter.) "Just move along a-zig-zag."—"London."

backed, v. Threw back. "She backed her ears and opened her mouth." --"Old Joe Clark."

103

'backer, n. Tobacco. "Wants a chew o' 'backer but he won't get mine."
—" 'Tain't Goin' to Rain No More.'

back step, v. phr. (Dance term.) Take short steps backward to keep
moving. "Back step a little if you can't dance Josie."—"Coffee Grows on
a White Oak Tree."

balance, v. (Dance term.) Move conversely with one's partner, usually
taking three or four short steps backward and forward.

bald-faced pony, n. Marked with white on the face. "I'll ride my bald-
faced pony."—"The Girl I Left Behind Me."

bar, n. A reference to the saloon in which Western dances often took
place (Dr. J. H. Combs). Probably thrown in for rhyme. "Gents to the
center and back to the bar."

barlow knife, n. "A knife probably so named after its English maker."
—Thornton. "Asked her if she'd be my wife. Said she wouldn't for a barlow knife."—"Tideo."

bat, v. Wink. "Quick as a bat can bat an eye."—"Billy Boy."

Battle-ax, n. A brand of chewing tobacco. "But I've got the Battle-
ax."—"You're from Virginny."

beegum hat. Shaped like or as big as a beehive (from the sections of
hollow gum-trees used for that purpose). "Gather corn in a bee-gum hat."
—" 'Tain't Goin' to Rain No More."

big-foot, n. (Satiric.) A big-footed, hence, awkward, clumsy, back-
ward person. "Stand there, big-foot, don't know what to do."—"Skip to
My Lou." "Big foot guy and can't jump Josie."—"Coffee Grows on a
White Oak Tree." See club foot.

big-footed, adj. "Big-footed nigger and can't jump Josey."—"Coffee
Grows on a White Oak Tree."

billy, n. Billy goat. "Old Dan Tucker went to town, Riding a billy
and leading a hound."

bird, n. (Figurative.) Girl. "Bird hop out and the crow hop in."—
"Buffalo Girls."

biscuit, n. (Figurative.) Waist swing. "If she don't like biscuit, feed
her cornbread," i. e., if she won't let you swing her by the waist, swing her
by the hand.—"Miller Boy."

black-jack, n. (*Quercus marilandica* Muench.) Commonly known as
"scrub oak." A small, slow-growing oak, occurring on dry or poorly
drained gravely, clay, or sandy upland soils where few other forest trees
thrive. The wood is used mostly as firewood. "Coffee grows on a black-
jack stump."

boosy (boozy?), adj. Drunk. "Then we'll all get boosy."—"Going
Down to Rowser."

bound, adj. Determined. "One more river I'm bound to cross."—"Sandy Land." "Mississippi river I'm bound to cross."—"The Irish Trot."

bow-ee. Bow ye. "Bow-ee down."

branch, n. "A stream smaller than a creek; a brook" (Thornton). "And throwed him in the branch."—"Old Joe Clark."

brandnew, adj. Different. "Same old boy and a brandnew lady."—"The Girl I Left Behind Me."

break, v. (Dance term.) Loose hands. "Now you break and now you swing."—" 'Tain't Goin' to Rain No More." See drop.

break and trail, v. "All loose hands and follow trail fashion" (Dudley and Payne, p. 11). "Break and trail in the Irish trot." Compare "Breaking the trail in sandy land."

break loose, v. See break. "Break loose, started home."—"Walk Along, John."

buck-eye, adj. Buck-eyed. Pop-eyed (?). (Like the eyes of a buck, or possibly a corruption of *bug-eyed.*) "Buckeye rabbit, hoot, hoot."—"I've Been to the East."

bug, n. Silly. "Oh, my, mamma, what a bug I'll be, When two young men come courting me."—"Star Promenade."

bum, n. (Satiric.) Boy. "Three old bums come to help them out."—"Three Old Maids."

bust, v. Burst. "The 'lasses worked, the hogshead bust."—"Old Dan Tucker."

calico, n. (Figurative.) Girl, dancer. "Fall in the arms of the calico."—"Jim Along Josie."

cane, n. The Chinese sugar-cane, from which sorghum-molasses is made; cultivated widely in the South during the Civil War as a substitute for sugar (Schele De Vere, p. 287).

> Went on top of a mountain
>   To sow a patch of cane
> To raise a barrel of 'lasses
>   To sweeten Liza Jane.
>   —"Liza Jane," "Old Joe Clark."

cane-brake, n. "A thicket of cane-bushes" (Thornton). "And we'll rally round the cane-brake."—"Shoot the Buffalo." "Here comes Jumbo through the canebrakes."—"Down in Alabama." Also "cane-break" (folk-etymological).

cast off, v. (Dance term.) "Go below the next couple" (*"Good Morning,"* p. 23). Also: "Turn outwards and proceed without one or other of the lines of dancers" (Wolford, p. 20).

caught a fall, phr. Had a fall. "The limb it broke and he caught a fall."—"Old Dan Tucker."

center, n. (Dance term.) Aisle. Also: Center of the ring or middle of the set. See middle.

chaw, n. Chew. "And I know you want a chaw."—"You're from Virginny." "And I've got to have a chaw."—"Shoot the Buffalo."

cheat, v. (Dance term.) Omit to swing (make off as if to swing your partner and then "grab" any girl). "Cheat 'er, Swing."

chigger, n. (Corruption of West Indian *chigoe.*) Seed-tick. "They chased a chigger round a stump."—"Old Joe Clark."

childern, n. Children.

chunk, n. Piece of firewood. "Fell in the fire and kicked out a chunk." —"Old Dan Tucker."

cinnamon, n. Term of endearment. "Turn, cinnamon, turn." See Newell, p. 231.

circle, v. (Dance term.) Make a complete circle.

clare, clar, v. (Negroism.) Clear. "Clar(e) de kitchen."

club foot, n. (Satiric.) "Stand there, club foot, don't know what to do."—"Skip to My Lou."

come handy, phr. Be at hand. "Charley he loves to kiss the girls When they come handy."—"Weevily Wheat."

cornbread, n. (Figurative.) Swinging by the hands. Compare biscuit.

corner, n. (Dance term.) "The position on the opposite hand from partner" (Piper, p. 286 n.). The lady to the left. "Swing your corner like you're swingin' on a gate."—"Star Promenade." "Break corners off Cecila." —"Old Doc Collins. "Swing your corner with the Irish Trot." See neighbor.

corner girl, n. (Dance term.) The girl in corner position. "Promenade your corner girl."—" 'Tain't Goin' to Rain No More."

cornstalk fiddle, n. A toy made by loosening an outside fibre of a cornstalk and placing a bridge under each end, and producing dull sounds by vibrating it (Schele De Vere, p. 47). See "I'll Come Back and Be Your Beau."

couple up, v. (Dance term.) Join hands. "Couple up four and round and round."—"Brown Jug." See round up.

cunning, adv. Cunningly. "Looking cunning down at me."—"Possum Pie."

dar, adv. (Negroism.) There.

darling, n. Partner. "Skip to my lou, my darling."

darned, adv. "Darned good girl for the shape she's in."—"Buffalo Girls."

dat, pron., conj. (Negroism.) That.

106

delight with, v. phr. Take delight in. "And if you delight with a handsome little man."—"Jolly Sailor Girls."

dey, pron. (Negroism.) They.

dis, pron. (Negroism.) This.

do, n. Treat. "What makes you do him so."—"Old Doc Collins."

do c, do-ce-do, v. Do-si-do.

dog-gone, int. See "Liza Jane."

domino, int. See "Coffee Grows on a White Oak Tree."

don't, v. Doesn't. "Old Gray's tied and don't need holding."—*ibid.*

do-see, v. Do-si-do. "Do-see, ladies, round and round."—"Brown Jug."

dosey do, adv. "Two little ladies come dosey do."—"Shoo Fly."

do-si-do, do-se-do (Fr. *dos-à-dos,* back to back), n. and v. A dance figure performed as follows: "Lady and gentleman forward, pass to left of each other; that is, right shoulder to right shoulder; having gone one step past each other, take one step to the right, which brings the couple back to back. Without turning, back around each other and walk backward to place" (*"Good Morning,"* pp. 23-24).

doth, v. (Facetious.) "Till daylight doth appear."—"We Won't Go Home Till Morning." (Archaic.) "The needle's eye that doth supply."

double whirl, n. (Dance term.) A swing twice-around. "Give that girl a double whirl."—" 'Tain't Goin' to Rain No More."

drop, v. (Dance term.) Loose hands. "Drop and trail in the sandy land." See break.

drop out, v. (Dance term.) Drop out of the ring. "Go drop out two to London."—"London."

drownded, part. "He got drownded in the ocean."—"John Brown Had a Little Indian."

dumbbell, n. (Satiric.) "Stand there, dumbbell, don't know what to do."—"Skip to My Lou."

dust, adv. (Scot., *adist.*) This way, come hither. "Dusty, dusty, dust." —"Walking on the Green Grass."

even dollar down, phr. "Sold the horse for fifteen cents And even dollar down."—"Old Joe Clark."

fair lady, n. (Complimentary.) "Next fair lady in the wilderness."— "On to Galilee."

falling from the sky, phr. "Falling weather." "Oh, it's a-raining and a-hailing and a-falling from the sky."—"London."

fare-ye-well, n. Farewell. "I remember that last fare-ye-well."—"Brown Jug."

fare-you-well, int. "Fare-you-well, Dick, and fare-you-well, Tom."— "Kila Ma Cranky." "Ladies, fare you well."—"Sandy Land." "Fare you well, Old Joe Clark."

figure eight, n. (Dance term.) The eight is formed as one couple dances around the lady in the next couple and back around the gentleman.

fixin' round, phr. Getting ready. "We'd have the old folks fixin' round For you and I to marry."—"Weevily Wheat."

fix up, v. Get ready. "Fix up, boys, and we'll go with them."—"Boston."

flippy, adj. Flippant. "I won't marry a flippy flirt."—"Weevily Wheat."

for to see, phr. "The Lawd his master for to see."—"Old Dan Tucker."

gal, n. (Often facetious.) "My gal lives in Baltimore." "Oh Suzanna Gal."—"Baltimore." "Whoop law, Lizzie pore gal."—"Liza Jane." "That gal I left behind me." "Buffalo Gals."

gap, n. A hurdle or low place in a fence; an opening for a gate. "He chased the big hogs through the gap."—"Old Joe Clark."

garden patch, n. "I ran all over his garden patch."—*ibid.*

garden spot, n. Same as above. "Can't get around his garden spot."—*ibid.*

gent, n. Conventional dance term for male dancer. Compare lady.

give, pret. "Give my horn a toot."—"Liza Jane."

give him a call, phr. "So go past your partner and give him a call."—"Steal Apples."

gonna, v. Going to. "Gonna get married."—"Green Leaf."

gosh sake, int. "For gosh sake, don't give it pepper sauce."—"The Ocean is Wide."

got a livin', phr. Make a living. "Dad's got a livin' in the sandy land."—"Sandy Land."

grandly, adj. Grand. "We'll have a grandly barbecue."—"Possum Pie."

green, adj. Ignorant. "Salute your pard if you're not green."—"Captain Jinks."

gwine, v. (Negroism.) Going, going to. "Hop along, Peter, where ya gwine?"—"Oh, Ain't I Sweet." " 'Tain't gwine rain."

halfway, adv. (Dance term.) Halfway between lines. "Meet halfway to your best like-em."—"Do-Si-Do."

Hally Hally Bum, int. (Corruption of "Hallelujah"?). "Hally Hally Bum, sugar and tea."

hands around. (Dance term.) Join hands and circle round. "Hands all around in the Irish trot." "Four hands round," etc. See all hands up.

heart, v. Husk (?). "He steals old marster's roasting ears And hearts them on a rail."—"Liza Jane."

he'p, v. Help. "I love you, and you can't he'p it."—"The Ocean is Wide."

high, low, jack, and (the) game, phr. High, ace; low, deuce. See "Old Joe Clark."

him. He's. "I hope him doing well."—*ibid.*

hit, n. (Children's word.) Blow. "Yes, she gave me some pie with a hit in the eye."—"Billy Boy."

hold your oats. (Folk-etymological or facetious for "hold your holts.") "Hold your oats and turn right back."—"Miller Boy."

holler, n. and adj. Hollow.

holt, n. (Dance term.) Hand-hold. "Just hold your holts and turn right back."—*ibid.* "Hold your holts and circle again."—"Gents to the Center."

home, adv. (Dance term.) Starting or resting place. "Break loose, started home."—"Walk Along, John."

honey, n. Partner. "Swing your honey, go round and through."—"Miller Boy."

honor, n. and v. (Dance term.) Bow. "Honor to your right."—"Getting Upstairs." "When you honor your partner, turn facing her and make a light bow. . . . " (*Old Time Dance Calls,* p. 12).

hop-up, v. Move closer or faster. "Hop-up a little or you can't dance Josie."—"Coffee Grows on a White Oak Tree."

hoss, n. Horse. "Hold my hoss while I jump Josey."—*ibid.*

howda do, phr. How do you do. "Back from Texas, howda do."—"Skip to My Lou."

immigrate west, phr. Circle left. "Join your hands and immigrate west."—"Captain Jinks."

Injun, n. and adj. Indian. "John Brown had a little Injun."

is, v. Are. "Me and my true love is marching on together."—"It Rains and It Hails."

Joe, Jo, n. (Scot.) Sweetheart. "There comes my Joe."—"Liza Jane."

keep a-hookin' on, v. phr. Swing down the line (originally, with the elbow-hook). "Keep a-hookin' on in sandy land."

Kentuck. Kentucky. "I wish I was back in old Kentuck."—"Old Virginny Never Tire."

kick 'em out, phr. Put them out. "Kick 'em out of the center if they can't dance Josie."—"Coffee Grows on a White Oak Tree."

kin, v. Can. "I kin get another one just as fair."—"Skip to My Lou."

lady, young lady. Conventional dance terms for female dancer. Compare gent.

laid, v. Lay. "The little old pig laid down and snored."—"Turkey in the Straw."

'lasses, n. Sorghum molasses. "To make a barrel of 'lasses."—"Liza Jane." "Sweet as 'lasses candy-O."—"Coffee Grows on a White Oak Tree."

lead, v. Move forward, swinging. "Lead her up and down, the old brass wagon."

109

leader, n. Lead horse. "The leaders had no line."—"Old Joe Clark."

learn, v. Teach. "To learn those ladies how to dance."—"Consolation Flowing Free."

left, n. (Dance term.) The one on your left. Also: The left hand. Compare right.

left go, phr. Let go. "Many a beau have I left go."—"Needle's Eye."

li'l, adj. Little. "Li'l Liza Jane."

lively, adv. "Swing those ladies lively."—"Coffee Grows on a White Oak Tree."

Lord a massy, Laws a massy, Lawsie Massa, int. See "Old Dan Tucker."

lou, n. (Southern.) Sweetheart. "Skip to my Lou, my darling." See Perrow, *JAFL*, 26:136.

make them joy, phr. Give them joy. "Can't we make them joy By raising up our arms?"—"Yonder She Comes."

mam, n. (Southern.) Mamma. "Dad's old hat and mam's old shoe."—"Skip to My Lou."

mammy, n. See mam. "Cannot leave my Mammy-Oh!"—"Consolation Flowing Free." "Too young to leave her mammy."—"Billy Boy." "My stepdad and mammy too."—"Weevily Wheat."

marse, marster, massa, massie, mushy. Master.

mashing, v. Trampling. "Without mashing down his rye."—"Old Joe Clark." See stomp.

maw, n. Mother. "Whether your maw says 'yes' or 'no'."—"Consolation Flowing Free."

me, pron. I. "Me and my true love is marching on together."—"It Rains and It Hails."

met with, v. Met. "Since I last met with you."—"Yonder She Comes."

middle, n. Center of the ring. "Four in the middle and can't jump Josey."—"Coffee Grows on a White Oak Tree."

mighty, adv. Very much. "You are mighty in the way."—"Little Fight in Mexico."

mo', adv. More. "It ain't a-goin' to rain no mo'."

Morgan Brown. Name of horse. See "Old Joe Clark."

muley, n. (Folk-etymological for "mulley.") Dehorned, as in muley cow, or ox. "And I will work the muley."—"The Girl I Left Behind Me."

'n, conj. Than. "I'll get another one prettier 'n (better 'n) you."—"Skip to My Lou."

neighbor, n. (Dance term.) The lady to the left. See corner.

none, in double negative. "I won't have none of your weevily wheat."

Noo Yawk. (Facetious.) "There's a building in Noo Yawk."—"Old Joe Clark."

o', prep. Of. "We got lots o' leather."—"It Rains and It Hails."

ol', ole, adj. Old. "You may ride the ol' gray hoss."—"In Somebody's Garden."

old bachelor, old bum, old hobo, n. (Satiric.) "First old bachelor in the wilderness."—"On to Galilee." See soapstick.

old folks, n. "We'll never mind the old folks."—"Going Down to Rowser."

Old Grady. Name of horse. "I saddled up Old Grady."—"Getting Upstairs."

Old Gray. Name of horse. "Hold Old Gray while I dance Josey."— "Coffee Grows on a White Oak Tree."

Old Nellie. Name of horse. "I'll pull Old Nellie blind."—"Old Joe Clark."

once and a half. (Dance term.) Swing one-and-a-half times round. "Once and a half if you can't jump Josey."—"Coffee Grows on a White Oak Tree."

other 'n, pron. Other one. "And the other 'n had a cornstalk round his neck."—" 'Tain't Goin' to Rain No More."

ought of been, phr. Ought to have been. "Four in the center where they ought of been two."—"Coffee Grows on a White Oak Tree."

ourself, pron. (For rhyme with "yourself.") Ourselves. "We'll bet you five dollars we'll better ourself."—"Hog Drovers."

Pap, n. (Southern.) Papa. "Pap's old hat and Mam's old shoe."— "Skip to My Lou."

pard, pardner, n. Partner. "Salute your pard if you're not green."— "Captain Jinks." "Swing your next pardner."

paw, n. Hand. "And present to me your paw."—"Shoot the Buffalo."

peachy, adj. Peach (perhaps with implied sense of "excellence"). "Just old peachy brandy-O."—"Coffee Grows on a White Oak Tree."

Peter Brown. Name of mule. See "Old Joe Clark."

pick up, v. (Dance term.) Take into the ring. "Pick up two to London."—"London." See couple up.

pink, n. (Figurative.) Term of affection or compliment. "My pretty little pink." "All around those pretty little pinks."

plenty good, plenty of good, phr. Good enough. "You're old enough and plenty of good."—"Consolation Flowing Free."

plug-ugly, n. (Satiric.) "Old brother plug-ugly, how merry were we." —"Sister Phoebe."

pore, adj. (Often facetious.) Poor. "Whoop law, Lizzie pore gal."— "Liza Jane."

promenade, n. and v. A dance figure performed as follows: Couples walk or skip to the right in a circle or round the room, one behind the other, with joined hands crossed in front or with the lady holding the man's arm.

pull blind, phr. Pull so tight that the eyes pop and the whites show. "I'll pull Old Nellie blind."—"Old Joe Clark."

pulled his freight, phr. Departed. "Rabbit skipped de garden gate, Picked a pea and pulled his freight."—" 'Tain't Goin' to Rain No More."

punkin, n. Pumpkin. "Little piece of puddin' An' a punkin pie."—"Jim Lane."

raggin', v. (From *rag,* a fast dance.) "Hold your holts, come a-raggin' right back."—"Miller Boy."

raising up, v. Raise. "Can't we make them joy, By raising up our arms."—"Yonder She Comes."

rared, v. Reared or raised; jumped(?). "Rared around old Joe Clark."

right, n. (Dance term.) The one on your right. Also: The right hand. Compare left.

right and left, or *grand right and left,* n. and v. "Right and left to Rowser's." A dance figure performed as follows: Boys and girls go in opposite directions, each boy swinging his partner by and with the right hand, then the next girl with her left hand in his left, and so on until he gets back to his partner. (The simple right and left is a different figure involving two couples. See *"Good Morning,"* p. 27.)

rise up, v. Rise. "Now sister rise up and choose you a man."—"Sister Phoebe." "Rise you up, my dearest dear."—"Shoot the Buffalo." "Rise you up, Bobby, and choose you a wife."—"Hog Drovers."

roasting ears, n. Green corn, so called from the method of preparing it for the table by roasting before a fire or in hot ashes. "He steals old marster's roasting ears."—"Liza Jane."

rock, v. A dance step. "Rock, rock, old Joe Clark." See White, p. 336.

round up, v. (Dance term.) Join hands. "Round up four in London." See couple up.

run, pret. Ran. "And run my nose in the butter."—"Old Joe Clark."

same old, phr. Same. "Same old boy and a brandnew lady."—"The Girl I Left Behind Me."

setting, v. sitting. "Setting on a rail."—"Old Joe Clark."

"Shucks for your daughter and fodder for yourself," phr. (Satiric.) Corn husks for your daughter to lie on and dried corn blades for you to eat. See "Hog Drovers."

shush, v. Hush. "Shush your talking."—"Walk Along, John."

silly, n. (Satiric.) Dude. "Silly came down the lane."—"Liza Jane."

'simmon, n. Persimmon. "Possum up the 'simmon tree."—"Possum Pie."

sister, n. (Dance term.) Girl. "Two little sisters form a ring."—" 'Tain't Goin' to Rain No More."

six-gun, n. A six-shooter, or revolver with six chambers. "With a six-gun in my hand."—"Granger."

skeeter, n. Mosquito. "Skeeter on a gate post, skip to my Lou."

skip, v. Jump. "Rabbit skipped the garden gate."—" 'Tain't Goin' to Rain No More."

smack, v. Kiss. "The boy in the middle says, Smack, boys, smack."—"Miller Boy."

soapstick, n. (Satiric.) "Next old soapstick in the wilderness."—"On to Galilee." "We're marching round the soapstick."—"Lead through That Sugar and Tea." See old bachelor.

sojer, n. (Negroism.) Soldier. "A bull frog dressed in sojer's clo'es."—"Old Virginny Never Tire."

some, adv. "And old Dan Tucker flew some too."

sparking, v. Courting. "And sparking Betty Brown."—"Old Joe Clark."

squirlie, n. Squirrel. "The squirlie yam a pretty bird."—"Liza Jane."

stepdad, n. Stepfather. "My stepdad and mammy too."—"Weevily Wheat."

sting, v. Omit to swing. "Swing the one, sting the other."—"Bird in the Cage." See cheat.

stomp, v. Stamp; trample. "Stomp that foot and everybody swing."—"Miller Boy." "And stomped down all his rye."—"Old Joe Clark." See mashing.

stumped, v. Stubbed. "And the monkey stumped his toe."—"Shoot the Buffalo." "Stumped my toe on the table leg."—"Old Joe Clark."

sugar lump, n. Sweetheart. "Somebody's rocking my sugar lump."—"Turn, Cinnamon, Turn."

Susie Brown. Name of horse. See "Old Joe Clark." ·

sweeten up, v. Sweeten (mollify). "To sweeten up Liza Jane."

swing, n. and v. "Partners take ball-room position (i.e., boy's right hand at his partner's waist, his left hand holding his partner's right hand, and the girl's left hand on his right arm) and turn on spot, usually taking eight steps" (Wolford, p. 19).

'tain't, v. " 'Tain't Goin' to Rain No More."

take in the town, phr. See the town on a spree. "Swore he'd take in the town."—"Old Joe Clark."

113

tater, n. Potato. "Hogs in the tater patch, two by two."—"Skip to My Lou." "Raisin' sweet taters in sandy land." "Grasshopper settin' on a sweet tater vine."—"'Tain't Goin' to Rain No More."

taw, n. (Dance term.) Partner. (From marble usage.)

tearing out, v. Galloping. "The old gray horse Came tearing out of the wilderness."

teeter up and down, v. phr. (Figurative for back-and-forth movements in the dance.) Seesaw. "Teeter up and down in your little brass wagon." —"Coffee Grows on a White Oak Tree."

tell it's her. Elliptical for "I can tell it's her." "Tell it's her by the rattle of the bushes."—"Down in Alabama."

them, adj. Those. "Swing them ladies, tu du la."—"Poor Old Joe."

they. There. "Four in the center, where they ought of been two."— "Coffee Grows on a White Oak Tree."

thou, pron. (Facetious.) "When I can get such boys as thou For sixteen cents a dozen."—"Weevily Wheat."

throwed, pret. Threw. "And throwed him in a branch." "Throwed up a wagon bed."—"Old Joe Clark."

tight, adj. Drunk. "Captain Jinks got tight last night."

tole, v. Told. "Jim along Josie tole me so."

track, n. (Dance term.) Lane or aisle between two lines of dancers. "In the same old track turn right back."—"The Girl I Left Behind Me." "Turn right round and don't lose track."—"Miller Boy."

trail, v. Follow trail fashion. "Break loose, trail home."—"'Tain't Goin' to Rain No More." "Drop and trail in the sandy land."

trip, v. Swing. "Trip her up and down as long as you love her."— "Do-Se-Do."

trot, n. Dance. "The Irish Trot."

turtle dove, n. (Complimentary.) Lady partner. "And now your turtle dove."—"Mollie Brooks."

twistification, n. (Southern Mountains.) A country dance. See Kephart, p. 263.

unto, prep. (For meter.) "And balance unto your partner."—"Buffalo Girls."

uster do, v. phr. Used to do; have done before. "Down the center as you uster do."

Virginny. Virginia. "You're from Virginny."

was'd, v. Were. "I wish't I was'd a granger."

weep and sigh. Elliptical for "I'll weep and sigh." "Weep and sigh till the day I die For the girl I left behind me."

weevily, adj. Full of weevils. "Weevily Wheat."

whoop law, int. (Southwestern.) "Whoop law, Lizzie pore gal."—
"Liza Jane."

wid, prep. (Negroism.) With.

wish't, v. Wish. "I wish't I was'd a granger."

wrong, adv. (Dance term.) Left. "Lady in the lead, All going
wrong."—"Walk Along, John."

wrop candy, phr. Rock candy. A dance step. See White, p. 162 n.

yaller, adj. Yellow. "Oh, Marse got him a yaller gal."—"Oh, Ain't I
Sweet."

yam, v. (Negroism.) Am. "The squirlie yam a pretty bird."—"Liza
Jane."

yes-sir-ee, int. "Yes-sir-ee, if you say so."—"All Around Those Pretty
Little Pinks."

yi, yi, yi, int. (Southwestern.) "Fly, Tucker, fly, yi, yi, yi."

zip, int. "Zip, I hit him in the eye."—"Possum Pie."

6. Literary Form and Content

Turning from variations to the themes on which variations are played
(some of which have already been considered in the first section of this
chapter), we find that the factor of change is in constant conflict with
that of standardization and that, as the former characterized the language,
so the latter distinguishes the poetic style of play-party songs. This con-
ventionalization is to be explained on the same basis as the dependence
of the play-party on folk-songs and popular songs for sources—as another
aspect, namely, of the strong tendency toward imitation that it shares in
common with other types of folk literature. In other words, just as play-
party songs themselves are improvised on the model of other songs, so
stanzas of play-party songs are improvised on the model of other stanzas.
In both these respects the play-party affords an excellent illustration of the
working of a principle that may be laid down as one of the axioms of
folk-songs: "Adaptation of something familiar is the first instinct in
popular improvisation." [208]

If we inquire into the causes and effects of the use of formulae, we
find that a double motivation and purpose exist. In the first place, the
use of type stanzas arises from the conservatism of oral tradition, the "need
of general currency" on which play-party songs depend for acceptance.
This conservatism depends partly on the psychology of memory and association, whereby only the familiar strikes an immediate response and is
capable of being remembered longest, and partly on the powerful levelling
and codifying force of custom and tradition, which are simply memory and

---

[208] Pound, *Poetic Origins and the Ballad,* p. 227 n.

association operating collectively. In the second place, the use of formulae arises out of and satisfies the aesthetic need of conventions that follow the line of least resistance or the principle of economy, which, in combination with the principle of unity-in-variety, produces form, structure, pattern, design.

In unwritten literature, on account of the absence of print and the greater degree of variation, the need of a regulator is all the greater. This is especially true of a spontaneous, extemporaneous, and ephemeral form like the play-party song, where improvisation calls repeatedly for stopgaps and stock devices. At the same time, this pouring of new wine into old bottles depends for its success as much on the constant shock of novelty in the wine as on the secure familiarity of the bottle.

Here enters the inevitable factor of variation from the norm. The combination of recognition and discovery is best accomplished by a simple bipartite structure like that of the "I wouldn't marry" stanzas in "Old Joe Clark." They begin with the announcement of an objection that strikes a familiar chord and arouses anticipation and suspense—

> (1) (Joe) Wouldn't marry. . . .
> I'll tell you the reason why

and they end with the humorous surprise of a reason that in the last line has something of the climax of an answer to a conundrum or the conclusion of a limerick. Thus for the old maid, the preacher's daughter, or the preacher gal:

> Her neck 'd be (neck 's) so long and stringy
> I'm afraid she'd (she'll) never die.[209]

For the old maid again:

> Her nose was always dripping
> And her chin was never dry.[210]

> Hung my foot in the corner of the fence
> An' tore down all her rye.[211]

[209] William Plaster, Meeker, Lincoln County; Paul Howard, Headrick, Jackson County. Compare Ames, p. 300; Cox, p. 495; Douthitt, p. 38; Dudley and Payne, p. 33; Parker, p. 247; Perrow, *JAFL*, 28:176; Talley, p. 63.

[210] L. E. Russell, Cyril, Caddo County. Compare Parker, p. 247; Perrow, p. 136. For other similar stanzas stating the color preferences of the Negro see Bales, *PTFS*, 7:104; Odum and Johnson, *The Negro and His Songs*, pp. 191-192; Talley, pp. 56, 63. Perrow (pp. 136-137, 175-177) gives similar stanzas for the yaller gal, the black gal, the widow, the pore gal, the preacher, the school-teacher, the country girl, and the city girl.

[211] Douthitt, p. 38. Compare Cox, p. 495.

For the widow:

> She'd have (She had) so many children
> They'd make (She made) those biscuits fly.[212]

For the yellow gal:

> She'd eat a barrel of sour krout
> And drink the river dry.[213]

For the young gal:

> Her kin folks come to see her,
> And call for chicken pie.[214]

For the school teacher:

> She blows her nose in yellow corn bread
> And calls it punkin pie.[215]

Another formula in the same song, combining humor with sentiment and fancy, is even simpler, consisting as it does of two words, "I wish" (sometimes replaced by "If"):

> I wish I had a needle and thread
>   As fine as I could sew.
> I'd sew the girls to my coat-tail
>   And down the road I'd go.[216]

> If I had a needle and thread,
>   I tell you what I'd do.
> I'd sew my true love to my side
>   And down the river I'd go.[217]

> (I) Wish I was a big red (an) apple,
>   Hanging on a tree,
> And every girl that came along
> (Some pretty little girl come along)
>   Would (And) take a bite of me.[218]

---

[212] William Plaster, Meeker, Lincoln County; L. E. Russell, Cyril, Caddo County. Compare Bales, p. 104; Perrow, p. 176.

[213] William Plaster, Meeker, Lincoln County.

[214] Dudley and Payne, p. 33.

[215] Mrs. Christine Clark, Norman, Cleveland County, who played it near Vinita, in Craig and Mayes Counties. Compare Perrow, p. 176.

[216] Mrs. Della I. Young, Cheyenne, Roger Mills County, from J. R. Weatherly, Elk City, Beckham County.

[217] Jane Bowman, Pauls Valley, Garvin County. Compare Ames, p. 300; Edmands, p. 131; Hamilton, pp. 302-303; Randolph, p. 223; Scarborough, pp. 124-125.

[218] William Plaster, Meeker, Lincoln County; Audra A. Plumlee, Norman, Cleveland County. Compare Talley, p. 133, and Scarborough, p. 127, for similar sentiments but different lines.

(I) Wish I had a lariat rope
    (As) Long as I could throw.
(I'd) Throw it around my sweetheart's neck (a pretty girl)
    And round and round we'd go.
    (And to Arkansas I'd go.) [219]

I wish I had a candy box
    To put my sweetheart in,
Take her out and kiss her twice
    And put her back again.[220]

I wish I had a sweetheart
    Sitting on a shelf.
I'd take her down and kiss her
    And get up there myself.[221]

If I had a sweetheart,
    I'd set her on a shelf,
And every time she'd grin at me
    I'd get up there myself.[222]

Well I wish I had a nickel,
    I wish I had a dime.
I wish I had a pretty gal
    To kiss and call her mine.[223]

I wish I had a pig in a pen,
    Corn to feed it on,
Pretty little girl to stay at home
    To feed it while I am gone.[224]

(I) Wish I was in Arkansaw,
    Setting on a rail,
Sweet potato in my hand
    (And a) Possum by the tail.[225]

---

[219] William Plaster, Meeker, Lincoln County; Helen Jacobs, Tulsa, Tulsa County.

[220] Mrs. Christine Clark, Norman, Cleveland County, who played it near Vinita, in Craig and Mayes Counties.

[221] Harold Roberts, Blackwell, Kay County.

[222] Gene Michael, Marietta, Love County.

[223] Paul Howard, Headrick, Jackson County.

[224] Gene Michael, Marietta, Love County. A similar stanza is reported by Dr. J. H. Combs, of Fort Worth, Texas, from Knott County, Kentucky.

[225] Ruby Pfautsch, Norman, Cleveland County; Lucy I. Pitts, Oklahoma City, Oklahoma County.

In "Old Dan Tucker":

> Old Dan Tucker went to town
> Riding a goat and leading a hound.
> The hound yelled, the goat jumped,
> Threw old Dan Tucker astraddle a stump.[226]

Or:

> The hound got loose in the middle of the street,
> And he couldn't catch him for his number ten feet.[227]

> Old Dan Tucker went to town,
> He swallowed a hogshead of 'lasses down.
> The 'lasses worked, the hogshead bust,
> And it throwed Old Dan in a thunder gust.[228]

> Old Dan Tucker went to town,
>   Riding a little pony.
> He stuck a feather in his cap
>   And called it macaroni.[229]

> Old Dan Tucker went to town,
>   He wore his daddy's trousers.
> He said he couldn't see the town
>   For so many houses.[230]

An example of a song made up entirely of a formula is "Granger," which begins

> I want to be a something
>   And with the somethings stand,
> With something on my shoulder
>   And something in my hand.[231]

and runs the gamut of the cowboy, the preacher, the farmer, the hobo, the soldier, the sailor, the rich man, the fireman, with their respective paraphernalia.

At times the formula, couching a bit of homely philosophy, has a touch of the proverbial. From the English saw—

> The higher the plum-tree the riper the plum,
> The richer the cobbler the blacker his thumb.[232]

---

[226] Louis E. Baily, Oklahoma City, Oklahoma County.
[227] Harold Roberts, Blackwell, Kay County.
[228] Ruby Burns, Noble, Cleveland County, from her mother.
[229] The same.
[230] The same.
[231] Creed Bogan, Duncan, Stephens County, who played it near Lawton, Commanche County.
[232] Northall, p. 522.

comes

> The higher up the cherry tree,
>> The riper grows the cherry.
> The more you hug and kiss the girls,
>> The sooner you'll get married.[233]

or:

> The higher up the cherry tree,
>> The sweeter are the cherries.
> Every pretty girl I meet
>> I always want to marry.[234]

> Never saw a pretty girl
> But what she wanted to marry.[235]

And from another English maxim—

> Bread when you're hungry, drink when you're dry,
> Rest when you're weary, and heaven when you die.[236]

comes

> Oh, it's beefsteak when I'm hungry
> And whiskey when I'm dry.
> And a pretty little girl to cheer me up
> In heaven when I die.[237]

In the next the proverbial expression takes the form of neat antithesis:

> You may ride the old gray horse,
>> And I may ride the roan.
> If you get there before I do,
>> Leave my honey alone.[238]

or:

> And I'll talk to your sweetheart,
> But you leave mine alone.[239]

> You may court (love) your own sweetheart,
> But you'd better leave (let) mine alone.[240]

---

[233] "Old Joe Clark," Mrs. Della I. Young, Cheyenne, Roger Mills County, from J. R. Weatherly. "The sooner they will marry"—Beatrice Jennings McMullin, Norman, Cleveland County, brought from Kentucky to Missouri, then to Kay and Grant Counties on the Oklahoma-Kansas border.

[234] The same.

[235] "Oh, Ain't I Sweet," Florette McNeese, Oklahoma City, Oklahoma County.

[236] Northall, pp. 501, 526.

[237] "London," Elsie Montgomery, Sunset, Beaver County, from Glendale and Overstreet districts in the Panhandle of Texas. See headnote to "London."

[238] Mrs. Della I. Young, Cheyenne, Roger Mills County, from J. R. Weatherly, Elk City, Beckham County. These excerpts are all from "Old Joe Clark," unless otherwise stated.

[239] Mrs. Christine Clark, Norman, Cleveland County, who played it near Vinita in Craig and Mayes Counties.

[240] Florette McNeese, Oklahoma City, Oklahoma County; "In Somebody's Garden," Clifford Chandler, Crescent, Logan County.

I will ride the old gray horse,
    And you will ride the roan.
I'll go see your sweetheart
    And you'd better leave mine alone.[241]

You may work the horned cow,
    And I will work the muley.
But give me back my fifteen cents,
    And I'll go home to July.[242]

You go down the newcut road,
    And I'll go down the lane.
You can hug the old gatepost
    While I'll hug Liza Jane.[243]

Here appears the device of introducing a direction or comment with a line or two of nonsense or *galimatias,* which often gives an opportunity for figurative or allusive expressions with a proverbial ring. Somehow the "apple" is a great favorite in these lines:

Apples fried and apples dried,
Kiss her on the other side,[244]

Apple cider, cinnamon beer,
Christmas comes but once a year.[245]

Peaches in the summertime,
    Apples in the fall.
If I can't get the girl I want,
    I won't have none at all.[246]

Sometimes the introductory line is not pure *galimatias* but involves a comparison that heightens the emotional effect. Thus, in "The Ocean is Wide":

The ocean is wide, and I can't step it.
I love you, and you can't he'p it.

Sure as the vine grows round the rafter,
You're the girl that I'm after.

---

241 William Plaster, Meeker, Lincoln County.
242 "The Girl I Left Behind Me," Walter Myers Gable, Norman, Cleveland County.
243 Florette McNeese, Oklahoma City, Oklahoma County.
244 "Consolation Flowing Free," Audra A. Plumlee, Norman, Cleveland County.
245 "Jim Along Josie," Mrs. L. T. Monnett, Norman, Cleveland County, who played it in Missouri.
246 "Old Joe Clark," Florette McNeese, Oklahoma City, Oklahoma County.

> Sure as the moss grows round the stump,
> You re my darling sugar lump.[247]

Or since the play-party is fond of satirizing love, an humorous allusion may take the edge off the sentiment.

> When you find a mule tied to a tree,
> Pull his tail and think of me.[248]

Or, conversely, a touch of the serious or mock-serious may invade the ludicrous:

> Oh, boys, you'd better be drowned
> Than fall in love with me.[249]

Looking more closely at the imagery of the play-party song, we find that its paradise on earth is a fool's paradise, where

> Coffee grows on a high oak tree,
> And the river flows with brandy free.
> The streets are lined with dollar bills
> And the girls are sweet as sugar pills.[250]

And the Promised Land (for the western emigrant) is a Happy Hunting Ground with plenty of land and strangely incongruous animals.

> Rise ye up, my dearest dear,
>   And present to me your hand,
> For I long to take a journey
>   To a far and distant land
> (And I'll put you in possession
>   Of ten thousand acres of land)
> Where the hunter killed the crow
> And the baboon stubbed his toe,
>   And we'll rally round the canebrake
> And shoot the buffalo.[251]

But the other occupations sound real enough.

> The boys can reap and mow,
> And the girls can knit and sew.

---

[247] Mrs. Christine Clark, Norman, Cleveland County, who played it near Vinita in Craig and Mayes Counties.

[248] The same.

[249] "Going Down to Rowser," Beatrice Jennings McMullin, Norman, Cleveland County, brought from Kentucky to Missouri, then to Kay and Grant Counties on the Oklahoma-Kansas border.

[250] Doris G. Waters, Ponca City, Kay County. Compare "The Big Rock Candy Mountain," *The Hobo's Hornbook*, edited by George Milburn.

[251] Glenn A. Roe, Oklahoma City, Oklahoma County, who played it at Frederick, Tillman County.

> The girls can card and spin,
> And the boys can sit and grin.[252]

There is an escape from the present situation into the play-party's Land of the Phoenix—

> Rain, hail, sleet, snow,
>   It ain't gonna rain no more.
> It rained last night and the night before,
>   It ain't gonna rain no more.[253]

Again, the reality may be harsh—

> Raisin' sweet 'taters in a sandy land,
>   Sandy land, sandy land,
> Raisin' sweet 'taters in a sandy land,
>   The way to make a living in a sandy land.[254]

But there is the consolation of

> Lot o' pretty girls in Sandy Land.[255]

Tall tale, animal fable, and extravagant nonsense abound. Gluttony is elaborated *ad nauseam* (literally) in the following composite stanza constructed from 12 Oklahoma variants:

> I went down to old Joe's house (Old Joe Clark's)
> (I went to see Old Joe Clark.)
> (Went down to see my girl.)
>   (And) He was (lying) sick in bed.
>   (I) Found him (her) sick in bed (abed).
> (I) Rammed (put) (ran) (run) (stuck) (poked) my finger (fist)
>   (right) down his (her) throat
>   And pulled out a chicken ('s) (turkey) (rabbit's) (pole-cat's) head
>   (wagon bed).
>   (He throwed up a wagon bed.)

Chicken or pumpkin pie is a spur to the imagination:

> Old Joe Clark had (built) a house (lives in a fine brick house),
> (There's a building in Noo Yawk)
>   (It was) (That's) Fifteen (Sixteen) (Twenty) (Forty) (Fifty) (Sixty)
>   stories high.
> (And) Every story (room) in (of) that house
>   Was (Is) filled (lined) (full) with (of) chicken (pumpkin) (apple) pie.
>   (Just smelled like chicken pie.)

252 Carl West, Perico, Texas, from Dallam County.
253 William Plaster, Meeker, Lincoln County.
254 Viola Harris, Porter, Wagoner County.
255 Mary Haxel, Purcell, McClain County, who played it near Noble, Cleveland County, and Washington, McClain County.

There is (was) a house in Garber (Garbar) town,
  Sixteen (Fourteen) stories high.
And every story in that house
  Is (Was) filled with pumpkin pie.

Many of the animal stanzas are borrowed from Negro song.

As I went down the newcut road,
There I spied a tarrepin and a toad.
Ever time the toad would sing
The tarrepin would cut the pigeon wing.[256]

A bull frog dressed in sojer's clo'es
Went in de field to shoot some crows;
De crows smell powder and fly away,
De bull frog mighty mad dat day.[257]

The raccoon's tail yam ringed all around,
  The possum's tail yam bare,
The rabbit has no tail at all,
  But a little bunch of hair.

The squirlie yam a pretty bird
  With a long and bushy tail,
He steal old marster's roasting ears,
  And hearts them on a rail.[258]

Old Joe Clark (he) had a horse,
  (His) Name was Morgan Brown,
And every tooth the old horse had
  Was fifteen inches round.[259]

Or:

And everywhere he went
He covered an acre of ground.[260]

Massa had a yaller cow,
  She had a holler horn.
And every tooth in her head
  Would hold a barrel (bushel) of corn.[261]

---

[256] "Liza Jane," Catherine Harris, Antlers, Pushmataha County, from S. B. Hackett, Norman, who played it in Arkansas.
[257] "Old Virginny Never Tire," Atlee M. Garrett, Loco, Stephens County.
[258] "Liza Jane," Catherine Harris, Antlers, Pushmataha County, from S. B. Hackett, Norman, who played it in Arkansas.
[259] Florette McNeese, Oklahoma City, Oklahoma County.
[260] Paul Howard, Headrick, Jackson County.
[261] "Oh, Ain't I Sweet," Florette McNeese, Oklahoma City, Oklahoma County.

Mushy had an old coon dog,
  Three-quarters hound.
Every tooth in that dog's head
  Was a mile and a quarter around.[262]

Although extravagance rather than delicacy is the keynote of the play-party, lonesome, lovesick "blue" stanzas are wistful and even tender.

Now I ain't got much money,
  Ain't got no place to stay,
Ain't got no place to lay my head
  Till roosters crow for day.[263]

Going down the lane,
  It was dark and hazy.
Every time I thought of my girl
  It nearly drove me crazy.[264]

Comin' down the mountain side,
  Comin' through the cane,
Every stalk that I broke down,
  I thought o' Liza Jane.[265]

Left her setting in a rocking-chair,
  I thought those tears would blind me.
I'll never forget the girl I left,
  The one I left behind me.[266]

Personal description is uncommon and, when it occurs, may be conventionally pretty—

She's pretty in the face and little round the waist,[267]

Dressed in blue with a buckle on her shoe [268]

Sky-blue eyes and sunny hair,
Rosy cheeks and a dimpled chin.[269]

---

[262] Lillie O. Heaton, Watonga, Blaine County.
[263] Jane Bowman, Pauls Valley, Garvin County.
[264] Sherman E. Hively, Coyle, Logan County.
[265] "Liza Jane," Professor Kenneth Kaufman, Norman, Cleveland County, who played it in Eastern Custer County.
[266] "The Girl I Left Behind Me," Gene Michael, Marietta, Love County.
[267] *Ibid.*, Professor Kenneth Kaufman, Norman, Cleveland County, who played it in Eastern Custer County.
[268] *Ibid.*, Faneta Fitchett, Billings, Noble County.
[269] "Getting Married," Leonard C. Dresser, Lahoma, Garfield County, who played it near Vernon, Garfield County.

but more often is extravagantly burlesque—

    Massa had a yaller gal,
        And she was from the South;
    She did her hair up so tight,
        She could not shut her mouth.[270]

    Her head is like a coffee pot,
        Her nose is like a spout.
    Mouth is like a fireplace
        With ashes taken out.[271]

    He took her to the blacksmith shop,
        To have her mouth made small.
    She backed her ears and opened her mouth
        And swallowed shop and all.[272]

    Went down to Dinah's house,
        Saw her standin' in the door,
    Shoes and stockin's in her hand
        And her feet all over the floor.[273]

    Old Joe Clark he had a wife
        And she was seven feet tall.
    She slept with her head in the kitchen,
        And her feet out in the hall.[274]

(a true tall tale!) or celebrating ugliness—

    Your mouth is like a cellar,
        Your foot is like a ham,
    Your eyes are like the owl's at night,
        Your voice is never calm.
    Your hair is long and curly.
        You just look like a crane.
    I looked her in the face and said,
        "Good-by, my Susan Jane." [275]

    I got a girl, freckles on her chin,
        Wart on her nose and her eyes turned in.
    Darn good girl for the shape she's in. . . . [276]

---

[270] "Oh, Ain't I Sweet," Florette McNeese, Oklahoma City, Oklahoma County.
[271] *Ibid.*, Helen Jacobs, Tulsa, Tulsa County.
[272] Lucy I. Pitts, Oklahoma City, Oklahoma County, played in Indian Territory.
[273] Paul Howard, Headrick, Jackson County.
[274] Cora Frances Starritt, Ada, Pontotoc County.
[275] "Susan Jane," Beatrice Jennings McMullin, Norman, Cleveland County, brought from Kentucky to Missouri, then to Kay and Grant Counties on the Oklahoma-Kansas border.
[276] "Buffalo Girls," Lois F. Bɔckham, Norman, Cleveland County, from Memphis, Tennessee.

References to rural customs and backgrounds are common but less so than they are in dance calls on account of the greater element of improvisation in the latter. "Join your hands and immigrate west" [277] and "We'll all go to Texas, two by two" [278] allude to the regular yearly movement of tenants in covered wagons, especially when they make a failure, to work on the harvest in Texas and come back in the summer drouth, then to go west again in the fall for cotton. Dry farming has inspired one play-party song.

> Sift your meal and save your bran,
> Dad's got a livin' in the Sandy Land.[279]

References to chewing tobacco and snuff are characteristic.

> Rise up to me, my dearest dear,
>   And present to me your paw,
> For I know you chew tobacco
>   And I know you want a chaw.[280]

> Chew it up and spit it out,
>   Best you ever saw,
> You an' me an' mother-in-law,
>   We all want a chaw.[281]

> I wouldn't give her up for a box of snuff.[282]

The circumstances—ardors, endurances, and humors—of the party and the players come in for their share of teasing mention:

> Those who go slow are not worth having.[283]

> Meet your honey with a pretty bouquet. . . .
> Flap your wings and fly away.

> Hands in your pockets and your head against the wall. . . .
> Take a chew of tobacco and promenade all.

---

277 "Captain Jinks," Harold Roberts, Blackwell, Kay County.
278 "Skip to My Lou." Compare the dance call, "All in your places, Hook up your traces, And come out West" (Frank A. Hanna, Drumright, Creek County). Compare Hudson, pp. xvii, 130.
279 Mrs. Anne McClure, Oklahoma City, Oklahoma County, who played it in Benton County, Arkansas.
280 Wallace N. McCown, Emporia, Kansas, from Earl Denton, Norman, Cleveland County.
281 Joseph Edward Terral, Oklahoma City, Oklahoma County.
282 "Turn, Cinnamon, Turn," Audra A. Plumlee, Norman, Cleveland County.
283 "Betsy Larkin," Florette McNeese, Oklahoma City, Oklahoma County.

Aces, diamonds, deuces, spades. . . .
It ain't raining now like it was a while ago.[284]

Shake the door and rock the floor.[285]

O law, mother, my toes are sore . . .
Dancing on your sandy floor.[286]

Trip her up and down as long as you love her.[287]

All night long in Ju Tang a Ju Tang Ju.[288]

Dance all night till broad daylight.
    Go home with the girls in the morning.[289]

The fiddler's drunk and he can't play,
    Hurrah for Wilson's Barroom.[290]

The way we play it is no sin.[291]

We're all church members, Celia.[292]

Take a (this) lady (her) by the (lily-white) hand,
    (And) Lead her like a pigeon.
Make her dance the Weevily Wheat.
    (Till) She loses her religion.
    (And scatter her religion.) [293]

As to the form of these stanzas, repetition is their chief structural element. It often takes the place of rhyme in both couplet and quatrain forms.

Round up four in Jutang, Jutang Ju.
Round up four in Jutang, Jutang Ju.

Go circle six to London,
    And so I heard them say.
Go circle six to London,
    And so I heard them say.

[284] William Plaster, Meeker, Lincoln County.
[285] "The Girl I Left Behind Me," Sam West, Duke, Jackson County.
[286] "Weevily Wheat," Miles, *Harper's Magazine,* 109:121; Van Doren, p. 496.
[287] "Do-Se-Do," Verla Summers, Snyder, Kiowa County, who played it near McLoud, Pottawatomie County.
[288] Melvin Culbertson, Amber, Grady County.
[289] "Buffalo Girls," Lela L. Conrad, Perry, Noble County.
[290] Mrs. T. H. Maness, Oswalt, Love County.
[291] "Boston," Glenn A. Roe, Oklahoma City, Oklahoma County, who played it at Frederick, Tillman County.
[292] "Old Doc Collins," Ezra Van Horn, Norman, Cleveland County.
[293] Dudley and Payne, pp. 17, 18; Wolford, p. 13. Compare Combs, *Folk-Songs du Midi des États-Unis,* p. 115.

Two stanza forms based on repetition are derived from the traditional game. One of these is the "London Bridge" type, in which the last half of the first line is sung twice in the second line and the third line is the same as the first, followed by a refrain.

> Buffalo girls, are you coming out to-night,
> Coming out to-night, coming out to-night,
> (Say) Buffalo girls, are you coming out to-night
> To dance by the light of the moon.

The other is the "Marching round the Levy" type, which the play-party seems to have made especially its own, since it is the most common form employed, whereas its use in the traditional game is limited to a very few instances.[294] This consists in singing a line three times (less frequently two) with (rarely without) a refrain.

> I sent my brown jug down town,
> I sent my brown jug down town,
> I sent my brown jug down town,
> So early in the morning.
>
> Gone again, what shall I do?
> Gone again, what shall I do?
> Skip-to-my-lou, my darling.
>
> Jack killed a rabbit, shoo-la-lay,
> Jack killed a rabbit, shoo-la-lay,
> Jack killed a rabbit, shoo-la-lay.

True couplets and quatrains are also found.

> I've got a girl in Baltimore,
> Street cars run right by her door.

Practically all forms of the quatrain are employed, except that with alternate rhymes, which apparently takes more rhyme than the play-party can muster. The simplest kind is the *aabb* type:

> Now you're married you must obey,
> You must be true to all you say.
> You must be kind, you must be good,
> And keep your wife in kindling wood.

Less common is the type rhyming *aaab*:

> Captain Jenks is here to-night,
> Clap your hands with pure delight,
> And salute your partner on the right,
> For that's the style of the army.

---

[294] It occurs in the following games in Gomme: "Click, Clock, Cluck," I, p. 70; "Green Grow the Leaves" (I), I, pp. 183-185; "Would You Know How Doth the Peasant," II, pp. 399-401.

Most common is the *abcb* scheme:

> Old Joe Clark is dead and gone,
>> Hope he is doing well.
>
> Made me wear the ball and chain
>> Till my old ankle swelled.

A six-line stanza often occurs:

> Hey, come a get along,
>> Get along Josie.
>
> Hey, come a get along,
>> Get along Jo.
>
> All you girls that want a beau,
> Fall in the arms of the calico.

And an eight-line stanza, as in the opening of "Shoot the Buffalo," previously cited.

Rhyme is often imperfect or displaced by assonance, although such extra graces as internal rhyme and feminine rhyme may be added. The most common irregularity in rhyme is caused by the addition of a suffix, as in the preterite (compare the "Old Joe Clark" stanza cited above) or the plural ending—

> When coffee grows on white oak trees,
>> And rivers flow with brandy,
>
> You swing around sugar and tea,
>> I'll swing around this candy.

or other extra consonants. From these causes proceed such combinations as washed-squash, jumped-stump, town-around, cross-lost, and the like.

Wrenched accent occurs frequently, in ballad fashion:

> Going down the river,
>> Going down below,
>
> Going down the river,
>> Going down to old Shiloh.

> They can get married
>> If they will agree,
>
> So march them down together
>> In sweet harmony.

Refrains are of several types. The refrain of meaningless syllables is not so common as one might expect, there being but a scant handful of examples: Fal-da-ral-de-ray; [295] Sing fa da ra, sing fa da ra; [296] Shoo-la-lay; [297] Tideo; Jutang; To-ri-rooly.[298]

---

295 "Brown Jug."
296 "Little Fight in Mexico."
297 "Jack Killed a Rabbit."
298 "Round the Mountain, To-Ri-Rooly," Dudley and Payne, p. 22.

130

Refrains employing the names of persons and places are more common: Oh, Suzanna gal; [299] Hello, Susie Brown; [300] My lovely Susie Brown; [301] Good-by, Liza Jane; [302] And good-by, Lucy Long; [303] Down in Alabama (Way down in Alabama); [304] Old Virginia style; [305] On to Galilee; Way down in Pawpaw land; Down in the valley; [306] Down in Jay Bird Town. [307]

Other refrains are borrowed from other songs: (With those) Golden Slippers on; [308] Shoo Fly, shoo fly, shoo; It ain't gonna rain no more.

Some are purely conventional, surviving from traditional game-songs and folk-songs: So early in the morning; [309] Cold and frosty morning; [310] (On a) Long summer day; [311] So I heard them say; [312] Ladies, fare you well. [313]

Most common, finally, is the allusive type, with special reference to the dance. You're the one, my darling; [314] Won't you be my darling; [315] Shoo-li-lo, my darling; [316] Skip to my Lou, my darling; And also my dear darling; [317] (For) I ain't got long to stay; [318] Rocky road to Jordan and we'll all roll away; [319] In the promised land; [320] Way down below; [321] What makes you treat me so; [322] Oh, turn cinnamon, turn; Rock-a-bye, ladies turn; [323] Oh, what a shame; [324] (And) Everybody knows; [325] You know very well what I mean. [326]

---

299 "Baltimore."
300 "Coffee Grows on a White Oak Tree," "Virginia."
301 "Susie Brown."
302 "Liza Jane," "Old Joe Clark."
303 "Old Joe Clark."
304 "Down in Alabama," "Virginia."
305 "Virginia." Compare the refrain "Old Virginny never tire," Van Doren, p. 492.
306 "Old Dan Tucker," Wolford, pp. 78-79.
307 Wolford, p. 39.
308 "Golden Slippers," "Old Joe Clark."
309 "All Down to Sleep," "Boston," "Brown Jug," "Old Gray Mare," "Three Old Maids," "Wilson's Barroom."
310 "Chase the Squirrel."
311 "Sweetheart a-Hunting," "Three Old Maids."
312 "London."
313 "Sandy Land."
314 "Betsy Larkin," "Do-Se-Do," "Old Brass Wagon." Compare "You're the one I love," in "Miss Liking," Gardner, pp. 112-113.
315 "Rosa Becky Diner."
316 "Shoo-Li-Lo."
317 "Stole My Partner."
318 "London," "Old Joe Clark."
319 "Sweetheart a-Hunting."
320 "Boston."
321 "The Irish Trot."
322 "Old Doc Collins."
323 "Have Two Prisoners Here in Jail."
324 "Virginia."
325 "Oh, Ain't I Sweet."
326 "Green Leaf," Wolford, pp. 49-50.

In all this mass of doggerel, jingle, and improvisation genuine musical or poetic quality is rare, and is apt to be the result of accident rather than deliberate art. But occasionally one comes upon a piece notable for lyric delicacy and grace like the following:

Lady on the green grass,
   Long summer day,
Lady on the green grass,
   Long summer day.

Come in upon the ocean,
   Long summer day,
Come in upon the ocean,
   Long summer day.

Choose your lover,
   Long summer day,
Choose your lover,
   Long summer day.

Now or never,
   Long summer day,
Now or never,
   Long summer day.[327]

Such lightness of syllables, unity of tone, harmony of parts, completeness of structure, and beauty of pattern are sufficiently rare in the play-party song to justify the use of these weighty critical terms, to which the foregoing slender trifle may seem out of all proportion.

For the most part, however, the play-party was not interested in perfection of form, and what little we find is of the artless variety. The songs were made to serve the eminently practical purpose of accompanying and directing movement, and there was no time for embellishment. And the tradition itself was hardly old enough to permit the smoothing off of rough edges, the rounding and polishing that often take place in the process of oral transmission, and that have resulted in the superior quality of the English singing-games. In the latter, moreover, it is perhaps not too fanciful to see the effects not only of greater antiquity but also of the stability and serenity of English village life in contrast to the raw and uprooted crudity of the American frontier.

But what the American play-party song lacks in the finer graces of art it more than makes up for in freshness, vitality, variety, and verve. If there are few flowers of fancy, the vigor of the growth is attested by a

[327] J. Kyle McIntyre, Ardmore, Carter County, from Montgomery County, East Tennessee.

wild, weedy rankness of invention. Surprise and novelty abound in the language, which is full of picturesque dialect and racy colloquialism, new combinations and formations, *galimatias,* and plays on words. Images and allusions drawn from country life are piled pell-mell on each other in a breathless hodge-podge, playing variations on a theme or ringing the changes on a rhyme with remarkable ingenuity. Irrelevance and impropriety reign supreme. Vulgar buffoonery mingles with wistful sentiment; satire treads on the heels of compliment; natural history runs into fable; snatches of other songs and ballads, seemingly remembered by chance, are interpolated at random, without regard to unity or coherence. In the same miscellaneous spirit all sorts of material are converted to the uses of the dance. Marching song, drinking song, sailor's chantey, emigrant song; nursery rhyme, hymn—all are roughly assimilable to the leveling spirit of the democratic play-party. The raw, half-grown poetry of a raw, half-grown civilization—irreverent, irresponsible, inconsequential, incongruous, but always good-humored and high-spirited—play-party songs have an inevitable rightness that is tantamount to art. The players did not know much about art but they knew what they liked, and in their rough-and-ready choice and handling of material, they arranged and combined a limited number of ideas, sentiments, game movements, and dance figures in the right proportions and in what seems like inexhaustible variety.

"The way we play it is no sin," sing the players in "Going to Boston." And yet it is not to but from Boston that they are going, turning their backs on the powers of propriety and solemnity that have ranged themselves against what John Cotton, in 1625, called "lascivious dancing to wanton ditties, and in amorous gestures and wanton dalliances." So romping and swinging, choosing, changing, stealing, and chasing partners, even claiming the forbidden kiss, the chanting, laughing players march around the room, as their elders have done before them and as youth will continue to do, in one form or another, after them, gaily defiant, though innocent enough for all their boisterous bravado—

> In somebody's big white house,
>   In somebody's garden,
> If you don't let me out, I will jump out
>   And swing somebody's darling.

PART TWO
OKLAHOMA TEXTS AND TUNES

I know no reason but that this harmless riddle
May as well be printed as sung to a fiddle.
                    —OLD BROADSIDE.

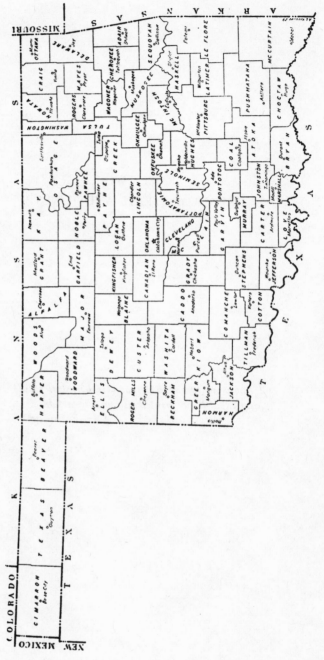

MAP OF OKLAHOMA

INTRODUCTORY NOTE

For the history and procedure of this collection, see Preface, Part One. The following material is included:

1. A headnote, with references (alphabetical according to author) to

    (a.) probable origins, possible sources, analogues, etc., in folk-songs, popular songs, ballads, nursery rhymes and songs, and traditional games, as well as parallel lines, stanzas, and allusions in, and borrowing, shifting, and interpolations from, other play-party songs;

    (b.) printed versions or mention in *The Journal of American Folk-Lore* (*JAFL*), *Publications of the Texas Folk-Lore Society* (*PTFS*), and other journals, collections, etc., dealing with the play-party and related song, game, and dance material, together with the place of collection or provenience, if identified, and the number of texts given;

    (c.) intrusive or parallel phrases, lines, and stanzas; similarities in tune, and other resemblances in the songs contained in this collection, titles of songs in this collection being set in capitals for cross-reference;

    (d.) other annotations—glossarial, textual, and descriptive.

(In bibliographical notes, when there is more than one work by an author or when the work is of a more general nature or only rarely cited, titles are usually given; otherwise, they are to be found by consulting the Bibliography.

When identical with the title in this collection, or without important variations, the titles of collated songs are omitted. First lines, often given in the absence of a title, are to be distinguished from titles by the fact that only the first word is capitalized.)

2. The texts of the most representative or interesting variants found in Oklahoma, with the variant title, if any; the name, town, and county (and state, if other than Oklahoma) of the informant, and the place of provenience, if known.

(Here, too, the title of the variant is understood to be the same as the general title unless a variant title or the note "No Title" appears.

Unless indicated as "Sung" or "Dictated," the text has been communicated in writing.)

3. A selection of important variant and additional lines and stanzas, together with the names and addresses of informants and the place of provenience.

4. An alphabetical list of informants (with addresses and the place of provenience) who reported other variants not printed, the list being in-

tended to serve as a record of material collected and as an index to the popularity and geographical distribution of the song.

5. A tune, wherever available.

(Those familiar with folk singing will recognize the impossibility of representing, in ordinary notation, the slurs and glides and other subtle variations in pitch which usually occur on the accented syllables. Thus, in the melody of "Sandy Land," the first note is recorded as "g," whereas in actuality the singer begins on a note less than a half-step below "g" and glides into it. Minor variations of the melody for succeeding stanzas have not been indicated.)

6. Directions or methods of playing the games, wherever available.

1
A. B. C. D.
(Mrs. L. T. Monnett, Norman, Cleveland County, who played it in Missouri.)

Cf. "A. B. C.," Piper (Montana), *JAFL*, 28:265, and, as a counting-out rhyme, Bolton (Cincinnati), p. 119.

A. B. C. D. E. F. G.,
H. I. J. K. L. M. N. O. P.,
Q. R. S. and T. U. V.,
W. and X. Y. Z.

2
ALL AROUND THOSE PRETTY LITTLE PINKS
A
(Kathryn C. Nicolett, Bache, Pittsburg County.)

For the term "pretty little pinks," see PRETTY LITTLE PINK.

1 All around, all around those pretty little pinks, (*Three times.*)
That grew in yonder garden.

2 Choose the one that you love best,   (*Three times.*)
Be sure you choose no other.

3 Say, kind miss, will you marry me, (*Three times.*)
So early in the morning.

4 Yes-sir-ee, if you say so, (*Three times.*)
I'll marry you to-morrow.

5 To-morrow night is the wedding night (*Three times.*)
For you and I to marry.

6 We'll have those old folks flyin' around, (*Three times.*)
A-fixin' for the weddin'.

7 God bless those good old folks (*Three times.*)
That gave to me their daughter.

8 You rascal, you — you told me a lie, (*Three times.*)
You stole me from my mamma.

B
God Bless That Good Old Man
(Bertha Matthews, Norman, Cleveland County, who played it in Texas.)

1 God bless that good old man, (*Three times.*)
For givin' me his daughter.

2 He knew I'd treat her well, (*Three times.*)
That's why he consented.

3

ALL DOWN TO SLEEP

(O. B. Campbell, Medford, Grant County.)

This is related to a large group of marriage games, including HOG
DROVERS, SISTER PHOEBE, and THREE DUKES, "All Down to
Sleep," "Hog Drovers," and "Sister Phoebe" being of the circle- or ring-
game type as distinct from the line-game type represented ·by "Three
Dukes." Like "Hog Drovers," in Ireland it is played at wakes (Gomme,
2:199).

For British versions, see the following in Gomme: "Here stands a
young man," 1:204-205 (two texts); "Poor Widow," 2:62-63 (three texts);
"Silly Old Man," 2:196-199 (six texts, including one from Carleton's *Traits
and Stories of the Irish Peasantry,* p. 107); in Northall: "Here stands a
young man who wants a sweetheart" (same as Gomme, No. I), p. 370;
"Silly old man he walks alone," pp. 378-379.

For American versions, see "There Was a Young Lady Who Sat
Down to Sleep," Babcock (Washington, D. C.) *American Anthropologist,*
1:252-253; "Sleepy Man," Dudley and Payne (Texas), *PTFS,* 1:27; "There
Sits an Old Woman," Gardner (Michigan), *JAFL,* 33:126; "Here's a
young lady," Heck (Cincinnati), *JAFL,* 40:39; "Here Sits a Young Lady,"
Isham (Virginia), *JAFL,* 34:117-119; "The Sleeping Beauty," Newell
(Massachusetts, Texas Negroes), pp. 224-225; "Here Sits a Young Man,"
Piper (Western Nebraska), *JAFL,* 28:269; "Melven Vine," Wolford (In-
diana), pp. 66-67.

Newell sees the idea of deliverance from enchantment, as in the Sleeping Beauty legend, underlying the song. The phrase "lies alone," found
in some English versions, suggests that "all down to sleep" may mean
"sleeping alone" as a euphemism for "lying alone."

1 Here sits a young lady all down to sleep,
   All down to sleep, all down to sleep.
 Here sits a young lady all down to sleep,
   So early in the morning.

2 She wants a young man to keep her awake,
   To keep her awake, etc.

3 So write his name down and send it by me,
   And send it by me, etc.

4 Mr. —— his name it shall be,
   His name it shall be, etc.

140

5 The way is open and he'll step in,
  And he'll step in, etc.

6 Here sits a young man all down to sleep, etc.

7 He wants a young lady to keep him awake, etc.

8 So write her name down and send it by me, etc.

9 Miss —— her name it shall be, etc.

10 The way is open and she'll step in, etc.

B

Young Lady Sit Down to Sleep

(Florette McNeese, Oklahoma City, Oklahoma County, from her pupils.)

1 There was a young lady, sit down to sleep,
  Sit down to sleep, sit down to sleep.
  There was a young lady, sit down to sleep,
  Sit down to sleep.
    Heigh-o to my hollie heigh-o.

2 She needs a young gentleman to keep her awake,
  Keep her awake, etc.

3 Mr. Joe Steel his name it shall be,
  Name it shall be, etc.

Other variants by Marguerite Durkee, Norman, Cleveland County; Audra A. Plumlee, Norman, Cleveland County.

4

ANGELINA

Cf. Ames (Missouri), *JAFL.,* 24:299; "Skip, Angelina," Clarke (Virginia Negroes), *JAFL,* 3:288.

An Oklahoma variant, "Aunt Jermima,"* reported by Walter L. Payne, Hobart, Kiowa County, from Mrs. S. J. Payne, Hobart, is related to "Aunt Jemima," Hamilton (Northeast Missouri), *JAFL,* 27:291.

---

* Cf. Aunt Jemima climbed a tree,
    Took a stick to boost her.
  There she sat a-throwing cobs
    At a bob-tailed rooster.

(Professor Kenneth C. Kaufman, Norman, Cleveland County, who heard it in Arkansas.)

A

(Mary Virginia Maloy, Norman, Cleveland County, from her father, Granbury, Texas.)

1 Angelina, do go home,
    Do go home, do go home,
  Angelina, do go home,
    And get your husband's supper.

2 Nothing there but bread and butter,
    Bread and butter, bread and butter,
  Nothing there but bread and butter,
    And a cup of tea.

3 Bread and butter is good enough for me,
    Is good enongh for me, is good enough for me,
  Bread and butter is good enough for me
    Without a cup of tea.

B

(Willis Goetzinger, Beaver, Beaver County, from Orlan Bell, Gray, Beaver County.)

1 Come, Angelina, do go home,
    Do go home, do go home.
  Come, Angelina, do go home,
    And get a little supper.

2 Bread and butter's good enough for me,
    Is good enough for me, is good enough for me,
  Bread and butter is good enough for me
    Without a cup of tea.

Directions: "All form and circle holding hands. Then circle to the left during the first stanza, and swing with a dance hold during the next."

5

BALTIMORE

Based on a bawdy song, popular in "Gentleman Jim" Corbett's time, some forty years ago, according to Dr. S. R. Hadsell, of the University of Oklahoma, who recalls that the circus concert (following the regular performance) helped to spread songs like this through the provinces, the children taking them up after the show's departure.

Cf. "Pairing Off," Davis (South Carolina plantation dance), *JAFL,* 27:252; "Baltimore," Dudley and Payne (Texas), *PTFS,* 1:19 (close to E); "Miss Mary Jane," Scarborough (South Carolina), p. 117; White (North Carolina), p. 296 and note.

Alonzo Lance, Bradley, Grady County, reports a dance call couplet:

    I gotta gal in Baltimore,
    But she's not mine any more.

Dr. Josiah H. Combs, of Texas Christian University, reports the following from Knott County, Kentucky:

'Way down yander in Kalamazine
Bullfrog sewed on a sewing machine;
He sewed so hard and he sewed so fast,
He sewed nine stitches in his a—.

I've got a gal in Kalamazoo,
She don't wear no —— yes, she do.
I've got a gal on the under square,
She don't wear no underwear.

George Milburn, of Pineville, Missouri, reports:

I've got a gal in Kalamazoo,
She eats ice cream and it runs right through.

See LIZA JANE.

A

(Sung by Professor Kenneth C. Kaufman, Norman, Cleveland County, who played it in Eastern Custer County.)

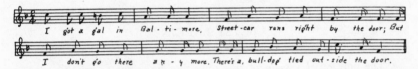

I got a girl in Baltimore,
Street-car runs right by the door;
But I don't go there any more:
There's a bull-dog tied outside the door.

B

(Margaret Hudson, Bartlesville, Washington County; Virginia R. Nelson, Clinton, Custer County.)

1 Here we go to Baltimore,
  Two behind and two before.

2 I've got a girl in Baltimore,
  Street cars run (right) by the door.

C

(Sam West, Duke, Jackson County, from Ruth Coleman, Jackson County.)

I've got a girl in Baltimore,
The street car passes right by her door.
She gets her hair cut pompadour,
And she's got sweethearts by the score
In Bal-ti-more.

D

(No Title)

(Hattie Bell Bethea, Marion, South Carolina.)

My gal lives in Baltimore,
Street car runs right by her door.

Ta-ra-ra-boom-de-ay,
Ta-ra-ra-boom-de-ay,

E

(Winnifred Spencer, Walters, Cotton County, from Jefferson, Marion County, Texas.)

1 Take your girl to Baltimore,
   Oh, Suzanna Gal.
   Take your girl to Baltimore,
   Oh, Suzanna Gal.

2 Turn your road to Baltimore,
   Oh, Suzanna Gal, etc.

Variant by Juanita Curtis, Glencoe, Payne County.

6

BETSY LARKIN

(Florette McNeese, Oklahoma City, Oklahoma County, from her pupils.)

The only other version of this song that has come to my attention is reported by Dr. Josiah H. Combs, of Texas Christian University, from Knott County, Kentucky, under the title "Old Betty Larkin," as follows:

1 Steal, steal old Betty Larkin, (*Three times.*)
   Also my dear darling.

2 You've got mine, I'll get another, etc.*

3 Needle in the haystack, old Betty Larkin, etc.

4 Hop around, skip around, old Betty Larkin, etc.

Played like OLD BRASS WAGON (B).
For the pattern, see DO-SE-DO.

1 Lead her up and down, sold Betsy Larkin. (*Three times.*)
   You're the one, my darling.

2 Never do to give her up, sold Betsy Larkin, etc.

3 Those who go slow are not worth having, sold Betsy Larkin, etc.

---

* This suggests "Skip to My Lou" in method of playing.

7

BILE DEM CABBAGE DOWN

(Sung by Professor Kenneth C. Kaufman, Norman, Cleveland County, who played it in Eastern Custer County.)

For the chorus, cf. "Mosquito He Fly High," Clarke (Virginia Negroes), *JAFL*, 3:289; "Bile Dem Cabbage Down," Scarborough (Virginia, South Carolina), pp. 124-125, 168; "Cooking Dinner," Talley, p. 156. See OLD JOE CLARK.

1 Wouldn't marry a widow,
    Tell you de reason why,
Got so many childern
    Dey make dem biscuits fly.

Chorus:
    Bile dem cabbage down.
    Bile dem cabbage down.
      I tell you gals, dere's no use foolin',
    But bile dem cabbage down.

8

BILLY BOY

(John V. Early, Oklahoma City, Oklahoma County.)

Based on the nursery song, generally considered a "comic derivative, or burlesque" of "Lord Randal" (Child, No. 12).

For British versions of the song, see Baring-Gould (*A Book of Nursery Songs and Rhymes*), pp. 36-39; Baring-Gould and Sheppard (*A Garland of Country Song*), p. 83; Halliwell (*Nursery Rhymes*), 5th and 6th editions, pp. 226-227; idem (*Popular Rhymes and Nursery Tales*), pp. 259-260; Herd (*Ancient and Modern Scottish Songs*), 2:1; Rimbault (*A Collection of Old Nursery Rhymes*), pp. 34-35; Sharp (*English Folk-*

145

Songs), 1, No. XLII; *idem* (*One Hundred English Folksongs*), pp. 132-133; Terry (*The Shanty Book*), Part I, pp. 2-3.

For American versions, see Campbell and Sharp, pp. 260-261 (two texts); Cox (West Virginia), pp. 484-488 (four texts, with annotations); Hudson (Mississippi), *JAFL,* 39:151-153 (four texts); Lomax (*American Ballads and Folk Songs*), pp. 320-322; Moore (Oklahoma), No. 120; Pound (Nebraska, *American Ballads and Songs*), pp. 231-232; *idem* (Nebraska, *Syllabus*), pp. 42-43; Shearin and Combs (Kentucky), pp. 30-31 (described); Shoemaker (*North Pennsylvania Minstrelsy*), pp. 131-132; Wyman and Brockway (Kentucky), p. 14; Wier (*Songs the Children Love to Sing*), p. 230.

For play-party use as a dramatic dialogue game, see Gardner (Michigan), *JAFL,* 33:92-93 (two texts); Wolford (Indiana), pp. 24-25.

> 1 Have you found you a wife, Billy Boy, Billy Boy,
> Have you found you a wife, bonny Billy?
> I've found me a wife, she's the joy of my life,
> Yet she's a young thing and cannot earn a living.
> (*Or:* She was a young thing and could not leave her mother.)

> 2 Did she put you to bed, Billy Boy, Billy Boy,
> Did she put you to bed, bonny Billy?
> She put me to bed with a bump on my head,
> She's a young thing and cannot earn a living.

> 3 Did she bake you a pie, Billy Boy, Billy Boy,
> Did she bake you a pie, bonny Billy?
> Yes, she gave me a pie with a hit in the eye,
> She's a young thing and cannot earn a living.

Directions: "The children form a circle with a chosen child in the center. The fun of the game was for the chorus to give Billy a 'hot one' in the way of a question, and Billy in return was supposed to ably give back an answer funny and thrilling, to the merriment of our gang."

Variants by Hattie Bell Bethea, Marion, S. C.; Jane Bowman, Pauls Valley, Garvin County; Mary Virginia Maloy, Norman, Cleveland County.

9

BIRD IN THE CAGE

Cf. "There's a Light in the Window," Ball (Idaho), *JAFL,* 44:7-8; "There's a Light in the Window," Piper (Montana), *JAFL,* 28:277-278. Stanza 2 in the former:

> There is somebody waiting, (*Three times.*)
> For me.

recalls the following lines from the sentimental song, "There is Somebody Waiting" (c. 1860), by Charles Glover (cited by Pound, *Syllabus,* p. 46):

There is somebody waiting,
There is somebody waiting,
There is somebody waiting for me.

See CHEAT 'ER SWING.

A

(No Title)

(Mrs. Della I. Young, Cheyenne, Roger Mills County, from Vashti Young.)

1 From the looks of your age
  You're a bird in the cage,
  But there's somebody waiting for you.
  There's somebody waiting,
  There's somebody waiting,
  There's somebody waiting for you.

Chorus:
  Choose the two, leave the other,
  Choose the two, leave the other,
  Choose the two, leave the other for me.

  Swing the one, leave the other,
  Swing the one, leave the other,
  Swing the one, leave the other for me.

2 From what I've been told
  You've been left in the cold,
  But there's somebody waiting for you,
  There's somebody waiting, etc.

B

Birdie in the Cage

(Lillie O. Heaton, Watonga, Blaine County.)

There is a birdie in the cage
And I know she is not engaged,
For there is somebody waiting for me.
Oh! there is somebody waiting,
Oh! there is somebody waiting for me.

C

Somebody Waiting

(Emma Vilhauer, Norman, Cleveland County.)

1 There is somebody waiting, (*Three times.*)
  There is somebody waiting for me.

2 Take the two, two together, (*Three times.*)
   Take the two, two together for me.

3 Swing the one, sting the other, (*Three times.*)
   Swing the one, sting the other for me.

D
BIRD IN THE CAGE
(Clifford Chandler, Crescent, Logan County.)

There's a bird in the cage,
And they say she's of age,
And there is somebody waiting for her.

Chorus:
   Choose the one, leave the other,
   Choose the one, leave the other,
   Choose the one, leave the other for me.

E
DOWN SOUTH IN THE HOLLER
(Mary Esther Coffman, Geary, Blaine County.)

1 Way down South in the holler,
   Where the pigs used to waller,
      There is somebody waiting for me.

2 There is somebody waiting,
   There is somebody waiting,
      There is somebody waiting for me.

Other variants by Katherine Harris, Norman, Cleveland County:
Harold Roberts, Blackwell, Kay County.

10
BOSTON

Cf. "Going to Boston," Dudley and Payne (Texas), *PTFS,* 1:16-17
(two texts); "Goodbye, girls, I'm going to Boston," Kittredge (Kentucky),
JAFL, 20:275; "Going to Boston," Lomax (*American Ballads and Folk
Songs*), pp. 297-298; "We'll All Go to Boston," Randolph (Ozarks, Missouri), *JAFL,* 42:215-216 (also *The Ozarks,* pp. 158-159); "Going to
Boston," Shearin and Combs (Kentucky), p. 36 (excerpt); "Go to Boston," Wolford (Indiana), p. 49.

The tune resembles that of PAWPAW LAND.

Oklahoma Texts and Tunes

A

(Sung by Charlie Carr, Noble, Cleveland County.)

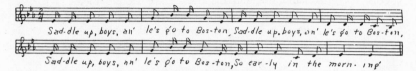

Sad-dle up, boys, an' le's go to Bos-ton, Sad-dle up, boys, an' le's go to Bos-ton,

Sad-dle up, boys, an' le's go to Bos-ton, So ear-ly in the morn-ing'

1 Saddle up, boys, an' le's go to Boston, (*Three times.*)
   So early in the morning.

2 Come on, girls, an' le's go with them, etc.

3 Uh-oh, Charlie, I'll tell your Mamma, (*Three times.*)
   How you are courtin'.

4 Courtin' that pretty girl, she won't have you. (*Three times.*)
   So early in the morning.

Directions: The boys and girls line up facing each other. At 1 the boys march around the girls and back to their places. At 2 the girls march around the boys and back to their places. At 3 the front couple swing. At 4 they swing down the center and take their places at the end of the line. The other couples follow suit.

B

(Florette McNeese, Oklahoma City, Oklahoma County, from her pupils.)

1 Where, oh, where is Belva Lockwood, (*Three times.*)
   Why, she's gone to Boston.

Chorus 1:
   Come along, girls, and we'll go to Boston, (Three times.)
    In the promised land.

2 Where, oh, where is Grover Cleveland,* (*Three times.*)
   Why, he's gone to Boston.

Chorus 2:
   Come along, boys, and we'll go to Boston, etc.

Chorus 3:
   Come along, folks, and we'll all go to Boston, etc.

Directions: "Boys and girls form lines opposite each other. As they sing the stanza, they keep time with their feet. With the chorus, the girls

---

* ". . . would at least indicate at what period the game was popular."—F. McN.

start marching and with a rude dancing step go completely around the boys (who remain in line) back to their original places. With the second chorus, the girls stand still and the boys dance around them. With the third chorus boys and girls take hands and promenade around the room with a hopping step. Other stanzas are frequently added."

C

(Glenn A. Roe, Oklahoma City, Oklahoma County, who played it at Frederick, Tillman County.)

1 Come along, girls, and let's go to Boston, (*Three times.*)
   So early in the morning.

2 Fix up, boys, and we'll go with them, etc.

3 Here we go round the mulberry bush, etc.

4 John Brown's dead and his wife's a widow, etc.

5 Maybe she'll die and she'll be with him, etc.

6 The way we play it is no sin, etc.

D

How You Go a-Courtin'

(Zelma Oliver, Norman, Cleveland County, from Eugene Nolen, Norman.)

1 ——*, Oh, ——, I'll tell your Mamma, (*Three times.*)
   How you go a-courtin'.
2 Courtin' ——, an' she won't have you, etc.

Other variants by Delphin Delmor Bledsoe, Marlow, Stephens County; Gerald Bond, Chickasha, Grady County; Harry L. Deupree, Oklahoma City, Oklahoma County, from Nebraska, Iowa, Missouri.

11

BUFFALO GIRLS

Based on the well-known Christy minstrel song. See Chapple (*Heart Songs*), p. 366; *Minstrel Songs Old and New,* pp. 130-131; Scarborough, p. 113; Spaeth (*Weep Some More, My Lady*), pp. 107-108; Sullivan (*Our Times*), 2:160-162.

For "I danced with the girl with a hole in her stocking," cf. "Charleston Gals," Allen, Ware, and Garrison (*Slave Songs of the United States*), p. 88 (also Scarborough, pp. 162-163); and "Purty Yaller Gal," Perrow (Mississippi Negroes), *JAFL,* 28:188. The line "Go home with the girls

---

* Name of player inserted.

in the morning" occurs as the last of four lines recorded by Van Doren (Eastern Illinois, *JAFL,* 32:496), beginning "Mother, O Mother! my toes are sore."

Cf. "Cincinnati Girls," Ball (Idaho), *JAFL,* 44:11; "Buffalo Girls," Hamilton (Northeast Missouri), *JAFL,* 27:300; "Louisiana Girls," Lomax (*American Ballads and Folk Songs*), pp. 288-290; Piper (Western Nebraska, Western Iowa), *JAFL,* 28:285-286; Scarborough, pp. 113-114; "Louisiana Gal," *idem,* p. 112; "The Lushbaugh Girls," Shoemaker (*North Pennsylvania Minstrelsy*), pp. 129-130; "Buffalo Girls," Van Doren (Eastern Illinois), *JAFL,* 32:487; "Cincinnati Girls," Wolford (Indiana), p. 32. Dr. Josiah H. Combs, of Texas Christian University, reports a version from Monongalia County, West Virginia, under the title, "Jim-Town Girls" (from the name of a local settlement).

A

(Lois Ferguson Beckham, Norman, Cleveland County, from Memphis, Tennessee. Tune from Charlie Carr, Noble, Cleveland County.)

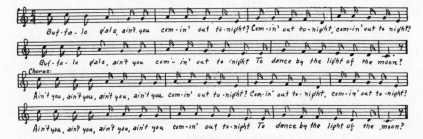

1 Buffalo girls, ain't you comin' out to-night?
    Comin' out to-night, comin' out to-night?
Buffalo girls, ain't you comin' out to-night?
    To dance by the light of the moon?

Chorus:
    Ain't you, ain't you, ain't you, ain't you comin' out to-night,
        Comin' out to-night, comin' out to-night?
    Ain't you, ain't you, ain't you, ain't you comin' out to-night
        To dance by the light of the moon?

2 I got a girl freckles on her chin,
    Wart on her nose and her eyes turned in.
Darn good girl for the shape she's in,
    Tell me ain't you comin' out to-night? *

---

* This is borrowed from the song "Ain't-cha, ain't-cha, ain't-cha, ain't-cha comin out to-night?" which in turn seems to be an adaptation of "Buffalo Girls."

B

(Lela L. Conrad, Perry, Noble County.)

1 Form a star, the right hands crossed,
   The right hands crossed, the right hands crossed.
   Form a star, the right hands crossed,
   The left hand back again.

2 Eight hands up and round we go,
   Round we go, round we go.
   Eight hands up and around we go.
   Ladies don't see any gents they know.

3 Buffalo girls a-coming by night,
   Coming by night, coming by night.
   Buffalo girls a-coming by night
   To dance by the light of the moon.

4 Dance all night till broad daylight,
   Till broad daylight, till broad daylight.
   Dance all night till broad daylight,
   Go home with the girls in the morning.

----

1 Got a little gal with a wooden leg,
   Wooden leg, wooden leg,
   Guess that's the reason that they call her Peg.
   Oh, tell me, ain't-cha comin' out to-night?

Chorus:
   Ain't-cha, ain't-cha, ain't-cha, ain't-cha comin' out to-night,
   Comin' out to-night, comin' out to-night?
   Oh, tell me, ain't-cha, ain't-cha, ain't-cha, ain't-cha comin' out to-night
   To dance by the light of the moon?

2 Got a little gal and she lives on a hill,
   Lives on a hill, lives on a hill.
   She's a moonshiner's daughter, but I love her still.
   Oh, tell me, ain't-cha comin' out to-night?

3 Got a little gal with freckles on her nose,
   Freckles on her nose, freckles on her nose,
   . . . .
   Oh, tell me, ain't-cha comin' out to-night?

4 Got a little gal with a wart on her chin,
   Wart on her chin, wart on her chin.
   Her nose sticks out and her eyes turn in,
   (*Spoken*) But she's a pretty good gal for the shape she's in.
   Oh, tell me, ain't-cha comin' out to-night?

(L. E. Russell, Cyril, Caddo County.)

C

(Fanny W. Kelly, Jefferson, Grant County; Evelyn Roach, Shamrock, Texas.)

1 One buffalo girl all around inside,
  All around inside, all around inside,
  One buffalo girl all around inside,
  With honors to your partner.

2 Swing 'em all around [inside],
  All around [inside], all around [inside],
  Swing 'em all around [inside],
  With honors to your partner.

D

(Florette McNeese, Oklahoma City, Oklahoma County, from her pupils.)

Buffalo girls, are you coming out to-night,
  Are you coming out to-night, are you coming out to-night?
Buffalo girls, are you coming out to-night,
  To spend the evening dancing?
Bird hop out and the crow hop in,
All hands up and circle again.
Balance eight till all get straight,
Swing pretty pard and promenade eight.

E

(Chester Harley Anderson, Guthrie, Logan County.)

1 Buffalo girls, are you coming out to-night,
  Coming out to-night, coming out to-night,
  Say, Buffalo girls, are you coming out to-night
  To dance by the light of the moon?

2 Oh, yes, pretty boys, we are coming out to-night,
  Coming out to-night, coming out to-night,
  Oh, yes, pretty boys, we are coming out to-night
  To dance by the light of the moon.

Variants:

Choctaw girls, ain't you coming out to-night,
  Ain't you coming out to-night, ain't you coming out to-night?
Choctaw girls, ain't you coming out to-night
  To dance by the light of the mooon, moon, moon?
      (Catherine Harris, Antlers, Pushmataha County, from S. B. Hackett,
      Norman, who played it in Arkansas.)

Dance to the girl with a hole in her heel,
  Hole in her heel, hole in her heel,
Dance to the girl with a hole in her heel,
  And I had one in mine.
      (Elizabeth Ducker, Tecumseh, Pottawatomie County.)

153

I danced with a girl with a hole in her stocking,
    And her heel kep' a-rockin', and her heel kep' a-rockin',
Danced with a girl with a hole in her stocking,
    Prettiest gal in the room.
        (Ella Hopkins, Tulsa, Tulsa County.)

I danced with a girl with a hole in her stockin',
    An' her heel kep' a-rockin', etc.
    An' her heel kep' a-rockin' to the moon.
        (Mrs. Anne McClure, Oklahoma City, Oklahoma County, who played it
        in Benton County, Arkansas.)

Other variants by Boyce Billingsley, Wayne, McClain County, from Northern Arkansas; Creed Bogan, Duncan, Stephens County; Jane Bowman, Pauls Valley, Garvin County; John Cunningham, Watonga, Blaine County, from his father, who played it at Homestead, Blaine County; Juanita Curtis, Glencoe, Payne County; Agnes Frick, Oklahoma City, Oklahoma County; Alice Flora Hare, Norman, Cleveland County, from Bernice Taylor, Norman; Louise James, Norman, Cleveland County; Beatrice Jennings McMullin, Norman, Cleveland County, from Kentucky to Kay and Grant Counties, on Oklahoma-Kansas border; Virginia R. Nelson, Clinton, Custer County; Audra A. Plumlee, Norman, Cleveland County; Ruth Revelle, Oklahoma City, Oklahoma County; Dorothy H. Smith, Oklahoma City, Oklahoma County; Cora Frances Starritt, Ada, Pontotoc County.

12

CAPTAIN JINKS

Based on the stage song, popular in the early seventies and possibly of Civil War origin (Wolford, p. 29). See Chapple (*Heart Songs*), p. 54; Spaeth (*Weep Some More, My Lady*), pp. 47-48.

Cf. Ames (Missouri), *JAFL*, 24:308-309; Ball (Idaho), *JAFL*, 44:14; Elsom and Trilling (*Social Games and Group Dances*), pp. 236-239; Gardner (Michigan), *JAFL*, 33:95 (two texts); Osborn (Catskill dance call), *American Speech*, 3:143; Piper (Western Iowa), *JAFL*, 28:285; "Captain Jenks," Pound (Nebraska, *Syllabus*), p. 68; Randolph (Ozarks, Missouri), *JAFL*, 42:231-232; Wolford (Indiana, Pennsylvania), pp. 27-29 (four texts).

It is interesting for the introduction of dance directions into the ballad and for the variations of "horse marines," of which "horse merinks (marinks)" (found in two Oklahoma variants and also reported by Dr. S. R. Hadsell, of the University of Oklahoma, from Adams County, Illinois) is the most curious.

A

(Sung by Clayton Black, east of Noble, Cleveland County.)

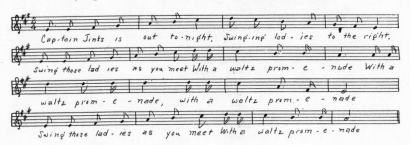

Cap-tain Jinks is out to-night, Swing-ing lad - ies to the right. Swing those lad ies as you meet With a waltz prom - e - nade With a waltz prom - e - nade, with a waltz prom - e - nade Swing those lad - ies as you meet With a waltz prom - e - nade

Captain Jinks is out to-night,
   Swinging (Dancing) ladies to the right.
Swing those ladies as you meet
   With a waltz promenade, *(Three times.)*
Swing those ladies as you meet
   With a waltz promenade.

Directions: The boys march around the girls (in the center ring) until they get back to their partners. They swing on the "promenade." Reverse for the girls, singing "Mrs. Jinks is out to-night."—Charlie Carr, Noble, Cleveland County.

B

(Sung by Charlie Carr, Noble, Cleveland County.)

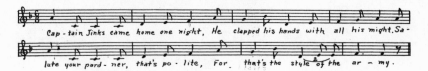

Cap-tain Jinks came home one night, He clapped his hands with all his might. Sa- lute your pard - ner, that's po - lite, For that's the style of the ar - my.

Captain Jinks came home one night,
He clapped his hands with all his might.
Salute your pardner, that's polite,
   For that's the style of the army.

C

(Emma Vilhauer, Norman, Cleveland County.)

1 Captain Jinks with a horse my ring,
   He clapped his hands and you may swing,
   Swing 'em around with all your might,
   For that's the style of the army.

Chorus:
> Circle hands and form a no (*sic*),
>> Formano, formano.
> Circle hands and form a no
>> For that's the style of the army.

2 Captain Jinks got tied (tight) last night,
  He clapped his hands with all his might,
  Gentlemen passes from one to the right.
  > For that's the style of the army.

3 Teach the ladies how to walk,
  > How to walk, how to walk,
  Teach the ladies how to walk,
  > For that's the style of the army.

D

(Ruby Home, Calumet, Canadian County.)

1 I'm Captain Jinks of the horse marine,
  I feed my horse good corn and bean
  Although it's quite beyond my mean,
  > For I'm captain in the army.

2 When I left my home my ma she cried,
  > My ma she cried, my ma she cried.
  When I left my home my ma she cried,
  > For I'm captain in the army.

3 I teach the ladies how to dance,
  > How to dance, how to dance,
  I teach the ladies how to dance,
  > For I'm captain in the army.

E

(Mrs. Della I. Young, Cheyenne, Roger Mills County, from Vashti Young,
Cheyenne.)

1 Captain Jinks, the horse marine,
  He fed his crew on corn and beans.
  Come swing the ladies in their teens,
  > For that's the style in the army.

Chorus:
> Teach the ladies how to dance,
>> How to dance, how to dance,
> Teach the ladies how to dance,
>> For that's the style in the army.

2 Captain Jinks went home one night.
    The gentleman passes to the right.
    We'll get married at first sight,
        For that's the style in the army.

F

(Rephord Hubert Stevens, Union City, Canadian County.)

1 Captain Jinks came home one night,
    He clapped his hands with all his might.
    Salute your pardner, that's polite,
        For that's the style of the army.

    All join hands and forward all,
        Forward all, forward all.
    All join hands and forward all,
        For that's the style of the army.

2 Captain Jinks came home one night.
    The gentleman passes to the right.
    Salute your pardner, that's polite,
        For that's the style of the army.

    All join hands and stand still,
        Stand still, stand still,
    All join hands and stand still,
        For that's the style of the army.

G

(Wanda Irene Dalton, Curtis, Woodward County.)

Captain Jenks is here to-night,
Clap your hands with pure delight,
And salute your pardner on the right,
    For that's the style of the army.
All join hands and circle to your right.
Swing your pardner and promenade to your right.
There's a hot time in the town to-night.

H

(The same.)

1 Captain Jenks, his horse marine,
    He claps his hand upon his knee.
    Swing your partner once and a half,
        For that's the style of the army.

2 Captain Jenks, his horse marine.
    He claps his hand upon his knees.
    Swing your pardner once and a half,
        For that's the style of the army.

157

3 Join hands and promenade,
   Promenade, promenade,
 Join hands and promenade,
   For that's the style of the army.

I

(Frances T. Henderson, Fort Cobb, Caddo County.)

1 Captain Jenks is out to-night.
 The lady dances to the right.
 The gentleman dances to the left,
   And we'll all promenade.

2 Captain Jenks got tight one night.
 The gentleman changes to the right
 And swings the lady with all his might,
   And we'll all promenade.

3 My ma she cried when I left home,
   When I left home, when I left home.
 My ma she cried when I left home,
   For that's the style of the army.

J

(Carl West, Perico, Texas, from Raymond Kiser, Perico.)

1 Captain Jenks, of the horse merinks,
 Claps his hands with all his minks.
 And swing your partner if you're not too green,
   For that's the style of the army.

2 We'll all join hands and circle left,
   And circle left, and circle left.
 We'll all join hands and circle left,
   For that's the style of the army.

3 Ladies to the center and back again,
   Gents to the center and form in a ring.
 And when you've formed then you may swing,
 And when you've swung remember my call.
 Skip one partner and promenade all.

K

(Doris G. Waters, Ponca City, Kay County, from her pupils.)

1 Captain Jinks, the horse marinks,
 He claps his hands and then he swings.
 He swings that lady with all his might,
   For that's the style of the army.

158

We'll all join hands and circle to the left,
    Circle to the left, circle to the left.
We'll all join hands and circle to the left,
    For that's the style of the army.

2 Captain Jinks got tight one night.
  Gentleman changes to the right,
  And swings that lady with all his might,
    For that's the style of the army.
  We'll all join hands and circle to the left, etc.

L

(No Title)

(Harold Roberts, Blackwell, Kay County.)

1 Captain Jenks, the horse marines,
  He claps his hands and then he swings.
  He swings his lady with all his might,
    For that's the style of the army.

2 Join your hands and immigrate west,
    Immigrate west, immigrate west,
  Join your hands and immigrate west,
    For that's the style of the army.

M

(Fanny W. Kelly, Jefferson, Grant County; Madeline Tarpley, Shamrock, Texas.)

Captain Jinks of the horse marines,
  He claps his hands beyond the ranks.
Salute your pard if you're not green,
  For that's the style of the army.

Other variants by Ethel Rose Baird, Bixby, Tulsa County; Raymond Hugh Guthrie, Wakita, Grant County; Catherine Harris, Antlers, Pushmataha County, from S. B. Hackett, Norman, who played it in Arkansas; Lillie O. Heaton, Watonga, Blaine County; Thelma Staggs, Guthrie, Logan County; Ralph W. Winstead, Forgan, Beaver County.

13

CHASE THE SQUIRREL (1)

A kissing game.

Cf. "Up and Down the Center We Go," Hamilton (Missouri), *JAFL*, 27:303; "Chase That Squirrel," Piper (Western Nebraska), *JAFL*, 28:266; "Up and Down the Center We Go," Wedgwood (Southwestern Nebraska, Southern Iowa, from Missouri), *JAFL*, 25:271; Wolford (Indiana), pp. 30-31; "Catch the Squirrel," *Social Plays, Games,* etc., p. 18.

"Hunt the Squirrel," Newell, pp. 168-169, is played like "Drop the Handkerchief." Also different in words and method of playing are the Negro games, "Hop, Old Squirrel," "Peep, Squirrel, Peep," Scarborough (Virginia, Washington, D. C.), pp. 134-136; "Peep Squirrel," Smiley, *JAFL*, 32:376-377; "Peep Squirrel," Talley, p. 78 (the first and last of which resemble C).

A

COLD AND FROSTY MORNING

(Lela Tilman, Sumner, Noble County. Played in Indian Territory over forty years ago.)

Each boy gets a partner and they stand in line facing each other. First couple starts back and forth between the two lines. All sing:

1 Up and down the center we go, (*Three times.*)
   Cold and frosty morning.

(*Girl ahead of boy*)
2 Out and around the ring we go, etc.

(*Walks faster*)
3 Little bit faster if you please, etc.

(*Boy chases girl*)
4 Now's the time to catch her if you can, etc.
   (*Or:* Catch 'er and kiss 'er if you can, etc.)

The couple, having played, goes to the foot of the line; and the next couple starts, and so on.

B

CHASE THE SQUIRREL

(Walter L. Payne, Hobart, Kiowa County, from Mrs. Jesse Fields, who played it at a rural school near Nashville, Tennessee, some forty-five years ago.)

This is the way to chase the squirrel —
   So say remember me.
This is the way to chase the squirrel —
   Moscow ladies, turn.
Turn, turn, Moscow ladies, (*Three times.*)
   Moscow ladies, turn.

C

(Delphin Delmor Bledsoe, Marlow, Stephens County; Agnes Frick, Oklahoma City, Oklahoma County; Ruth Revelle, Oklahoma City, Oklahoma County.)

Peep squirrel, hey diddle dinctum.
Catch that squirrel, hey diddle dinctum.
Chase that squirrel, hey diddle dinctum.
   Lady in the center an' a-all hands round,

14

CHASE THE SQUIRREL (2)

(Sung by Raburn Linton, Mountain Park, Kiowa County.)

Related to the square dance, of the same name, involving a "chasing" figure. For the music and calls, see Burchenal (*American Country-Dances*), pp. 16-17, and for borrowings, cf. "Fare You Well," Ames (Missouri), *JAFL,* 24:316, and Hamilton (Northeast Missouri), *JAFL,* 27:300.

Fourteen variants of the dance call were reported under this title from Oklahoma, most of them containing the couplets:

> Chase the rabbit, chase the squirrel,
> Chase the pretty girl around the world.

> Chase the rabbit, chase the coon,
> Chase the pretty girl around the moon.

Cf. "Fragment," Pound (Nebraska, *Syllabus*), p. 69.
For the pattern, cf. JUTANG, LONDON, and OLD DOC COLLINS.

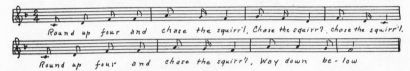

1 Round up four and chase the squirr'l,
    Chase the squirr'l, chase the squirr'l.
Round up four and chase the squirr'l,
    Way down below.

2 Break and swing and chase the squirr'l, etc.

3 Round up six, etc.

4 Break and swing, etc.

5 Round up eight, etc.

6 Break and swing, etc.

15

CHEAT 'ER SWING

(Sung by Orville Nichols, Mountain Park, Kiowa County, from Cordell, Washita County.)

Related to the square dance.
See BIRD IN THE CAGE.

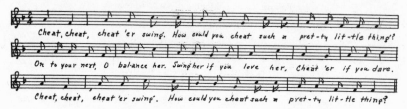

Cheat, cheat, cheat 'er swing. How could you cheat such a pret-ty lit-tle thing?

On to your next, O bal-ance her. Swing her if you love her, Cheat 'er if you dare.

Cheat, cheat, cheat 'er swing. How could you cheat such a pret-ty lit-tle thing?

> Cheat, cheat, cheat 'er swing.
> How could you cheat such a pretty little thing?
> On to your next,
> O balance her.
> Swing her if you love her,
> Cheat 'er if you dare.
> Cheat, cheat, cheat 'er swing.
> How could you cheat such a pretty little thing?

Variant by Mrs. Bertha Downing, Norman, Cleveland County, who played it in Southern Noble, Northeastern Logan, and Northern Payne Counties.

16

THE CHIMNEY SWEEPER

(Walter Payne, Hobart, Kiowa County.)

Cf. "Old Chimney Sweeper," Hamilton (Northeast Missouri), *JAFL,* 27:295; Thomas (Kentucky), pp. 7-8, 74-75; "I'm a Poor Old Chimney Sweeper," Van Doren (Eastern Illinois), *JAFL,* 32:491-492; "I'm a Poor Old Chimney Sweeper," Wolford (Indiana), p. 58; "Old Chimney Sweeper" (Massachusetts), *JAFL,* 10:325.

For "this broomstick step over," cf. "Slave Marriage Ceremony Supplement," Talley, p. 143.

> I am a poor old chimney sweeper,
> I have but one daughter but can't keep her;
> And as you have resolved to marry,
> Go choose your mate and no longer tarry.
> Since you have one of your choosing,
> You have no time to be losing.
> So join your right hand, this broomstick step over,
> And kiss the lips of your true lover.

17

CIRCLE LEFT

(Sung by Clayton Black, east of Noble, Cleveland County.)

Related to the square dance.

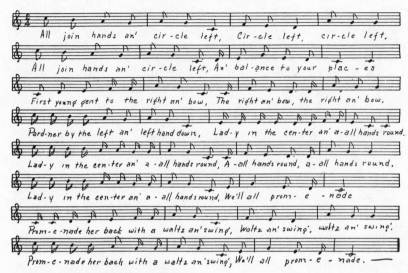

1 All join hands an' circle left,
    Circle left, circle left.
All join hands an' circle left,
    An' balance to your places.
First young gent to the right an' bow,
    The right an' bow, the right an' bow.
Pardner by the left an' left hand down,
    Lady in the center an' a-all hands round.
Lady in the center an' a-all hands round,
    A-all hands round, a-all hands round,
Lady in the center an' a-all hands round,
    We'll all promenade.
Promenade her back with a waltz an' swing,
    Waltz an' swing, waltz an' swing,
Promenade her back with a waltz an' swing,
    We'll all promenade.

2 All join hands an' circle left, etc.
Next young gent to the right an' bow, etc.

163

18

COFFEE GROWS ON A WHITE OAK TREE* (JOSEY)

For "coffee grows" variants, see headnote to PRETTY LITTLE PINK.

For "Josey," cf. "Mr. Cooler," Davis (South Carolina plantation dance), *JAFL*, 27:253-254; Douthitt (Kentucky), p. 33; Dudley and Payne (Texas), *PTFS*, 1:21-22; "Josey," *ibid.*, p. 12; Hudson (Mississippi, *Specimens*), pp. 129-130; "Four in the Middle," Randolph (Ozarks, Missouri), *JAFL*, 42:213-214 (also *The Ozarks*, pp. 154-156); "Hold My Mule," Scarborough, pp. 105-106; Wolford (Indiana), pp. 33-35.

For "fiddler's drunk," see (LITTLE) BROWN JUG, WILSON'S BARROOM, WINDING UP THE BALLROOM.

For the "raging canal," see (LITTLE) BROWN JUG, RAILROAD (AND) STEAMBOAT.

For "big white house," see DOWN IN ALABAMA, VIRGINIA.

For "coffee grows," see LEAD THROUGH THAT SUGAR AND TEA (D), PRETTY LITTLE PINK.

A

(Sung by Clayton Black, east of Noble, Cleveland County.)

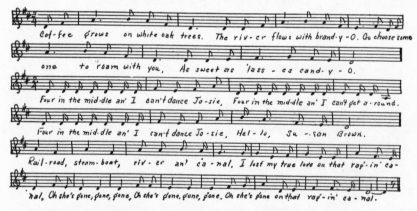

1 Coffee grows on white oak trees,
   The river flows with brandy-O.
   Go choose some one to roam with you,
   As sweet as 'lasses candy-O.

---

* Also, "Coffee Grows on White Oak Trees."

2 Four in the middle an' I can't dance Josie,
    Four in the middle an' I can't get around.
Four in the middle an' I can't dance Josie,
    Hello, Susan Brown.

("Just sing such little old verses as the last there until you get tahrd.")

3 Wheel around an' whirl around, I can't dance Josie, etc.

4 Rats in the boots an' the boots turned over, etc.

5 Hold Old Gray while I dance Josie, etc.*

6 Briar in the heel an' can't dance Josie, etc.

("You ought to get some of these young fellers that sings them all the time to give you the words. Just before the end you sing:")

7 *Railroad, steamboat, river an' canal,*
   I lost my true love on that ragin' canal.
   Oh, she's gone, gone, gone,
   Oh, she's gone, gone, gone,
   Oh, she's gone on that ragin' canal.

8 Coffee grows on white oak trees, etc.

9 Coffee grows on black jack stumps,
   The river flows with sugar lumps, etc.

B

(Sung by Raburn Linton, Mountain Park, Kiowa County.)

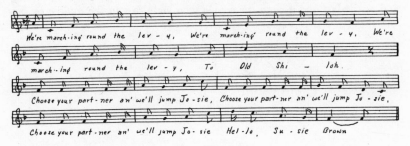

1 We're marching round the levy, (*Three times.*)
   To Old Shiloh.

2 Choose your partner an' we'll jump Josie, (*Three times.*)
   Hello, Susie Brown.

---

* Hold my dog till I tree a possum.—Charlie Carr, Noble, Cleveland County.

C

HELLO, SUSIE BROWN

(Vonnie B. Hill, Tahlequah, Cherokee County, from Pebble Smyth, Norman, Cleveland County.)

1 Oh, coffee grows on white oak trees,
   The river flows with brandy, O!
Go choose some one to roam with you
   As sweet as 'lasses candy, O!

2 Four in the middle and can't jump Josey,
   Four in the middle and can't get around.
Four in the middle and can't jump Josey.
   Hello, Susie Brown.

3 Big-footed nigger and can't jump Josey, etc.

4 Hold Old Gray while I jump Josey, etc.

5 Big white house and nobody livin' in it,
   Big white house and nobody livin' in it.
I'll take you and we'll be livin' in it.*
   Hello, Susie Brown.

6 Get out of there if you can't jump Josey, etc.

Directions: All the boys and girls form a ring with the exception of a boy and a girl who remain in the center. All sing the first stanza as the two in the center choose partners. Then the following stanzas are sung, and as the last one is sung the couple who were first in the middle go out and the dance is repeated.

D

HELLO, SUSAN BROWN

(Walter Myers Gable, Norman, Cleveland County.)

1 Briar in my heel and I can't jump Joseph,
   Briar in my heel and I can't get around.
Briar in my heel and I can't jump Joseph,
   Hello, Susan Brown.

Chorus:
   Railroad, steamboat, river and canal.
   Lost my true love on that raging canal.
   Oh, she gone, gone, gone!
   Oh, she gone, gone, gone!
   Oh, she gone on that raging canal!

---

* We'll get married, we'll live in it.—Charlie Carr, Noble, Cleveland County.

166

2 Four in the middle and I can't jump Joseph, etc.

3 Frog in the pond and the pond run over, (*Three times.*) *
Hello, Susan Brown.

E

Coffee Grows

(The same.)

1 Coffee grows on a black jack stump,
  The river flows with brandy, O.
Choose some one to roam with you,
  Just old peachy brandy, O.

2 Coffee grows on white oak trees,
  Brandy flows from here to the sea, etc.

F

(No Title)

(Professor Kenneth C. Kaufman, Norman, Cleveland County, who played it in
Eastern Custer County.)

1 Two in the middle and they can't dance Josie,
  Two in the middle and they can't dance Jo.
Two in the middle and they can't dance Josie.
  Hello, Susan Brown.

Chorus:
  We're going down the river,
  We're going down below.
  We're going down the river,
  To old Shiloh.†

2 Fiddler's drunk and we can't dance Josie, etc.

3 Hold my mule while I dance Josie, etc.

(There must have been a hundred different verses. They made them up—
just get one line.—K. C. K.)

---

* Frog in the pond, pond froze over.—Charlie Carr, Noble, Cleveland County.
† On Deer Creek, near Hydro, they used to sing the chorus:
  We're going down Old Deer Creek,
  We're going down below.
  We're going down Old Deer Creek,
  To Old Hydro.

G

Coffee Grows on a High Oak Tree

(Doris G. Waters, Ponca City, Kay County, from her pupils.)

1 Coffee grows on a high oak tree
And the river flows with brandy free.
The streets are lined with dollar bills
And the girls are sweet as sugar pills.
Go choose your love to roam with you
Over the dreary ocean blue.

2 Four in the center where they ought of been two, (*Three times.*)
Swing that couple about you.

3 You're all in trouble and you don't know what about, (*Three times.*)
You've done very well, so you better get out.

H

Four in the Middle

(Bertha Matthews, Norman, Cleveland County, from Chickasha, Grady County.)

1 Ladies to the center with a ding dong ding.
Gents to the center and form a little ring.
Tra la la la la la la.
Tra la la la la la la.
Four in the middle and I can't jump Josie,
Four in the middle and I can't get away.
Four in the middle and I can't jump Josie,
Four in the middle and I can't get away.

2 Gents to the center with a ding dong ding.
Ladies to the center and form a little ring, etc.
Four in the middle and I can't jump Josie,
Four in the middle and I can't get away.
Hold my mule while I jump Josie,
Hold my mule while I get away.
Hold my mule while I jump Josie,
Hold my mule while I get away.

I

(No Title)

(Mrs. Ellye S. Kilgo, Ringling, Jefferson County.)

1 I sent my brown jug down town, (*Three times.*)
So early in the morning.

2 It came back with a waltz around, etc.

168

3 Four in the middle and can't dance Josie, (*Three times.*)
   Hail! Oh, Susian Gal!

4 Cow is in the well and can't dance Josie, etc.

5 Pig is in pen and I can't dance Josie, etc.

6 Fiddler gone and I can't dance Josie, etc.

Directions: "This can be played with 4, 8, or even number of 4's. 1. Catch hands and all go around the same way when first stanza is sung. 2. The same, except reverse. 3. 4. 5. 6. Break up in fours and dance the same as in country dance."

J

Green Coffee Grows

(Florette McNeese, Oklahoma City, Oklahoma County, from her pupils.)

1 Green coffee grows on a white oak tree,
   The river flows with brandy-O.
Go choose your love to walk with you,
   Sweet as 'lasses candy-O.

Chorus:
   Four in the middle and you'd better get about, (Three times.)
   Swing those ladies lively.

2 Six in the middle and they keep a-comin' on, etc.

3 When you're married, jump for joy, etc.
   Domino.

Directions: "As the stanza is sung, all circle around a couple in the middle. With the third line, these choose another couple. At the end of the stanza, those in the circle stop and drop hands. As the chorus is sung, the four in the middle swing, right hand to partner, left to neighbor, and back to partner. Sometimes two more are chosen, and the six 'right and left.' The word 'Domino' marks the end. The last couple chosen remain in the middle and the stanza is sung again."

K

Jump Josie

(The same.)

1 We're going down the river,
   We're going down below.
We're going down the river
   To old Shilo.

2 Two in the middle and they can't jump Josie, (*Three times.*)
   Hello, Susie Brown.

169

3 Choose a couple in and then jump Josie, etc.

4 Hold my mules till I jump Josie, etc.

5 Big-foot guy and can't jump Josie, etc.

6 My shoes untied and I can't jump Josie, etc.

7 Get out of the way if you can't jump Josie, etc.

Directions: "As this game was reported, the first stanza has nothing to do with the rest of the game and is undoubtedly a stray bit from another game. Whenever this is sung, it is used as a starting stanza and the couples merely get ready and circle to its rhythm. Then the real game begins. A circle is formed with two couples in the center, who 'right, left, and swing' as the stanzas are being sung. At the last stanza, the first couple rejoins the ring and another is chosen."

Other variants by Boyce Billingsley, Wayne, McClain County; Delphin Delmor Bledsoe, Marlow, Stephens County; Bonnie Mae Close, Oklahoma City, Oklahoma County; J. O. Conner, Shawnee, Pottawatomie County; Ruth Davis, Fort Worth, Texas; Leonard C. Dresser, Lahoma, Garfield County; Alice Flora Hare, Norman, Cleveland County; Viola Harris, Porter, Wagoner County; Mary Haxel, Purcell, McClain County, who played it near Noble, Cleveland County, and Washington, McClain County; Lillian A. Jasper, Roosevelt, Kiowa County; Mrs. T. H. Maness, Oswalt, Love, County; Wallace M. McCown, Emporia, Kansas, from Earl Denton, Norman, Cleveland County; Mark H. McKinsey, Ardmore, Carter County, who played it near Tuttle, Grady County; Geraldine Miller, Norman, Cleveland County; Ruby Pfautsch, Norman, Cleveland County; William Plaster, Meeker, Lincoln County; Thelma Wild Rose, Chickasha, Grady County, from Waurika, Jefferson County; L. E. Russell, Cyril, Caddo County; Joseph Edward Terral, Oklahoma City, Oklahoma County; Mrs. Della I. Young, Cheyenne, Roger Mills County, from J. R. Weatherly, Elk City, Beckham County.

19
COME, ALL YE YOUNG MEN IN YOUR WICKED WAYS
(Hattie Bell Bethea, Marion, South Carolina.)

For British versions, see "Joggle Along," Gomme, 1:285-286; Northall, p. 361.

For American versions, see "Come, all ye young people that's wending your way," Ames (Missouri), *JAFL,* 24:314; "The Baptist Game," Newell, pp. 101-102, and note: "Such is the peculiar title of this amusement in Virginia, where it is said to be enjoyed by pious people who will not dance. There is a row of couples, with an odd player at the head. At the sudden close of the song occurs a grand rush and change of partners." For the change of partners there is usually another couplet and chorus (missing in the version given below); e.g.

> The night is far spent, and the day's coming on,
> So give us your arm, and we'll jog along,
> > You shall be happy, etc.
> > (Newell.)

Cf. also "Old Maids," Backus (Connecticut), *JAFL,* 14:297.

> Come, all ye young men in your wicked ways.
> Come, sow your wild oats in your youthful days,
> And you shall be happy,
> And you shall be happy when you grow old.

20

COME, MY LOVE

Cf. "Come, My Love," Hamilton (Northeast Missouri), *JAFL,* 27:299-300; "Thus the Farmer Sows His Seed," Wolford (Indiana), pp. 94-95.

For the dialogue in A, see CONSOLATION FLOWING FREE.

For "low-ly-low," cf. "Low-Ly-Low," Hamilton, *ibid.,* p. 297 (otherwise unlike B).

For Stanza 1 of B, cf. "O My Laura Lee!" Perrow (North Carolina), *JAFL,* 28:175.

For "buckeye rabbit," cf. "Buck-Eyed Rabbit! Whoopee!", Talley, p. 175.

For B and C, see I'VE BEEN TO THE EAST.

A

(Marguerite M. Durkee, from Mrs. P. R. Durkee, Norman, Cleveland County.)

1 Come go along, my love, with me, (*Three times.*)
  And I'll be good to thee.

2 I am too young, I cannot go, (*Three times.*)
  I cannot leave my mother.

3 You're old enough, you are just right, (*Three times.*)
  I asked your mother last Saturday night.

4 You have lied, you were not there, (*Three times.*)
  And now deny it if you dare.

B
LOW-LY-LOW, *or* COME, MY LOVE

(Beatrice Jennings McMullin, Norman, Cleveland County, brought from Kentucky to Missouri, then to Kay and Grant Counties, on Oklahoma-Kansas border.)

1 Come, my love, and go with me,
    And hear my money jingle.
  If you love me as I love you,
    We'll live no longer single.

Chorus:
  Low-ly, low-ly, low-ly, low, (Three times.)

2 I've been to the East, I've been to the West,
    I've been to the jaybird's altar.
  The prettiest girl I ever knew
    Was sailing o'er the water.

C
(Louise James, Norman, Cleveland County.)

1 Come, my love, and go with me.
    Yes, my love, I'll meet you;
  Meet you down in Tennessee,
    I'll meet you by and by.

2 I've been to the East, I've been to the West,
    I've been to North Carolina.
  Prettiest girl I ever did see
    Was buckeye rabbit's daughter—
  Buckeye rabbit, hoot, hoot,
  Buckeye rabbit's daughter.

21
COME, PHILANDERS
(O. B. Campbell, Medford, Grant County.)

Cf. "Philander's March," Newell, pp. 58-59; "Come, Philander, Be a-Marching," Pound (Nebraska, *Syllabus*), p. 75.
See POLLY, PUT THE KETTLE ON.

1 Come, Philanders,
    Let's be marching,
  All ye true lovers,
    Let's be marching.

Chorus:
  Ring farewell.
    To my love, farewell.
  We are all marching
    Around very well.

2 Choose your true love
    Now or never.
Take her by the hand
    And tell her how you love her.

3 My heart you've gained,
    My hand I'll give you.
One sweet kiss,
    And it's honey, I must leave you.

4 O, my little honey,
    You don't know how I love you.
There's none on this earth
    That I love like I love you.

22

CONSOLATION * FLOWING FREE

Stanza 1 is based on the hymn.† Stanza 3 recalls "I'm Seventeen Come Sunday," Sharp (*One Hundred English Folksongs*), No. 61, pp. 138-140, for Stanzas 1 and 3 of which, cf. "Weevily Wheat," Dudley and Payne (Texas), *PTFS,* 1:17-19, and for Stanza 3, "Toddy O'," Douthitt (Kentucky), p. 31.

Cf. "Consolation Flowing Free," Ames (Missouri), *JAFL,* 24:301-302.
See COME, MY LOVE; KILA MA CRANKY.

A

(Sung by Leondis Brown, Noble, Cleveland County. Additional tune from Professor Kenneth C. Kaufman, Norman, Cleveland County, who played it in Custer County. For the hymn tune, see Jackson, (*White Spirituals in the Southern Uplands*), p. 145.)

* Would be sung "Cancellation flowing free." I had an idea the children had gone that far along in arithmetic. They didn't know consolation, but they did know cancellation.—Professor Kenneth C. Kaufman, Norman, Cleveland County.

† Come and taste along with me
Consolation flowing free.
All that come with a free good will
Make the banquet sweeter still.

Now I go rejoicing home
From the banquet of perfume,
Gleaning manna all the way
Falling from the mouth of God.

(Chester Harley Anderson, Guthrie, Logan County; Louise James, Norman, Cleveland County; Dorothy H. Smith, Norman, Cleveland County.)

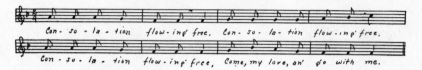

1 Consolation flowing free, (*Three times.*)
Come, my love, an' go with me.

2 Oh, I'm too young, I cannot go, (*Three times.*)
Cannot leave my mother (mamma)-O.

3 You're old enough an' a plenty of good, (*Three times.*)
Leave your mother if you would.

4 Go tell your Maw to hold her tongue, (*Three times.*)
She loved boys when she were (*sic*) young.

5 Tell your Dad to do the same, (*Three times.*)
For he used to play the same old game.

6 Sweet sixteen an' twenty-nine, (*Three times.*)
I'll be yours if you'll be mine

7 Irish potatoes, tops an' all, (*Three times.*)
Kiss her now or not at all.
(*Or:* Kiss her now or wait till fall.)

8 My sweetheart has gone to France, (*Three times.*)
To learn those ladies how to dance.

9 My sweetheart she's comin' home, (*Three times.*)
As sweet as any honeycomb.

("I know a lot of funny ones that I sing just for meanness.")

B

(Audra A. Plumlee, Norman, Cleveland County.)

1 Consolation flowing free, (*Three times.*)
Come, my love, and go with me.

2 Come, my love, and go with me, (*Three times.*)
We'll go back to Tennessee.

3 Oh, I'm too young, I cannot go, (*Three times.*)
Because I love my mamma so.

4 You're old enough and plenty good, (*Three times.*)
You could leave her if you would.

5 Sweet sixteen and twenty-nine, (*Three times.*)
I'll be yours if you'll be mine.

6 Apples fried and apples dried, (*Three times.*)
Kiss her on the other side.

C

(No Title)

(Pauline Goodson, Blackwell, Kay County, from Northern Oklahoma and Southern Kansas.)

1 Consolation flowing free, (*Three times.*)
Come, my honey, and go with me.

Chorus:
No, no, no, I'm too young.
Yes, yes, yes, you're all right.
Ask your ma for Saturday night.

2 Tell your ma to hold her tongue, (*Three times.*)
For she had beaux when she was young.

D

Cream and Peaches

(Lonnie D. Huddleston, Norman, Cleveland County, from his pupils in Adair School, Cleveland County.)

1 Cream and peaches twice a week, (*Three times.*)
Kiss her on the other side [cheek?].

2 Apples fried and apples dried, (*Three times.*)
Kiss her on the other side.

3 Irish potatoes tops and all, (*Three times.*)
Kiss her now or not at all.

4 Consequences flowing free, (*Three times.*)
Come, my love, and go with me.

5 I am too young, I cannot go, (*Three times.*)
Because I love my mother so.

6 Old enough and plenty of good, (*Three times.*)
You could leave her if you would.

7 Sweet sixteen and forty-nine, (*Three times.*)
I'll be yours if you'll be mine.

Variants:

I am too young, I cannot go, (*Three times.*)
For my mother told me so.

You're not too young, you are just right, (*Three times.*)
For I ask your father last Saturday night.

> (Mrs. Bertha Downing, Norman, Cleveland County, who played it in South-
> ern Noble, Northeastern Logan, and Northern Payne Counties.)

You're old enough, that will do.
Twice sixteen makes thirty-two.

If I'm old enough then I will go.
Whether my ma says yes or no.

> (Juanita Curtis, Glencoe, Payne County; Margaret Hudson, Bartlesville,
> Washington County; Virginia R. Nelson, Clinton, Custer County.)

You're not too young, you are just right. (*Three times.*)
Go ask your Maw for Saturday night.

If that be so, why, then we'll go. (*Three times.*)
Whether your Maw says yes or no.

> (Lela L. Conrad, Perry, Noble County.)

You're old enough and plenty of good.
Do my cooking if you would.

> (Alec Gilbreath, Atoka, Atoka County, who played it at Lehigh, Coal
> County.)

'Tween sixteen and ninety-nine, (*Three times.*)
I'll be yours if you'll be mine.

> (Sue Marguerite Patterson, Erick, Beckham County, from Jackson County;
> Logan Earl Hysmith, Wilburton, Latimer County, from Sebastian County,
> Arkansas.)

Ask your mother if you may go, (*Three times.*)
For she had beaux when she was young.

Chorus:
> Consolation flowing free, (*Three times.*)
> Come, my love, and dance with me.

> (Lavelle McDaniel, Norman, Cleveland County, from Opal Poindexter,
> Covington, Garfield County.)

23
DO-SE-DO

(Vera Summers, Snyder, Kiowa County, who played it near McCloud, Pottawatomie
County. Tune from Levi Wilcox, Noble, Cleveland County.)

Cf. "The Virginia Reel," Ball (Idaho), *JAFL,* 44:9-10 (two texts, with
"likeness" for "liking"); "Miss Liking," Gardner (Michigan), *JAFL,*

33:112-113; "Meet Half Way," Piper (Western Iowa, Nebraska), *JAFL,* 28:281-282 (two texts).

For the pattern, see BETSY LARKIN.

Meet half way to your best like-'em, Meet half way to your best like-'em,

Meet half way to your best like-'em, You're the one, my dar-ling'.

1 Meet half way to your best like-em, (*Three times.*)
You are the one, my darling.

2 Right hand around to your best like-em, etc.

3 Left hand around to your best like-em, etc.

4 Both hands around to your best like-em, etc.

5 Docey Do and don't you touch her, etc.

6 Trip her up and down as long as you love her, etc.

Variants:

Meet half way to your best liking, (*Three times.*)
You're the one, my darling.

***

Five dollars if you touch her, (*Three times.*)
For you are my darling.
(Elsie Montgomery, Sunset, Beaver County, from Bessie Oneal, Follett, Texas, who played it at Darrouzett, Texas.)

Do-se-do to your best liking, (*Three times.*)
You're the one, my darling.
(Glenn A. Roe, Oklahoma City, Oklahoma County, from Frederick, Tillman County.)

24

DOWN IN ALABAMA

Cf. "Topsy through the Window," Blair (Kentucky), *JAFL,* 40:96; Piper (Western Nebraska, Western Iowa), *JAFL,* 28:266-267 (two texts); "Old Virginny Never Tire," Van Doren (Eastern Illinois), *JAFL,* 32:492-493; "There Goes Topsy through the Window," Wolford (Indiana), pp. 92-93.

"Jingle at the Window ("Jingle at th' winder tideo") is the title of a song given by Randolph (Ozarks, Missouri), *JAFL,* 42:214-215 (also *The Ozarks,* pp. 156-158). See TIDEO. "I knew it was her by the jingle of the window" occurs in "Down in Jay Bird Town," Wolford (Indiana), pp. 39-40.

"Big white house" occurs in "Four in the Middle," Randolph (Ozarks, Missouri), *JAFL*, 42:213. See COFFEE GROWS ON A WHITE OAK TREE, VIRGINIA.

The tune is a variant of (THE) OLD GRAY MARE.

A

(Sung by Raburn Linton, Mountain Park, Kiowa County.)

Hop, skip, down the wilderness, Down the wilderness, down the wilderness.
Hop, skip, down the wilderness, Down in Alabama.

Hop, skip, down the wilderness,
    Down the wilderness, down the wilderness.
Hop, skip, down the wilderness,
    Down in Alabama.

B

Topsy, *or* Down in Alabama

(Leonard C. Dresser, Lahoma, Garfield County, who played it near Vernon, Garfield County; Cecil Enochs, Drumright, Creek County.)

1 Here comes Topsy through the window,*
    Through the window, through the window.
Here comes Topsy through the window,
    Down in Alabama.†

---

* Here comes Sambo through the windows.
    (Doris G. Waters, Ponca County, Kay County, from her pupils.)

Here comes Topsy through the timber.
    (Rephord Hubert Stevens, Union City, Canadian County.)

Here comes Jumbo through the timber.
    (Sam West, Duke, Jackson County, from Om Earl Hitt.)

Here comes Topsy around the corner.
    (Emma Vilhauer, Norman, Cleveland County.)

Here comes Jumbo round the corner.
    (John Cunningham, Watonga, Blaine County, from his father, who played it at Homestead, Blaine County; Lillie O. Heaton, Watonga, Blaine County.)

† Way down in Alabama.
    (Fanny W. Kelly, Jefferson, Grant County; Evelyn Roach, Shamrock, Texas; Madeline Tarpley, Shamrock, Texas.)

Directions: "Girls and boys form two circles, the girls on the inside and the boys on the outside, facing each other, with extra boys in between who try to beat the other boys to their places as they swing on the third stanza."

2 Nothing was heard but a jingle on the window,
    Jingle on the window, jingle on the window,
Nothing was heard but a jingle on the window,
    Down in Alabama.

3 A great big house and nobody living in it,
    Nobody living in it, nobody living in it.
A great big house and nobody living in it,
    Down in Alabama.

C

TOPSY THROUGH THE WINDOW

(Florette McNeese, Oklahoma City, Oklahoma County, from her pupils.)
1 Here goes Topsy through the window,
    Through the window, through the window.
Here goes Topsy through the window,
    Down in Alabama.

Chorus:
    All promenade with hands on shoulders, etc.

Directions: "In this game all the boys get partners and form a circle with the girls facing the boys, but leaving enough space for the extra boy to march through while singing the stanza. As the chorus begins, the 'Topsy' tries to secure a partner."

D

HERE COMES JUMBO

(Mrs. Bertha Downing, Norman, Cleveland County, who played it in Southern Noble, Northeastern Logan, and Northern Payne Counties.)

1 Here comes Jumbo through the wilderness,
    Through the wilderness, through the wilderness.
Here comes Jumbo through the wilderness,
    All run away.

2 Here comes Jumbo through the canebrakes, etc.

Bound for Alabama.
    (Lillie O. Heaton, Watonga, Blaine County; Lucille Parker, Norman, Cleveland County.)

Bound for Alabam.
    (Emma Vilhauer, Norman, Cleveland County.)

179

E

Here Comes Topsy Through the Bushes

(Cleve Turner, Cheyenne, Roger Mills County.)

1 Here comes Topsy through the bushes, (*Three times.*)
  Skip to my Lou, my darling.

2 Tell it's her by the rattle of the bushes, (*Three times.*)
  Down in Alabama.

Other variants by Orville Nichols, Mountain Park, Kiowa County, from Cordell, Washita County; Naomi Maye Porter, Ringling, Jefferson County, from Glen Ballenbach.

25

DOWN IN SHILOH TOWN

(Alec Gilbreath, Atoka, Atoka County, who played it at Silverton, Texas.)

For "Jawbone Walk," cf. "Walk, Jaw Bone," *Minstrel Songs Old and New,* pp. 210-211; also *The Negro Forget-Me-Not Songster,* pp. 248-250; "De Jawbone Walk," "Lula Gal," Scarborough (Virginia), pp. 103-104; "Brer Rabbit put on Brer Rabbit's hat," Smiley, *JAFL,* 32:358-359; "Jawbone," Talley, p. 12. The jawbone is also mentioned in "Rise, Ole Napper," "Bile dem Cabbage Down," Scarborough (Virginia), pp. 102-103, 125.

1 Way down in Shiloh town, rats come butting them houses down.
  Walking and riding, slipping and sliding.
  Quit your walking, quit your riding,
  Quit your slipping and all go sliding.

2 Ain't going to walk, ain't going to ride,
  Ain't going to slip, ain't going to slide.
  Walking and riding, slipping and sliding,
  [Quit your slipping and all go sliding.]

3 Jawbone walk, jawbone talk,
  Jawbone eat with a knife and fork.
  Quit your walking, quit your riding,
  Quit your slipping [and] all go sliding.

26

DOWN THE RIVER

Based on a minstrel song. See "Down the River — Down the Ohio," *The Negro Forget-Me-Not Songster,* 1:88-89.

Cf. Piper (Western Iowa), *JAFL,* 28:267; Wolford (Indiana), pp. 40-41.

For E, cf. "Come, Love, Come," Finger (*Frontier Ballads*), pp. 165-166.

Oklahoma Texts and Tunes

A

(Sung by Orville Nichols, Mountain Park, Kiowa County, from Cordell, Washita County.)

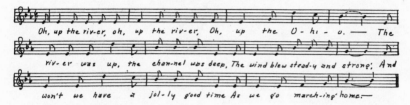

Oh, up the river, oh, up the river,
    Oh, up the O-h-i-o.
The river was up, the channel was deep,
    The wind blew steady and strong.
And won't we have a jolly good time
    As we go marching home.

B

(Mrs. Bertha Downing, Norman, Cleveland County, who played it in Southern Noble, Northeastern Logan, and Northern Payne Counties.)

O down the river, O down the river,
    O down the Ohio.
The river was up, the water was deep,
    The current was steady and strong.
We buffet the waves as we go by,
    As we go marching along.
O down the river, etc.

C

(Elsie Montgomery, Sunset, Beaver County.)

1 Down the river, down the river, down the river we go, (*Three times.*)
    Down the river we flow to the Ohio.

2 The river was wide and the canal was deep,
    And the winds blow sturdy and strong.
We watched the waves sail by
    As we went marching along.

3 Down the river, etc.

D

(No Title)

(Florette McNeese, Oklahoma City, Oklahoma County, from her pupils.)

The "right and left" figure is an especial favorite. The following stanza is one that is sung over and over again as the couples circle and swing:

181

Oh, down the river we go,
Oh, Oh, Oh!
The river is wide and the channel's deep
As we go marching along.

E

(No Title)

(Hattie Bell Bethea, Marion, South Carolina.)

Down in the cane brick (*sic*)
　Close by the mill,
There lived a pretty girl,
　And her name was Nancy Lil.
Come, boys, come, the boat lies low,
　Take you down the Ohio.
Come, boys, come, the boat lies low,
　Take you down the Ohio.

Other variants by Alta Lonnie Hays, Spearman, Texas, who played it at Arch, New Mexico; Verla Summers, Kiowa County, from near Mc-Cloud, Pottawatomie County.

27

EIGHTEEN POUNDS OF MEAT A WEEK

(Florette McNeese, Oklahoma City, Oklahoma County.)

For Stanza 1, cf. "Old Joe Clark," Dudley and Payne (Texas), *PTFS,* 1:32-34.

For Stanza 2, cf. the minstrel song, "Lucy Long," * by T. G. Booth. See Chapple (*Heart Songs*), p. 289; Marsh's *Selection or Singing for the Million,* 1:115-116; White, pp. 449-450. Cf. "Scoldin' Wife," Perrow (Mississippi Negroes), *JAFL,* 28:188; "Ain't I Goin'," Piper (Western Nebraska, from Arkansas), *JAFL,* 28:271-272; "Bile dem Cabbage Down," Scarborough (Virginia), pp. 124-125; "Roving Bachelor," Tolman and Eddy (Indiana), *JAFL,* 35:431-432.

1 Eighteen pounds of meat a week,
　Whiskey here to sell,
How can the boys stay at home
　When the girls all look so well,
　And the girls all look so well?

---

* Oklahoma fragments:
　It took six days to make this earth,
　　That wasn't very long.
　But I think it would have taken seven days
　　To visit Lucy Long.

2 If I had a scolding wife
  I'd whip her as sure as she's born;
I'd take her down to New Orleans,
  And trade her off for corn,
  And trade her off for corn.*

28

GARBER TOWN

See OLD JOE CLARK.

A

Git Along, Mah Cindy

(Sung by Raburn Linton, Mountain Park, Kiowa County.)

Git a long. mah Cin - dy, Mah Cin - dy, I say. —
Git a - long, mah Cin - dy, An' don't for - get the way. —

Chorus:
  Git along, mah Cindy,
    Mah Cindy, I say,
  Git along, mah Cindy,
    An' don't forget the way.

Chorus:
  Oh, rock that cradle, Miss Lucy,
    Miss Lucy, Lucy Long.
  Oh, rock that cradle, Miss Lucy,
    And keep the children warm.
      (Mrs. L. T. Monnett, Norman, Cleveland County.)

Oh! I just come out afore you,
  To sing a little song.
I plays it on de banjo,
  An' dey calls it Lucy Long.

Chorus:
  Oh! take your time, Miss Lucy,
    Take your time, Miss Lucy Long.
  Oh! take your time, Miss Lucy,
    Take your time, Miss Lucy Long.
      (Atlee Garrett, Loco, Stephens County.)

---

* If I had a scolding wife,
  I'd whip her down sho as you're born.
I'd take her down to New Orleans
  And trade her off for corn.
    (Hattie Bell Bethea, Marion, South Carolina.)

1 Rabbit stole a punkin,
   It started down to town.
Heard the hounds a-comin',
   It throwed the punkin down.

Chorus:
   Hurry up, mah Cindy, etc.

2 I wish't I had a billy goat,
   A stall to put him in.
(I'd) Take him out an' feed him,
   An' put him in again.

Chorus:
   Git along, mah Cindy, etç.

B

(Pauline Goodson, Blackwell, Kay County, from Northern Oklahoma and
Southern Kansas.)

1 There is a house in Garber town
   Sixteen stories high,
And every story * in that house
   Is filled with pumpkin pie.

Chorus:
   Run away home, run away home,
   Run away home, I say;
   Run away home, my little blue eyes,†
   And don't forget the way.

2 A rabbit ‡ stole a pumpkin,
   And started for the town.
He heard them darkies yelling
   And dropped the pumpkin down.

29

GENTS TO THE CENTER

(Sung by Charlie Carr, Noble, Cleveland County, and Professor Kenneth C. Kaufman,
Norman, Cleveland County, who played it in Eastern Custer County.)

Related to the square dance. See Chapter III.
Cf. "Arkansas Style," Ball (Idaho), *JAFL,* 44:19-20; Hamilton (Northeast Missouri), *JAFL,* 27:299; "St. Patrick's Day," Piper, *JAFL,* 28:286-287; Wilson (Ozarks), pp. 77-78.
Tune: "The Irish Washerwoman."

* Window (Jessie Lee Bryant, Billings, Noble County).
† Little brown eyes (the same).
‡ Johnnie (the same).

184

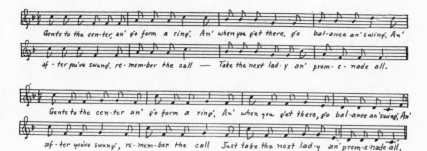

1 Gents to the center, an' go form a ring,*
An' when you get there, go balance an' swing,
An' after you've swung, remember the call —
(Just) Take the next lady an' promenade all,
Promenade, promenade, promenade all,
Take the next lady an' promenade all.

2 Ladies to the center, etc.

Other variants by Ethel Rose Baird, Bixby, Tulsa County; Clifford
Chandler, Crescent, Logan County; Anita Shaw, Thomas, Custer County;
Emma Vilhauer, Norman, Cleveland County.

30

GETTING MARRIED

For Stanza 1, cf. "Sailing at High Tide," Newell (Connecticut), pp.
238-239.

For Stanza 2 and variants (as in OATS, PEAS, BEANS, AND
BARLEY GROWS), cf. "Marriage by the Knife," Babcock (Washington,
D. C.), *American Anthropologist*, 1:267-268; "Marriage," Backus (Con-
necticut), *JAFL*, 14:297-298; "Merry-Ma-Tansa," Gomme, 1:371-372;
"Oats and Beans and Barley," *idem*, 2:1-13; "Sally Water," *idem*, 2:151-167
(especially 153); "Three Old Bachelors," *idem*, 2:282; "Oats, Pease, Beans,
and Barley Grows," Newell, pp. 80-84; "Oats, Peas, Beans, and Barley,"
Piper (Illinois), *JAFL*, 28:273; "King William Was King James's Son,"
Van Doren (Eastern Illinois), 32:493-494.

---

* Often prefaced by a couplet reminiscent of dances held in saloons:
  Gents to the center and back to the bar,
  Ladies to the center and form in a star.
  (Professor Kenneth C. Kaufman; William Plaster, Meeker, Lincoln County.)

Cf. "Choose Your Mate," Owens (Texas), *Southwest Review,* pp. 170-171; "In This Ring Comes a Lady," Van Doren (Eastern Illinois), *JAFL,* 32:495.

See OATS, PEAS, BEANS, AND BARLEY GROWS.

A

(Leonard C. Dresser, Lahoma, Garfield County, who played it near Vernon, Garfield County.)

1 In this ring is a lady fair,
　Sky-blue eyes and sunny hair,
　Rosy cheeks and a dimpled chin,
　Please consider: won't you step in?

2 Now you're married and you must obey,
　You must be careful what you say,
　Live together all your life,
　And I'll pronounce you man and wife.

3 In this ring is a gentleman fair,
　Sky-blue eyes and sunny hair,
　Rosy cheeks and a dimpled chin,
　Please consider, won't you step in?

4 Now you're married and you must obey,
　You must be careful what you say.
　Live together all your life,
　And I'll pronounce you man and wife.

B

(No Title)

(Florette McNeese, Oklahoma City, Oklahoma County, from her pupils.)
Round and round all in this ring,
Choose your true love while I sing.
Choose the one that you profess
To be the one that you love best.
Now you're married, I wish you joy,
You're my son, a great big boy;
You're my son, and daughter too,
Kiss her twice if once won't do.

31

GETTING UPSTAIRS

Based on a minstrel song. See "Sich a Gittin Upstairs," *The Negro Forget-Me-Not Songster,* 1:242-244; 2:167-168.

Cf. "Getting Upstairs," Wolford (Indiana), pp. 44-45 (four texts). Requested by Payne (Texas), *PTFS,* 1:35-38.

The tune of A is a variant of "The Irish Washerwoman."

A

(Sung by Orville Nichols, Mountain Park, Kiowa County, from Cordell, Washita County.)

Such a gittin' upstairs
  I never did see.
Such a gittin' upstairs
  It don't suit me.

B

(The same.)

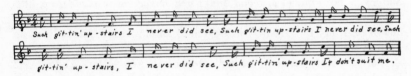

Such gittin' upstairs
  I never did see,
Such gittin' upstairs
  I never did see,
Such gittin' upstairs
  I never did see,
Such gittin' upstairs
  It don't suit me.

C

(Fanny W. Kelly, Jefferson, Grant County.)

1 First gent out,
  Swing that lady with a right hand about,
  Partner by the left as you come around,
  Lady in the center and you'll all run around.

2 Such a kitten (*sic*) upstairs,
  Well, I never did see.
Such a kitten upstairs,
  Well she don't suit me.

D

(Ethel Rose Baird, Bixby, Tulsa County.)

1 I got up in the morning,
  The rain was pouring down.
I saddled up old Grady
  And bound for —— [*name*] town.

187

2 Honor to your right,
   Honor to your left,
   Swing your next partner
   And promenade to your left.

3 Such getting upstairs
   I never did see.
   Such getting upstairs
   Don't suit me.

32

THE GIRL I LEFT BEHIND ME

Based on the song. See Chappell (*Popular Music of the Olden Time*), pp. 172-173 (where the tune is given as that of an English march of the eighteenth century and the date of the words as 1759); Chapple (*Heart Songs*), p. 66; Ford (*Vagabond Songs and Ballads of Scotland*), pp. 101-104 (two texts); Lomax (*Cowboy Songs*), pp. 342-343; Spaeth (*Read 'Em and Weep*), pp. 16-17 (where it is given as an old Irish folk-tune, with an English version, "Brighton Camp," and the words dated about 1770).

For play-party versions, see Ball (Idaho), *JAFL,* 44:15; "Toddy, O'," Douthitt (Kentucky), p. 31 (one stanza); Dudley and Payne (Texas), *PTFS,* 1:28-29; "Swing the Girls," *ibid.,* pp. 24-25; Gardner (Michigan), *JAFL,* 33:99-100; Hamilton (Northeast Missouri), *JAFL,* 27:297; "The Gal I Left Behind Me," Lomax (Texas), *American Ballads and Folk Songs,* pp. 280-281; Piper (Western Nebraska, Iowa), *JAFL,* 28:286 (two texts); Randolph (Ozarks, Missouri), *JAFL,* 42:230-231; Wolford (Indiana), pp. 46-47.

For "If ever I travel this road again," cf. "Old Joe Clark," Dudley and Payne (Texas), *PTFS,* 1:32-34; "Shady Grove," Perrow (Kentucky), *JAFL,* 28:182-183; "The Jaybird Died," *idem* (Mississippi), *JAFL,* 26:133.

A

(Sung by Charlie Carr, Noble, Cleveland County.)

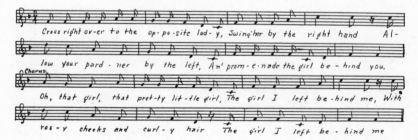

Cross right ov-er to the op-po-site lad-y, Swing her by the right hand Allow your pard-ner by the left, An' prom-e-nade the girl be-hind you.
Oh, that girl, that pret-ty lit-tle girl, The girl I left be-hind me, With
ros-y cheeks and curl-y hair The girl I left be-hind me

1 Cross right over to the opposite lady,
    Swing her by the right hand.
Allow your pardner by the left,
    An' promenade the girl behind you.

Chorus:
    Oh, that girl, that pretty little girl,
      The girl I left behind me,
    With rosy cheeks and curly hair,
      The girl I left behind me.

2 Same old boy an' a different lady, etc.

3 I'll travel that road, I'll travel it again,
    Just as long as those tears don't blind me,
Till I get back with a rat in a sack
    And the girl I left behind me.

B

PROMENADE THE GIRL BEHIND YOU

(Gerald Bond, Oklahoma City, Oklahoma County, who played it at Chickasha, Grady County; Glenn A. Roe, Oklahoma City, Oklahoma County, who played it at Frederick, Tillman County.)

1 Same old boy and brand new girl,
    Swing her by the right hand,
Now your partner by the left,
    And promenade the girl behind you.

Chorus:
    Oh, that girl, that pretty little girl,
      That girl I left behind me.
    The more I drink, the less I think
      Of the girl I left behind me.

2 If ever I travel this road again,
    That is, if they don't blind me,
I'll stop and see that pretty little girl,
    The girl I left behind me.

C

(Walter Myers Gable, Norman, Cleveland County.)

1 The more I drink, the less I think,
    Of the girl I left behind me,
With rosy cheeks and curly hair,
    That girl I left behind me.

Chorus:
> *Oh, that girl, that pretty little girl,*
> *That girl I left behind me,*
> *With rosy cheeks and curly hair,*
> *That girl I left behind me.*

2 You may work the horned cow,
   And I will work the muley,
But give me back my fifteen cents,
   And I'll go home to July.

D

(Bernice Penn, Cordell, Washita County.)

1 If ever I go that road again
   And the Boston boys don't find me,
I'm going to see that pretty iittle girl,
   The girl I left behind me.

Chorus:
> *Oh, that girl, pretty little girl,*
> *The girl I left behind me.*
> *With rosy cheeks and curly hair,*
> *The girl I left behind me.*

2 She jumped in bed, covered up her head,
   And kicked out the lights behind her.
Oh, that girl, that pretty little girl,
   The girl I left behind me.

E

DOWN IN NEW ORLEANS

(Winnifred Spencer, Walters, Cotton County.)

1 I went down to New Orleans,
   I landed there on Sunday;
Put me in the calaboose,
   And I got drunk on Monday.
Balance on the corner,
   Swing that girl behind you.
Swing your partner by the left,
   Promenade the girl behind you.

Chorus:
> *Oh, that girl, that pretty little girl,*
> *Oh, that girl I left behind me.*
> *I'll weep and sigh till the day I die*
> *For the girl I left behind me.*

190

F

(Gene Michael, Marietta, Love County.)

1 Swing the opposite lady,
   Swing her by the right hand.
Swing your partner by the left.
   Promenade the girl behind you.

2 Left her setting in a rocking-chair.
   I thought those tears would blind me.
I'll never forget the girl I left,
   The one I left behind me.

3 If you ever come to town,
   I'll tell you where to find me.
I think I'll stop and stay all night
   With the girl I left behind me.

Variants:

That girl, that girl, that pretty little girl,
   The girl I left behind me.
The less I drink, the more I think,
   That girl I left behind me.
      (Clifford Chandler, Crescent, Logan County.)

Oh, that girl, that pretty little girl,
   The girl I left behind me.
Dressed in blue with a buckle on her shoe,
   The girl I left behind me.
      (Faneta Fitchett, Billings, Noble County.)

Oh, where's that girl, that pretty little girl,
   The girl I left behind me?
But the prettiest girl that ever I saw
   Is the girl I got beside me.
      (Catherine Harris, Antlers, Pushmataha County, from Mrs.Bonnie G. Harris.)

That gal, that gal, that pretty little gal,
   That gal I left behind me.
She's pretty in the face and little round the waist,
   That gal I left behind me.
      (Professor Kenneth C. Kaufman, Norman, Cleveland County, who played
      it in Eastern Custer County.)

If ever I travel that road again,
    I'll stop and see my darling.
I'll stop and see that pretty little girl,
    The girl I left behind me.
        (Carl West, Perico, Texas.)

If ever I travel that road again,
    I'll ride my bald-faced pony.
I'll stop and see the pretty little girl,
    The girl I left behind me.
        (Audra A. Plumlee, Norman, Cleveland County.)

Oh, that gal, that pretty little gal,
    That gal I left behind me.
Shake the door and rock the floor,
    Oh, how it does remind me.
        (Sam West, Duke, Jackson County.)

Other variants by Bonnie Mae Close, Oklahoma City, Oklahoma County; Fanny Kelley, Jefferson, Grant County; Raburn Linton, Mountain Park, Kiowa County; Madeline Tarpley, Shamrock, Texas; Thelma Wild Rose, Chickasha, Grady County, from Waurika, Stephens County.

33

GOING DOWN THE RIVER
(Clarence W. Anthony, Norman, Cleveland County.)

See COFFEE GROWS ON A WHITE OAK TREE.

Going down the river,
    Going down below,
Going down the river,
    Going down to ole Shiloh.

Directions: "Played by an equal number of boys and girls. The boys choose their partners, and every one makes a ring by holding hands. Each boy has his partner on his right. When the music starts, each boy swings the girl on his right, and every one dances around in a circle at the same time singing. At the end of each singing the boys swing their partners to the left and form a ring. Then the singing is started again, and the boys again swing the girl on the right and dance until the end of the stanza. The singing and dancing are repeated until the boys get to the partners they started with."

192

34

GOING DOWN TO ROWSER

Cf. "We'll All Go Down to Rowser," Ames (Missouri), *JAFL,* 24: 297-298; "Rowser's," Ball (Idaho), *JAFL,* 44:14-15; "Rouser," Douthitt (Kentucky), p. 33; "Rouser," Dudley and Payne (Texas), *PTFS,* 1:12; "Rowser's," Gardner (Michigan), *JAFL,* 33:122; "Rowser's," Hamilton (Northeast Missouri), *JAFL,* 27:290; "We're Marching Down to Rauser's" ("evidently a German saloon-keeper who kept 'good beer'"), Miller, p. 31 (listed); "Pig in the Parlor," Pound (Iowa, *American Ballads and Songs*), p. 237; "To Rowser's" Pound (Nebraska, *Syllabus*), p. 71; "We'll All Go Down to Rowser's," Randolph (Ozarks, Missouri), *JAFL,* 42:217-218 (also *The Ozarks,* pp. 160-161); "To Rowser's," Shearin and Combs (Kentucky), p. 39 (listed); "Going Down to Rousie's," Van Doren (Eastern Illinois), *JAFL,* 32:492; "All Go Down to Rowser's," Wolford (Indiana), pp. 22-23.

To the tune of WE WON'T GO HOME TILL MORNING.
See RAILROAD (AND) STEAMBOAT.

A

We'll All Go Down to Rowser's

(Audra A. Plumlee, Norman, Cleveland County, from Northwest Arkansas.)

1 We'll all go down to Rowser's,
   Rowser's, Rowser's,
   We'll all go down to Rowser's
   To get some Irish stew.

2 Oh, the duck flew over the ocean,
   The ocean, the ocean,
   Oh, the duck flew over the ocean
   To see what he could see.

3 We'll all go down to Rowser's,
   Rowser's, Rowser's,
   We'll all go down to Rowser's
   To get a bottle of beer.

4 Right and left to Rowser's,
   Rowser's, Rowser's
   Right and left to Rowser's
   To get a glass of beer.

5 Never mind the old folks,
   The old folks, the old folks,
Never mind the old folks,
   The young ones, they don't care.

B

WE'LL ALL GO DOWN TO ROWSER'S

(Mary Haxel, Purcell, McClain, County, who played it at Noble, Cleveland County, and Washington, McClain County.)

1 We'll all go down to Rowser's,
   To Rowser's, to Rowser's.
We'll all go down to Rowser's
   To get some good ol' beer.

Chorus:
   Rowser he's a jolly boy,
   A jolly boy, a jolly boy.
   Rowser he's a jolly boy,
   We'll have a jolly time.

2 We'll all go down to Lexington,
   To Lexington, to Lexington.
We'll all go down to Lexington
   To measure up some barley.

C

(No Title)

(Tephia Folsom, Atoka, Atoka County, from Pat Lowry, Atoka County.)
1 We'll all go down to Rowsey's, (*Three times.*)
   To get some lager beer.

2 Then we'll all get boosy, (*Three times.*)
   As we are going home.

D

GOING DOWN TO ROWSER

(Beatrice Jennings McMullin, Norman, Cleveland County, from Kentucky to Missouri then to Kay and Grant Counties, on Oklahoma-Kansas border.)

1 We're going down to Rowser, (*Three times.*)
(*Couples catch hold of hands and march in circle.*)

2 Oh, where they keep sweet beer, (*Three times.*)
(*Stop, and couples rock arms to and fro.*)

194

3 Oh, boys, you'd better be drowned (*Three times.*)
    Than fall in love with me.
  (*Swing and promenade.*)

E
Four Go Down to Rowser
(Lillian A. Jasper, Roosevelt, Kiowa County.)

1 Four go down to Rowser,
    Rowser, Rowser.
Four go down to Rowser
    To get a log of beer.

Chorus:
  Railroad, steamboat, river, and canal,
  I lost my true love down the raging canal.
  Oh, she's gone, gone, gone,
  Oh, she's gone, gone, gone,
  Down the raging canal.

2 Six go down to Rowser, etc.

3 Eight go down to Rowser, etc.

F
Going Down to Rouser
(William Plaster, Meeker, Lincoln County.)

1 Four hands down to Rouser,
    To Rouser, to Rouser,
Four hands down to Rouser
    To get a keg of beer.
They won't be back until morning,
    Morning, morning.
They won't be back until morning,
    Just before daylight.

Chorus:
  Railroad, steamboat, railroad engineer.
  Lost my true love on that raging canal.
  Oh, she's gone, gone, gone,
  Let her go, go, go,
  Let her go to that land, fare-ye-well.

2 Six hands down to Rouser, etc.

3 Eight hands down to Rouser, etc.

4 Never mind the ol' folks.
  Ol' folks, ol' folks.
Never mind the ol' folks
  For they don't care any more.

G

Down to Rowsers

(Florette McNeese, Oklahoma City, Oklahoma County, from her pupils.)

1 We'll all go down to Rowsers,
    To Rowsers, to Rowsers,
  We'll all go down to Rowsers
    Because he is so gay. (*Three times.*)
  We'll all go down to Rowsers
    Because he is so gay.

2 We'll all go down to Rowsers,
  All go down to Rowsers,
  All go down to Rowsers,
    To get some lager beer,
    Sweet lager beer, good lager beer.
  We'll all go down to Rowsers
    To get some lager beer.

3 Oh, Russel keeps the best, sir,
  Russel keeps the best, sir,
  Russel keeps the best, sir,
    The best of lager beer,
    Sweet lager beer, good lager beer.
  Russel keeps the best, sir,
    The best of lager beer.

4 We'll never mind the old folks,
    The old folks, the old folks,
  We'll never mind the old folks,
    For they're away from home, (*Three times.*)
  We'll never mind the old folks,
    For they're away from home.

H

(The same.)

1 Two round two to rouse her,
    To rous'er, to rous'er,
  Two round two to rouse her,
    To get a glass of beer.

196

Round the gent to rouse him,
  To rouse him, to rouse him,
Round the lady to rouse her,
  To get a glass of beer.
Four hands up to rouse her,
  To rouse her, to rouse her,
Four hands up to rouse her,
  To get a glass of beer.

Chorus:
  Right and left to Rowsers,
    To Rowsers, to Rowsers,
  Right and left to Rowsers,
    To get a glass of beer.

Directions: "The participants form a circle and drop hands. One couple stands out from the others. The leader and his partner skip around this isolated couple, first around the boy, then around the girl, as the song directs. The leader and his partner then take hands with the isolated couple, making four in the ring. These 'right and left' as the chorus is sung. Another couple steps aside and the four now go around 'to rowser'."

Other variants by Delphin Delmor Bledsoe, Marlow, Stephens County; Helen A. Cook, Norman, Cleveland County, from Indian Territory; Dr. E. E. Dale, Norman, Cleveland County; Lucy I. Pitts, Oklahoma City, Oklahoma County, from Middle Tennessee (with "Rosea" for "Rowser"); J. E. Terral, Oklahoma City, Oklahoma County; Sam West, Duke, Jackson County, from Dorothy Edwards, Jackson County.

35

GOLDEN SLIPPERS

(Catherine Harris. Antlers, Pushmataha County, from A. A. Dilbeck, Miller, Pushmataha County, who played it in Arkansas.)

The refrain is derived from the minstrel song. See "Oh! Dem Golden Slippers" (words and music by James A. Bland), *Good Old-Time Songs,* 1:68; *Minstrel Songs Old and New,* pp. 195-197.

The original is more nearly preserved in "Dem Golden Slippers," Wolford (Indiana), pp. 38-39. The chorus appears in "Raccoon Up in de 'Simmon Tree," Scarborough, p. 172; and "With (the) golden slippers on" occurs in "Four Hands Round in the Euchre Ring," Wedgwood (Southwestern Nebraska, Southern Iowa, from Missouri), *JAFL,* 25:273; "Cuckoo Waltz," Wolford (Indiana), pp. 36-37; "Down to New Orleans," *idem,* p. 41.

See OLD JOE CLARK, SUSIE BROWN.

1 Round up four, my darling girl,
    Round up four, I'm gone,
  Round up four, my darling girl,
    Golden slippers on.

2 Right and left, my darling girl.
    Right and left, I'm gone.
  Right and left, my darling girl.
    Golden slippers on.
  (*This can be repeated up to twenty, taking in two each time.*)

36

GOOD OLD CIDER WINE

(Mrs. T. H. Maness, Oswalt, Love County.)

1 Lead her up and down the valley on that good old cider wine.
  Lead her up and down the valley on that good old cider wine.

2 Oh, wouldn't you like to have some of that good old cider wine?
  Oh, wouldn't you like to have some of that good old cider wine?

37

GOT A LITTLE HOME TO GO TO

(Audra A. Plumlee, Norman, Cleveland County.)

For Stanza 1, see OLD JOE CLARK.

For Stanza 2, cf. "When I Was a Little Boy," Halliwell (*The Nursery Rhymes of England*), pp. 135-137; Perrow (Indiana), *JAFL,* 28:184; Talley, p. 168.

For Stanza 3, see LIZA JANE.

1 Wish I was an apple,
    Hanging on a tree.
  Some pretty little girl come along
    And take a bite of me.

Chorus:
  Home an' a home,
  Home an' a home,
  I've got a little home to go to.

2 I can wash the dishes,
    I can sweep the floor,
  I can kiss some pretty little boy
    Behind the parlor door.

3 Went upon the mountain,
    Gave my horn a blow,

Thought I heard my sweetheart say:
"Don't come here any mo'."

38

GRANGER

Adapted from the hymn. See "I Want to Be an Angel," Pound (Nebraska, *Syllabus*), p. 54:

I want to be an angel, and with the angels stand,
A crown upon my forehead, a harp within my hand.

Aldrich, in *The Story of a Bad Boy* (pp. 7-8), refers to the hymn as follows: "I didn't want to be an angel and with the angels stand. . . . "

Cf. Piper (Western Iowa), *JAFL*, 28:283; "I Want to Be a Cowboy," Pound (Nebraska, *Syllabus*), p. 22 (also *American Ballads and Songs*, p. 173).

A

Granger Boy

(Sung by Leondis Brown, Noble, Cleveland County.)

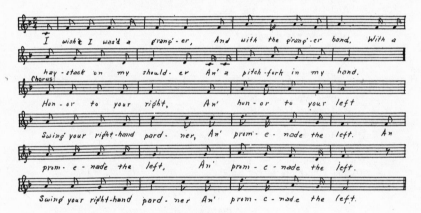

1 I wish't I was'd a granger,
    And with the granger band,
  With a haystack on my shoulder
    An' a pitchfork in my hand.

("It's supposed to be sung sorta slow—not too fast.")

Chorus:
  Honor to your right,
    An' honor to your left.
  Swing your right-hand pardner,
    An' promenade the left. (Three times.)
  Swing your right-hand pardner
    An' promenade the left.

199

2 I wish't I was'd a cowboy,
    An' with the cowboy band,
With a lasso on my shoulder
    An' a six-shooter in my hand.

3 I wish't I was'd a schoolboy,
    An' with the schoolboy band,
With a book satchel on my shoulder
    An' a pencil in my hand.

4 I wish't I was'd a preacher,
    An' with the preacher band,
With a church-house on my shoulder
    An' a bible in my hand.

B

I Long to Be a Granger

(Frances T. Henderson, Fort Cobb, Caddo County, from New Mexico.)

1 I got up in the morning
    And I looked up in the sky,
And I saw two little angels,
    And how was that for I?

Chorus:
    Honor to your pardner,
      Also on the corner.
    Swing your right hand lady
    And promenade the left.

2 I long to be an angel
    And with the angels stand,
With a crown upon my forehead
    And a pitchfork in my hand.

C

Granger

(Lillie O. Heaton, Watonga, Blaine County.)

1 Oh, I long to be a granger
    And live in granger land,
With a haystack on my shoulder
    And a pitchfork in my hand.

Chorus:
    Honors to your right,
      Honors to your left.
    Swing your right hand pardner
    And promenade the left.

D

I'd Love to Be a Granger

(Erma Malthy, Billings, Noble County.)

1 I'd love to be a granger;
    A granger, a granger;
    I'd love to be a granger
    And join the granger band.

Chorus:
    All promenade,
        All promenade.
    Go left unto your pardner
        And all promenade.

2 With a haystack on my shoulder,
    My shoulder, my shoulder;
    With a haystack on my shoulder
    And a pitchfork in my hand.

E

(No Title)

(Raymond Hugh Guthrie, Wakita, Grant County.)

1 I wish I was a cowboy,
    A cowboy I would stand,
    With a lariat on my shoulder
    And a six-gun in my hand.

Chorus:
    Honor to your right,
        And honor to your left.
    Swing your right hand partner,
        And promenade to the left.

F

I Want to Be a Something

(Creed Bogan, Duncan, Stephens County, who played it near Lawton, Comanche
County.)

1 I want to be a something
    And with the somethings stand,
    With something on my shoulder
    And something in my hand.

Chorus:
    It's honor to your right hand,
        It's honor to your left.
    So swing your right hand pardner
        And promenade your left.

201

2 I want to be a cowboy
    And with the cowboys stand,
With a saddle on my shoulder
    And a bridle in my hand.

3 I want to be a preacher
    And with the preachers stand,
With a church-house on my shoulder
    And a bible in my hand.

4 I want to be a farmer
    And with the farmers stand,
With a haystack on my shoulder
    And a pitchfork in my hand.

5 I want to be a hobo
    And with the hoboes stand,
With a knapsack on my shoulder
    And a bundle in my hand.

6 I want to be a soldier
    And with the soldiers stand,
With a rifle on my shoulder
    And a pistol in my hand.

7 I want to be a sailor
    And with the sailors stand,
With a steamboat on my shoulder
    And a compass in my hand.

8 I want to be a rich man
    And with the rich men stand
With a money-bag on my shoulder
    And a coin in my hand.

9 I want to be a fireman
    And with the firemen stand,
With a ladder on my shoulder
    And a fire-hose in my hand.

Directions: "The song has about forty verses and the game is played until every one is tired. At the beginning every one forms a ring with a boy and girl alternating. Every one helps sing the song. When they come to the chorus, the boy looks first to the right and bows, then to the left. Then he swings his right-hand pardner and promenades his left."

G

(Mrs. Mary Axelson, Norman, Cleveland County.)

Oh, I want to see an Ozark,
  And on an Ozark stand,
With a notebook in my pocket
  And a kodak in my hand.

Other variants by Leonard C. Dresser, Lahoma, Garfield County, who played it near Vernon, Garfield County; Mary Haxel, Purcell, McClain County, who played it at Noble, Cleveland County, and Washington, Mc-Clain County; Dorothy Long, Billings, Noble County, from her pupils; Rephord Hubert Stevens, Union City, Canadian County; Ralph W. Winstead, Forgan, Beaver County; Doris G. Waters, Ponca City, Kay County, from her pupils; Mrs. Della I. Young, Cheyenne, Roger Mills County, from Vashti Young and J. R. Weatherly, Elk City, Beckham County.

39

GREEN LEAF

For "Went to Mr. Johnston," cf. "Rocking Chair," Babcock (Washington, D. C.), *American Anthropologist,* 1:250-251.

Cf. "Green Leaves," Dudley and Payne (Texas), *PTFS,* 1:25-26 (like B); Wolford (Indiana), pp. 49-50 (dissimilar).

A

(Winnifred Spencer, Walters, Cotton County, from Jefferson, Marion County, Texas.)

Green leaf, green leaf, yellow and brown,
King goes up and the king goes down.
Went to Mr. Johnston to borrow his knife.
There sat Mr. Johnston a-courting his wife.

B

(Martin Odom, Checotah, McIntosh County.)

The green leaf, the green leaf that grows on the vine.
Go choose you a pardner the fairest you can find.
Gonna get married, joy, joy, joy, it's bound to be.
Gonna get married, joy, joy, joy has come at last.

40

HAVE TWO PRISONERS HERE IN JAIL

(Kathryn C. Nicolett, Bache, Pittsburg County.)

For "Yankee dime," cf. Perrow (Mississippi), *JAFL,* 28:181.
1 Have two prisoners here in jail, (*Three times.*)
  Rock-a-bye, ladies, turn, turn, turn.
  Rock-a-bye, ladies, turn.

2 Robbed a house and stole the girl, etc.

3 Yankee dime will set you free, etc.

(*Repeat, with four, six, eight, and ten prisoners.*)

41

HAY-O-MY-LUCY-O

(Beatrice Jennings McMullin, Norman, Cleveland County, brought from Kentucky to Missouri, then to Kay and Grant Counties, on Oklahoma-Kansas border.)

Cf. "Sunday Night," Gomme, 2:221-222 (two texts); "Hay-o-My-Lucy-o," Wolford (Indiana), pp. 51-52 (two texts).

1 (*Marching around.*)
Hay-O-my-Lucy-O, hay-O-my-Lucy-O,
  My darling, darling Lucy-O,
I'd give this world and all I know
  To turn and swing my Lucy-O.

Chorus:
  (*Promenade.*)
  Lucy-O, Lucy-O,
  Lucy-O, Lucy-O.

Variants:
To break and swing my (darling) Lucy-O.
  (Lillian A. Jasper, Roosevelt, Kiowa County; Geraldine Miller, Norman, Cleveland County.)

If I could swing my Mandy-O.
  (Professor Kenneth C. Kaufman, Norman, Cleveland County, who played it in Caddo and Eastern Custer Counties.)

42

HEEL AND TOE POLKA

Cf. Piper (Western Nebraska, Western Iowa), *JAFL,* 28:280-281 (two texts). Requested by Payne (Texas), *PTFS,* 1:35-38.

For "bounce around," cf. "Bounce Around," Ames (Missouri), *JAFL,* 24:296-297.

See KILA MA CRANKY.

A

(Margaret Hudson, Bartlesville, Washington County; Virginia R. Nelson, Clinton, Custer County.)

Heel and toe, we always go,
  We always go together,
Rain or shine, sleet or snow,
  No matter what's the weather.

B

(Dorothy A. Smith, Norman, Cleveland County.)

Heel and toe and a polka-O,
Heel and toe and a polka-O,
Heel and toe and a polka-O,
Heel and toe and away we go.

C

(Mary Coffman, Geary, Blaine County, from Canadian County.)

Heel and toe the way we go,
    Can't you dance a polka-O?
Heel and toe the way we go,
    Can't you dance a polka-O?

D

Bounce Around

(Walter L. Payne, Hobart, Kiowa County.)

Pick her up and lay her down,
But don't you touch her, bounce around.

First the heel and then the toe,
That's the way the poker (*sic*) goes.
Heel, toe, and a one, two, three,
Heel, toe, and a one, two, three.

E

Dancing the Poker

(Harry L. Deupree, Oklahoma City, Oklaohma County, from Nebraska, Iowa, and Missouri.)

See me dance the poker,
    See me cover the ground,
See my coat tail flying,
    As I go dancing round.

Other variants by Juanita Curtis, Glencoe, Payne County; Louise James, Norman, Cleveland County; Mary Virginia Maloy, Norman, Cleveland County; Bertha Matthews, Norman, Cleveland County.

43

HOG DROVERS

Cf. "The Nine Daughters," Duncan, *Folk-Lore,* 5:190, an Irish game played at wakes, which contains the stanza:

"A fig for your daughter, and a fig for yourself,
    For three-halfpence more I'd get a far better wife."

It opens thus: "Two masters having been appointed, nine men are sent out and brought in singly each having chosen a trade" (such as that of tailor), and closes with the following forfeit which seems to be the high point of the game: "The father is then persuaded to give him one of his daughters, but asks what fortune would be wanted with her. Finally he insists on giving her a good fortune, but says he cannot pay it all at once, and asks in how many 'gales' the young man will have it, always endeavouring to fix the gales at a high number. This having been settled the other trades follow. As a conclusion, each one is hoisted on the back of one of the masters, and receives for each gale of his fortune a prick with a 'pound' pin, to the amusement, doubtless, of the company."

Cf. also "Three Sailors," Gomme, 2:282-289 (six texts), in which occurs the request:

> "Can we have a lodging here, here, here?
> Can we have a lodging here?"

Among occupations rejected in favor of kings are sailors and soldiers, in the first variant, and in other variants, tinkers and soldiers; sweeps and bakers; tailors, sailors, and blacksmiths. "Three Sailors" is also given by Walter (*Old English Singing Games*), pp. 22-23.

For American versions, see "Three Kings," Babcock (Washington, D. C.), *American Anthropologist*, 1:259-260; "Hog Drovers (Hog Rovers)," Dudley and Payne (Texas), *PTFS*, 1:15-16; "Two Wagoners," Gardner (Michigan), *JAFL*, 33:131; Hogue (*Back Yonder*), pp. 87-88; Hudson (Mississippi), *JAFL*, 39:191-193 (two texts; also *Specimens*, pp. 125-126); "Swine Herders," Newell (two texts, North Carolina), pp. 232-234; "Three Kings" (two texts, West Virginia, Washington, D. C.), *idem*, pp. 46-47, 234-236.

See SISTER PHOEBE.

A

(Sung by Levi Wilcox, Noble, Cleveland County.)

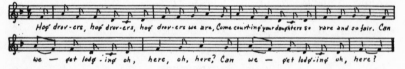

Hog drovers, hog drovers, hog drovers we are,
Come courting your daughters so rare and so fair.
Can we get lodging oh, here, oh, here?
Can we get lodging oh, here?
(Continues like B.)

206

B

(Florette McNeese, Oklahoma City, Oklahoma County, from her pupils.)

1 Hog drovers, hog drovers, hog drovers we are,
   Come courting your daughters so rare and so fair.
   Can we get lodging here, oh, here?
   Can we get lodging here.

2 This is my daughter that sets by my side,
   And none of you hog drovers can have her for a bride,
   And you can't get lodging here, oh, here;
   You can't get lodging here.

3 Don't care for you daughter, much less for yourself.
   I'll bet you five dollars we better ourselves,
   And we don't want lodging here, oh, here;
   We don't want lodging here.

4 John Smith can get her for a bride
   By choosing another to sit by my side,
   And he can get lodging here, oh, here,
   And he can get lodging here.

5 Rise you up, Bobby, and choose you a wife.
   Make the best choice that you can for your life.
   So rise you up, Bobby, and go, oh, go;
   So rise you up, Bobby, and go.

6 Rise you up, Phoebe, and choose you a man,
   And make the best choice that ever you can.
   So rise you up, Phoebe, and go, oh, go;
   So rise you up, Phoebe, and go.

C

(The same, from Pearl Mobley, Rubottom, Love County.)

(A man sits in one of two chairs in center of yard or room. Girl sits down beside him. Two men come marching, singing:)

1 Hog drovers, hog drovers, hog drovers we are,
   Come courting your daughter so rare and so fair.
   Can we get lodging here, oh, here?
   Can we get lodging here?

   (*Man sings:*)
2 This is my daughter that sets by my side,
   And none of you hog drovers can have her for a bride,
   And you can't get lodging here, oh, here;
   And you can't get lodging here.

207

(*Men hang heads and sing:*)

3 It's bread for your daughter and hay for yourself,
   We'll go on a piece farther and better ourselves.
   And we won't take lodging here, oh, here;
   We won't take lodging here.
   (*March off.*)

(*Two more men come and sing:*)

4 Rich merchants, rich merchants, rich merchants we are,
   A-courting your daughter so rich and so fair.
   Can we get lodging here, oh, here?
   Can we get lodging here?

5 This is my daughter that sets by my side,
   And one of you merchants can have her for bride,
   By bringing another one here, oh here,
   By bringing another one here.

(Girl gets up, catches hands with one man. Man left chooses girl to sit by man in center and rich merchant is left alone. Girl in middle chooses man to march with him. Man and girl out march around couple in middle, starting the circle. Same play is repeated with various occupations and results; for example:

Gold miners — accepted.
Cowboys—rejected. They sing at leaving:
"We've been through Arkansas and bettered ourselves."
   Man sings on this occasion:
"This is my daughter that sets in my lap,
   And none of you cowboys can take her from her pap."
School teachers — accepted.
Farmers — sometimes accepted, sometimes rejected.
Oil drillers — not accepted, etc.

My informant went on to say that when boys were rejected, the circle jeered and teased them. She also said that they made up new verses all the time.

Other variants by Boyce Billingsley, Wayne, McClain County, from Northern Arkansas; Delphin Delmor Bledsoe, Marlow, Stephens County; Gerald Bond, Oklahoma City, Oklahoma County, who played it in Chickasha, Grady County; Dr. E. E. Dale, Norman, Cleveland County; Atta LeGate, Muskogee, Muskogee County; Mary Virginia Maloy, Norman, Cleveland County, from her mother, Texas; Martin Odom, Checotah, McIntosh County; Cora Frances Starritt, Ada, Pontotoc County; James E. White, Norman, Cleveland County, who played it in Bradley, Grady County.

44

HOGS IN THE CORNFIELD

For "Hogs in the Cornfield," cf. Ames (Missouri), *JAFL,* 24:318.
For "Tell them pretty gals I'm coming over," cf. "The Courting Boy,"
Talley, p. 141.
See JIM ALONG JOSIE.

A

(Sam West, Duke, Jackson County, from Ruth Coleman, Jackson County. Tune from
Orville Nichols, Mountain Park, Kiowa County, from Cordell, Washita County.)

Hogs in the corn-field, Cows in the clov-er. Tell them pret-ty gals I'm com-ing' o -ver.

Hogs in the cornfield,
    Cows in the clover.
Tell them pretty gals,
    I'm coming over.

B

(Dorothy A. Smith, Oklahoma City, Oklahoma County.)

1 Hogs in the cornfield,
    How do you know?
Met a little boy,
    And he told me so.

2 Her eyes were blue,
    Her cheeks were red,
And her lips were as sweet
    As gingerbread.

She showed me the hole the hogs got in.

45

I'LL COME BACK AND BE YOUR BEAU.

(Christine Bettis, Norman, Cleveland County.)

Cf. Ames (Missouri), *JAFL,* 24:312; "Heel and Toe," Piper (Western
Nebraska, Western Iowa), *JAFL,* 28:280-281 (two texts); White (Ala-
bama), p. 270.
See JIM LANE.

Cornstalk fiddle and a shoe-string bow,
I'll come back and be your beau,
Be your beau, be your beau.
I'll come back and be your beau.

46

IN EIGHTEEN HUNDRED AND SIXTY-FOUR

For this Civil War parody of "Three Crows," cf. Davis, p. 145.

Cf. "Eighteen Hundred and Sixty," Ames (Missouri), *JAFL,* 24:314-315; Randolph (Ozarks, Missouri), *JAFL,* 42:218-219 (both dissimilar in text).

A

(Kaspar and Lacie Huff, Norman, Cleveland County, from Mrs. W. T. Huff.)

In eighteen hundred and sixty-four
We'll all go home and fight no more.
We'll all drink stone blind.
Johnny, fill up the bowl,
Johnny, fill up the bowl again,
Johnny, fill up the bowl.
We'll all drink stone blind.
Johnny, fill up the bowl.

B

(Sue Patterson, Erick, Beckham County.)

1 In eighteen hundred and sixty-four, hurrah! hurrah! (*Bis.*)
In eighteen hundred and sixty-four was when that war first begun.

Chorus:
Drink stone bine O, Johnny fill up the bowl.

2 In eighteen hundred and sixty-five, hurrah! hurrah! (*Bis.*)
In eighteen hundred and sixty-five, there'll not be a nigger left behind.

3 In eighteen hundred and sixty-six, hurrah! hurrah! (*Bis.*)

47

IN SOMEBODY'S GARDEN

(Clifford Chandler, Crescent, Logan County. Tune from Professor Kenneth C. Kaufman, Norman, Cleveland County, who played it in Eastern Custer County.)

Cf. "I'm in some lady's garden," Fauset (Mississippi), *JAFL,* 40:303; "Do, Do Let Me Out," Kennedy (*Black Cameos*), p. 196; "Do, Do, Pity My Case," Newell (Louisiana), pp. 87-88 (also Scarborough, pp. 140-141); "Brick House," Owens (Texas), *Southwest Review,* 18:176; "Fine Brick House," Piper (Western Nebraska), *JAFL,* 28:267-268; "In Some Lady's Garden," Scarborough (Texas), pp. 114-115, 140; "The Closet Key," *idem* (Virginia), p. 139; "Ransum Scansum," "Aransom Shansom," *idem* (Louisiana), p. 131.

For Stanza 2, see OH, AIN'T I SWEET, OLD JOE CLARK.

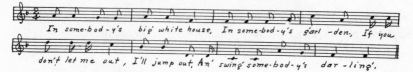

In some-bod-y's big white house, In some-bod-y's garl-den, If you
don't let me out, I'll jump out, An' swing some-bod-y's dar-ling'.

1 In somebody's big white house,
    In somebody's garden,
If you don't let me out, I will jump out,
    And swing somebody's darling.

2 You may ride the ol' gray hoss,
    And I will ride the roan,
You may love your own sweetheart,
    But you'd better leave mine alone.

48

THE IRISH TROT, *or* MISSISSIPPI RIVER

(Bertha Matthews, Norman, Cleveland County, from Chickasha, Grady County. Tune
from Levi Wilcox, Noble, Cleveland County.)

"They also had a dance called 'the Irish trot' from which it seems
that the word trot as the name for a dance is not so modern after all."—
Mary Newton Stanard, *Colonial Virginia, Its People and Customs*, p. 144.
Cf. "The Irish Trot," Dudley and Payne (Texas), *PTFS*, 1:10-11.
For stanza 1, see SANDY LAND (E).

Mississippi Riv'r I'm bound to cross, Mississippi Riv'r I'm bound to cross,
Mississippi Riv'r I'm bound to cross, Way down be-low.

1 Mississippi River I'm bound to cross, (*Three times.*)
    Way down below.

2 Hands all around in the Irish trot, etc.

3 Turn right back in the Irish trot, etc.

4 Ladies in the center and the boys take a walk, etc.

5 Mississippi River they are bound to cross, etc.

6 Gents to the center and the girls run away, etc.

7 Mississippi River they did get across, etc.

Variants by Gerald Bond, Oklahoma City, Oklahoma County, who
played it at Chickasha, Grady County; Catherine Harris, Antlers, Push-

mataha County, from A. A. Dilbeck, Miller, Pushmataha County, who played it in Arkansas; J. Kyle McIntyre, Ardmore, Carter County; Gilbert Morehead, Oklahoma City, Oklahoma County.

49

IT RAINS AND IT HAILS

Cf. "It's a-Hailin'," Bales (Texas Negroes), *PTFS,* 7:107; Bass (South Carolina), *JAFL,* 44:432; "It's Raining," Clarke (Virginia Negroes), *JAFL,* 3:288; "Miller Boy," Dudley and Payne (Texas), *PTFS,* 1:13; "I'll Be the Reaper," Gardner (Michigan), *JAFL,* 33:103-104; "Cold, cold, frosty morning," Heck (Cincinnati), *JAFL,* 40:14; "Who'll Be the Binder," Newell, pp. 84-86; Piper (Western Nebraska), *JAFL,* 28:270; "Fragment," Pound (Nebraska, *Syllabus*), p. 72; "Cold, Stormy Morning," Spenney (North Carolina), *JAFL,* 34:112. Dr. Josiah H. Combs, of Texas Christian University, reports this from Gilmer County, West Virginia, as the chorus of "The Dusty Miller."

See YONDER SHE COMES.

A

(Dr. E. E. Dale, Norman, Cleveland County.)

It rains and it hails and it's cold stormy weather.
In comes the farmer with a big jug of cider.
Who'll be the reaper and who'll be the binder?
Lost my true lover and right here I find her.

B

(Ethel Rose Baird, Bixby, Tulsa County, from Logan Summers, Bixby, who played it in Vernon County, Missouri.)

1 It rains and it hails
    And it's cold and stormy weather,
I've lost my true love
    And I don't know where to find her.

2 Oh, it's yonder she comes,
    And it's how-do-ye-do.
How have you been
    Since I parted from you?

C

(Mary Virginia Maloy, Norman, Cleveland County.)

It rains and it hails, and it's cold stormy weather.
The old cow died, and we got lots of leather.

Other variants by Christine Bettis, Norman, Cleveland County; Agnes Frick, Oklahoma City, Oklahoma County; Alice Flora Hare, Norman, Cleveland County, from Bernice Taylor, Norman, Cleveland County;

J. Kyle McIntyre, Ardmore, Carter County; Martin Odom, Checotah, Mc-
Intosh County; Ruth Revelle, Oklahoma City, Oklahoma County; Winnifred Spencer, Walters, Cotton County, from Jefferson, Marion County,
Texas; Sam West, Duke, Jackson County, from Mrs. F. P. Dowdy, Jackson County; James E. White, Norman, Cleveland County, who played it
at Bradley, Grady County.

50

I'VE BEEN TO THE EAST

Cf. "I've been to the east," Ames (Missouri), *JAFL*, 24:303-304;
"Buck-Eyed Rabbit! Whoopee!", Talley, p. 175.

"Big (Pop) eye, Brer Rabbit, hoo, hoo!" occurs in the Negro folk-tale
"Brer Rabbit put on Brer Rabbit's Hat," Smiley (Virginia), *JAFL*, 32:
358-359.

See COME, MY LOVE.

A

(Louise James, Norman, Cleveland County; Dorothy H. Smith, Oklahoma City,
Oklahoma County.)

I've been to the East, I've been to the West,
  I've been to North Carolina.
Prettiest girl I ever did see
  Was buckeye rabbit's daughter.
Buckeye rabbit, hoot, hoot,
Buckeye rabbit's daughter.

B

(Agnes Frick, Oklahoma City, Oklahoma County; Ruth Revelle, Oklahoma City,
Oklahoma County, from her father, Haywood County, Tennessee.)

I've been to the East and I've been to the West,
  I've been to South Carolina.
I've lost my true love
  And don't know where to find her.

51

JACK KILLED A RABBIT

(Marguerite M. Durkee, Norman, Cleveland County, from Mrs. P. R. Durkee; Zelma
Oliver, Norman, Cleveland County, from Eugene Nolen, Norman.)

See SHOO-LI-LO.

1 Jack killed a rabbit, shoo-la-lay. (*Three times.*)

2 We'll all get married, shoo-la-lay. (*Three times.*)

3 Next Sunday morning, shoo-la-lay. (*Three times.*)

4 All invited, shoo-la-lay. (*Three times.*)

5 No one slighted, shoo-la-lay. (*Three times.*)

6 On to the next, shoo-la-lay. (*Three times.*)

52

JERSEY BOYS

(Walter L. Payne, Hobart, Kiowa County.)

Cf. "Jersey Boy," Wolford (Indiana), p. 61; "Georgy Boys," *Godey's Lady's Book*, 89:62.

See MICHIGAN GIRLS.

Jersey boys, hear the call,
An invitation to you all.
The way is broad, the track is clear,
Jersey boys, come volunteer, volunteer, volunteer,
Jersey boys, come volunteer.

53

JIM ALONG JOSIE

Based on the minstrel song.* See "Jim Along Josey," Marsh's *Selection or Singing for the Million*, 2:161-164; *Minstrel Songs Old and New*, pp. 118-119; Scarborough (Mississippi), p. 105; Spaeth (*Weep Some More, My Lady*), pp. 103-104.

Johnson (*What They Say in New England*, p. 177) gives

Fire on the mountain,
Run, boys, run;
The cat's in the cream-pot,
Run, girls, run!

---

* Oklahoma fragment:
Oh, I'se from Lusianna, as you all know,
Dar whar Jim Along Josey's de scream.
Dem riggahs all rise w'en de bell does ring,
An' dis is de song dat dey do sing.

Chorus:
  Hey, git along, git along, Josey,
    Hey, git along, Jim along Joe!
  Hey, git along, git along, Josey,
    Hey, git along, Jim along Joe!

My sister Rose de ober night did dream,
Dat she was floatin' up an' down de stream,
An' when she 'woke she began to cry,
An' de white cat pick'd out de black cat's eye.

(Atlee Garrett, Loco, Stephens County.)

as "the proper thing to shout out to the one in chase" in a game of tag. Cf. "Fire on the Mountains," Gomme, 2:421 (given as origin of "Round Tag").

Cf. "Jim Along Jo," Ames (Missouri), *JAFL,* 24:298; "Mill Pond," Dudley and Payne (Texas), *PTFS,* 1:21; Finger (*Frontier Ballads*), p. 164; "Jim Along Jo," Gardner (Michigan), *JAFL,* 33:105-106 (five texts); Hamilton (Northeast Missouri), *JAFL,* 27:290; "Jim Along Jo," Mahan and Grahame (Iowa), pp. 61-62; "Hi, Come Along!", Piper (Western Nebraska, Western Iowa), *JAFL,* 28:268 (three texts); Scarborough (Mississippi), pp. 104-105; "As I was going up a new-cut road," *idem* (Virginia), p. 106; "Come a High Jim Along," Shearin and Combs (Kentucky), p. 39 (listed); "Fire on the Mountain," Van Doren (Illinois), *JAFL,* 32:493.

See HOGS IN THE CORNFIELD.

A

(Sung by Orville Nichols, Mountain Park, Kiowa County, from Cordell, Washita County.)

Hey, Jim a - long, Jim a - long Jo-sie, Hey, Jim a - long', Jim a - long' Jo.

Hey, Jim along, Jim along Josie,
  Hey, Jim along, Jim along Jo.
Hey, Jim along, Jim along Josie,
  Hey, Jim along, Jim along Jo.

B

Get Along Josie

(Florette McNeese, Oklahoma City, Oklahoma County, from her pupils.)

1 Hey, come a get along,
    Get along, Josie.
  Hey, come a get along.
    Get along Jo.
  All you girls, that want a beau,
  Fall in the arms of the calico.

2 Fire's in the mountain,
    Fun, boys, fun, boys.
  Fire in the mountain,
    Fun, boys, fun.
  All you boys, etc.

3 Cat's in the cream jar,
　　Run, girls, run, girls.
Cat's in the cream jar,
　　Run, girls, run.
All you girls, etc.

C

JIM ALONG JOSIE

(Mrs. L. T. Monnett, Norman, Cleveland County, who played it in Missouri.)

1 Apple cider, cinnamon beer,
Christmas comes but once a year.

Chorus:
　　Hey, get along,
　　Jim along Josie.
　　Hey, get along,
　　Jim along Jo.

D

HEY, JIM ALONG, JIM ALONG JOE

(Alvin Meixner, Alva, Woods County, from Capron, Woods County; Wanda Irene
Dalton, Curtis, Woodward County; Corwin Quinn, Alva, Woods County.)

1 Fire in the mountain,
　　Run, boys, run.
Take your partners as you go.
Hey, Jim along, Jim along Joe.

2 Cat's in the cream jar,
　　Run, girls, run, etc.

E

HOGS IN THE CORNFIELD

(Juanita Curtis, Glencoe, Payne County; Margaret Hudson, Bartlesville,
Washington County.)

Hogs in the cornfield, I don't know,
Jim along Josie tole me so.
Hey, Jim along, Jim along Josie.
Hey Jim along, Jim along, Joe.

54

JIM LANE

Dr. Josiah H. Combs. of Texas Christian University, reports this from
Knott County, Kentucky, under the title of "My Love Sat Down in a
Sad Condition," and from West Virginia under the title of "Sad Station."
Cf. "The Boatman," Shearin and Combs (Kentucky), p. 36 (excerpt).
The text of "My Love Sat Down in a Sad Condition" follows:

1 My love sat down in a sad condition,
　Mourning for the loss of her own true-love;
　Some say she (*sic*) was taken in the wars of Germany.

2 Hi lee, hi low,
　I'll turn my back and be your beau;
　I'll turn my elbow to my wrist,
　And then turn back in a double twist.*

3 Bow, bow, bow to the right,
　We bow down in Inland's might;
　Every time you kiss her, jump like a crow,†
　Never mind the weather so the wind don't blow.

Also Kittredge, *JAFL*, 20:276.
See I'LL COME BACK AND BE YOUR BEAU.

A

(Bertha Matthews, Norman, Cleveland County.)

1 All down with the wars of old Jim Lane,
　Since he's been slain, since he's been slain.
　All down with the wars of old Jim Lane.

Chorus:
　Oh, no, no, it can't be so,
　He's come back to be my beau.
　Little piece of puddin' an' a punkin pie.
　If the girls ain't pretty, I hope I'll die.

B

I'LL COME BACK AND BE YOUR BEAU

(Marguerite M. Durkee, Norman, Cleveland County, from Mrs. P. R. Durkee.)

1 She sat down in meditation,
　Mourning the loss of her true love.
　It has been said that he was slain
　In the war with General Lee.

Chorus:
　Oh, no, no, it is not so,
　He's come back to be your beau.

C

I'LL COME BACK AND BE YOUR BEAU

(J. Kyle McIntyre, Ardmore Carter County, from Montgomery County, East Texas.)

1 She sat down in a sad way station
　To mourn the loss of her own true love.

---

* See KILA MA CRANKY.
† See JUMP, JIM CROW.

It has been said that he was slain
All in the war of General Wayne.

Chorus:
No, no, 'tis not so,
For he's come back to be my beau.
To be my beau, to be my beau.
He's come back to be my beau.

Note: "The first stanza of this song is in slow 3/4 time and the second is rapid 2/4 for dancing."

D

HE'LL COME BACK AND BE YOUR BEAU

(Martin Odom, Checotah, McIntosh County.)

1 As she sits down in hesitation,
    Mourning the loss of her old true love,
  It has been said that he was slain
    In the wars of General Lane.

Chorus:
Oh, no, no, it is not so,
For he'll come back and be your beau.

Directions: "Girl sits with head bowed in arms during the slow part. When the fast part starts, she jumps up and joins the group, singing above, alone, first, then the group repeating it with her. The circle skips during this part."—Josiah H. Combs.

55

JOHN BROWN HAD A LITTLE INDIAN

Based on a counting-out rhyme. Cf. Leland, *JAFL,* 2:113-114, who assigns 1847 as the earliest date for the game in the United States and traces it back to "additive and subtractive magic songs" for "reducing a disease by counting it off."

Cf. "Indian Boys," Ames (Missouri), *JAFL,* 24:310; "Ten Little Niggers," Chapple (*Heart Songs*), p. 357; "John Brown," Douthitt (Kentucky), p. 37; "Ten Little Indians," Newton (*Graded Games*), pp. 12-13; "John Brown and His Little Injuns," Pound (Nebraska, *Syllabus*), p. 75; "John Brown's Little Indians," Shearin and Combs (Kentucky), pp. 34-35 (described); "Ten Little Indians," Wier (*Songs the Children Love to Sing*), p. 10. It is probably related to "Tom Brown's Two Little Indian Boys," Halliwell (*The Nursery Rhymes of England*), p. 110.

For "What will we do with the drunken sailor," cf. the chanteys: "The Drunken Sailor," Colcord (*Roll and Go*), p. 30; "What To Do with a Drunken Sailor." Davis and Tozer (*Sailors' Songs or "Chanties"*), pp. 46-47; "Drunken Sailor," Sharp (*English Folk-Chanteys*), p. 8; "What Shall We Do with the Drunken Sailor," Terry (*The Shanty Book*), Part I:30-31; and the play-party song, "Sailor," Piper (Western Iowa), 28:277; Wolford (Indiana), p. 85.

A

(Sung by Charlie Carr, Noble, Cleveland County.)

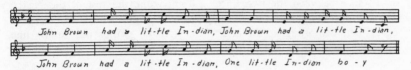

1 John Brown had a little Indian, (*Three times.*)
    One little Indian boy.

Chorus:
    One little, two little, three little Indian,
    Four little, five little, six little Indian,
    Seven little, eight little, nine little Indian,
        Ten little Indian boys.
    Ten little, nine little, eight little Indian,
    Seven little, six little, five little Indian,
    Four little, three little, two little Indian,
        One little Indian boy.

2 Ship went sailing over the ocean, (*Three times.*)
    So early in the morning.

3 They all got back but one little Indian, (*Three times.*)
    One little Indian boy.

4 He got drowned in the ocean, etc.

5 Put him in a boat and sail him over, etc.

B

Seven Little Indian Boys

(Walter Myers Gable, Norman, Cleveland County.)

1 Do-ce-do and don't you touch her, (*Three times.*)
    One little Indian boy.

Chorus:
    One little Indian, two little Indian.
    Three little Indian, four little Indian,
    Five little Indian, six little Indian,
        Seven little Indian boys.

2 Do-ce-do to your best likings, (*Three times.*)
  Two little Indian boys.

3 Fall of the year comes in October, (*Three times.*)
  Three little Indian boys.

Directions: "This game is played by the boys lining up on one side and the girls lining up on the other side and the boy on one end of the line meeting a girl who is on the other end of the other line, half way in distance between the two lines. All this time the rest of the players are singing. On the chorus the boy swings the girl who is at the center once, then beginning at the end of the line he swings one in the line, then her again, etc., until he finishes the line."

C
(No Title.)

(Mrs. Edna Muldrow, Norman, Cleveland County, from her pupils.)

1 John Brown had a little Indian, (*Three times.*)
  One little Indian boy.

2 Ten little, nine little, eight little Indians,
  Seven little, six little, five little Indians,
  Four little, three little, two little Indians,
  One little Indian boy.

3 ——, Nine little, eight little Indians, etc.

Etc.

Directions: "Every time you sing it you leave out one number until you get down to 'One little Indian boy.' If you don't come in at the right time, you have to quit. When you leave out a number, you say it to yourself so you will get the right time."

Variants:

Ships come sailing o'er the ocean.
   (Lucile Parker, Norman, Cleveland County; Thelma Staggs, Guthrie, Logan County.)

Put him in a boat and he'll sail over.
   (Mrs. Edna Muldrow, Norman, Cleveland County, from her pupils.)

What will we do with the drunken sailor?
Put him in a boat and he'll sail over.
Sometimes drunk and sometimes sober,
The fall of the year comes in October.
   (Karl Herdi, Billings, Noble County.)

Way down in the poppy bed.
   (Mrs. Bertha Downing, Norman, Cleveland County, who played it in Southern Noble, Northeastern Logan, and Northern Payne Counties.)

Do-ci-do and don't you touch 'em.
(Mary Virginia Maloy, Norman, Cleveland County.)

Other variants by Ruth Davis, Fort Worth, Texas; Mrs. L. T. Monnett, Norman, Cleveland County, who danced it in Missouri like a Virginia reel; Elsie Montgomery, Sunset, Beaver County, from Bessie Oneal, Follett, Texas, who played it at Darrouzett, Texas; Maude Markham Vaughan, Pawhuska, Osage County; Doris G. Waters, Ponca City, Kay County, from her pupils.

56
JOHN BROWN'S BODY

(Florette McNeese, Oklahoma City, Oklahoma County, from her pupils.)

For the song, cf. Lomax (*American Ballads and Folk Songs*), pp. 528-529.

For the play-party, cf. Piper (Western Nebraska), *JAFL*, 28:270.

Tune: "Battle Hymn of the Republic."

1 John Brown's body lies a-mouldering in the grave, (*Three times.*)
   As we go marching on.

Chorus:
   Glory, glory, hallelujah, (*Three times.*)
   As we go marching on.

2 Hang Jeff Davis to a sour apple tree,
   As we go marching on.

Directions: Danced like Virginia reel.

57
JOLLY SAILOR GIRLS

(Bertha Matthews, Norman, Cleveland County, from Chickasha, Grady County.)

For British versions, see "Here comes our jolly, jolly sailors," Douglas, p. 81; "Jolly Sailors," Gomme, 1:294-296 (six texts); "Jolly Lads, Bold," *idem*, 2:436; "Here comes four jolly sailor boys," Northall, p. 369 (two texts).

For American versions, see "Tailor Boy," Babcock (Washington, D. C.), *American Anthropologist*, 1:253-254 (two texts); "Jolly Rover," "The Sailor Boys," Hamilton (Northeast Missouri), *JAFL*, 27:295, 301-302; "There came one jolly, jolly sailor boy," Heck (Cincinnati), *JAFL*, 40:24-25; "Three Jolly Sailors," Newell, p. 124.

1 There were three jolly, jolly sailor girls
   Just lately come on shore.
   They spent their days in a many foolish ways
   Just as they've done before.

And now they'll take another road,
And now they'll take another road.
And if you delight with a handsome little man,
Just bring him on the floor.

2 There were two jolly, jolly sailor girls, etc.

3 There was one jolly, jolly sailor girl, etc.
(*Repeat from beginning, substituting "boys" for "girls."*)

Variant:
And we'll take another oar,
And row the boat to shore.
If he delights in a pretty little wife
Let him lead her to the shore.

> (Dr. S. R. Hadsell, Norman, Cleveland County, who notes: "Imitate the motion of the boat rocking. This was a good game to start a party with and get acquainted—an ice-breaker. Three girls choose three boys, and when you got a circle you could go on to play 'Ugly Mug.' ")

58
JUMP, JIM CROW

(Danny Kay, Mannford, Creek County, who played it at Stillwater, Payne County.)

For the folk sources and variants, with "jump Jim Crow" as a dance step, cf. Davis (South Carolina), *JAFL,* 27:250 (listed); Harris (*Uncle Remus, His Songs and His Sayings*), p. 147 (" 'Make a bow ter de Buzzard en den ter de Crow, Takes a limber-toe gemmun fer ter jump Jim Crow' "); Gaines (*The Southern Plantation*), pp. 96-96n. (where the source of Rice's inspiration is given variously as a Cincinnati stage-driver and a Cincinnati, Pittsburgh, and Louisville Negro); Goldberg (*Tin Pan Alley*), pp. 37-38 (where the song is assigned to the Columbia Street Theatre, Cincinnati, 1828-29, and a Negro version from Kentucky is cited, with the chorus: "First on de heel tap, den on de toe, Ebery time I wheel about I jump Jim Crow"); Scarborough, p. 127; Talley, p. 13; White (North Carolina), pp. 162-163. *Addendum:* Bass (South Carolina), *JAFL,* 44:427-428.

For the minstrel song, by Thomas D. Rice, introduced by him at the Bowery Theatre, New York, November 12, 1832 (Gaines, p. 96), cf. Ashton (*Modern Street Ballads*), pp. 349-350 ("the first of the flood . . . the original 'Jim Crow,' Thomas D. Rice, or, as he was better known, 'Adelphi Rice,' . . . introduced it, in 1836, into a play called 'A Flight to America' "); *Minstrel Songs Old and New,* p. 209; Paskman and Spaeth, pp. 11-14 (where "Jim Crow car" is traced to the song); Scarborough, pp. 125-127; White, pp. 452-453.

1 Jump, jump, jump Jim Crow,
   Take a little partner and away we go.

2 Jump, jump, point your toe.
   Slide, slide, take another partner and you jump Jim Crow.

Directions: Boys and girls hop on one foot, take hands, and turn around, during first stanza; then do-ce-do. When all have exchanged partners, make a little bow. (Played at church socials.)

59

JUTANG

Cf. Dudley and Payne (Texas), *PTFS*, 1:11; "Hands All 'Round," Spenney (North Carolina), *JAFL*, 34:113-114.

For the pattern, cf. LONDON and OLD DOC COLLINS.

See WILSON'S BARROOM (C).

A

(Mary Haxel, Purcell, McClain County, who played it near Noble, Cleveland County, and Washington, McClain County. Tune from Charlie Carr, Noble, Cleveland County.)

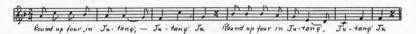

Round up four in Jutang, Jutang Ju,
Round up four in Jutang, Jutang Ju.
Doce do in Jutang, Jutang Ju,
Doce do in Jutang, Jutang Ju,
Change and swing in Jutang, Jutang Ju,
Change and swing in Jutang, Jutang Ju,
Treat 'em all alike in Jutang, Jutang Ju,
Treat 'em all alike in Jutang, Jutang Ju,
One more time in Jutang, Jutang Ju,
One more time in Jutang, Jutang Ju,
Promenade home in Jutang, Jutang Ju.
Promenade home in Jutang, Jutang Ju.

Round up six, etc.

Round up eight, etc.

B

JU TANG

(Melvin Culbertson, Amber, Grady County.)

Circle four in Ju Tang a Ju Tang Ju,
Circle four in Ju Tang a Ju Tang Ju,
Work right and left in Ju Tang a Ju Tang Ju,
Work right and left in Ju Tang a Ju Tang Ju,
Once in a half a Ju Tang a Ju Tang Ju,

223

Once in a half a Ju Tang a Ju Tang Ju,
On down the line to the next pretty girl a Ju Tang Ju,
On down the line to the next pretty girl a Ju Tang Ju,
Next young lady to your right a Ju Tang Ju,
Next young lady to your right a Ju Tang Ju,
On down the line in Ju Tang a Ju Tang Ju,
On down the line in Ju Tang a Ju Tang Ju,
Meet your partner in Ju Tang a Ju Tang Ju,
Meet your partner in Ju Tang a Ju Tang Ju,
All night long in Ju Tang a Ju Tang Ju,
All night long in Ju Tang a Ju Tang Ju,

Circle six, etc.

Circle eight, etc.

Etc.

"This is generally stopped for a while when they have rounded up ten and sometimes twelve. If they want to play some more they start with four again. Practically the same thing is sung over and over again during the whole game."

C

JUE TAIN

(Audra A. Plumlee, Norman, Cleveland County.)

1 Four hands round Jue tain,
    Jue tain jue.
  Four hands round Jue tain,
    Jue tain jue.

2 Right hand cross in Jue tain,
    Jue tain jue.
  Right hand cross in Jue tain,
    Jue tain jue.

3 Right hands back in Jue tain,
    Jue tain jue.
  Right hands back in Jue tain,
    Jue tain jue.

D

(Professor Kenneth C. Kaufman, Norman, Cleveland County, who played it in Eastern Custer County.)

Once-and-a-half, shoe string,
  Shoe string, shoe.
Once-and-a-half, shoe string,
  Shoe string, shoe.

224

Other variants by Catherine Harris, Antlers, Pushmataha County, from A. A. Dilbeck, Miller, Pushmataha County, who played it in Arkansas ("Jew Tong"); Lillian A. Jasper, Roosevelt, Kiowa County; Florette McNeese, Oklahoma City, Oklahoma County, from her pupils ("U-Tang-U"); Geraldine Miller, Norman, Cleveland County; Thelma Wild Rose, Chickasha, Grady County, from Waurika, Jefferson County; Cleve Turner, Cheyenne, Roger Mills County; Sam West, Duke, Jackson County, from Ed Stockton, Jackson County ("Shoo Tang").

60
KILA MA CRANKY

Based on a Jacobite song. Cf. "Killicrankie," Macquoid (*Jacobite Songs and Ballads*), pp. 40-41. The lines

Frinkum frankum is a fine song
An' we will dance it all along;

occur in "Cushion Dance," Gomme, 1:88.

Cf. "Crinkely, Cronkely," Gardner (Michigan), *JAFL,* 33:95; "Crinny My Cranky," Hamilton (Northeast Missouri), *JAFL,* 27:297; "Kilma-crankie," Piper (Western Iowa), *JAFL,* 28:272-273; "Creel-My-Crankie," Van Doren (Eastern Illinois), *JAFL,* 32:489; "Kilamakrankie," Wolford (Indiana), p. 61.

For Stanza 6 of B, cf. "Oats, Peas, Beans, and Barley," Piper (Illinois), *JAFL,* 28:273; "Negro Reel," Sandburg (Kentucky and Tennessee), pp. 134-135.

For B, see CONSOLATION FLOWING FREE.

A
DANCING ON A SHEEPSKIN

(Beatrice Jennings McMullin, Norman, Cleveland County, brought from Kentucky to Missouri, then to Kay and Grant Counties, on Oklahoma-Kansas border.)

1 If you have been where I have been
And have seen the sights that I have seen,
Four-and-twenty Irishmen
All dancing on a sheepskin.

2 Fare-you-well, Dick, and fare-you-well, Tom,
Fare-you-well, little Frankie.
Every time I think of you,
I'm dancing fiddle-ma-cranky.

3 Fiddle-ma-cranky is my song.
Now we'll dance and promenade along,
From the elbow to the wrist,
And now is the time to make the twist.

Directions: "Choose partners and form circle with one person in center. Circle and sing first stanza. Girls swing boys and boys swing girls during second stanza. Odd person in center tries to seize a partner. Promenade and while singing last line of stanza turn a 'dishrag'."

B

KILA MA CRANKY

(Florette McNeese, Oklahoma City, Oklahoma County, from her pupils.)

1 Consolation flowing free, (*Three times.*)
Come and go along with me.

Chorus:
   Kila ma cranky, here we go.
   Kila ma cranky, here we go.
   From my heel unto my toe.
   Kila ma cranky, here we go.

2 You're not too young, you are just right, (*Three times.*)
I'll see you home next Saturday night.

3 It is too far, I cannot go, (*Three times.*)
I cannot leave the old folks so.

4 As to the distance, need not mind, (*Three times.*)
I've been there many a time.

5 Tell your mother to hold her tongue, (*Three times.*)
She had beaux when she was young.

6 Lord! Lord! what have I done? (*Three times.*)
Married the old man instead of the son.

7 If you had been where I had been
And seen the sights that I have seen.
Four-and-twenty Irish girls
Dancing on a sheepskin.

61

KING WILLIAM WAS KING JAMES' SON

(Florette McNeese, Oklahoma City, Oklahoma County, from her pupils.)

Pound (*JAFL,* 26:355-356) notes: "It sounds as though it derived from about 1688, when William of Orange succeeded James the Second, but such may not be the case."

For British versions, see Gomme, 1:302-304 (three texts). For Stanza 2, cf. "Sally Water," Northall, pp. 374, 376, 377, 378, and for Stanza 3, the same, pp. 372, 373.

For American versions, see Ames (Missouri), *JAFL,* 24:313; Babcock (Washington, D. C.), *American Anthropologist,* 1:247-248; Ball (Idaho), *JAFL,* 44:10-11; "King Arthur Was King James's Son," Champlin, p. 447; "King William," Gardner (Michigan), *JAFL,* 33:107-109 (four texts); Hamilton (Northeast Missouri), *JAFL,* 27:295; "King William," Hudson (Mississippi), *JAFL,* 39:191 (also *Specimens,* p. 121); "King William Was King Jamie's Son," Mahan and Grahame (Iowa), pp. 57-58; "King Arthur Was King William's Son," "King William Was King George's Son," "King Charles He Was King James's Son," Newell, pp. 73-75, 246-248; Pound, *loc. cit.,* also *Syllabus* (Nebraska), p. 74; Randolph (Ozarks, Missouri), *JAFL,* 42:226-227; "King William," *Social Plays, Games,* etc., pp. 24-25; "King William Was King George's Son," Spenney (North Carolina), *JAFL,* 34:111; "Kneel on This Carpet," Talley, p. 82; Van Doren (Eastern Illinois), *JAFL,* 32:493-494; "King William Was King Jamie's Son," Wolford (Indiana), pp. 62-64 (two texts).

Dr. Josiah H. Combs, of Texas Christian University, reports as the opening of one of two texts from Gilmer County, West Virginia, the lines, "Here stands a lovely creature," cited under YONDER COMES A HEAVENLY CREATURE.

1 King William was King James' son,
  Around the royal race he run.
  He wore a star upon his breast
  As big as any hornet's nest.

2 Come choose your east, come choose your west,
  Come choose the one you love the best.
  If she's not here, just take your part,
  And choose another with all your heart.

3 Down on the carpet you must kneel
  As sure as the grass grows in the field,
  And when you rise upon your feet,
  Then hug your bride and kiss her sweet.

Variants by Mrs. Anne McClure, Oklahoma City, Oklahoma County, who played it in Benton, Arkansas, and describes it as a Jacobean song; Beatrice Jennings McMullin, Norman, Cleveland County, brought from Kentucky (where it was played when Daniel Boone was a boy) to Missouri, then to Kay and Grant Counties, on Oklahoma-Kansas border; Mrs. L. T. Monnett, Norman, Cleveland County, who played it in Missouri; Ada M. Scheirman, Kingfisher, Kingfisher County.

227

62

LEAD THROUGH THAT SUGAR AND TEA

Cf. "Sugar and Tea," Randolph (Ozarks, Missouri), *JAFL,* 42:219-220; "Sugar Loaf Tea," Talley, p. 81; "Sugar and Tea," Wilson (Ozarks), pp. 82-83.

For D, cf. "We're Marching Round a Pretty Girl," Van Doren (Illinois), *JAFL,* 32:495.

See COFFEE GROWS ON A WHITE OAK TREE.

A

(Sung by Charlie Carr, Noble, Cleveland County.)

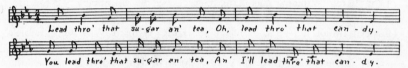

Lead through that sugar and tea,
  Oh, lead through that candy.
You lead through that sugar and tea,
  And I'll lead through that candy.

B

(Dictated by Katherine Harris, Norman, Cleveland County.)

1 Lead through that sugar and tea,
   You lead through that candy.
  I'll lead through that sugar and tea,
   And you'll lead through that candy.

2 You swing that sugar and tea,
   I'll swing that candy.
  We'll swing that sugar and tea,
   And I'll swing that candy.

Directions: The boy and girl at the foot of the lines march through to the head. He swings the head girl, while the head boy swings his girl. Repeat until all have been swung by the head couple.

C

(Lorena Collings, Norman, Cleveland County.)

1 Lead through that sugar and tea,
   Lead through that candy.
  You lead through that sugar and tea,
   While I lead through that candy.

228

2 Hi, oh, that sugar and tea,
 Hi, oh, that candy.
 You hi, oh, that sugar and tea,
 While I hi, oh that candy.

3 Promenade that sugar and tea,
 Promenade that candy.
 You promenade that sugar and tea,
 While I promenade that candy.

Directions: "The boys line up in a straight line opposite the girls, with about eight feet between the boys and the girls. The boy and the girl at the head of the rows will begin the game. During the first stanza the boy swings the girl at the end of the line and the girl (the boy's partner) swings the boy opposite the girl. After each swings a boy and a girl, they return to the center and swing each other. During the third stanza each boy grasps the hand of his partner and promenades. The boy and the girl who started the game go to the end of the line, and the next couple begins."

D

(No Title)

(Catherine Harris, Antlers, Pushmataha County, from Mrs. Clay Roberts, Antlers.)

1 We're marching round the soapstick,
 The soapstick, the soapstick,
 We're marching round the soapstick,
 Do-se, ladies, do.

2 And if you want a sweetheart,
 A sweetheart, a sweetheart,
 If you want a sweetheart,
 Choose one so gaily.

3 Hally, hally, bum, sugar and tea,
 Hally, hally, bum with candy,
 Hally, hally, bum, sugar and tea,
 Swing the little Miss Handy.

4 Sometimes get about ladies, (*Three times.*)
 Get about on the floor.

5 Don't you hear my heel and toe, (*Three times.*)
 Skipping on the floor.

E

(No Title)

(Audra A. Plumlee, Norman, Cleveland County.)

When coffee grows on white oak trees
  And rivers flow with brandy,
You swing around sugar and tea,
  I'll swing around this candy.

Other variants by Alec Gilbreath, Atoka, Atoka County, who played it in Lehigh, Coal County; Mary Haxel, Purcell, McClain County, who played it near Noble, Cleveland County, and Washington, McClain County; Thelma Staggs, Guthrie, Logan County.

63

(LITTLE) BROWN JUG

Cf. Ball (Idaho), *JAFL*, 44:8; Douthitt (Kentucky), p. 32; Dudley and Payne (Texas), *PTFS*, 1:9; Hamilton (Northeast Missouri), *JAFL*, 27:296-297; Owens (Texas), *Southwest Review*, 18:177; Randolph (Ozarks, Missouri), *JAFL*, 42:224. These texts use only the title and the phrase, "(Little) Brown Jug." For play-party versions closer to the popular song by Eastburn (*Minstrel Songs Old and New*, pp. 30-32), see Gardner (Michigan), *JAFL*, 33:109-110, and Hamilton, *op. cit.*, p. 301.

For the canal lines, see COFFEE GROWS ON A WHITE OAK TREE, RAILROAD (AND) STEAMBOAT.

For "fiddler's drunk," see COFFEE GROWS ON A WHITE OAK TREE, WILSON'S BARROOM, WINDING UP THE BALLROOM.

A

(Sung by Professor Kenneth C. Kaufman, Norman, Cleveland County, who played it in Eastern Custer County.)

1 Sent my brown jug down to town, (*Three times.*)
    To get some lager beer.

B

(The same.)

Sent my brown jug down to town,
  Down to town, down to town,
Sent my brown jug down to town,
  To get some lager beer.

2 It came back so round and brown, etc.
    Full of lager beer.

C

(Willis Goetzinger, Beaver, Beaver County, from Orlan Bell, Gray, Beaver County.)

1 Sent my brown jug down to town, (*Three times.*)
    So early in the morning.

2 It came back with a waltz around, etc.

3 Swing your lady with a do-se-do, etc.

Directions: All form circle and join hands. During the first stanza circle to the left. During the second stanza circle to the right. During the third stanza swing with a dance hold.

D

(Florette McNeese, Oklahoma City, Oklahoma County, from her pupils.)

Like C with the following chorus added, variants of which are reported by Artelee Derrell, Norman, Cleveland County; Eula Savage, Oklahoma City, Oklahoma County; Mrs. Della I. Young, Cheyenne, Roger Mills County, from Vashti Young, Cheyenne, and J. R. Weatherly, Elk City, Beckham County:

> Railroad, steamboat, river and canal,
> Lost my true love on the raging canal.
> Do, si, ladies, bow, wow, (*Three times.*)
> So early in the morning.
> Oh, she's gone, gone, gone,
> Let her go, go, go,
> Oh, she's gone, gone, gone,
> Gone o'er the raging canal.

E

(Glenn A. Roe, Oklahoma City, Oklahoma County, who played it at Frederick, Tillman County.)

1 Took my little brown jug down town, (*Three times.*)
    Fal-da-ral-de-ray.

2 It came back with a bounce around, etc.

Additional stanzas:

Fiddler's drunk and he can't play, (*Three times.*)
    So early in the morning.
        (Tephia Folsom, Atoka, Atoka County, from Ed Butler (Negro), Atoka.)

I'm my mamma's darling child, (*Three times.*)
    Early in the morning.
        (Zelma Oliver, Norman, Cleveland County, from Eugene Nolen, Norman.)

231

Do see, ladies, round and round, (*Three times.*)
So early in the morning.
(Cora Frances Starritt, Ada, Pontotoc County.)

Other variants by Boyce Billingsley, Wayne, McClain County, from Northern Arkansas; Alice Lucile Jackson, Supply, from Ray Cunningham, Supply, Woodward County; Lavelle McDaniel, Norman, Cleveland County, from Opal Poindexter, Covington, Garfield County; Thelma Wild Rose, Chickasha, Grady County, from Waurika, Jefferson County; Winnifred Spencer, Walters, Cotton County, from Jefferson, Marion County, Texas; Jack H. Watson, Oklahoma City, Oklahoma County, from C. F. Wallas, Norman, Cleveland County.

64
LITTLE FIGHT IN MEXICO

Cf. the chantey celebrating General Zachary Taylor's defeat of Santa Anna at Monterey. See "On the Plains of Mexico," Davis and Tozer (*Sailors' Songs or "Chanties"*), p. 34; "Santy Anna," "General Taylor," Sharp (*English Folk Chanteys*), pp. 2, 38-39. Taylor instead of Santa Anna is represented as running away in "Santy Anna," Colcord (*Roll and Go*), pp. 34-35; "Santa Anna," Terry (*The Shanty Book*), pp. 18-19 (cf. B).

Cf. "Fight in Mexico," Dudley and Payne (Texas), *PTFS*, 1:14; Hamilton (Northeast Missouri), *JAFL*, 27:296; "Had a Big Fight in Mexico," Hudson (Mississippi, *Specimens*), p. 120; "Mexico," Piper (Western Kansas), *JAFL*, 28:277.

Had a Little Fight in Mexico
A

(O. B. Campbell, Medford, Grant County. Tune from Professor Kenneth C. Kaufman, Norman, Cleveland County, who played it in Eastern Custer County.)

1 Had a little fight in Mexico.
If it wasn't for the girls the boys wouldn't go.

Chorus:
Sing *ja da ra, sing ja da ra.*
Sing *ja da ra, sing ja da ra da ra.**

---
* *Sing jol de rol, sing jol de ray,*
Sing jol er rol er rol, sing jol er rol er ray.

(K. C. K.)

2 Come to the place where the blood was shed,
  The girls turned back and the boys went ahead.

3 When those girls and boys do meet,
  They do hug and kiss so sweet.*

4 You had better get up, you are mighty in the way.
  Choose you a partner and come along and play.

B

LITTLE FIGHT IN MEXICO

(Cora Frances Starritt, Ada, Pontotoc County.)

1 Oh, that little fight in Mexico.
  None was killed but John Taylor-O.

2 Come to the place where the blood was shed,
  The boys slowed up and the girls went ahead.

Directions: "Players in couples with odd boy. Promenade with partners. When 'come to the place where blood was shed,' girls continue
forward and boys step back so that partners are changed. If singer (odd
boy) finds girl he wants for his partner he takes her and song continues."

C

(John Cunningham, Watonga, Blaine County, from his father William, who played it
at Homestead, Blaine County.)

1 Had a little fight in Mexico,
  Hi-O, ladies-O.
  Had a little fight in Mexico,
  Come-a-hike-O, ladies turn.

Chorus:
  Come-a-hike-O, ladies turn, turn, turn.
  Come-a-hike-O, ladies turn.

2 Come to the place where the blood was shed, etc.

3 The war's all over and we'll turn back, etc.

Other variants by J. Kyle McIntire, Ardmore, Carter County; Forest
Nelson, Duncan, Stephens County; James E. White, Norman, Cleveland,
County, who played it at Bradley, Grady County.

---

* Oh, the boys and the girls, when they do meet,
  They hug and they kiss and they court about a week.
  (K. C. K.)

233

65

LITTLE GIRL ROCKIN'
(Roxy Ann)

Of Negro origin.

Cf. "Fooling," Douthitt (Kentucky), pp. 33-34; "Roxy Anne," Dudley and Payne (Texas), *PTFS*, 1:19; "Roxy Anne," Hamilton (Northeast Missouri), *JAFL*, 27:298; "Foolin' Roxie," Owens (Texas), *Southwest Review*, 18:176-177; "Roxie Anne," Randolph (Ozarks, Missouri), *JAFL*, 42:225; "Roxie Anne," Van Doren (Eastern Illinois), *JAFL*, 32:492.

For "rock candy," see WROP CANDY.

See OLD JOE CLARK.

A

(Sung by Professor Kenneth C. Kaufman, Norman, Cleveland County, who played it in Eastern Custer County.)

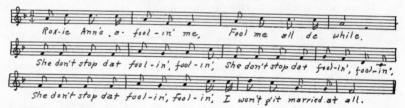

1 Roxie Ann's a-foolin' me,
  Fool me all de while.
  She don't stop dat foolin', foolin', (*Three times.*)
  I won't git married at all.

2 Sixteen months a-foolin' me,
  Sixteen months in all.
  She don't stop dat foolin', foolin', etc.

3 Fool me in de summeh time,
  Fool me in de fall.
  She don't stop dat foolin', foolin', etc.

B

(Florette McNeese, Oklahoma City, Oklahoma County, from her pupils.)
1 Roxy Ann's a-foolin' me,
  She fooled me all the while.
  She's been a long time foolin', foolin',
  Three long years a-foolin' me.
  She fooled me all the while.
  She's been a long time foolin', foolin',
  She's been a long time foolin' me.

Chorus:
>*Little girl rockin', she can't rock me, (Three times.)*
>*Get up a little higher, (Three times.)*
>*And learn to rock candy.*

2 She fooled me in the summer,
>She fooled me in the fall,
>She fooled me in the kitchen,
>She fooled me in the hall.
>Long time she's been a-foolin', foolin',
>Long time she's been a-foolin' me;
>Long time she's been a-foolin', foolin',
>Long time she's been a-foolin' me.

66
LIZA JANE

Cf. the minstrel song, "Good Bye, Liza Jane," arranged by Eddie Fox (*Minstrel Songs Old and New,* pp. 112-114), and the popular song, "Good-Bye, Liza Jane," copyright, 1903, by Harry Von Tilzer (Spaeth, *Read 'Em and Weep,* p. 230).

"Black the boots and make them shine" is related to the Negro shine reels given by Scarborough (Texas), pp. 213-214.

M is related to "The Squirrel," Sharp (*Nursery Songs from the Appalachian Mountains*), No. 9. For the triple comparison of tails, cf. also "Brudder Eph'em," Bass (South Carolina), *JAFL,* 44:429-430; "Shady Grove," Combs (Kentucky), *Folk-Say: 1930,* p. 243; "Old Napper," Hudson (Mississippi), *JAFL,* 39:178 (also *Specimens,* p. 103); "Old Bee Make de Honeycomb," "I Went to My Sweetheart's House," "Boil dem Cabbage Down," Scarborough (Mississippi, Virginia, South Carolina), pp. 165, 166-167, 168, 169, 170; "Tails," Talley, p. 5; "Buck-Eyed Rabbit! Whoopee!", *idem,* p. 175; "Old Virginia Breakdown," Webb (Texas), *JAFL,* 28:298; "Do Come Along, Ole Sandy Boy," White, pp. 316-317n. (also pp. 451-452); *idem* (Alabama), pp. 234-236 (three texts).

For Stanza 4 of A, cf. "Jinny Git Around," reported by Dr. Josiah H. Combs, of Texas Christian University, from Knott County, Kentucky:

1 Eighteen miles away from home,
>Chickens a-crowin' for day;
>I'm in bed with another man's wife,
>And I'd better be a-gittin' away.

Chorus:
>*Jinny, git around, O my love,*
>*Jinny, git around, I say.*
>*Jinny, git around, O my love,*
>*I'm a-goin' away to-day.*

Of this Dr. Combs notes: "Puttenham, in his *Art of English Poesie* (1589), p. 12, mentions William Gray (author of *Fantasies of Idolatry*) as having been favored by Henry VIII, and afterward by the Duke of Somerset, 'for making certain merry ballads, whereof one chiefly was, The hunt is up, the hunt is up.' Ritson, in his *Ancient Songs and Ballads* (1790, 1829), in the Introduction, quotes the following lines from an old song:

> The hunt is up, the hunt is up,
>> And now it is almost day,
> And he that's in bed with another man's wife,
>> It's time to get him away.

See also Perrow (Kentucky), *JAFL,* 28:183; White (Alabama), p. 269.

Cf. "Oh, Ain't I Gone," Ames (Missouri), *JAFL,* 24:299-300; "Shiloh," *ibid.,* p. 317; Blair (Kentucky), *JAFL,* 40:97-98; "Go On, Lize," Clarke (Virginia Negroes), *JAFL,* 3:290; "Liza Jane," "High Low Jack an' the Game," Douthitt (Kentucky), pp. 35-36; "Liza Jane, or Black dem Boots," Dudley and Payne (Texas), *PTFS,* 1:31-32; Edmands (North Carolina), *JAFL,* 6:131; "Susan Jane," Hamilton (Northeast Missouri), *JAFL,* 27: 291-292; "Eliza Jane," Henry (North Carolina), *JAFL,* 45:165-167 (two texts); Lomax (*American Ballads and Folk Songs*), pp. 284-286; "Get Along Home," Owens (Texas), *Southwest Review,* 18:171; Perrow (East Tennessee, Kentucky, Mississippi, and Indiana whites and Mississippi Negroes), *JAFL,* 28:178-180 (eight texts); "Ain't I Goin'," Piper (Western Nebraska from Arkansas), *JAFL,* 28:271-272; "Good-by, Liza Jane" (minstrel song), Sandburg, p. 51; *idem* (Kentucky), pp. 132-133 (two texts); "Liza in the Summer Time (She Died on the Train)," *idem* (North Carolina), pp. 308-309; "Boil dem Cabbage Down," Scarborough (Virginia), p. 169; "Hawkie is a Schemin' Bird," *idem* (Mississippi), p. 192; "Rejected by Eliza Jane," Talley, p. 134; Thomas (Kentucky), pp. 91-93; Truitt (Kentucky), *JAFL,* 36:378-379; "Eliza Jane," White (Alabama, North Carolina), pp. 172-175 (seven texts, with annotations); "Black the Boots," Wolford (Indiana), pp. 25-26.

From Knott County, Kentucky, Dr. Josiah H. Combs, of Texas Christian University, reports "I went up to the top of the hill" as part of "Walk, Georgie, Row":

> I went up to the top of the hill,
>> I gave my horn a blow:
> Thought I heard those pretty girls say,
>> "Yonder comes my beau."

Chorus:
> *Walk, Georgie-row, (Three times.)*
> *Give your horn a blow.*

For this stanza, see GOT A LITTLE HOME TO GO TO, OLD JOE CLARK.

For Stanza 3 of A, see GOT A LITTLE HOME TO GO TO.

For H, I, and J, see OLD VIRGINNY NEVER TIRE.

For Stanza 2 of O, see BALTIMORE.

See SHOO FLY (A), SUSAN JANE.

A

(Sung by Professor Kenneth C. Kaufman, Norman, Cleveland County, who played it in Caddo County.)

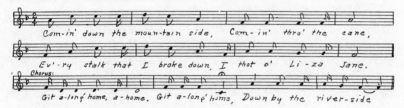

1 Comin' down the mountainside,
    Comin' through the cane,
Every stalk that I broke down,
    I thought o' Liza Jane.

Chorus:
> *Git along home, a-home,*
> *Git along home.*
> *Down by the riverside.*

2 Went up on the mountain-top,
    Give my horn a blow,
Though I heard my Liza say,
    "Yonder comes my beau." *

3 When I was a little boy,
    Sixteen inches high,
I'd kiss the girls and pull their curls
    And make their mammas cry.

---

* Went up on the mountain-top,
    Give my horn a toot,
Thought I heard my Liza say,
    "Yonder comes my Newt."

4 Forty miles away from home,
    Chickens crowin' for day.
Laid my head in a yaller gal's lap,
    And the yaller gal fainted away.*
(*Or*: Me in bed with another man's wife,
    I'd better be gittin' away.)

B

STANDING ON A PLATFORM

(Sung by Clayton Black, east of Noble, Cleveland County.)

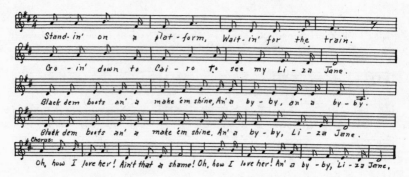

1 Standin' on a platform,
    Waitin' for the train.
Goin' down to Cairo
    To see my Liza Jane.

2 Black dem boots an' a-make 'em shine,
    An' a by-by, an' a by-by.
Black dem boots an' a-make 'em shine,
    An' a by-by, Liza Jane.

Chorus:
    Oh, how I love her!
    Ain't that a shame!
    Oh, how I love her!
    An' a by-by, Liza Jane.

3 Jaybird pullin' at a four-horse plow,
    An' a by-by, an' a by-by, etc.

4 Hawk caught a chicken an' flew upstairs, etc.

---

* Cf. "I Went Down to New Orleans," Bales (Texas), *PTFS*, 7:100.

C

BLACK THE BOOTS

(Emma Vilhauer, Norman, Cleveland County.)

1 Black the boots and make them shine,
    Good-bye, Liza Jane.
  Swing old Liza, swing old Liza,
    Swing old Liza Jane.

2 I went up the mountain
    To give my horn a blow.
  I thought I heard some one say,
    "Yonder comes my beau."

Chorus:
  Oh, how lovers!
    And ain't that a shame.
  Oh, how lovers!
    And good-bye, Liza Jane.

D

(No Title)

(Boyce Billingsley, Wayne, McClain County, from Northern Arkansas.)

1 Hawk caught a chicken and flew upstairs,
    Flew upstairs, flew upstairs.
  Hawk caught a chicken and flew upstairs,
    Good-bye, Liza Jane.

Chorus:
  Oh, how I love her!
    Ain't that a shame.
  Oh, how I love her!
    Good-bye, Liza Jane.

E

(No Title)

(Harold Roberts, Blackwell, Kay County.)

1 Black them boots
    And make them shine.
  I got to go see
    That pretty girl of mine.

Chorus:
  Oh, how I love her!
    Ain't that a shame.
  Oh, how I love her!
    It's a good-bye, Liza Jane.

F

(No Title)

(Tephia Folsom, Atoka, Atoka County, from Pat Lowry, Atoka.)

Blacken boots and make 'em shine, (*Three times.*)
Good-bye, Susie Jane.

G

HAWK CAUGHT A CHICKEN

(Alec Gilbreath, Atoka, Atoka County, who played it at Lehigh, Coal County.)

1 Hawk caught a chicken and flew upstairs,
Good-bye, Lizzie Jane.

2 Hawk flew down and picked that goose.
Good-bye, good-bye, Lizzie Jane.

3 Standing on a platform, waiting for a train,
Going down to Cairo, to see Miss Lizzie Jane.

4 Black them boots, make them shine,
Good-bye, Miss Lizzie Jane.

H

LIZA JANE

(Ben Hennessy, Oklahoma City, Oklahoma County, who played it in Logan County.)

1 As I was going down the road
Sally (Silly*) came down the lane.
She stubbed her toe on a horseshoe track,
Down came Liza Jane.

Chorus:
  O, Liza, Liza, Jane,
    O, Liza, Liza, Jane,
  She stubbed her toe on a horseshoe track,
  Down came Liza Jane.

I

(Frank Henry Dearden, Britton, Oklahoma County.)

You go down the rocky road,
I'll go down the lane.
You'll stub your toe and down you'll go,
Good-bye, Liza Jane.

J

(No Title)

(Winnifred Spencer, Walters, Cotton County, from Jefferson, Marion County, Texas.)

As I went down the Newport road,
She came up the lane.

---

* Satirical for *dude.*

240

As I went down the Newport road,
   I met Miss Liza Jane.

K

(Catherine Harris, Antlers, Pushmataha County, from S. B. Hackett, Norman,
who played it in Arkansas.)

1 I went up on the mountain,
   To give my horn a blow.
I thought I heard my Liza say,
   "There comes my Joe."

Chorus:
   Get along home, home, Cinda.
   Get along home, I say.
   Get along home, home, Cinda.
   Get along home to-day.

2 I went up on the mountain
   To get some sugar cane
To make a barrel of 'lasses
   To sweeten Liza Jane.

L

(Catherine Harris, Antlers, Pushmataha County, from Mrs. Clay Roberts, Antlers.)

1 See that frog walking that log,
   Good-bye, good-bye.
See that frog walking that log,
   Good-bye, Liza Jane.

2 Hawk caught a chicken and it flew so high,
   Good-bye, good-bye.
Hawk caught a chicken and it flew so high,
   Good-bye, Liza Jane.

Chorus:
   Oh, how I love her,
   And I'm telling no lie.
   Oh, how I love her,
   And I'll love her till I die.

M

(Catherine Harris, Antlers, Pushmataha County, from S. B. Hackett, Norman,
who played it in Arkansas.)

1 The raccoon's tail yam ringed all around,
   The possum's tail yam bare,
The rabbit has no tail at all
   But a little bunch of hair.

241

2 The squirlie yam a pretty bird
   With a long and bushy tail.
   He steals old marster's roasting-ears
   And hearts them on a rail.

3 When you want to travel
   Travel on the train.
   When you want to marry,
   Back to Liza Jane.

N

WHOOP LAW, LIZZIE

(Jane Bowman, Pauls Valley, Garvin County.)

Whoop law, Lizzie, pore gal,
   Whoop law, Lizzie Jane.
Whoop law, Lizzie, pore gal,
   She died carryin' the ball and chain.
Doggone!

O

LI'L LIZA JANE

(Joseph Edward Terral, Oklahoma City, Oklahoma County.)

1 I've got a gal and you've got none.
   Li'l Liza Jane.
   I've got a gal and you've got none.
   Li'l Liza Jane.

Chorus:
   Oh, Eliza,
      Little Liza Jane,
   Oh, Eliza,
      Little Liza Jane,

2 House by the side of Baltimore,
   Li'l Liza Jane, etc.

3 Children playin' round the door,
   Li'l Liza Jane, etc.

67

LONDON

Cf. "Twenty-Five Miles to London," Ames (Missouri), 24:315; "London," Douthitt (Kentucky), p. 34; "To London," Dudley and Payne (Texas), *PTFS*, 1:11; "Round That Lady," Hamilton (Northeast Missouri), *JAFL*, 27:302; "Rally, Boys, Rally," Hudson (Mississippi, *Specimens*), p. 127.

Stanza 3 of E has been reported under the titles "Rye Whiskey" and "Beefsteak," as follows:

Rye whiskey, rye whiskey, rye whiskey, says I,
If a tree don't fall on me, I'll live till I die.

I'll eat when I'm hungry, I'll drink when I'm dry,
If a tree don't fall on me, I'll live till I die.
> (Mrs. Anne D. McClure, Oklahoma City, Oklahoma County, from Benton
> County, Arkansas.)

Beefsteak when I'm hungry,
   Corn liquor when I'm dry;
Pretty little girl when I'm lonesome,
   Sweet heaven when I die.

Pretty little girl when I'm lonesome,
   Good water when I'm dry;
Good whiskey when I'm rowdy,
   Sweet heaven when I die.
> (Dr. Josiah H. Combs, Texas Christian University, from Knott County,
> Kentucky.)

Hudson (*Culture in the South,* p. 534) notes, among Civil War songs:
" 'I'll Eat When I'm Hungry, I'll Drink When I'm Dry' is a ribald frag-
ment to the tune of 'Old Hundred' "; and, under "Songs of the Civil
War" (*Specimens,* p. 85) cites:

> I'll eat when I'm hungry,
>   I'll drink when I'm dry.
> If the Yankees don't git me,
>   I'll live till I die.

The expression is proverbial. Cf. Northall, pp. 501, 526:

> Bread when you're hungry, drink when you're dry,
> Rest when you're weary, and heaven when you die.

> A roof to cover you, and a bed to lie,
> Meat when you're hungry, and drink when you're dry.
> And a place in heaven when you come to die.

It also occurs in "Here, Under the Green-Wood Bushes," by M'Nally
(*Universal Songster,* 2:439), as

> I eat when I'm hungry,
> Drink when I'm dry.

Again it appears in "Farewell, Sweet Mary" (Cox, West Virginia, pp.
433-434):

> I'll eat when I'm hungry,
>   And drink when I'm dry;
> I'll think of sweet Mary,
>   And sit down and cry.

243

and in "Farewell, Sweet Mollie Mary (Farewell Sweet Polly)" (Moore, Oklahoma, No. 83), as in Stanza 2 of "Rye Whiskey" above, or with the variant:

> If the Devil don't get me,
> I'll live till I die.

For other variants, cf. "Don't Grow Weary, Boys," Dobie, *PTFS*, 6:157; "Rye Whiskey," Gaines, *PTFS*, 7:153-154; "Rye Whiskey," Lomax (*American Ballads and Folk Songs*), pp. 170-173; "Jack o' Diamonds," *idem* (*Cowboy Songs*), pp. 292-296; Miles (Southern Mountains), *Harper's*, 109:120; "The Drunkard's Song," Perrow (East Tennessee, Mississippi, Missouri), *JAFL*, 28:129, 181-182 (four texts); "I'll Eat When I'm Hungry," Talley, p. 114; "Eat When Yo're Hongry," Thomas (South Texas Negroes), *PTFS*, 5:169; "Way Up on Clinch Mountain," Thomas (Kentucky), pp. 128-129; "Sourwood Mountain," Wilson (Ozarks), p. 61.

For the pattern, cf. CHASE THAT SQUIRREL, JUTANG, OLD DOC COLLINS.

A

(Sung by Charlie Carr, Noble, Cleveland County.)

1 Round up four in London,
   That's all I heard 'em say.
   Round up four in London,
   That's all I heard 'em say.

2 Lad' (lady)-do-se in London, etc.

3 Oncet and a half in London, etc.

4 Treat 'em all alike in London, etc.

5 One more time in London, etc.

6 Keep a-hookin' on in London, etc.

7 Hooray, boys, in London, etc.

8 Change and swing in London, etc.

B

(Mary Haxel, Purcell, McClain County, who played it near Noble, Cleveland County,
and Washington, McClain County.)

1 Round up four in London,
    So I heard them say.
  Round up four in London,
    So I heard them say.

2 Do-ce-do in London, etc.

3 Break and swing in London, etc.

4 Treat 'em all alike in London, etc.

5 Lots of pretty girls in London, etc.

6 One more time in London, etc.

7 Promenade home in London, etc.

(Repeat for "Round up six," etc., "Round up eight," etc.)

C

CIRCLE SIX

(Leonard C. Dresser, Lahoma, Garfield County.)

1 Go circle six to London,
    And so I heard them say.
  Go circle six to London,
    And so I heard them say.

2 Go right and left, etc.

3 Go once-and-a-half, etc.

4 Go circle six, etc.

5 Go pick up two, etc.

6 Go promenade, etc.

7 Go drop out two, etc.

D

(Mrs. Christine Clark, Norman, Cleveland County, who played it near Vinita in
Mayes and Craig Counties.)

Eighteen miles to Ketchem,
Eighteen miles to Ketchem,
    So I heard them say.
Eighteen miles to Ketchem,
    Hug the pretty girls on the way.

E

(Elsie Montgomery, Sunset, Beaver County, from Glendale and Overstreet districts, in the Panhandle of Texas.)

1 Cut a figure eight in London,
   And so I heard them say.
   Cut a figure eight in London,
   And so I heard them say.
   Oh, just cut a figure eight in London,
   For I ain't got long to stay.

2 Oh, it's a-raining and a-hailing,
   And a-falling from the sky.
   Oh, I fell in love with a pretty little girl,
   And I thought to my soul I'd die.

3 Oh, it's beefsteak when I'm hungry
   And whiskey when I'm dry,
   Oh, it's beefsteak when I'm hungry
   And whiskey when I'm dry,
   And a pretty little girl to cheer me up
   In heaven when I die.
   Just move along a-zig-zag,
   For I ain't got long to stay.

Other variants by Clifford Chandler, Crescent, Logan County; Lillian A. Jasper, Roosevelt, Kiowa County; Geraldine Miller, Norman, Cleveland County.

68

LONDON TOWN

(Warren Barnhill, Yukon, Canadian County.)

See OH, AIN'T I SWEET, OLD JOE CLARK (F), WEEVILY WHEAT.

To the tune of WEEVILY WHEAT.

1 Oh, to marry you, to marry you!
   Do you think I'd marry my cousin
   When I can get such girls as these
   For fifteen cents a dozen.

2 Higher up the cherry tree,
   Riper grow the cherries.
   The more you hug and kiss the girls,
   The sooner you will marry.

69

MILLER BOY

Newell (p. 103) notes: " 'Round and Round, the Mill Goes Round' is mentioned as an English dance of the seventeenth century. A song of 'The Happy Miller' is printed in 'Pills to Purge Melancholy' (1707), of which the first verse is—

> How happy is the mortal that lives by his mill!
> That depends on his own, not on Fortune's wheel;
> By the sleight of his hand, and the strength of his back,
> How merrily his mill goes, clack, clack, clack!

This song was doubtless founded on the popular game; but the modern children's sport has preserved the idea, if not the elegance, of the old dance better than the printed words of a hundred and seventy years since." Wolford (p. 68) adds: "D'Urfey in 'Pills to Purge Melancholy' (vol. III, pp. 151 ff. of 1707 edition) mentions this as being used in several ballad operas, e.g., 'The Quakers' Opera,' 'The Devil to Pay,' and 'The Fashionable Lady' or 'Harlequin's Opera,' under the name of 'The Budgeon It Is a Delicate Trade.' The tune to the 'The Jolly Miller' was in 1624 harmonized by Beethoven for George Thomson (*Pills to Purge Melancholy*, i, p. 169)." Among the numerous references to the song in literature she cites "The Miller of Dee" in Dryden's *Miscellany* and *The Convivial Songster* (1782) and "The Dusty Miller" in Walsh's *Compleat Country Dancing Master*. Dr. Josiah H. Combs, of Texas Christian University, points out that the song is known in Canada and in Sweden and cites this line of a French folk-song:

> J'entends le moulin, tique, tique, tique.

For British versions, see "There Was a Jolly Miller," Douglas, p. 73; "Jolly Miller," Gomme, 1:289-293, 2:436-437 (eight texts, including "A Hunting We Will Go"); "Jolly Miller," Northall, p. 366.

For American versions, see "The Jolly Old Miller," Ames (Missouri), *JAFL*, 24:306; Ball (Idaho), *JAFL*, 44:15; Dudley and Payne (Texas), *PTFS*, 1:13 (two texts); "Jolly Is the Miller," Elsom and Trilling (*Social Games and Group Dances*), pp. 218-219; "Happy Miller," Gardner (Michigan), *JAFL*, 33:101-102 (four texts); "Jolly Miller," Hamilton (Northeast Missouri), *JAFL*, 27:293; "Happy is the Miller," Heck (Cincinnati), *JAFL*, 40:20; "The Happy Miller," Hudson (Mississippi), *JAFL*, 39:193; "The Jolly Miller," *idem* (Mississippi, *Specimens*), p. 129; Mahan and Grahame (Iowa), pp. 38-40 (four texts); "Happy Is the Miller," Newell, pp. 102-103; "The Jolly Miller," Newton (*Graded Games and Rhythmic Exercises*), pp. 40-41; "Jolly Miller," Perrow (East Tennessee), *JAFL*,

26:139; Pound (Nebraska, *Syllabus*), p. 73; Randolph (Ozarks, Missouri), *JAFL*, 42:205-206 (also *The Ozarks*, pp. 145-146); "The Jolly Miller," Shearin and Combs (Kentucky), p. 37 (excerpt); "The Miller," *Social Plays, Games,* etc., p. 25; "Happy is the Miller," Van Doren (Eastern Illinois), *JAFL*, 32:490-491 (two texts); Wedgwood (Southwestern Nebraska, Southern Iowa, from Missouri), *JAFL*, 25:269; Wolford (Indiana), pp. 67-70 (two texts, with annotations).

A

(Sung by Leondis Brown, Noble, Cleveland County.)

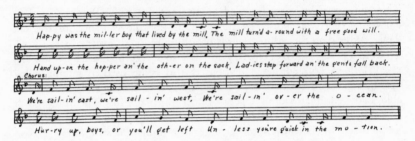

Hap-py was the mil-ler boy that lived by the mill, The mill turn'd a-round with a free good will.

Hand up-on the hop-per an' the oth-er on the sack, Lad-ies step forward an' the gents fall back.

Chorus:

We're sail-in' east, we're sail-in' west, We're sail-in' ov-er the o-cean.

Hur-ry up, boys, or you'll get left Un-less you're quick in the mo-tion.

1 Happy was the miller boy that lived by the mill.
The mill turned around with a free good will.
Hand upon the hopper an' the other on the sack,
Ladies step forward an' the gents fall back.

("The way to get 'em mixed up is to sing it, 'The gents step forward an' the ladies step back,' an' you get 'em so bumfoozled you can steal a partner.")

Chorus:

("Here all the boys get in the center an' wait until 'Unless you're quick' before they grab partners.")

We're sailin' east, we're sailin' west,
   We're sailin' over the ocean.
Hurry up, boys, or you'll get left
   Unless you're quick in the motion.

2 Happy was the miller boy, etc.
Hold your pardners an' turn right back.

3 Happy was the miller boy, etc.
Hand upon the hopper an' the other on the slab.
Every time the mill turns,
Grab, boys, grab.

B

(Lynn Scott, Holliday, Texas; Evelyn Roach, Shamrock, Texas.)

1 Happy is the miller boy that lives by the mill.
The mill turns around with a free good will.
Hand in the hopper and other in the sack.
Hold your holts, come a-raggin' right back.

Chorus:

> *We're sailing east, we're sailing west,*
> *We're sailing all over the ocean.*
> *If there's any young man who wants a young wife,*
> *They'd better get quick in the motion.*

2 Happy is the miller boy that lives by the mill.
The mill runs around with a good free will.
· Hand in hopper and the other in the sack,
Ladies step forward, and the gents fall back.

Call:

First gent out, swing that lady
With a right hand about.
Partner by the left as you come around,
Lady in the center and you'll all run around.
Such a kitten upstairs, well, I never did see.
Such a kitten upstairs, well, she don't suit me.

First couple down center and divide the ring,
Lady go right and gent go left.
When they meet, everybody swing.
Alemond a left, go round the ring.
Down the center as you uster do.
Down the center and a-cast off two.
When you meet, everybody swing.
Alemond a left, go round the ring.

First couple out to the right of the ring.
Honor that lady with a howdy do, do,
Swing your honey, go round and through,
Swing your honey, go through and around.
When you meet, four hands up
And around you go.
Two little ladies, come dosey do.
One more change and on you go.

249

C

(Nieto Looney, El Reno, Canadian County, who played it at Hennepin,
Garvin County.)

1 Miller boy, miller boy, living by the mill.
The mill turned around with a free good will.
Hand on the hopper and the other on the sack,
Gents step forward and ladies step back.

Chorus:
  Sailing east, sailing west,
    Sailing over the ocean.
  All you boys who want a good cook
    Had better be quick in the motion.

2 Happy was the miller boy that lived by the mill.
If he hadn't moved away, he'd be living there still.
Hand on the hopper and the other on the ground,
Ladies stand still and gents go round.

3 Happy was the miller boy that lived by the mill.
The mill turned round with a free good will.
Hand on the hopper and the other on the sack,
Turn right around and go right back.

D

(Walter Myers Gable, Norman, Cleveland County; Myrtle Walter, Covington, Garfield
County, who played it near Enid, Garfield County.)

1 Once there was a miller boy, he lived by the mill.
The mill turned around with its own free will.
Hand upon the hopper and the other on the sack.
The boy in the middle says: Smack, boys, smack.

2 Once there was a miller boy, he lived by the mill.
The mill turned around with its own free will.
Hand upon the hopper and the other on the jug.
The boy in the middle says: Hug, boys, hug.

3 Once there was a miller boy, he lived by the mill.
The mill turned around with its own free will.
Hand upon the hopper and the other on the sack.
The boy in the middle says: Ladies step forward, and the gents fall back
three (*or any number*).

Other variants by Louise Ann Aldridge, Quinton, Pittsburg County;
Mrs. Marjorie Allen, Lexington, Cleveland County; Kendall Andrews,
Chickasha, Grady County; Louis E. Baily, Oklahoma City, Oklahoma
County; Ethel Rose Baird, Bixby, Tulsa County; John Troy Baker, Turley,

Tulsa County; Warren Barnhill, Yukon, Canadian County; Lois Ferguson Beckham, Norman, Cleveland County; Creed Bogan, Duncan, Stephens County; Gerald Bond, Oklahoma City, Oklahoma County, who played it at Chickasha, Grady County; Jane Bowman, Pauls Valley, Garvin County; B. F. Brewer, Oklahoma City, Oklahoma County; Jessie Lee Bryant, Billings, Noble County; Clifford Chandler, Crescent, Logan County; Mary Esther Coffman, Geary, Blaine County; J. O. Conner, Shawnee, Pottawatomie County; Bert H. Cook, Binger, Caddo County; C. L. Cowan, Okemah, Okfuskee County, from Mrs. J. T. Baker, Norman, Cleveland County; Wanda Dalton, Curtis, Woodward County, who played it near Cheney, Kansas; Delmer Denton, Blackwell, Kay County; Harry L. Deupree, Oklahoma City, Oklahoma County, from Nebraska, Iowa, Missouri; Alma Dixon, Norman, Cleveland County; Leonard C. Dresser, Lahoma, Garfield County, who played it near Vernon, Garfield County; Elbert Durkee, Norman, Cleveland County; Ruth Edwards, Waurika, Jefferson County; Evalyne Ellis, Ochelata, Washington County; Faneta Fitchett, Billings, Noble County; Atlee Margaret Garrett, Loco, Stephens County; Raymond Hugh Guthrie, Wakita, Grant County; Catherine Harris, Antlers, Pushmataha Country, from S. B. Hackett, Norman, who played it in Arkansas; Mabel Harryman, Lexington, Cleveland County; Mary Haxel, Purcell, McClain County, who played it near Noble, Cleveland County, and Washington, McClain County; Harold L. Heiple, Oklahoma City, Oklahoma County; Ruby Home, Calumet, Canadian County; Ellen Hopkins, Tulsa, Tulsa County; George O. Hopkins, Norman, Cleveland County; Paul Howard, Headrick, Jackson County; Cora Huddleston, Norman, Cleveland County; Ben Huey, Norman, Cleveland County; Helen Jacobs, Tulsa, Tulsa County; Walter Jordan, Apperson, Osage County; Fanny W. Kelly, Jefferson, Grant County; Mary Virginia Maloy, Norman, Cleveland County; Mrs. T. H. Maness, Oswalt, Love County; Bertha Matthews, Norman, Cleveland County, who played it in Texas; Beatrice Jennings McMullin, Norman, Cleveland County, brought from Kentucky to Missouri, then to Kay and Grant Counties on Oklahoma-Kansas border; Florette McNeese, Oklahoma City, Oklahoma County, from her pupils; Alvin C. Meixner, Alva, Woods County; Gene Michael, Marietta, Love County; Esca Milne, Oklahoma City, Oklahoma County; Forest N. Nelson, Duncan, Stephens County; Zelma Oliver, Norman, Cleveland County, from Eugene Nolen, Norman; Seth Payton, Rhea, Dewey County; Ruby Pfautsch, Norman, Cleveland County, from St. Louis, Missouri, and vicinity; William Plaster, Meeker, Lincoln County; Audra A. Plumlee, Norman, Cleveland County, from Northwestern Arkansas; Ruth Prutsman, Spearman, Ochitree County, Texas; Opal Roberts, Enid, Garfield

County; L. E. Russell, Cyril, Caddo County; Eula Savage, Oklahoma City, Oklahoma County; Anita Shaw, Thomas, Custer County; Rephord Hubert Stevens, Union City, Canadian County; A. J. Strange, Clinton, Custer County; Verla Summers, Snyder, Kiowa County, who played it near Mc-Cloud, Pottawatomie County; Madeline Tarpley, Shamrock, Texas; Lela Tilman, Sumner, Noble County; Fern Tuttle, Norman, Cleveland County, from his grandmother who played it in Indiana; Maude Markham Vaughan, Pawhuska, Osage County; Emma Vilhauer, Norman, Cleveland County; Doris G. Waters, Ponca City, Kay County, from her pupils; Carl West, Perico, Texas; James E. White, Norman, Cleveland County, who played it near Bradley, Grady County; Gerald Whitlaw, Waynoka, Woods County; Ralph W. Winstead, Forgan, Beaver County; Mrs. Della I. Young, Cheyenne, Roger Mills County, from Vashti Young.

70

MOLLIE BROOKS

Cf. "Molly Brooks," Randolph (Ozarks, Missouri), *JAFL,* 42:218; Wolford (Indiana), p. 71.

A

(Fanny Kelly, Jefferson, Grant County; Evelyn Roach, Shamrock, Texas.)

1 Mollie Brooks has gone to the isle,
    To the isle, to the isle.
Mollie Brooks has gone to the isle,
    And she'll never return, they say, (*Three times.*)
Mollie Brooks has gone to the isle,
    And she'll never return, they say.

2 Bow to your opposite pard,
    And now to your own true love.
Swing your opposite once and a half
    And now your turtle dove.
Four hands half and ladies dosey do,
And on to the next you go.

B

MOLLY BROOKS HAS GONE TO THE ISLES

(John Cunningham, Watonga, Blaine County, from his father, William, who played it at Homestead, Blaine County.)

1 Molly Brooks has gone to the isles, (*Three times.*)
    And they say she'll never return.

Chorus:
    And they say she'll never return,
    And they say she'll never return,
        Molly Brooks has gone to the isles,
    And they say she'll never return,

71

NELLIE GRAY

(Florette McNeese, Oklahoma City, Oklahoma County, from her pupils.)

See "that touching ballad, 'Darling Nelly Gray'" (Paskman and Spaeth, "*Gentlemen, Be Seated!*", pp. 118-120), by Hanby, "of the grief of family separation" (Gaines, *The Southern Plantation*, p. 135).

Cf. Piper, *JAFL*, 28:265 (listed; "'Nelly Gray' escaped mutilation, perhaps because its length was satisfactory and all its verses familiar").

Danced like Virginia reel.

1 There's a low green valley on the old Kentucky shore,
    Where I've whiled many happy hours away
A-sitting and a-singing by the little cottage door
    Where lived my darling Nellie Gray.

Chorus:
  Oh, my darling Nellie Gray,
  They have taken her away
    And I'll never see my darling any more;
  I am sitting by the river and I'm weeping all the day,
    Since you've gone from the old Kentucky shore.

2 One night I went to see her, but "she's gone" the neighbors say,
    "The white man hath bound her with his chain,
They have taken her to Georgia for to wear her life away
    And she's toiled in the cotton and the cane."

Chorus:
  Oh, my poor Nellie Gray, they have taken her away
    And I'll never see my darling any more;
  They have taken her to Georgia for to wear her life away
    And she's gone from the old Kentucky shore.

3 My eyes are getting blinded and I cannot see the way;
    Hark! there's somebody knocking at the door;
I hear the angels calling and I see my Nellie Gray,
    Farewell to the old Kentucky shore.

Chorus:
  Oh, my darling Nellie Gray, up in heaven, so they say,
    They will never take you from me any more,
  I am coming, coming, coming, as the angels clear the way,
    Farewell to the old Kentucky shore.

72

OATS, PEAS, BEANS, AND BARLEY GROWS

(Amy Etta Bly, Dale, Pottawatomie County; Margaret Hogan, Tuttle, Grady County; Mary Virginia Maloy, Norman, Cleveland County.)

For British versions, see "Oats and Beans," Broadwood and Maitland (*English County Songs*), p. 87; "Oats and Beans and Barley," Gomme, 2:1-13 (eighteen texts); "Peas, Beans, Oats, and the Barley" (English catch), *Journal of the Folk-Song Society,* 1:67; "Oats and beans and barley grow," Northall, pp. 370-372 (two texts); "Oats and Beans," Walter (*Old English Singing Games*), pp. 26-27.

For American versions, see "I Like Coffee and I Like Tea," Babcock (Washington, D. C.), *American Anthropologist,* 1:251-252; "O sweet beans and barley grows," *ibid.,* p. 252; "Oats-Peas-Beans," Champlin, p. 508; Eggleston (*The Circuit Rider*), p. 22; "Old Sweet Peas and Barley Grows," Hoke (North Carolina), *JAFL,* 5:118 (listed); "Oats, Pease, Beans, and Barley Grows," Newell, pp. 80-84; "Oats, Peas, Beans, and Barley Grow," Newton (*Graded Games and Rhythmic Exercises*), pp. 38-39; "Oats, Peas, Beans, and Barley," Piper (Illinois), *JAFL,* 28:273; "Oats and Beans and Barley," Pound (Nebraska, *Syllabus*), p. 74; "We're on the Way to Baltimore," Rourke (*Davy Crockett*), pp. 27-28; "Oats, Pease, Beans, and Barley Grows," Van Doren (Eastern Illinois), *JAFL,* 32:494; "Oats, Beans, and Barley Grow," Wier (*Songs the Children Love to Sing*), p. 107; "Thus the Farmer Sows His Seed," Wolford (Indiana), pp. 94-95.

For use as a counting-out rhyme, see Bolton (Iowa), p. 119.

For Stanza 4, see GETTING MARRIED.

1 Oats, peas, beans, and barley grows.
   Oats, peas, beans, and barley grows.
   Nor you, nor I, nor nobody knows
   How oats, peas, beans, and barley grows.

2 Thus the farmer sows his seed.
   Thus he stands and takes his ease,
   Stamps his foot and claps his hands.
   And turns around to view his lands.

3 A-waiting for a partner,
   A-waiting for a partner,
   So open the ring and choose one in.
   Make haste and choose a partner.

4 Now you're married, you must obey,
   You must be true to all you say.
   You must be kind, you must be good,
   And keep your wife in kindling wood.

Directions: "Any number of children clasp hands and form a circle, one of their number remaining in the center. They move left as they sing the first four lines. They then stand still and, dropping hands, go through the various motions suggested in the next four lines. The children again clasp hands and continue in the same direction as before while singing the first two lines of the third stanza. On the two lines following, all drop hands again and stand while the one in the center either beckons to or takes a partner, who joins her in the center. All those in the circle now shake their forefinger warningly at the couple in the center as the last stanza is sung. The game is repeated with the one who was chosen remaining in the center."—Margaret Hogan.

Variants by Hattie Bell Bethea, Marion, South Carolina; Evalyne E. Ellis, Ochelata, Washington County; Helen Jacobs, Tulsa, Tulsa County; Bertha Matthews, Norman, Cleveland County, who played it in Texas; Ed Mills, Oklahoma City, Oklahoma County, from Atchison, Kansas; Vernon T. Sanford, Chickasha, Grady County.

73
THE OCEAN IS WIDE

(Mrs. Christine Clark, Norman, Cleveland County, who played it near Vinita, in Craig and Mayes Counties.)

For Stanza 1, cf. "The Road Is Wide," Perrow (East Tennessee), *JAFL,* 28:187.

For Stanza 2, cf. White (Alabama), p. 328.

For Stanza 3, cf. "Roses Red," Talley, p. 128.

For Stanzas 2 and 3, cf. Henry (Georgia), *JAFL,* 47:340.

Cf. "I'll Sail on the Sea," reported by Dr. Josiah H. Combs, of Texas Christian University, from Knott County, Kentucky.

1 The world is round and the sea is deep, (*Three times.*)
   And in your arms, I long to sleep.

Chorus:
   I'll cut my way where the bullets fly, (*Three times.*)
   I'll sail on the sea till the day I die.

2 Sure as the grape grows on the vine, (*Three times.*)
   I will be yours if you'll be mine.

3 Sure as the vine runs round the stump,
   You are my own sweet sugar lump.

4 Sure as the fruit grows on the tree,
   Some time you will my wife be.

5 The rose is red and the violet blue,
Candy is sweet, and so are you.

6 If you love me as I love you,
No knife can cut our love in two.

See WALKING ON THE GREEN GRASS.

1 The ocean is wide, and I can't step it.
I love you, and you can't he'p it.

2 Sure as the vine grows round the rafter,
You're the girl that I'm after.

3 Sure as the moss grows round the stump,
You're my darling sugar lump.

4 When you get married and your old man gets cross,
Pick up the broom and show him who's boss.

5 When you get married and your baby gets cross,
For gosh sake, don't give it pepper sauce.

74
OH, AIN'T I SWEET

"The spirit of the words and the formation of the stanzas recall 'Old Joe Clark,' but it is usually considered a separate song."—Florette Mc-Neese.

Based on a Negro song. Cf. Bass (South Carolina), *JAFL*, 44:433-434; "Oh, Susan Quit Your Fooling," Dobie, *PTFS*, 6:134-135; "Massa Had a Little Yaller Gal," Henry (North Carolina), *JAFL*, 45:170-171; "When de Band Begins to Play," Odum and Johnson (*The Negro and His Songs*), pp. 235-237; "Hump-Back Mule," *idem* (*Negro Workaday Songs*), p. 179; "Goin' Down to Town," Sandburg, p. 145; "Massa Had a Yaller Gal," Scarborough (Louisiana, South Carolina, Kentucky), pp. 66-68 (three texts); "Brother Ephrum Got de Coon and Gone On," *idem* (Virginia), p. 101; "Massa Had a Yaller Gal," White (Alabama, North Carolina), pp. 152-156, 324 (eight texts, with annotations); "The Gal from the South," *idem*, pp. 450-451. For Stanza 2 of B, cf. also "Edmund Had an Old Gray Horse," "That Mule," Perrow (East Tennessee, Mississippi), *JAFL*, 26:124, 126.

Cf. "Oh, Ain't I Gone," Ames (Missouri), *JAFL*, 24:299-300; "Ain't I Goin'," Piper (Western Nebraska, from Arkansas), *JAFL*, 28:271-272.

See IN SOMEBODY'S GARDEN, LONDON TOWN, OLD JOE CLARK, SUSAN JANE.

A

(Sung by Levi Wilcox, Noble, Cleveland County.)

1 You may ride the old gray horse,
    And I will ride the roan.
  You may court vour own sweetheart,
    But I will court my own.

Chorus:
    Oh, ain't I sweet, (Three times.)
    Everybody knows.

B

(Florette McNeese, Oklahoma City, Oklahoma County, from her pupils.)

1 You may ride the old gray horse,
    And I will ride the roan.
  You may court your own sweetheart,
    But you'd better let mine alone.

Chorus:
    Oh, ain't I sweet, sweet, sweet, (Three times.)
    Everybody knows.

2 Massa had a yellow cow,
    She had a holler horn;
  And every tooth in her head
    Would hold a barrel of corn.

3 Massa had a yaller gal,
    And she was from the South.
  She did her hair up so tight
    She could not shut her mouth.

4 Higher in the cherry tree,
    Riper grows the cherry;
  Never saw a pretty girl
    But what she wanted to marry.

Directions: Right and left figure.

C

(No Title)

(Ruth Davis, Fort Worth, Texas.)

1 Massie had a yellow cow
    That had a crumpled horn.
Every tooth in her head
    Held a bushel of corn.
I love Cindy, Cindy,
    And everybody knows.

2 I wish I had a nickle,
    I wish I had a dime.
I wish I had a dollar bill,
    I'd go see that girl of mine.
Oh! I love Cindy, Cindy,
    And everybody knows
I love Cindy.

D

Marsa's Yaller Gal

(Helen Jacobs, Tulsa, Tulsa County.)

1 Oh, Marsa got 'im a yaller gal,
    He got 'er way down South.
Her hair was curled so very tight
    She couldn't shut her mouth.

Chorus:
    Hop along, Peter; it's hop along, Peter.
    Hop along, Peter, where ya gwine?

2. Her head is like a coffee pot,
    Her nose is like a spout.
Mouth is like a fireplace
    With ashes taken out.

3 He took her to the tailor shop
    To git her mouth made small.
She opened her mouth so big and wide
    She swallowed shop and all.

75

(THE) OLD BRASS WAGON

Cf. Ames (Missouri), *JAFL*, 24:307-308; Ball (Idaho), *JAFL*, 44:13;
Dudley and Payne (Texas), *PTFS*, 1:17; Hamilton (Northeast Missouri),
JAFL, 27:293-294, 298; Piper (Western Nebraska), *JAFL*, 28:282-283;
Randolph (Ozarks, Missouri), *JAFL*, 42:216-217 (also *The Ozarks*, pp.

159-160); Sandburg (Indiana), p. 159; Wolford (Indiana), pp. 76-77 (two texts).

Tune of chorus: SKIP TO MY LOU.

A

LITTLE BRASS WAGON

(Sung by Leondis Brown, Noble, Cleveland County.)

1 Lead 'er up an' down, the little brass wagon, (*Three times.*)
  One wheel off an' the axle draggin'.

Chorus:
  Skip, skip, skip to my Lou, (*Three times.*)
  Skip to my Lou, my darling.

(Played like SKIP TO MY LOU. "There's a whole lot of verses that are sung to different songs.")

B

LEAD HER UP AND DOWN THE AISLE, *or* OLD BRASS WAGON

(Beatrice Jennings McMullin, Norman, Cleveland County, brought from Kentucky to Missouri, then to Kay and Grant Counties, on Oklahoma-Kansas border.)

1 Lead her up and down (the aisle) to the old brass wagon, (*Three times.*)
  You're the one, my darling.

2 Turn and swing the old brass wagon, etc.

3 Wouldn't kiss a pretty boy if I didn't love him, etc.

4 Wheels run off and double-trees dragging, etc.

5 All run away with the old brass wagon, etc.

Directions: "Boys and girls form an aisle facing each other. First couple at end goes up and down the aisle while first stanza is sung. The boy swings girls and the girl swings the boys, then swinging each other. When the line has been swung, all promenade, singing last stanza."

C

(Professor John Alley, Norman, Cleveland County, from North Texas.)

1 One wheel off the old brass wagon, (*Three times.*)
    You're the one, my darling.

Chorus:
    Swing and turn the old brass wagon, etc.

2 Two wheels off the old brass wagon, etc.

3 Three wheels off the old brass wagon, etc.

4 Four wheels off the old brass wagon, etc.

6 Tongue came out of the old brass wagon, etc.

Variants:

(Oh, we'll) Lead her up and down the old brass wagon, (*Three times.*)
    (So) Early in the morning.

> (Gerald Bond, Oklahoma City, Oklahoma County, who played it in
> Chickasha, Grady County; Mrs. T. H. Maness, Oswalt, Love County;
> Elizabeth Stewart, Chelsea, Rogers County, from Mrs. Jane Ida Hicks,
> Chelsea.)

O, Mr. Right, I'll tell your daddy. (*Three times.*)
    How you court the ladies.
        (Florette McNeese, Oklahoma City, Oklahoma County, from her pupils.)

Tripping up and down the old brass wagon, (*Three times.*)
    You're the one, my darling.
        (C. B. Williams, Elk City, Beckham County.)

Other variants by Mary Esther Coffman, Geary, Blaine County; Helen
A. Cook, Norman, Cleveland County; Roger Givens, Oklahoma City,
Oklahoma County, played in the Choctaw Nation, Indian Territory; Lillie
O. Heaton, Watonga, Blaine County; Mrs. L. T. Monnett, Norman, Cleve-
land County, who played it in Missouri; Beatrice Penn, Cordell, Washita
County; Florence Whitelock, Norman, Cleveland County, from Indiana.

76

OLD DAN TUCKER

Based on the "celebrated banjo song" (c. 1840) by Dan D. Emmett.
    Cf. Gaines, *The Southern Plantation,* p. 132; Pound, *Poetic Origins
and the Ballad,* p. 319. Although not of Negro origin (cf. Sullivan, *Our
Times,* 2:165-167), it is reported as sung by slaves before the war and
"fiddled" for Negro dancers (Scarborough, Arkansas, p. 199). See Chapple

(*Heart Songs*), p. 174; *Good Old-Time Songs*, No. 2, p. 43; *Ideal Home Music Library*, 10:273; Marsh's *Selection or Singing for the Million*, 2:1-3 (where the composer's name is spelled "Emmit"); *Minstrel Songs Old and New*, pp. 150-151 (also White, pp. 446-447); Paskman and Spaeth (*"Gentlemen, Be Seated!"*), pp. 42-44.

Cf. "Sam, Sam dirty old man," Douglas (*London Street Games*), p. 55; "Sam, Sam" and "My son John is a nice old man," Johnson (*What They Say in New England*), pp. 183-184; Lomax (*American Ballads and Folk Songs*), pp. 258-262; "Captain Dime," Talley, p. 5; "Old man Baker was a good old man," White (North Carolina), pp. 160-161.

Burchenal (*American Country-Dances*, 1:62-63) gives the music and calls for the square dance of the same name, and Bolton gives counting-out rhymes concerning Old Dan Tucker (*The Counting-Out Rhymes of Children*, p. 123; *JAFL*, 10:321).

For Old Dan Tucker as a legendary figure, cf. Rourke (*American Humor*), p. 85.

For "Old Dan Tucker climbed a tree," cf. Finger (*Frontier Ballads*), p. 165; "Zaccheus Climbed the Sycamo' Tree," Scarborough (Virginia), pp. 200, 286.

For "Fell in the fire and kicked out a chunk," cf. Bass (South Carolina), *JAFL*, 44:427; "Aunt Dinah Drunk," "Animal Fair," Talley, pp. 53, 159-160.

For "Riding a goat and leading a hound," cf. "Ole Aunt Dinah," Scarborough, p. 188.

For "Old Dan Tucker sang for his supper," cf. "Little Tom Tucker," *Mother Goose* (Dent and Dutton), p. 79.

For "Hog and sheep goin' to the pasture," cf. Bass (South Carolina), *JAFL*, 44:435; "Cotton Field Song," Lomax (*American Ballads and Folk Songs*), p. 242; "Sheep and Shote," Perrow (Virginia Negroes), *JAFL*, 26:131; "Sheep and Goat," Talley, p. 17.

For the "darby ram" stanza, cf. Stanza 3 of Version B, "My True-Love Has Gone to France," Tolman and Eddy, *JAFL*, 35:403.

For game, dance, and play-party versions, see Ames (Missouri), *JAFL*, 24:309-310; Ball (Idaho), *JAFL*, 44:16; Blair (Kentucky), *JAFL*, 40:96-97; Douthitt (Kentucky), p. 37; Dudley and Payne (Texas), *PTFS*, 1:14-15 (two texts); Gardner (Michigan), *JAFL*, 33:116-117 (four texts); Heck (Cincinnati), *JAFL*, 40:23; Mahan and Grahame (Iowa), pp. 54-56; Perrow (East Tennessee), *JAFL*, 28:131-132; Piper (Eastern Nebraska), *JAFL*, 28:284; Pound (Nebraska, *Syllabus*), p. 73; Randolph (Ozarks, Missouri), *JAFL*, 42:209-210 (also *The Ozarks*, pp. 149-151); Shearin and

Combs (Kentucky), p. 38 (listed); *Social Plays, Games,* etc., p. 17; Van Doren (Eastern Illinois), *JAFL,* 32:488-489; Wedgwood (Southwestern Nebraska, Southern Iowa, from Missouri), *JAFL,* 25:272-273; Wolford (Indiana, Texas), pp. 78-80 (three texts).

A

(Sung by Charlie Carr, Noble, Cleveland County.)

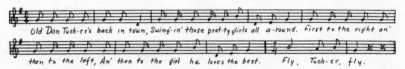

Old Dan Tucker's back in town,
    Swinging' those pretty girls all around,
First to the right an' then to the left,
    An' then to the girl he loves the best.
    Fly, Tucker, fly.

("We were havin' a dance. The music had to leave pretty early, an' we were sittin' around there, so we said we'll have some party games.")

B

(Florette McNeese, Oklahoma City, Oklahoma County, from her pupils.)

1 Old Dan Tucker came to town,
    Saluting his partners all around,
    First to the right and then to the left,
    And then to the one that you love best.

Chorus:
    Get out of the way for old Dan Tucker,
    He's too late to get his supper.
    Supper's over, and the cook's in bed.
    And old Dan Tucker's got a pain in his head.

2 Old Dan Tucker's a fine old man,
    Washed his face in the frying pan,
    Combed his hair with a wagon wheel,
    And died with the toothache in his heel.

Chorus 2:
    Get out of the way for old Dan Tucker,
    He's too late to get his supper.
    Supper's over, breakfast's cookin',
    Old Dan Tucker stands a-lookin'.

3 Old Dan Tucker's a nice old man,
   He used to ride the darby ram.
   He sent him whizzing to the foot of the hill;
   If he's not got up he's lying there still.

Chorus 3:
   Get out of the way for old Dan Tucker,
   He's too late to get his supper.
   Supper's over and the dishes washed,
   And nothing's left but a piece of squash.

4 Old Dan Tucker, he got drunk,
   He fell in the fire and kicked up a stump.
   Fire was hot, and the ashes flew,
   And old Dan Tucker flew some too.

5 Old Dan Tucker went out shootin',
   First thing he saw was an old sow rootin',
   Her nose in the ground and her tail a-shakin',
   Get out of the way, or 'll save your bacon.

Variant and additional stanzas:

Old Dan Tucker came home drunk,
Fell in the fire and kicked out a chunk.
Coal of fire got in his shoe.
O Lordamassie! how the ashes flew!

   (Professor John Alley, Norman, Cleveland County, who played it in North
   Texas.)

Old Dan Tucker went to town,
Riding a goat and leading a hound.
The hound yelled, the goat jumped,
Threw Old Dan Tucker astraddle a stump.

Old Dan Tucker, he got drunk,
Fell into the fire and kicked up a chunk.
A red hot coal fell down his shoe,
And oh, my Mamma, how the ashes flew!

   (Louis E. Bailey, Oklahoma City, Oklahoma County, through Lena E.
   Misener.)

Old Dan Tucker climbed a tree
Just for his Lord to see.
Limb did break and he did fall,
And he didn't see his Lord at all.

   (Gerald Bond, Chickasha, Grady County, through Lena E. Misener).

Old Dan Tucker, the other day,
Took a ride in a one-horse sleigh.
Horse ran away, sleigh upset,
And I haven't seen anything of Daniel yet.

> (Beatrice Jennings McMullin, Norman, Cleveland County, brought from
> Kentucky to Missouri, then to Kay and Grant Counties, on Oklahoma-Kansas
> border.)

Hog and sheep goin' to the pasture,
Hog says, "Sheep, let's get a little faster."
Sheep shell corn and rattle the horn.
Never heard like since I been born.

> (Christine Bettis, Norman, Cleveland County.)

Old Dan Tucker he went a-shootin'.
There he spied a wild hog a-rootin'.
Hog bristled up and set Dan to shakin';
That was all that saved his bacon.

> (Professor Kenneth C. Kaufman, Norman, Cleveland County, who played
> it in Eastern Custer County.)

Old Dan Tucker was a fine old soul,
He washed his face in the creamery bowl;
He combed his hair in (*sic*) a wagon wheel;
He died with a toothache in his heel.

> (William Lorenzen, El Reno, Canadian County.)

Old Dan Tucker went to town,
He swallowed a hogshead of 'lasses down.
The 'lasses worked, the hogshead bust,
And it throwed old Dan in a thunder gust.

Old Dan Tucker went to town,
  Riding a little pony.
He stuck a feather in his cap
  And called it macaroni.

Old Dan Tucker went to town,
  He wore his daddy's trousers.
He said he couldn't see the town
  For so many houses.

> (Ruby Burns, Noble, Cleveland County, from her mother.)

Old Dan Tucker and his wife one day
Went out in a one-horse shay.
The shay it broke, the horse went blind,
And he had no hair on his tail behind.

Old Dan Tucker went to town,
Riding a goat and leading a hound.
The hound got loose in the middle of the street,
And he couldn't catch him for his number ten feet.

(Harold Roberts, Blackwell, Kay County.)

Old Dan Tucker sang for his supper.
What shall we eat? White bread and butter.
How can we eat without a knife?
How can he marry without a wife?

(Bernice Penn, Cordell, Washita County.)

Other variants by Warren Barnhill, Yukon, Canadian County; Lois
Beckham, Norman, Cleveland County, from Nacona, Texas; Hattie Bell
Bethea, Marion, South Carolina; Jane Bowman, Pauls Valley, Garvin
County; Jewel Collings, Norman, Cleveland County; Helen A. Cook,
Norman, Cleveland County, from the Big Pasture, Tillman County; Ruth
Davis, Fort Worth, Texas; Dessie Deal, Billings, Noble County; Lucile
Dean, Weleetka, Okfuskee County; Harry L. Deupree, Oklahoma City,
Oklahoma County, from Nebraska, Iowa, Missouri; Joe C. Edwards,
Enid, Garfield County; Mrs. Bertha Downing, Norman, Cleveland County,
who played it in Southern Noble, Northeastern Logan, and Northern
Payne Counties; Thelma A. Epler, Norman, Cleveland County; Tephia
Folsom, Atoka, Atoka County, from Ed Butler (colored), Atoka; Agnes
Frick, Oklahoma City, Oklahoma County; Alta LeGate, Muskogee,
Muskogee County; Roger Givens, Oklahoma City, Oklahoma County,
from the Choctaw Nation, Indian Territory; Virginia Godfrey, Oklahoma
City, Oklahoma County; Alice Flora Hare, Norman, Cleveland County,
from Mrs. Hollis Bound, Norman; Catherine Harris, Antlers, Pushmataha
County, from S. B. Hackett, Norman, who played it in Arkansas; Frank
Henry, Dearden, Britton County; G. O. Hopkins, Norman, Cleveland
County; Helen Jacobs, Tulsa, Tulsa County; Mary Virginia Maloy, Nor-
man, Cleveland County, from her father who played it in Granbury,
Texas; Mrs. T. H. Maness, Oswalt, Love County; Syrian E. Marbut,
Eufaula, McIntosh County; Bertha Matthews, Norman, Cleveland County,
from Texas; Ralph J. May, Oklahoma City, Oklahoma County, from Iowa;
Gene Michael, Marietta, Love County; Mrs. Demma Ray Oldham, Okla-
homa City, Oklahoma County, who played it in Arkansas; Bernice Penn,
Cordell, Washita County; Ruby Pfautsch, Norman, Cleveland County,
from Tryon, Lincoln County; Audra A. Plumlee, Norman, Cleveland
County, from Arkansas; Anita D. Shaw, Thomas, Custer County; Cora
Frances Starritt, Ada, Pontotoc County; Doris G. Waters, Ponca City,

Kay County, from her pupils; Florence Whitelock, Norman, Cleveland County, from Indiana.

77
OLD DOC COLLINS

Requested by Payne (Texas), *PTFS,* 1:35-38. "Ceiling" in B is obviously a corruption of "Cecilia." The name "Cecilia" occurs in "Good-Day, Cecilia," an old French game "much like the English one of 'The Muffin Man'" (Kidson and Moffat, *Eighty Singing Games,* p. 59).

For the pattern, cf. CHASE THE SQUIRREL (2), JUTANG, LONDON.

A

CELIE

(Sung by Levi Wilcox, Noble, Cleveland County.)

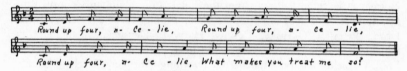

Round up four, a-Celie, (*Three times.*)
    What makes you treat me so?
    (*Continues like D, with "a-Celie" for "Celia."*)

B

(Leora Austin, Foss, Washita County.)

1 (*Sung while marching around in a circle.*)
Old Doc Collins is a married man.
    A married man, a married man.
Old Doc Collins is a married man,
    What makes you treat him so?

2 (*Sung while swinging your partner.*)
Wheel and turn the ceiling, (*Three times.*)
    What makes you treat him so?

3 (*Swinging partner in opposite direction.*)
The other way the ceiling, etc.

4 (*Changing partners and promenading.*)
The corners of the ceiling, etc.

266

C

CECILA

(Mary Haxel, Purcell, McClain County, who played it near Noble, Cleveland County, and Washington, McClain County.)

1 Old Doc Collins is a married man,
 Married man, married man,
 Old Doc Collins is a married man,
 What makes you do him so?

2 All go down to Cecila,
 To Cecila, to Cecila.
 All go down to Cecila,
 What makes you Cecila so?

3 Round up eight in Cecila, etc.

4 Break corners off Cecila, etc.

5 Treat 'em all alike, Cecila, etc.

6 Promenade home, Cecila, etc.

D

CELIA

(Ezra Van Horn, Norman, Cleveland County.)

1 Round up four, Celia, (*Three times.*)
 What makes you treat me so?

2 Do-si-do, Celia, etc.

3 Once-and-a-half, Celia, etc.

4 Treat 'em all alike, Celia, etc.

5 Promenade home, Celia, etc.

6 Round up six, Celia, etc.

7 Do-si-do, Celia, etc.

8 Once-and-a-half, Celia, etc.

9 Treat 'em all alike, Celia, etc.

10 We're all church members, Celia, etc.

267

11 Promenade home, Celia, etc.

12 Round up eight, Celia, etc.

13 Do-si-do, Celia, etc.

14 Once-and-a-half, Celia, etc.

15 Treat 'em all alike, Celia, etc.

16 We're all church mmbers, Celia, etc.

17 Last old time, Celia, etc.

18 Promenade home, etc.

19 Round up ten, Celia, etc.

78
(THE) OLD GRAY MARE

"The melody here is directly appropriated from the Negro spiritual, 'The Old Gray Mare Came Tearin' out the Wilderness.' "—Sandburg, p. 102. This is also a college song.

Cf. "Old Gray Hoss," Ames (Missouri), *JAFL*, 24:311; "Tearin' Out-a Wilderness" (cotton chopping song), Lomax (*American Ballads and Folk Songs*), pp. 336-338; "Down in Alabama," Piper (Western Nebraska), *JAFL*, 28:266; Sandburg, pp. 102-103; Scarborough, p. 183; White (North Carolina), p. 230.

Combs (*Dialect Notes*, 4:318) reports "williners" for "wilderness," with the query, "Willows?"

> Old gray horse come a-trottin' through the *williners*
> Down in Alabamy.

A

(Catherine Harris, Antlers, Pushmataha County.)

1 The old gray mare ain't what she used to be,
    Ain't what she used to be, ain't what she used to be.
  The old gray mare ain't what she used to be,
    Many long years ago.

2 The old gray horse came tearing out of the wilderness.
    Tearing out of the wilderness, tearing out of the wilderness.
  The old gray horse came tearing out of the wilderness,
    Early in the morning.

B

(Mrs. Bertha Downing, Norman, Cleveland County, who played it in Southern Noble, Northeastern Logan, and Northern Payne Counties.)

> The old gray mare, she ain't what she used to be,
>> Ain't what she used to be,
> The old gray mare, she ain't what she used to be,
>> Twenty long years ago.

79

OLD JOE CLARK

This potpourri of Southern song, with its rough and tumble nonsense, is one of the most carefree mixtures in the play-party canon, having attracted to it scores of stanzas from other songs as well as a "wild medley" of figures from other dance games (Randolph, p. 221).

The following stanza in a Texas version (Dudley and Payne, p. 34)—

> Yes, old Joe Clark, that good old man.
>> We will never see him any more,
> He left here wearing an overcoat
>> All buttoned-up down before.

points to a source in the opening of Albert Gordon Green's comic poem, "Old Grimes" (1827):

> Old Grimes is dead — that good old man,
>> We ne'er shall see him more,
> He wore a single-breasted coat
>> That buttoned down before.

For "Old Grimes," see Bryant (*The Family Library of Poetry and Song*), pp. 878-879; Pound (*Syllabus*), p. 38 (excerpt); Spaeth (*Weep Some More, My Lady*), pp. 150-151 (sung to the tune of "Auld Lang Syne"); Thornton (*An American Glossary*), 2:974-975.

Cox (*Folk-Songs of the South*, p. 490) cites another derivative of Greene's poem, under the same title, beginning:

> Old Grimes is dead, that good old man,
>> We ne'er shall see him more;
> He used to wear an old gray coat,
>> All buttoned up before, my boys,
>> All buttoned up before.

Cf. also the Yorkshire rhyme to the chime of a house clock (tune, "York"; Alice B. Gomme, *Folk-Lore*, 20:79):

> Old Brigg is dead, that good old man,
>> We shall see him no more;
> Then let us chime six, four, nine,
>> As we have done before.

269

Cox's "Old Grimes" contains a stanza suggestive of the hogs in "Old Joe Clark":

> I wish I had a load of wood,
> > To fence my garden round;
> For the neighbors' pigs they do get in
> > And root up all my ground, my boys,
> > And root up all my ground.

Cf. "Goin' Down to Town" (Virginia Negroes), Perrow, *JAFL,* 28:139:

> Goin' down tuh town,
> Goin' down tuh town,
> Goin' down tuh Lynchburg town tuh take my baccer down;
> Buy me a load uh pos',
> Fence my grave aroun',
> Keep Bob Ridley's ole gray sow fum rootin' me out de groun'.

Below is an attempt to collate typical stanzas of this vigorously and fabulously vulgar comic epic of cards, chickens, courting, chains, coons, coon dogs, and other critters, indicating the allusiveness and elusiveness of play-party tradition.

For "made me wear the ball and chain," cf. the "only stanza my cousin could remember of a song in which a member of the chain gang curses the Judge, or state's attorney, who was responsible for the sentence" (Perrow, East Tennessee, *JAFL,* 28:135):

> God damn old Alexander! I wish he wuz in hell!
> He made me wear the ball en chain en caused my ankles ter swell.

Cf. "Oh, Ain't I Gone," Ames (Missouri), *JAFL,* 24:300.

For "high, low, jack, and game," cf. "High Low Jack an' the Game," Douthitt (Kentucky), pp. 35-36.

For "I wouldn't marry" stanzas, cf. "Oh, Ain't I Gone," Ames (Missouri), *JAFL,* 24:300; "A Black Gal," Bales (Texas Negroes), *PTFS,* 7:104; "Cindy," Bass (South Carolina), *JAFL,* 44:428-429; "Liza Jane," Blair (Kentucky), *JAFL,* 40:98; "Hurry, Boys, Hurry, *or* " 'Tain't Gonna Rain No More," Douthitt (Kentucky), p. 38; "Hop Right," Odum and Johnson (*The Negro and His Songs*), p. 191; Parker (North Carolina), *JAFL,* 20:247; "Oh, Mourner!", Perrow (Mississippi Negroes), *JAFL,* 28:136-137; "O My Laura Lee!", (North Carolina, Tennessee, Mississippi, and Kentucky whites and Mississippi Negroes), *ibid.,* pp. 175-177 (six texts); "I'll Not Marry at All" (popular song), Pound, *American Ballads and Songs,* pp. 208-209; *Poetic Origins,* p. 225n.; "I Would Not Marry a Black Girl," "I Wouldn't Marry a Yellow or a White Negro Girl," Talley, pp. 56, 63; Truitt (Kentucky), *JAFL,* 36:379; White (Alabama), pp. 323-324 (two texts).

For "I wish I had a needle and thread," cf. "Oh, Ain't I Gone," Ames (Missouri), *JAFL*, 24:300; "Liza Jane," Edmands (North Carolina), *JAFL*, 6:131; "Up and Down," Hamilton (Northeast Missouri), *JAFL*, 27:303; "Get Along Home," Owens (Texas), *Southwest Review*, 18:171; "Liza in the Summer Time," Sandburg (North Carolina), p. 309; "Bile dem Cabbage Down," Scarborough (Virginia), p. 125.

For "I wish I was an apple," cf. "Cindy," Henry (North Carolina), *JAFL*, 45:168; "I Wish I Was an Apple," Talley, p. 133; Truitt (Kentucky), *JAFL*, 36:379.

For "I wish I had a candy box," cf. "Oh, Ain't I Gone," Ames (Missouri), 24:300; "O My Laura Lee," Perrow (North Carolina), *JAFL*, 28:175; "Bile dem Cabbage Down," Scarborough (Virginia), p. 124.

For "I wish I was in Arkansaw," cf. "The Monkey," Perrow (Mississippi Negroes), *JAFL*, 26:131.

For "Peaches in the Summertime," cf. "Shady Grove," Combs (Kentucky), *Folk-Say: 1930*, p. 242; "Get Along Home," Owens (Texas), *Southwest Review*, 18:171; "O My Laura Lee," Perrow (Kentucky), *JAFL*, 28:176; "Shady Grove," (Kentucky), *ibid.*, p. 183; "My Luluh," Thomas (South Texas Negroes), *PTFS*, 5:165.

For "You may ride the old gray horse," cf. "Oh, Ain't I Gone," Ames (Missouri), *JAFL*, 24:300; " 'Liza Jane," Edmands (North Carolina), *JAFL*, 6:131; "Up and Down," Hamilton (Northeast Missouri), *JAFL*, 27:303; "Liza Jane," Perrow (Mississippi), *JAFL*, 28:180; "Ain't I Goin'," Piper (Western Nebraska, from Arkansas), *JAFL*, 28:271; "Harvest Song," Talley, p. 57; "My Luluh," Thomas (South Texas Negroes), *PTFS*, 5:165; Truitt (Kentucky), *JAFL*, 36:379. (Cf. also the speech of the Elf Knight to Lady Isabel in "Lady Isabel and the Elf Knight," Scarborough, p. 44:

> "An' you may ride your milk-white steed
> An' I my apple bay.")

For "The higher up the cherry tree," cf. "Oh, Ain't I Gone," Ames (Missouri), *JAFL*, 24:300; "Weevily Wheat," Dudley and Payne (Texas), *PTFS*, 1:18; "Weevily Wheat," Hamilton (Northeast Missouri), *JAFL*, 27:291; "Up and Down," *ibid.*, p. 302; Truitt (Kentucky), *JAFL*, 36:379; "Weevily Wheat," Wolford (Indiana), p. 103. Cf. the old saw:

> The higher up the plum-tree the riper the plum,
> The richer the cobbler the blacker his thumb.—Northall, p. 522.

For "a house full of chicken pie," cf. "Miss Mary Jane," Scarborough (South Carolina), p. 117; "Karo Song," *idem* (Texas), p. 171; White (Alabama), pp. 155, 288, 366.

For "Mushy had an old coon dog," cf. "Karo Song," above.

For "Some one stole my old coon dog," cf. Bass (South Carolina), *JAFL,* 44:434; "My Coon Dog," Perrow, *JAFL,* 26:128; White (Alabama, North Carolina), pp. 232, 283.

For "To roll up her dirty sleeves," cf. "Care in Bread-Making," Talley, p. 112.

For versions of "Old Joe Clark," see "Old Joe Clog," Cox (West Virginia), p. 495; Dudley and Payne (Texas), *PTFS,* 1:32-34; Lomax (Kentucky, *American Ballads and Folk Songs*), pp. 277-280; Owens (Texas), *Southwest Review,* 18:173-174; Perrow (East Tennessee, Mississippi), *JAFL,* 25:152 (two texts); Randolph (Ozarks, Missouri), *JAFL,* 42:221-223; Thomas (Kentucky), pp. 56, 106-107; White (North Carolina), pp. 336-337; Wilson (Ozarks), pp. 76-77.

References for other stanzas are given under the title to which they originally belong: "I went up a mountain top," LIZA JANE; "new-cut road, OLD VIRGINNY NEVER TIRE; "Massa had a yellow girl" and Old Joe Clark's horse and mule, OH, AIN'T I SWEET; "She fooled me in the summer time," LITTLE GIRL ROCKIN'; "Went down to Dinah's house," SUSAN JANE.

"Sweeten Liza Jane" is found in LIZA JANE and SHOO FLY (A); "chicken pie" becomes "punkin pie" in GARBER TOWN.

In the chorus "Lucy Long" and "golden slippers" are borrowed from the minstrel songs.

For "walk the chalk," cf. "Walk-a Chalk," Harris (*Uncle Remus and His Friends*), p. 204.

See BILE DEM CABBAGE DOWN, GOT A LITTLE HOME TO GO TO.

A

(Sung by Clayton Black, east of Noble, Cleveland County.)

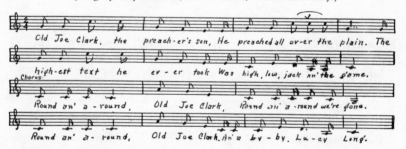

1 Old Joe Clark, the preacher's son,
    He preached all over the plain.
The highest text he ever took
    Was high, low, Jack an' the game.

Chorus:
  Round an' around, Old Joe Clark,
    Round an' around we're gone.
  Round an' around, Old Joe Clark,
    An' a by-by, Lucy Long.

'2 Old Joe Clark he had a dog,
    As blind as he could be.
Ran a redbug round a stump,
    And a coon up a holler tree.

3 If you see that girl of mine,
    Tell her if you please
Whenever she goes to roll that dough
    To roll up her dirty sleeves.

4 If you see that girl of mine,
    Tell her if you can
Whenever she goes to roll that dough
    To wash her dirty hands.

B

(Mabel Harryman, Lexington, Cleveland County.)

1 Old Joe Clark is dead and gone,
    Hope he is doing well.
Made me wear the ball and chain
    Till my old ankle swelled.

Chorus:
  Round and round, old Joe Clark,
    Round and round, I'm gone.
  Round and round, old Joe Clark,
    And good-by, Lucy Long.

2 I went down to old Joe's house,
    He was sick in bed;
Rammed my finger down his throat
    And pulled out a chicken head.

Chorus 2:
  Farewell, old Joe Clark,
    Farewell, I'm gone.
  Farewell, old Joe Clark,
    And good-by, Lucy Long.

273

3 I went down to old Joe's house,
　　He was eating supper.
　Stumped my toe on the table leg
　　And rammed my nose in the butter.*

4 I went down to see my gal,
　　She met me at the door
　With her shoes and stockings in her hands
　　And her feet all over the floor.

5 Old Joe Clark had a dog,
　　He was as blind as he could be.
　He chased a Negro round a stump,
　　I believe that dog could see.

6 Some one stole my old coon dog,
　　Wish they'd bring him back.
　He chased the big hogs through the fence
　　And the little ones through the crack.

7 Old Joe Clark was a preacher,
　　He preached all over Spain.
　The only text that he could take
　　Was high, low, jack, and the game.

8 Old Joe Clark had a house,
　　It was sixteen stories high,
　And every room in that house
　　Just smelled like chicken pie.

---

* Cf. "Chewing Gum":
　I took my girl to the ball one night.
　I thought I'd have some fun.
　But all in the world she would do
　Is set and chew her gum.

　Chorus:
　　Set and chew her gum,
　　Set and chew her gum—
　　All in the world she would do
　　Is set and chew her gum.

　I took my girl to the ball one night.
　I took her out to supper.
　She stubbed her toe on the table leg
　And stuck her nose in the butter.
　　(Sherman E. Hively, Coyle, Logan County. Cf. Pound, *Syllabus,* p. 59.)

C

(Paul Howard, Headrick, Jackson County.)

1 Old Joe Clark a preacher,
    Preached on the plains.
But the highest text he ever took
    Was high, low, jack and game.

Chorus:
    Fare ye well, old Joe Clark,
      Good-by, Betsy Brown.
    Fare ye well, old Joe Clark,
      I'm going to leave this town.*

2 Met a possum in the road,
    Blind as he could be,
Jumped the fence and whipped my dog
    And bristled up at me.

3 Chicken on a haystack,
    Hawk came flying by,
Grabbed the chicken by the neck
    And feathers began to fly.

4 Wouldn't marry a preacher gal,
    I'll tell you the reason why,
Her neck's so long and stringy,
    I'm afraid she'll never die.

5 Went down to Dinah's house,
    Saw her standin' in the door,
Shoes and stockin's in her hand
    And feet all over the floor.

6 Old Joe Clark had a house,
    Forty stories high,
And every story in that house
    Was filled with chicken pie.

7 Old Joe Clark had a horse,
    Name was Morgan Brown,
And everywhere he went
    He covered an acre of ground.

---

* From a popular song of about thirty years ago, "When That Evening Sun Goes Down."—P. H.

8 Well, I wish I had a nickle,
　　I wish I had a dime,
　I wish I had a pretty gal
　　To kiss and call her mine.

D

(Sherman E. Hively, Coyle, Logan County.)

1 Going down the lane,
　　It was dark and hazy.
　Every time I thought of my girl
　　It nearly drove me crazy.

Chorus:
　Fare you well, old Joe Clark,
　　Fare you well, I'm gone.
　Fare you well, old Joe Clark,
　　With those golden slippers on.

2 Driving an old mule team,
　　Leading Old Gray behind,
　Before I'll see my true love walk,
　　I'll pull Old Nellie blind.

3 I had an old gray mule,
　　As blind as he could be,
　I rode him under a chicken roost
　　And pulled off ninety-three.

E

(Helen Jacobs, Tulsa, Tulsa County.)

1 Joe Clark killed a man,
　　Killed him with a knife.
　I'm so glad he killed that man,
　　Now I'll get his wife.

Chorus:
　Fly around, old Joe Clark,
　Fly around, old Joe Clark,
　Good-by, Lucy Long.

2 Wish I had a lariat rope,
　　Long as I could throw.
　Throw it around a pretty girl,
　　And to Arkansaw I'd go.

F

(Mrs. Della I. Young, Cheyenne, Roger Mills Co., from J. R. Weatherly, Elk City, Beckham County.)

1 Old Joe Clark's the preacher's son,
　　He preached all over the plain,
　And every time he takes his text,
　　It's high, low, Jack, and the game.

Chorus:
 Rock, rock, old Joe Clark,*
  Rock, rock, I say.
 Rock, rock, old Joe Clark,
  You'd better be getting away.

2 You may ride the old gray horse,
  And I may ride the roan.
 If you get there before I do,
  Leave my honey alone.

3 The higher up the cherry tree,
  The sweeter are the cherries.
 Every pretty girl I meet
  I always want to marry.

4 The higher up the cherry tree,
  The riper grows the cherry.
 The more you hug and kiss the girls,
  The sooner you'll get married.

5 I wish I had a needle and thread,
  As fine as I could sew,
 I'd sew the girls to my coat-tail,
  And down the road I'd go.

6 Old Joe Clark is dead and gone,
  I hope him doing well.
 He made me wear the ball and chain
  That made my ankle swell.

G

(Lucy I. Pitts, Oklahoma City, Oklahoma County, from Indian Territory.)

1 Massa had an old gray horse,
  He rode him down in town.
 Sold the horse for fifteen cents
  And even dollar down.

Chorus:
 Fly around, old Joe Clark,
  Fly around, I'm gone.
 Fly around, old Joe Clark,
  Good-by, Lucy Long.

2 Massa had an old coon dog,
  Blind as he could be.
 Trace a chigger on a stump,
  I believe that dog could see.

---

* " 'Rock, rock,' evidently refers to the 'Rock candy' dance."—White, p. 336n.

3 Massa had an old gray horse,
     Rode him down to town,
Before he got his trading done,
     The buzzards had him down.

4 Massa had a yellow girl,
     Brought her from the South.
Black eyes and curly hair—
     She could not shut her mouth.

5 He took her to the blacksmith shop
     To have her mouth made small.
She backed her ears and opened her mouth,
     And swallowed shop and all.

6 I wish I was in Arkansaw,
     Setting on a rail,
Sweet potato in my hand
     And a possum by the tail.

H

(Jane Bowman, Pauls Valley, Garvin County.)

1 Fare ye well, old Joe Clark,
     Fare ye well, I'm gone,
Fare ye well, old Joe Clark,
     Good-bye, Betsy Brown.
Fare ye well, old Joe Clark,
     I'm going to leave this town.

2 Now I ain't got much money,
     Ain't got no place to stay,
Ain't go no place to lay my head
     Till roosters crow for day.

Variant and additional stanzas:

Old Joe Clark built a house,
     Sixteen stories high.
Every story of that house
     Was lined with chicken pie.

When I see that girl of mine,
     I have a thing to tell her.
She need not fool her time away,
     But court some other feller.

(Gerald Bond, Oklahoma City, Oklahoma County, who played it at Chicka-sha, Grady County.)

Old Joe Clark is dead and gone,
  And I ain't goin'-a cry.
Can't get round his garden spot
  Without mashing down his rye.

  (Roger Givens, Oklahoma City, Oklahoma County, played in the Choctaw
  Nation, Indian Territory.)

Mushy had an old coon dog,
  Three-quarters hound.
Every tooth in that dog's head
  Was a mile and a quarter round.

  (Lillie O. Heaton, Watonga, Blaine County.)

Old Joe Clark he had a horse,
  His name was Morgan Brown.
And every tooth the old horse had
  Was fifteen inches round.

Peaches in the summertime,
  Apples in the fall.
If I can't get the girl I want,
  I won't have none at all.

Chorus:
  Slippin', slidin' round, I say, (Three times.)
  I ain't got long to stay.

You go down the new-cut road,
  And I'll go down the lane.
You can hug the old gatepost,
  While I'll hug Liza Jane.

Went on top of a mountain
(*Or:* Goin' up the mountain)
  To sow a patch of cane,
To raise a barrel of 'lasses
  To sweeten Liza Jane.

She fooled me in the summer time,
  She fooled me in the fall,
She fooled me in the kitchen,
  And fooled me in the hall.

Chorus:
  Long time she's been a-foolin', foolin',
    Long time she's been a-foolin' me.
  Long time she's been a-foolin', foolin',
    Long time she's been a-foolin' me.

  (Florette McNeese, Oklahoma City, Oklahoma County, from her pupils.)

279

I went to see old Joe Clark,
   I found him sick in bed.
I rammed my finger down his throat,
   And pulled out a rabbit's head.

I wouldn't marry a widow,
   I'll tell you the reason why.
She'd have so many children
   They'd make those biscuits fly.

I wouldn't marry a yellow gal,
   I'll tell you the reason why,
She'd eat a barrel of sauerkraut
   And drink the river dry.

I wish I had a lariat rope,
   As long as I could throw.
I'd throw it around my sweetheart's neck
   And around and around we'd go.

I wish I was a big red apple,
   Hanging on a tree,
And every girl that came along
   Would take a bite of me.

I will ride the old gray horse,
   And you will ride the roan.
I'll go see your sweetheart,
   And you'd better leave mine alone.
      (William Plaster, Meeker, Lincoln County.)

Old Joe Clark had a girl,
   She was as blind as she could be.
She caught a beau the other night,
   I swear I believe that girl can see.
      (Mayo Roberts, Norman, Cleveland County.)

Chorus:
   Walk the chalk, old Joe Clark.
   Good-by, I'm gone.
   Walk the chalk, old Joe Clark.
   With the golden slippers on.

An India-rubber overcoat,
   A gumbo lassie's shoe,
Old Joe writes a telegram,
   Trying to get the news.

Old Joe on the mountain top,
    Can see him very well.
Nigger in the watermelon patch,
    Giving them watermelons hell.

Joe wouldn't marry an old maid,
    I'll tell you the reason why,
Her nose was always dripping,
    And her chin was never dry.
        (L. E. Russell, Cyril, Caddo County.)

Old Joe Clark he killed a man,
    And throwed him in the branch.
Old Joe Clark he's going to hang,
    There ain't no other chance.

There's a building in Noo Yawk
    That's sixteen stories high.
And every story in that house
    Is full of chicken pie.

He used to live in the country,
    But now he lives in town,
Living at the James Hotel,
    And sparking Betty Brown.

Old Joe Clark he had a wife,
    And she was seven feet tall.
She slept with her head in the kitchen,
    And her feet in the hall.

And that's the end of old Joe Clark,
    For he is dead and gone.
And that's the end of old Joe Clark,
    As well as Lucy Long.
        (Cora Frances Starritt, Ada, Pontotoc County.)

I went down to old Joe's house,
    He was lying sick in bed.
I put my fingers down his throat
    And pulled out a turkey-head (*or* wagon bed).

        (Jack H. Watson, Oklahoma City, Oklahoma County, from C. F. Wallas,
        Norman, Cleveland County.)

Went down to Lexington,
    Didn't know the route,
Put me in the coffee pot
    And poured me out the spout.

281

Old Joe Clark had a house,
　　Twenty stories high,
And every story in that house
　　Was filled with pumpkin pie.

Old Joe Clark had a dog,
　　Blind as he could be,
And that dog on the darkest night
　　Put a chigger up a tree.

Went down to see my girl,
　　Found her sick in bed,
Ran my finger down her throat
　　And pulled out a chicken head.

Went down to see my girl,
　　Never been there before.
Locked me in a chicken coop,
　　Ain't going back no more.

　　　　(Marguerite M. Durkee, Norman, Cleveland County.)

I went to see old Joe Clark,
　　Found him sick in bed.
Rammed my finger down his throat
　　And pulled out a pole-cat's head.

　　　　(Sam West, Duke, Jackson County, from Ruth Coleman, Jackson County.)

Old Joe lives in a fine brick house,
　　Fifteen stories high,
And every room in that house
　　Is lined with apple pie.

　　　　(James E. White, Norman, Cleveland County, who played it at Bradley, Grady County.)

Old Joe had a mule,
　　His name was Peter Brown.
Every tooth he had in his head
　　Was a mile and a quarter around.

　　　　(Mary Haxel, Purcell, McClain County, who played it near Noble, Cleveland County, and Washington, McClain County.)

Went down to Summerset (Lexington),
　　Didn't know the route,
Put me in the coffee pot
　　And poured me out the spout.

　　　　(Zelma Oliver, Norman, Cleveland County, from Eugene Nolen, Norman.)

282

I went to see old Joe Clark,
    And he was sick in bed.
I run my finger down his throat,
    He throwed up a wagon bed.

Old Joe Clark had a horse,
    Name was Susie Brown.
Every tooth that was in her head
    Was a mile and a quarter around.
        (Tephia Folsom, Atoka, Atoka County.)

I went upon a mountain top
    To give my horn a blow.
I thought I heard my true love say,
    "Yonder comes your Beau."
        (Ruby Pfautsch, Norman, Cleveland County.)

If I had a sweetheart,
    I'd set her upon a shelf,
And every time she'd grin at me,
    I'd get up there myself.

Old Joe Clark he had a hat,
    It didn't have any crown.
He put that hat upon his head
    And swore he'd take in the town.

Old Joe Clark he had a mule,
    Didn't have no ears.
Reminded me of a farmer
    Workin' on the shears.
        (Ruby Burns, Noble, Cleveland County.)

Old Joe Clark is mad at me,
    I'll tell you the reason why,
I ran all over the garden patch
    And stomped down all his rye.

I wish I had a pig in a pen,
    Corn to fed it on,
Pretty little girl to stay at home
    To feed it while I am gone.*

Sixteen horses in my team,
    The leaders had no line.
I whip them around a rocky road
    To see that girl of mine.
        (Gene Michael, Marietta, Love County.)

I wish I had a great big town,
    Fourteen stories high,
And every story in that town
    Was filled with chicken pie.

I wish I had a sweetheart
    Sitting on a shelf.
I'd take her down and kiss her
    And get up there myself.
        (Harold Roberts, Blackwell, Kay County.)

I wouldn't marry a school teacher,
    I'd tell you the reason why.
She blows her nose in yellow corn bread
    And calls it punkin pie.

I wish I had a candy box
    To put my sweetheart in,
Take her out and kiss her twice
    And put her back again.

---

* Dr. Josiah H. Combs, of Texas Christian University, reports this stanza from Knott County, Kentucky, as part of "The Devil Is Dead," a variant of "Charlie.":

    All I want's a big fine horse,
        And corn to feed him on,
    A pretty girl to stay at home,
        And feed him when I'm gone.

For wishing stanzas, cf. also his version of "Turtle Dove":
    Wish I was a little turtle dove,
        Sitting on a tree so high;
    I'd take my true-love on my knee,
        And bid this world good-bye.

Chorus:
    I love my honey, yes I do,
        I'll love her till the day I die;
    I love my honey, it ain't no use,
        I'll love her till the seas run dry.

Wish I was a little turtle dove,
    Sitting on a tree so high;
I'd take a dose of old morphine,
    And bid this world good-bye.

You ride the gray horse,
    And I'll take the roan,
And I'll talk to your sweetheart,
    But you leave mine alone.

        (Mrs. Christine Clark, Norman, Cleveland County, who played it near
        Vinita, in Craig and Mayes Counties.)

If I had a needle and thread,
    I tell you what I'd do.
I'd sew my true love to my side
    And down the river I'd go.
Doggone!

        (Jane Bowman, Pauls Valley, Garvin County.)

Chorus:
    Row around, old Joe Clark,
        Sail away and gone.
    Row around, old Joe Clark,
        With golden slippers on.

        (Mrs. T. H. Maness, Oswalt, Love County.)

80
OLD VIRGINNY NEVER TIRE

Based on a minstrel song attributed to Thomas D. Rice. See "Clar de Kitchen," Marsh's *Selection or Singing for the Million,* 2:153-154; "Clare de Kitchen," *Minstrel Songs Old and New,* pp. 152-153; Scarborough, pp. 110-112. This, in turn, was probably based on the Negro dance-song, "Old Virginny Never Tire." Cf. Scarborough (Virginia, Florida, South Carolina, West Virginia), pp. 108-110; White (Virginia), p. 459. "And ole Varginny never tire" appears in the chorus of the minstrel song, "Ginger Blue" (White, pp. 448-449). "Old Virginny Never Tire" is the title and chorus of Van Doren's Eastern Illinois version of "Down in Alabama" (*JAFL,* 32:492-493).

For "As I went down the new-cut road, cf. "Charleston Gals," Allen, Ware, and Garrison (*Slave Songs of the United States*), p. 88 (also Scarborough, pp. 162-163); "Turkey in the Straw," Sandburg, pp. 94-97; "As I was going up a new-cut road," Scarborough (Virginia), p. 106; "As I was walkin' 'long the new-cut road," *idem* (Virginia), pp. 164-165; "Miss Terrapin and Miss Toad," Talley, p. 162; White (Alabama), pp. 247-248 (with a reference to the minstrel song, "Jinny Come Along"). See LIZA JANE, OLD JOE CLARK.

For "I went to de creek, I couldn't get across," cf. "I Went to the River," Bass (South Carolina), *JAFL,* 44:435; "Run, Nigger, Run!",

Lomax (Virginia, *American Ballads and Folk Songs*), p. 231; "The Old
Gray Horse," "Hook and Line," Perrow (East Tennessee, Mississippi,
Virginia, Kentucky), *JAFL*, 26:124, 127 (four texts); "Went to the River"
(minstrel swapping song), Randolph (*The Ozarks*), pp. 205-206; Scarborough, pp. 184-185; "Polly Wolly-Doodle," Spaeth (*Read 'Em and
Weep*), pp. 92-93; "Crossing the River," "He Is My Horse," Talley, pp.
6, 16; White (Alabama), pp. 194-195.

For "A bull frog dressed in sojer's clo'es," cf. "Bullfrog Put on the
Soldier Clothes," Talley, p. 20.

A

(Catherine Harris, Antlers, Pushmataha County, from S. B. Hackett, Norman, who
played it in Arkansas.)

1 As I went down the new-cut road,
There I spied a terrapin and a toad,
Every time the toad would sing
The terrapin would cut the pigeon wing.

Chorus:
So clear the kitchen, old folks, young folks.
Old folks, young folks, Old Virginny never tires.

B

(No Title)

(Ruth Davis, Fort Worth, Texas; Ruby Pfautsch, Norman, Cleveland County, from
Arkansas.)

1 Dar was a gal in our town,
She had a yellow striped gown.
And every time she put her foot down
De hollow of her heel made a hole in the ground.*

Chorus:
Children! don't get weary, (Three times.)
Love come a-trinklin' down.

C

(No Title)

(Ruth Davis, Fort Worth, Texas; Ruby Pfautsch, Norman, Cleveland County, from
Arkansas.)

1 I wish I was back in old Kentuck',
For since I left I had no luck.
De gals so proud dey won't eat mush,
And when you go to court 'em, dey say, Hush!

---

*Warren Barnhill, of Yukon, Canadian County, reports the line in a dance call:
Hollow in your foot makes a wholly (?) in the ground.

Chorus:
> Oh, clare de kitchen, old folks, young folks.
> Clare de kitchen, old folks, young folks,
> Old Virginny neber tire.

2 I went to de creek, I couldn't get across.
  I'd nobody wid me but an old blind horse;
  But old Jim Crow came riding by,
  Says he, "Old feller, your horse will die."

D

CLARE DE KITCHEN

(Atlee M. Garrett, Loco, Stephens County.)

1 In old Kentuck in de arternoon,
  We sweep de floor wid a brand new broom,
  And arter dat we form a ring,
  And dis de song dat we do sing:

Chorus:
> Oh, clare de kitchen, old folks, young folks.
> Clare de kitchen, old folks, young folks,
> Old Virginny neber tire.

2 I went to de creek, I couldn't get across,
  I'd nobody wid me but an old blind horse;
  But old Jim Crow come riding by,
  Says he, "Old feller, your horse will die."

Chorus:
> It's clare de kitchen, etc.

3 A bull frog dressed in sojer's clo'es
  Went in de field to shoot some crows;
  De crows smell powder and fly away,
  De bull frog mighty mad dat day.

Chorus:
> So clare de kitchen, etc.

81

ONE LITTLE GIRL

(Florette McNeese, Oklahoma City, Oklahoma County, from her pupils.)

1 One little girl all around inside,
  All around inside, all around inside.
  One little girl all around inside,
    And balance to your places.

Chorus:

Swing 'em all around and then promenade,
And then promenade, and then promenade.
Swing 'em all around and then promenade.
And balance to your places.

2 Two little girls all around inside, etc.

(*Repeat until all the girls have joined the leader in the center.*)

82

ON TO GALILEE

"Below Galilee" occurs as the refrain of a North Carolina kissing game noted by Newell, pp. 232-233.

For the pattern and the tune, cf. DOWN IN ALABAMA.

A

IN THE WILDERNESS

(Sung by Clayton Black, east of Noble, Cleveland County.)

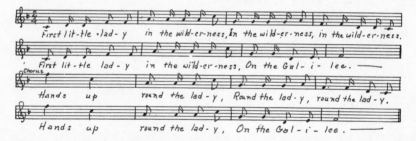

1 First little lady in the wilderness,
   In the wilderness, in the wilderness.
First little lady in the wilderness,
   On the Galilee.

Chorus:

Hands up round the lady,
   Round the lady, round the lady.
Hands up round the lady,
   On the Galilee.

2 Swing that lady out of the wilderness, etc.

3 Second little lady, etc.

Directions: "The lady is in the center. You keep going round her. Then hands up and go the other way. Then you swing her if it's your

288

partner. Repeat till all the girls have been swung. Then the boys get in the center with

First old soapstick (toothpick, slopbucket, gentleman), etc."

B

(Mary Haxel, Purcell, McClain County, who played it near Noble, Cleveland County, and Washington, McClain County.)

1 First young lady go down the wilderness,
  Down the wilderness, down the wilderness,
  First young lady go down the wilderness,
      On to Galilee.

Chorus:
  Hands up around the lady,
      Around the lady, around the lady.
  Hands up around the lady,
      On to Galilee.

2 Swing that lady out of the wilderness, etc.

3 Next old married lady go down the wilderness, etc.

4 Next old maid go down the wilderness, etc.

5 Swing all the ladies out of the wilderness, etc.

Variants:
First old hobo in the wilderness, etc.

Next old soapstick in the wilderness, etc.

Next fair lady in the wilderness, etc.

(Etc., according to personal appearance or actions.)
  (Alma Dixon, Norman, Cleveland County.)

First old bachelor in the wilderness, etc.
  (William Plaster, Meeker, Lincoln County.)

83
PAWPAW LAND

Cf. "Bouquet Patch (Pawpaw Patch)," Shearin and Combs (Kentucky), p. 38 (excerpt); "Way Down in the Paw Paw Patch," Wolford (Indiana), p. 101.

Played like BOSTON, to a similar tune.

A

(Sung by Levi Wilcox, Noble, Cleveland County.)

Come along, boys, an' le's go an' see her, (*Three times.*)
Down in Pawpaw land.

B

(Fanny W. Kelly, Jefferson, Grant County; Madeline Tarpley, Shamrock, Texas.)

1 Come along boys, and we'll all go see her, (*Three times.*)
Way down in Pawpaw land.

2 Here, oh, here comes —— [*name of girl*], etc.

(*Repeat, using names of other girls and boys.*)

84

PIG IN THE PARLOR

Rorie (*Folk-Lore,* 25:356) reports the following from the parish of Cruden in his "Stray Notes on the Folk-Lore of Aberdeenshire and the North-East of Scotland":

My father an' mither wis Irish,
    An' I am Irish too.
I boucht a fiddle for ninepence,
    An' it was Irish too.
An' a' the tunes 'at it could play
Wis "owre the hills an' far away."
I bruck it here, I bruck it there,
An' I bruck it through the middle.

See also "Father's Fiddle," Gomme, 1:120-121; Northall, pp. 564-565.

Cf. "Bull in the Park," Gomme, 1:50-51, which is similar in method of playing and in the lines, "Pig in the middle and can't get out," "Cat's i' t' cream-pot up t' knees." See SKIP TO MY LOU.

Cf. Ames (Missouri), *JAFL,* 24:298; "My Father and Mother Were Irish," Ball (Idaho), *JAFL,* 44:12; Gardner (Michigan), *JAFL,* 33:117-118 (three texts); Heck (Cincinnati), *JAFL,* 40:22; Mahan and Grahame (Iowa), pp. 44-46; Piper (Eastern Nebraska), 28:283-284; Pound (Nebraska, *Syllabus*), p. 74; "We'll All Go Down to Rowser's," *idem* (Iowa, *American Ballads and Songs*), pp. 237-238; Randolph (Ozarks, Missouri), *JAFL,* 42:211 (also *The Ozarks,* pp. 151-153); Wolford (Indiana), pp. 81-82.

Oklahoma Texts and Tunes

A

(Sung by Clayton Black, east of Noble, Cleveland County.)

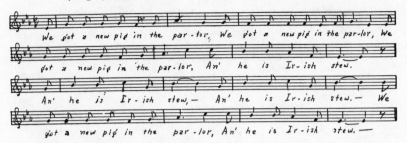

We got a new pig in the par-lor, We got a new pig in the par-lor, We got a new pig in the par-lor, An' he is Ir-ish stew. An' he is Ir-ish stew, — An' he is Ir-ish stew. — We got a new pig in the par-lor, An' he is Ir-ish stew. —

1 We got a new pig in the parlor, (*Three times.*)
  An' he is Irish stew, (*Three times.*)
We got a new pig in the parlor,
  An' he is Irish stew.

Chorus:
  Oh, it's right hand to your pardner,
  Oh, it's left hand to your neighbor,
  It's right hand to your pardner,
    An' we'll all promenade,
    We'll all promenade,
    We'll all promenade.
  It's right hand to your pardner,
    An' we'll all promenade.

B

(Karl Herdi, Billings, Noble County.)

1 My father and mother were Irish, (*Three times.*)
  And I am Irish too, (*Three times.*)
My father and mother were Irish,
  And I am Irish too.

2 We kept the pig in the parlor, (*Three times.*)
  And that is Irish too, (*Three times.*)
Etc.

3 We baked the pig in the boiler, etc.

4 We have a new pig in the parlor, etc.

5 The same old pig in the parlor, etc.

C

MY FATHER AND MOTHER WERE IRISH

(Florette McNeese, Oklahoma City, Oklahoma County, from her pupils.)

1 Oh, my father and mother were Irish,
   My father and mother were Irish,
   My father and mother were Irish,
   And I am Irish too.

Chorus:
   Oh, your right hand to your partner,
   Your left hand to your neighbor,
   Your right hand to your partner,
   And all promenade. (Three times.)
   Your right hand to your partner,
   And all promenade.

2 We kept the pig in the parlor, etc.

3 We kept the cat in the cream jug, etc.

4 We kept the cow in the kitchen, etc.

Directions: "A circle is formed with an extra boy in the center. Circle skips around as stanza is being sung. While singing the chorus, the players follow directions given in it. The extra boy tries to secure a partner for the promenade, as in 'Miller Boy.' If he fails, the next stanza is modified to: 'The same old pig in the parlor,' etc. Sometimes as a variation, a new boy is greeted with 'A brand new pig in the parlor,' etc."

Other variants by Mrs. Marjorie Allen, Lexington, Cleveland County; Ethel Rose Baird, Bixby, Tulsa, County; Lois Ferguson Beckham, Norman, Cleveland County; Gladys Mary Bednor, Luther, Oklahoma County; Hattie Bell Bethea, Marion, South Carolina; Clifford Chandler, Crescent, Logan County; Mary Esther Coffman, Geary, Blaine County; Bert H. Cook, Binger, Caddo County; J. O. Conner, Shawnee, Pottawatomie County; William Cunningham, Watonga, Blaine County; Harry L. Deupree, Oklahoma City, Oklahoma County, from Nebraska, Missouri, through Lena E. Misener; Lillie O. Heaton, Watonga, Blaine County; Gregory Hutchison, Tulsa, Tulsa County, from Norman, Cleveland County; Helen Jacobs, Tulsa, Tulsa County; William Lorenzen, El Reno, Canadian County; Erma Malthy, Billings, Noble County; Beatrice J. McMullin, Norman, Cleveland County, brought from Kentucky to Missouri, then to Kay and Grant Counties, on Oklahoma-Kansas border; Gene Michael, Marietta, Love County; Elsie Montgomery, Sunset, Beaver County, from Overstreet district, in the Panhandle of Texas; Lloyd Osborne, Carter, Beckham County; Ruth Prutsman, Spearman, Texas, from Ochitree County; L. E. Russell, Cyril, Caddo County; Rephord Hubert Stevens, Union City, Canadian County; Emma Vilhauer, Norman, Cleveland County; Doris G. Waters, Ponca City, Kay County, from her pupils.

85
POLLY, PUT THE KETTLE ON
(Mrs. L. T. Monnett, Norman, Cleveland County, who played it in Missouri.)

Cf. Dearmer and Shaw (*Song Time*), p. 38; Graham (*Traditional Nursery Rhymes*), p. 40; "Sally, put the kettle on," Heck (Cincinnati), *JAFL*, 40:35; *Mother Goose* (Dent and Dutton), p. 76; "Housekeeping," Newell, p. 173; "Molly, Put the Kettle on," Perrow (East Tennessee, sung with "Drop the Handkerchief"), *JAFL*, 26:138; "Mollie, Put the Kettle on," Sullivan (*Our Times*), 2:183 (as a popular song); Wier (*Songs the Children Love to Sing*), p. 235; Wolford (Indiana), p. 83.
See COME, PHILANDERS.

1 Polly, put the kettle on,
    Kettle on, kettle on.
Polly, put the kettle on,
    We'll all take tea.

2 Slice your bread and butter thin,
    Thin enough for you and me.
Choose the one you love the best,
    And call her in the ring.

3 Oh, you dearest dear,
    You don't know how I love you.
There is no one in this world
    That I adore above you.

4 My heart you have gained,
    My right hand I give you.
One sweet kiss
    And then I'll have to leave you.

Directions: "Players dance round in a circle with one child in the center who does the choosing."

86
POOR OLD JOE
(Ruby Pfautsch, Norman, Cleveland Co., from near Springfield, Douglas County, Missouri.)

Cf. "Oh! Dear! What Can the Matter Be?", *Old English Ditties from W. Chappell's Popular Music of the Olden Time,* pp. 202-203 (eighteenth century); "Oh dear! what can the matter be?", Dearmer and Shaw (*Song Time*), p. 34; "Johnny's So Long at the Fair," Perrow (Mississippi), *JAFL,* 28:169; "What Can the Matter Be?", Pound (Nebraska, *Syllabus*), p. 76; "O, Dear! What Can the Matter Be?", Shoemaker (*North Pennsylvania Minstrelsy*), p. 69; "Oh, Dear, What Can the Matter Be?", Sullivan (*Our Times*), 2:183 (as a popular song of the early 1900's); "Oh, Dear, What Can the Matter Be?", Thomas (Kentucky), pp. 144-145.

> 1 Poor old Joe, what is the matter,
>   Poor old Joe, what is the matter,
>   Poor old Joe, what is the matter,
>   You stay so far behind?
>
> 2 You promised you'd buy me a ring and gold locket
>   And lots of fine [things] to go in my pocket
>   An old straw hat and a bunch of blue ribbon
>   To tie up my bonnie brown hair.
>
> 3 Swing them ladies, tu du la, (*Four times.*)
>   Swing them ladies, tu du la de.
>   Swing them if you love them, tu du la. (*Four times.*)

Directions: "When the play was started the girl would lead and the boy would follow, acting as if he were old and crippled. They would march around the circle singing. When they came to 'Swing them ladies,' all the kids who had been standing in the circle would start swinging."

87

POSSUM PIE

(*Spoken*)

Cf. "Carve 'Im to De Heart," "An Opossum Hunt," Odum and Johnson (*The Negro and His Songs*), pp. 240-241; "An Oppossum Hunt," Talley, pp. 23-24.

Cf. "Possum Pie," Ames (Missouri), *JAFL,* 24:313-314 (a counting-out game).

For Stanza 1 of C, cf. "Old Bob Ridley," *The Negro Forget-Me-Not Songster,* pp. 155-157; Scarborough, p. 191.

A

(Beatrice Jennings McMullin, Norman, Cleveland County, brought from Kentucky to Missouri, then to Kay and Grant Counties, on Oklahoma-Kansas border.)

> Possum pie, made of rye,
>   Possum am de meat.
> It was rough enough and as tough enough
>   And as much as we all could eat.

B

(Sam West, Duke, Jackson County, from L. F. Holm, Jackson County.)

Possum, possum, possum pie—
I could eat 'em till I die.
P-o-s-s-u-m spells possum
And p-i-e spells pie.

Other variants by Agnes Frick, Oklahoma City, Oklahoma County; Catherine Harris, Antlers, Pushmataha County, from S. B. Hackett, Norman, who played it in Arkansas; Ruth Revelle, Oklahoma City, Oklahoma County, from her father, Haywood County, Tennessee.

C

POSSUM

(Ruth Davis, Fort Worth, Texas; Ruby Pfautsch, Norman, Cleveland County)

1 Possum up the 'simmon tree,
   Looking cunning down at me.
   I picked up a rock and on the sly
   Zip! I hit him in the eye.

Chorus:
   Swing them around with the rig, gig, gig,
   We'll have no holiday.
   Possum fried and possum stewed.
   We'll have a grandly barbecue.

2 Possum pie is made of rye,
   Possum was the meat,
   Rough enough and tough enough —
   More than we all could eat.

88

POSSUM UP A 'SIMMON TREE

Based on Negro songs of folk and minstrel origin.

For A, cf. "Brudder Eph'em," Bass, *JAFL,* 44:430; "Cotton Field Song," Lomax (*American Ballads and Folk Songs*), p. 241; "Old Bob Ridley," *The Negro Forget-Me-Not-Songster,* pp. 155-157; Perrow (Eastern North Carolina, Mississippi), *JAFL,* 26:131-132 (two texts); "Karo Song," "Raccoon Up in de 'Simmon Tree," Scarborough, pp. 170, 172, 173; "Shake the Persimmons Down," Talley, pp. 34-35; White (Alabama), pp. 138, 236-237 (four texts).

For B, cf. "Shady Grove," Combs (Kentucky, *Folk-Say: 1930*), p. 242; "Little Gal at Our House," Lomax (*American Ballads and Folk Songs*), p. 238; Perrow, *loc. cit.*; Scarborough, p. 177; "Possum up a Gum-Stump,"

Shearin and Combs (Kentucky), p. 38 (listed); "Possum up the Gum Stump," Talley, p. 3; White (Alabama), pp. 237, 238, 239 (four texts).

A

(Sung by Orville Nichols, Mountain Park, Kiowa County, from Cordell, Washita County.)

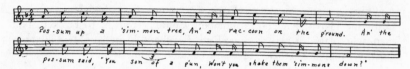

Possum up a 'simmon tree,
 An' a raccoon on the ground.
An' the possum said, "You son of a gun,
 Won't you shake them 'simmons down?"

B

OLD RACCOON

(Lois F. Beckham, Norman, Cleveland County, who played it at Memphis, Tennessee.)

Ol' possum in a gum stump,
 Coonie in the holler,
Pretty girl at our house,
 As fat as she can waller.

89

PRETTY LITTLE PINK

Of Mexican War origin (Hudson, *Culture in the South,* p. 533).

Cf. "Daisy," Edmands (North Carolina), *JAFL,* 6:134; Henry (Georgia), *JAFL,* 44:89-90; "Ring Game," Kennedy (*Black Cameos*), p. 197; Mooney (Carolina), *JAFL,* 2:104; Newell (East Tennessee), p. 245; "Coffee Grows on White Oak Trees," Perrow (Virginia), *JAFL,* 28:187; "Old Quebec," Randolph (*The Ozarks*), pp. 146-147; Sandburg (Kentucky), p. 166; Talley, p. 127; "Coffee Grows on White Folks' Trees," *idem,* p. 107; "Weevily Wheat," Wolford (Indiana), p. 103.

See COFFEE GROWS ON A WHITE OAK TREE, WE'RE MARCHING TO QUEBEC.

A

(O. B. Campbell, Medford, Grant County.)

1 My pretty little pink, I once did think
 That you and I would marry,
But now I've lost all hope of that,
 And I have no time to tarry.

2 I'll take my knapsack on my back,
  My rifle on my shoulder,
And I'll march away to the old Rio Grande
  And there I'll be a soldier.

3 There coffee grows on tall oak trees
  And the rivers flow with brandy,
The rocks and hills are covered with gold,
  And the girls are sweeter than candy.

4 Now the war's all over and we'll turn back
  To the place where we first started,
So open the ring and choose another
  To relieve the broken-hearted.

B

(No Title)

(Mrs. T. H. Maness, Oswalt, Love County.)

I'll take my knapsack on my back
  And my rifle on my shoulder,
And march away to New Mexico
  To be a gallant soldier.

90

RAILROAD (AND) STEAMBOAT

For the "raging canal," cf. "The Raging Can-all," Lomax (*American Ballads and Folk Songs*), pp. 471-474; "The Raging Canal," Marsh's *Selection or Singing for the Million,* pp. 83-88; "Raging Canawl," Sandburg, pp. 178-179. Professor Kenneth C. Kaufman, of the University of Oklahoma, assigns "She's gone on the raging canal" to an old college song.

Cf. "Railroad, Steamboat, River, and Canal," Dudley and Payne (Texas), *PTFS,* 1:9.

See (LITTLE) BROWN JUG, COFFEE GROWS ON A WHITE OAK TREE, GOING DOWN TO ROWSER.

A

(Mrs. T. H. Maness, Oswalt, Love County.)

1 Railroad, steamboat, river, and canal,
  I lost my poor love on that last farewell.
Oh, she's gone, gone, gone; let her go, go, go.
Oh, she's gone on that raging canal.

2 Oh, never mind the old folks,
  The old folks, the old folks.
Oh, never mind the old folks
  For they're at home in bed.

B

(Emma Vilhauer, Norman, Cleveland County.)

Railroad, steamboat, river and canal.
Lost my true love on the ridge of the canal.
  Oh, we're going, going; yes! we're going, going,
Yes! we're going to the ridge of the canal.

C

(No Title)

(William Lorenzen, El Reno, Canadian County.)

Railroad, steamboat, river, and canal.
Oh, my beloved, the raging canal.
  Oh, she's gone, gone, gone: let her go, go, go,
To the bottom of the raging canal.

D

RAILROAD, STEAMBOAT

(Elsie Montgomery, Sunset, Beaver County, from Bessie O'Neal, Follett, Texas, who
played it at Darrouzett, Texas.)

Railroad, steamboat, river, and canal.
I lost my poor darling on the raging canal.
Oh, she's gone, gone, gone, (*Four times.*)
On that raging canal.

91

RIG-A-JIG

A

Ee-I-Ee-I-O

(Danny Kay, Manford, Creek County, who played it at Stillwater, Payne County.)

As I was strolling down the street
Down the street, down the street,
A pretty girl I chanced to meet,
  Ee-i-ee-i-o.
Rig-a-jig-jig, and away we go,
Away we go, away we go,
Rig-a-jig-jig, and away we go,
  Ee-i-ee-i-o.

Directions: Boys and girls form a circle, with one couple inside, who
stroll around, one behind the other. At the third line the boy takes a girl
and the girl takes a boy, and they skip around the circle. Then the
couples break and repeat the process until all are taken in. (Played at
church socials.)

298

B

(Louise James, Norman, Cleveland County.)

1 As I was walking down the street,
   Heigh-o, heigh-o, heigh-o, heigh-o,
A prettier girl I chanced to meet,
   Heigh-o, heigh-o, heigh-o, heigh-o,

Chorus:
   Rig-a-jig-jig, and away we go,
      Away we go, away we go.
   Rig-a-jig-jig, and away we go,
      Heigh-o, heigh-o, heigh-o.
   Rig-a-jig-jig, and away we go,
      Away we go, away we go.
   Heigh-o, heigh-o, heigh-o, heigh-o,
      Heigh-o, heigh-o, heigh-o.

2 Said I to her, "What is you trade?"
   Heigh-o, heigh-o, heigh-o.
Said she to me, "I'm a weaver's maid."
   Heigh-o, heigh-o, heigh-o.

92

ROSA BECKY DINER

(Mrs. Ora Morris, Oklahoma City, Oklahoma County, who played it at Buena Vista, Carroll County, and in Benton County, Arkansas.)

Cf. "Rosa Betsy Lina," Douthitt (Kentucky), pp. 36-37; "Rosa-Betsy-Lina," Dudley and Payne (Texas), *PTFS*, 1:17; "Lead Her Up and Down," Randolph (Arkansas, *The Ozarks*), pp. 163-164.
Played like BOSTON.

Lead 'er up an' down, Rosa Becky Diner,
Lead 'er up an' down, Rosa Becky Diner,
Lead 'er up an' down, Rosa Becky Diner,
   Won't you be my darling?

93

RUN, NIGGER, RUN

Based on a slave song.
Cf. Allen, Ware, and Garrison (*Slave Songs of the United States*), p. 89; "Pateroll Song," Fauset (Mississippi), *JAFL*, 40:303; Harris (*Uncle Remus and His Friends*), pp. 200-201; *idem* (*Uncle Remus: His Songs and His Sayings*), p. 32n.; Lomax (North Carolina, Virginia; *American Ballads and Folk Songs*), pp. 228-231 (three texts); Perrow (Virginia Negroes), *JAFL*, 28:138; "Oh, Mourner!", *ibid.* (Mississippi Negroes), p. 135; Sullivan (*Our Times*), 2:173; Talley, p. 34; White (Alabama,

North Carolina), pp. 168-169 (four texts, with note on the origin of the song in the ante-bellum "patterolers" or patrols).

A

(Sung by Orville Nichols, Mountain Park, Kiowa County, from Cordell, Washita County.)

1 Run, nigger, run,
    Paterol 'll get you.
Run, nigger, run,
    You better get away.

2 Run, nigger, run,
    Paterol 'll get you.
Run, nigger, run,
    It's almost day.

B

(Ethel Rose Baird, Bixby, Tulsa County, from near Cheney, Kansas.)

1 Ladies to the center
    And then right back.
Gents to the center
    And then around the track.

2 Run, nigger, run.
    The white man will get you if you don't.
Run, nigger, run.
    Get away if you can.

3 The ladies step forward
    And the gents fall back

C

(Tephia Folsom, Atoka, Atoka County, from Ed Butler (colored), Atoka County.)

Run, nigger, run, or Pat will catch you,
Run, nigger run, you better get away.
Nigger run, nigger flew.
Nigger tore himself in two.
Nigger run, nigger flew.
Nigger tore his Sunday shoes in two.

94

SANDY HE BELONGED TO THE MILL

For a British version, see "Sandy He Belongs to the Mill," Northall, p. 366.

For B, cf. "Big Boy, Little Boy," Ames (Missouri), *JAFL,* 24:318.
Cf. Ames (Missouri), *JAFL,* 24:303; "Sandy," Hamilton (Northeastern
Missouri), *JAFL,* 27:292; "Sandy," Henry (Georgia), *JAFL,* 45:159.

A
(No Title)
(William Plaster, Meeker, Lincoln County.)

1 Oh, say, Mr. Sammie, won't you loan me your mill,
  Loan me your mill, loan me your mill?
  Oh, say, Mr. Sammie, won't you loan me your mill?
  Sammie, he says, "No, sir."

2 Sammie, he belongs to the mill,
  Belongs to the mill, belongs to the mill.
  Sammie, he belongs to the mill,
  And the mill belongs to Sammie.

3 Now we'll all promenade with Sammie in the lead,
  Sammie in the lead, Sammie in the lead.
  Now we'll all promenade with Sammie in the lead,
  At the rate of full speed.

B
SANDERS
(Rephord Hubert Stevens, Union City, Canadian County.)

1 Sanders, he belongs to the mill, (*Three times.*)
  And the mill belongs to Sanders.

2 Big boy, little boy, can't you dance, etc.

C
SANDY
(Ben Hennessy, Oklahoma City, Oklahoma County, who played it in McPherson County, Kansas, and north of Guthrie, Logan County.)

O, Mr. Sandy, won't you loan me your mill?
Yes, said Sandy, I guess I will.
I'll take my corn to Sandy's mill
And Sandy he will grind ut (*sic*).

D
(No Title)
(Ruby Pfautsch, Norman, Cleveland County.)

1 Sandy he belong to the mill, (*Three times.*)
  And the mill belong to Sandy,
  Tra la la la la la la.
  (*Repeat three times and then repeat "Sandy."*)

301

95

SANDY LAND

Cf. Dudley and Payne (Texas), *PTFS*, 1:8; "Sandy Lan'," Lomax (*American Ballads and Folk Songs*), pp. 236-237. Sullivan (*Our Times*, 2:173) notes: "Another negro dancing song, recalling a distinction between 'meal' and 'bran,' familiar in the days of grist mills, but now almost as unknown as slavery, was:

> Sif' dat meal and save de bran,
> Gwine to de weddin' with Sally Ann.
> Oh, shake dat wooden leg, Dinah, Oh...."

For Stanza 4 of B, see LONDON.

For Stanza 4 of D, cf. White (Alabama), p. 155.

For the chorus of E (see THE IRISH TROT), cf. the camp meeting song, Jackson (*White Spirituals in the Southern Uplands*), p. 295; the parody, "The animals came in two by two," White, pp. 141-142; and the comic song, "One More Ribber for to Cross," *Good Old-Time Songs*, 3:31; "There's One More River to Cross." Pound (Nebraska, *Syllabus*), p. 76.

A

(Sung by Clayton Black, east of Noble, Cleveland County.)

1 Make my livin' in sandy land, (*Three times.*)
Ladies, fare you well.

2 Keep a-hookin' on in sandy land, etc.

3 Lotsa pretty girls in sandy land, etc.

4 Raise (Grow) sweet p'taters in sandy land, etc.

5 Right 'n' left to sandy land, etc.

("We always just sing whatever come into our minds.")

302

B

(Mary Haxel, Purcell, McClain County, who played it near Noble, Cleveland County, and Washington, McClain County.)

1 Oh, come my pretty little miss,
    And do come, my honey.
  Oh, come my pretty little miss,
    I'll marry you next Sunday.

Chorus:
    We'll make our livin' in Sandy Land, (*Three times.*)
    Ladies, fare-you-well.

2 Right and left in Sandy Land, (*Three times.*)
    Ladies, fare-you-well.

3 On to the next in Sandy Land, etc.

4 Lot o' pretty girls in Sandy Land, etc.

5 Hurry up, boys, in Sandy Land, etc.

6 Promenade home in Sandy Land, etc.

C

(Mrs. Anne McClure, Oklahoma City, Oklahoma County, who played it in Benton County, Arkansas.)

1 Dad's got a livin' in the sandy land,
  Dad's got a livin' in the sandy land,

2 Sift the meal and save the bran,
  Dad's got a livin' in the sandy land,

3 Dad's go a livin', etc.

4 Big sweet potato in the sandy land,
  Big sweet potato in the sandy land.

5 Sift the meal, etc.

D

I Make My Livin' in Sandy Land

(Zelma Oliver, Norman, Cleveland County, from Eugene Nolen, Norman.)

1 I make my livin' in Sandy Land, (*Three times.*)
  Oh, ladies, fare ye well.

303

2 The raccoon he's a-choppin' wood,
   The possum he's a-haulin',
My old dog fell off a log
And killed himself a-bawlin'.

3 I make my livin', etc.

4 Once I had an old banjo,
   Strings were made of twine,
And all that old banjo could play
   Was "I wish that girl was mine."

5 I make my livin', etc.

E

RAISIN' SWEET 'TATERS IN A SANDY LAND

(Viola Harris, Porter, Wagoner County.)

1 Raisin' sweet 'taters in a sandy land,
   Sandy land, sandy land.
Raisin' sweet 'taters in a sandy land —
   The way to make a living in a sandy land.

2 Ladies in the center and the gents take a walk,
   Gents take a walk, gents take a walk.
Ladies to the center and the gents take a walk
   Till I reach my darling.

Chorus:
   And then one more river then [sic] I am bound to cross,
      Bound to cross, bound to cross.
   One more river I am bound to cross
      Till I reach my darling.
(*Repeat chorus till original partner is reached.*)

Other variants by Wilma Harrel, Fletcher, Comanche County; Paul Howard, Headrick, Jackson County; Fanny W. Kelly, Jefferson, Grant County; Evelyn Roach, Shamrock, Texas; Kenneth Tiger, Okmulgee, Okmulgee County.

96

SHOO FLY

Based on the minstrel song, with words by Billy Reeves and music by Frank Campbell (Spaeth, *Read 'Em and Weep,* p. 631). See "Shoo Fly, Don' Bother Me," *Good Old-Time Songs,* 2:39; Scarborough (Mississippi), pp. 200-201; Sullivan (*Our Times*), 2:173 (as a Civil War song).

For Stanza 3 of C, cf. "Karo Song" (Texas), Scarborough, p. 171; "Nobody Looking," Talley, p. 48.

"Shoo Die" is requested by Payne (Texas), *PTFS,* 1:35-38.

For "big white house," see COFFEE GROWS ON A WHITE OAK TREE, DOWN IN ALABAMA, VIRGINIA.

See LIZA JANE, OLD JOE CLARK, SHOO-LI-LO, SKIP TO MY LOU.

A

(Leon Kidd, Billings, Noble County. Tune from Professor Kenneth C. Kaufman, Norman, Cleveland County.)

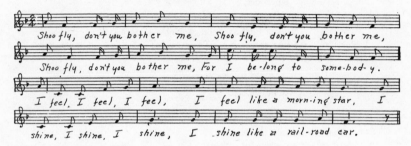

Shoo fly, don't you bother me, Shoo fly, don't you bother me,
Shoo fly, don't you bother me, For I belong to somebody.
I feel, I feel, I feel), I feel like a morning star, I
shine, I shine, I shine, I shine like a railroad car.

1 Shoo (shoo) fly, don't you bother me. (*Three times.*)
   For I belong to somebody.*

2 I feel, I feel, I feel,
   I feel like a morning star.
  I shine, I shine, I shine.†
   I shine like a railroad car.‡

3 Going up on a mountain
   To plant a patch of cane,
  To make a barrel of molasses
   To sweeten up Liza Jane.

4 And oh, how I love her!
   And ain't that a shame!
  To make a barrel of molasses
   To sweeten up Liza Jane.

---

* My mommee.—K. C. K.
† I feel, I feel, I feel.—K. C. K.
‡ I feel like a big cigar.—K. C. K.

The American Play-Party Song

B

(Sung by Orville Nichols, Mountain Park, Kiowa County, from Cordell, Washita County.)

Shoo fly, don't bother me, (*Three times.*)
For I belong to somebodee.

C

(Faneta Fitchett, Billings, Noble County.)

1 Shoo fly, don't you bother me, (*Three times.*)
  For I belong to Company G.

2 Right and left, shoo fly, (*Three times.*)
  Shoo fly, shoo fly, shoo.

3 I went down to shoo fly's house,
    Shoo fly wasn't home,
  Seated myself in a big arm chair
  And wait until shoo fly comes.

4 Once and a half, shoo fly, (*Three times.*)
  Shoo fly, shoo fly, shoo.

5 Shoo fly, don't you bother me, (*Three times.*)
  For I belong to somebodee.

6 We'll all promenade, shoo fly, (*Three times.*)
  Shoo fly, shoo fly, shoo.

D

(Mrs. Bertha Downing, Norman, Cleveland County, who played it in Southern Noble, Northeastern Logan, and Southern Payne Counties.)

1 Shoo fly, don't you bother me, (*Three times.*)
  For I belong to somebody else.

Chorus:
  Then right and left a shoo fly, (Three times.)
  Shoo fly, shoo fly, shoo.

2 Left hand round a shoo fly, etc.

3 Both hands round a shoo fly, etc.

4 Elaman left a shoo fly, etc.

306

5 Elaman right, a shoo fly, etc.

6 Do-se-do a shoo fly, etc.

E
(Emma Vilhauer, Norman, Cleveland County.)

1 Shoo fly, don't you bother me, (*Three times.*)
  For I belong to somebody.

Chorus:
    I feel, I feel, I feel,
        I feel like a morning star.
    I feel, I feel, I feel,
        I feel like an old box-car.
(*Repeat.*)

2 Mary had a little lamb,
        A little lamb, a little lamb.
  Mary had a little lamb,
        Its fleece was white as snow.

3 I feel, I feel religion in my soul,
  I feel, I feel religion in my soul.
  There'll be a hot time in the old town to-night, my baby.

4 Shoo fly, don't you bother me, etc.

Variant and additional stanzas:

Shoo flies, don't bother me, (*Three times.*)
For I belong to somebodee.

Big white house and nobody living in it.
    Nobody living in it, nobody living in it,
Big white house and nobody living in it,
    You're the one, my darling.
        (Fanny K. Kelly, Jefferson, Grant County; Evelyn Roach, Shamrock, Texas;
        Lynn Scott, Holliday, Texas.)

I feel, I feel, I feel just like a morning star.
I feel, I feel, I feel just like a smoked cigar,
And I wonder where in this wide world you are,
'Cause there'll be a hot time in the old town to-night.
        (Naomi Maye Porter, Ringling, Jefferson County.)

I went into the kitchen,
    Something to deceive,
And there I spied a bedbug,
    A-flirting with a flee.
        (Elsie Montgomery, Sunset, Beaver County, from New Home district in the
        Panhandle of Texas.)

I went down to the kitchen
    To see what I could see,
And there I saw a shoo, shoo fly,
    Wrestling with a bee.
    (Harold Roberts, Blackwell, Kay County.)

Other variants by Dessie Deal, Billings, Noble County; Madeline Tarpley, Shamrock, Texas.

97
SHOO-LI-LO

(Hattie Bell Bethea, Marion, South Carolina.)

See SHOO FLY.

1 Yonder comes a bachelor, shoo-li-lo, (*Three times.*)
    Shoo-li-lo, my darling.

2 I'll get another one quick as the other one, etc.

3 I feel, I feel, I feel like a morning star.
    Shoo fly, don't you bother me,
    Shoo fly, don't you bother me,
    For I belong to the busy bee.

Directions: Boys and girls form circle with extra boy in center called the "bachelor," who chooses partner.

98
SHOOT THE BUFFALO

Based on an emigrant song, "The Hunting of the Buffalo" (Belden, *JAFL,* 25:16).

Cf. Ames (Missouri), *JAFL,* 24:301; Ball (Idaho), *JAFL,* 44:16; "Pop Goes the Weasel," Douthitt (Kentucky), p. 34; Dudley and Payne (Texas), *PTFS,* 1:30-31; Hudson (Mississippi, *Specimens*), pp. 126-127; Lomax (*American Ballads and Folk Songs*), pp. 296-297; Perrow (Mississippi), *JAFL,* 26:137; Randolph (Ozarks, Missouri), *JAFL,* 42:212 (also *The Ozarks,* pp. 153-154); "Buffalo," Shearin and Combs (Kentucky), p. 38 (excerpt); *Social Plays, Games,* etc., pp. 26-27; "The Juniper Tree," Wilson (Ozarks), pp. 81-82; "Chase the Buffalo," Wolford (Indiana), pp. 29-30 (three texts).

See YOU'RE FROM VIRGINNY.

Oklahoma Texts and Tunes

A

(Sung by Clayton Black, east of Noble, Cleveland County.)

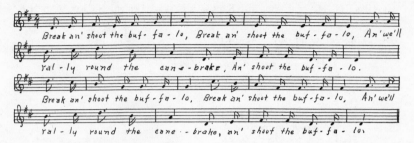

1 Break an' shoot the buffalo,
  Break an' shoot the buffalo,
    An' we'll rally round the canebrake,
  An' shoot the buffalo.
  Break an' shoot the buffalo,
  Break an' shoot the buffalo,
    An' we'll rally round the canebrake,
  An' shoot the buffalo.

2 An' the buffalo is dead,
  For I've shot him in the head, etc.

3 Break an' shoot the shoot shoot,
  Break an' shoot the shoot shoot, etc.

4 The girls go to school
  An' the boys love to fool, etc.

("Take back five or six years ago, an' I could sing nearly all them verses pretty
  nearly.")

B

(Sung by Professor Kenneth C. Kaufman, Norman, Cleveland County, who played
it in Eastern Custer County.)

Break an' shoot the buffalo,
Break an' shoot the buffalo,
  An' we'll rally round the canebrake,
An' shoot the buffalo.

C

RALLY ROUND THE CANEBRAKE AND SHOOT THE BUFFALO

(Wallace N. McCown, Emporia, Kansas, from Earl Denton, Norman, Cleveland
County.)

1 Rise up to me, my dearest dear,
　　And present to me your hand,
　For I know you want to marry
　　And I want to be the man.

　Or:
　Rise up to me, my dearest dear,
　　And present to me your paw,
　For I know you chew tobacco
　　And I know you want a chaw.

2 Oh, the hawk shot the buzzard,
　　And the buzzard shot the crow.
　Oh, we'll rally round the canebrake
　And shoot the buffalo.

3 Oh, the buffalo will die
　For I shot him in the eye.
　　For we'll rally round the canebrake
　And shoot the buffalo.

4 Oh, the buffalo is dead.
　For I shot him in the head.
　　Oh, we'll rally round the canebrake
　And shoot the buffalo.

Directions: "All in a circle, girls on right, commence chanting 'Rise
up, my dearest dear,' etc. Boys drop left hands, girls drop right hands,
circle in and out, taking hands each time. Boys go to the right, girls go
to the left. Singing and circling continues until partners are reached. The
boy places arm around waist of partner and swings her to the right once
around; then takes the girl next to the right and does the same with her.
This is continued until each person has returned to his partner. The chant
of the above continues throughout the game."

D

(Glenn A. Roe, Oklahoma City, Oklahoma County, who played it at Frederick,
Tillman County.)

1 Rise you up, my dearest dear,
　　And present to me your hand,
　For I long to take a journey
　　To a far and distant land,

Where the hunter killed the crow
And the baboon stubbed his toe,
    And we'll rally round the canebrake
And shoot the buffalo.

Chorus:
   And we'll shoot the buffalo,
   And we'll shoot the buffalo,
      And we'll rally round together
   And shoot the buffalo.

2 Rise ye up, my dearest dear,
    And present to me your hand,
And I'll put you in possession
    Of ten thousand acres of land,
Where the hunter killed the crow,
And the baboon stubbed his toe,
    And we'll rally round together
And shoot the buffalo.

E

(Carl West, Perico, Texas, from Dallam County.)

1 We'll shoot the buffalo,
We'll shoot the buffalo,
    We'll ramble in the canebrake
And shoot the buffalo.

2 The boys can reap and mow,
And the girls can knit and sew.
    We'll ramble in the canebrake
And shoot the buffalo.

3 The hawk shot the monkey
And the monkey stumped his toe.
    We'll ramble in the canebrake
And shoot the buffalo.

4 The girls can card and spin,
And the boys can sit and grin.
    We'll ramble in the canebrake
And shoot the buffalo.

F

RISE YOU UP

(Mrs. Bertha Downing, Norman, Cleveland County, who played it in Southern Noble,
Northwestern Logan, and Northern Payne Counties.)

Rise you up, my dearest dear,
    And present to me your paw,
For they say he has terbaccer,
    And I'd like to have a chaw.
O, Ma.

311

Or:

Rise ye up, my dearest dear,
   And present to me your hand,
And we'll journey on together
   Through a strange and distant land.

Other variants by Ethel Rose Baird, Bixby, Tulsa County; Delphin Delmar Bledsoe, Marlow, Stephens County; Mary Esther Coffman, Geary, Blaine County, from Carroll County, Missouri; Tephia Folsom, Atoka, Atoka County; Mrs. T. H. Maness, Oswalt, Love County; Bertha Matthews, Norman, Cleveland County, from Chickasha, Grady County, the same from Texas; Florette McNeese, Oklahoma City, Oklahoma County; Audra A. Plumlee, Norman, Cleveland County, from Northwestern Arkansas; L. E. Russel, Cyril, Caddo County; H. N. Scott, Fairland, Ottawa County; Cora Frances Starritt, Ada, Pontotoc County; Rephord Hubert Stevens, Union City, Canadian County; Elizabeth Stewart, Chelsea, Rogers County, from Mrs. Jane Ida Hicks, Chelsea; Jack H. Watson, Oklahoma City, Oklahoma County, from C. E. Wallas, Norman, Cleveland County; Sam West, Duke, Jackson County, from L. F. Holm, Jackson County.

99
SISTER PHOEBE

Cf. "The Juniper-Tree," Ames (Missouri), *JAFL*, 24:305-306; "Oh Sister Phoebe," Ball (Idaho), *JAFL*, 44:13-14; "The Juniper-Tree," Gardner (Michigan), *JAFL*, 33:107; "The Juniper-Tree," Hamilton (Northeastern Missouri), *JAFL*, 27:292-293; "Old Sister Phoebe, How merry were we," Hoke (North Carolina), *JAFL*, 5:118 (listed); "Under the Juniper Tree," Hudson (Mississippi, *Specimens*), pp. 127-128; "The Juniper Tree," Mahan and Grahame (Iowa), pp. 43-44; "The Widow with Daughters to Marry," "Quebec Town," Newell, pp. 57, 246; Parker (North Carolina), *JAFL*, 20:248 (listed); "Juniper Tree," Piper (Western Nebraska), *JAFL*, 28:269; "The Juniper Tree," Randolph (Ozarks, Missouri), *JAFL*, 42:225-226; Shearin and Combs (Kentucky), p. 37 (excerpt); "Presenting a Hat to Phoebe," Talley, p. 140; "The Juniper-Tree," Van Doren (Eastern Illinois), *JAFL*, 32:489-490; "The Juniper-Tree," Wedgwood (Southwestern Nebraska, Southern Iowa, from Missouri), *JAFL*, 25:272; Wilson (Ozarks), pp. 81-82; Wolford (Indiana), pp. 80-81.

For "I put on a nightcap to keep her head warm," cf. "Poor Widow," Gomme, 2:452. For a game played with hats, cf. "King Arthur Was King William's Son," Champlin, p. 447.

See HOG DROVERS.

A

(Florette McNeese, Oklahoma City, Oklahoma County, from her pupils.)

1 Sister Phoebe, how merry were we,
   The night we sat under the juniper tree,
       Heigh-ho, heigh-ho!
   Put this hat on your head and keep your ears warm,
   And take a sweet kiss — it will do you no harm,
       But a great deal of good, I know.
   Now, sister, rise up and choose you a man,
   The fairest that ever you can.

2 Brother Rogers, how merry were we,
   The night we sat under the juniper tree.
       Heigh-ho, heigh-ho!
   Put this hat upon your head to keep your ears warm,
   And take a sweet kiss — it will do you no harm,
       But a great deal of good, I know.
   Now, brother, rise up and go choose you a wife,
   And go choose you a wife for life.

B

That June Apple Tree

(O. B. Campbell, Medford, Grant County.)

1 Old Sister Pheobe, how merry were we,
   The night we sat under the June apple tree,
   That June apple tree, high-o, high-o,
   That June apple tree, high-o.

2 Put this hat on your head to keep your head warm.
   A thousand sweet kisses will do you no harm,
   But a great deal of good, I'm sure, I'm sure,
   But a great deal of good, I'm sure.

3 So rise you up, sister, go choose you a man,
   Go choose you the fairest that ever you can.
   So rise you up, sister, and go, go, go;
   So rise you up, sister, and go.

4 Old Brother Plug-Ugly, how merry were we, etc.

5 Put this hat on your head to keep your head warm, etc.

6 So rise you up, brother, go choose you a wife,
   Go choose you the fairest you can for your life.
   So rise you up, brother, and go, go, go;
   So rise you up, brother, and go.

Variant by Delmer Denton, Blackwell, Kay County.

100
SKIP TO MY LOU
(William Plaster, Meeker, Lincoln County.)

Cf. "Bull in the Park," Gomme, 1:50-51, which is similar in method of playing and in the lines, "Hen's i' t' hurdle crowing for day, Cock's i' t' barn threshing corn." (See PIG IN THE PARLOR.)

Cf. Ames (Missouri), *JAFL*, 24:304-305; Ball (Idaho), *JAFL*, 44:20-21; "The Miller," Belden (*A Partial List of Song-Ballads and Other Popular Poetry Known in Missouri*), No. 145; Blair (Kentucky), *JAFL*, 40:98; Douthitt (Kentucky), pp. 31-32; Dudley and Payne (Texas), *PTFS*, 1:15; "Skip Come a Lou," Gardner (Michigan), *JAFL*, 33:123-125 (seven texts); Hudson (Mississippi, *Specimens*), pp. 128-129; Lomax (*American Ballads and Folk Songs*), pp. 294-295; Mahan and Grahame (Iowa), pp. 40-42; Perrow (East Tennessee, Indiana, Mississippi), *JAFL*, 26:136-137 (four texts; note: "Lou, a common term for 'sweetheart' in East Tennessee. Probably derived from the proper noun."); Piper (Western Nebraska), *JAFL*, 28:276-277; Pound (Nebraska, *Syllabus*), p. 73; Randolph (Ozarks, Missouri), *JAFL*, 42:203-204 (also *The Ozarks*, pp. 141-142); "Waltz the Hall," *ibid.*, pp. 204-205 (also *The Ozarks*, pp. 143-145); Richardson (*American Mountain Songs*), p. 82; Shearin and Combs (Kentucky), p. 36 (excerpt); Van Doren (Eastern Illinois), *JAFL*, 32:493; Wedgwood (Southwestern Nebraska, Southern Iowa, from Missouri), *JAFL*, 25:270-271; Wolford (Indiana), pp. 89-90.

For tune, see chorus of (THE) OLD BRASS WAGON.

1 Gone again, what shall I do?
Gone again, what shall I do?
  Skip-to-my-lou, my darling.

Chorus:
  Skip, skip, skip-to-my-lou,
  Skip-to-my-lou, my darling.

2 I get another one, better than you, etc.

3 My wife skip and I'll skip too, etc.

4 If you can't get a white one, a black one will do, etc.

5 Little red wagon painted blue, etc.

6 An old rubber boot and a run-down shoe, etc.

7 Pig in the yard fence and he can't get through, etc.

8 If I can't get a red bird, a blue bird will do, etc.

9 Stand there, big foot, don't know what to do, etc.

10 If I had a rock, I'd throw it at you, etc.

11 Flies in the sugar bowl, two by two, etc.

Note: "Any kind of line that had the right rhythm would do."— Professor Kenneth C. Kaufman, Norman, Cleveland County.

Variants by Mrs. Marjorie Allen, Lexington, Cleveland County; Professor John Alley, Norman, Cleveland County, from North Texas; Warren Barnhill, Yukon, Canadian County; Virginia Bartley, Duncan, Stephens County; Lois Ferguson Beckham, Norman, Cleveland County; Gladys Mary Bednar, Luther, Oklahoma County; Jane Bowman, Pauls Valley, Garvin County; Frank Roger Campbell, Norman, Cleveland County; Raymond Coffelt, Duncan, Stephens County; Mary Esther Coffman, Geary, Blaine County; J. O. Conner, Shawnee, Pottawatomie County, from Leone Comstock, Shawnee; Bert H. Cook, Binger, Caddo County, from Mabel Cook; Dessie Deal, Billings, Noble County; Hattie Dupy, Billings, Noble County; Evalyne Ellis, Ochelata, Washington County; Thelma A. Epler, Norman, Cleveland County; Faneta Fitchett, Billings, Noble County; Lloyd B. Flood, Norman, Cleveland County; Walter Myers Gable, Norman, Cleveland County; Catherine Harris, Antlers, Pushmataha County, who played it at Miller, Pushmataha County; Mary Haxel, Purcell, McClain County, who played it near Noble, Cleveland County, and Washington, McClain County; Alta Lonnie Hays, Spearman, Texas; Lillie O. Heaton, Watonga, Blaine County; Ruby Home, Calumet, Canadian County; Alice Lucile Jackson, Supply, Woodward County; Helen Jacobs, Tulsa, Tulsa County; Louise James, Norman, Cleveland County; Lillian A. Jasper, Roosevelt, Kiowa County; Walter Jordan, Apperson, Osage County; Professor Kenneth C. Kaufman, Norman, Cleveland County, who played it in Eastern Custer County; Leon Kidd, Billings, Noble County; Nieto Looney, El Reno, Canadian County, who played it at Wayne, McClain County; Mary Virginia Maloy, Norman, Cleveland County; Erma Malthy, Billings, Noble County; Mrs. T. H. Manness, Oswalt, Love County; Wallace N. McCown, Emporia, Kansas, from Earl Denton, Norman, Cleveland County; Lavelle McDaniel, Norman, Cleveland County, from Opal Poindexter, Covington, Garfield County; Mark H. McKinsey, Ardmore, Carter County, who played it near Tuttle, Grady County; Beatrice Jennings McMullin, Norman, Cleveland County, brought from Kentucky to Missouri, then to Kay and Grant

Counties, on Oklahoma-Kansas border; Esca Milne, Oklahoma City, Oklahoma County; Mrs. Edna Muldrow, Norman, Cleveland County, from her pupils; Dr. L. B. Nice, Norman, Cleveland County, who played it in Ohio; Marjorie Nice, Norman, Cleveland County, from Ohio; Zelma Oliver, Norman, Cleveland County, from Eugene Nolen, Norman; Naomi Maye Porter, Ringling, Jefferson County; Opal Roberts, El Reno, Canadian County, from Enid, Garfield County, at opening of Oklahoma; Glenn A. Roe, Oklahoma City, Oklahoma County, who played it at Frederick, Tillman County, through Lena E. Misener; L. E. Russell, Cyril, Caddo County; Anita Shaw, Thomas, Custer County; Thelma Staggs, Guthrie, Logan County; Cora Frances Starritt, Ada, Pontotoc County; Rephord Hubert Stevens, Union City, Canadian County; A. J. Strange, Clinton, Custer County; Verla Summers, Snyder, Kiowa County, who played it near McCloud, Pottawatomie County; Helen Marie Swartz, Manitou, Tillman County; Joseph Edward Terral, Oklahoma City, Oklahoma County; Kenneth Tiger, Okmulgee, Okmulgee County; Maude Markham Vaughan, Pawhuska, Osage County, from near Enid, Garfield County; Emma Vilhauer, Norman, Cleveland County; Myrtle Walter, Covington, Garfield County; Sam West, Duke, Jackson County, from Om Earl Hitt, Jackson County; James E. White, Norman, Cleveland County, who played it at Bradley, Grady County; Florence Whitelock, Norman, Cleveland County, from Texas; Mrs. Della I. Young, Cheyenne, Roger Mills County, from Vashti Young and J. B. Weatherly, Elk City, Beckham County.

101
STAR PROMENADE

(Willis Goetzinger, Beaver, Beaver County, from Orlan Bell, Gray, Beaver County.)

Related to the square dance.

Cf. "Star Promenade," Wolford (Indiana), pp. 91-92.

See GENTS TO THE CENTER; TWINKLE, TWINKLE, LITTLE STAR.

1 Ladies to the center with a right hand cross.
Be careful now that you don't get lost.
Back to the left and don't be afraid,
Meet your partner with a star promenade.

2 Oh, my! mamma, what a bug I'll be,
What a bug I'll be, what a bug I'll be!
Oh, my! mamma, what a bug I'll be
When two young men come courting me!

102

STEAL APPLES

Related to the square dance.

For the words and the tune of the chorus, see GENTS TO THE CENTER.

A

(Sung by Orville Nichols, Mountain Park, Kiowa County, from Cordell, Washita County.)

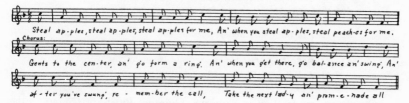

1 Steal apples, steal apples.
  Steal apples for me,
An' when you steal apples.
  Steal peaches for me.

Chorus:

  Gents to the center, an' go form a ring,
  An' when you get there, go balance an' swing,
  An' after you've swung, remember the call,
  Take the next lady an' promenade all.

B

WHEN YOU STEAL APPLES

(Emma Vilhauer, Norman, Cleveland County.)

1 Oh, when you steal apples,
  Steal peaches for me.
And when you steal peaches,
  Steal apples for me.

Chorus:

  It's ladies to the center and form a ring,
  And when you get there, just balance and swing.
  And when you have swung, remember my call.
  Take the next lady and promenade all.

2 Oh, when you take Susie,
  Leave Lizzie for me,
And when you take Lizzie,
  Leave Susie for me.

  It's gents to the center, etc.

317

C
IT'S WRONG TO STEAL APPLES
(J. O. Conner, Shawnee, Pottawatomie County, from Leone Comstock, Shawnee; L. E. Russell, Cyril, Caddo County.)

1 It is wrong to steal apples from another man's tree, (*Three times.*)
  If you want to steal apples, steal apples from me.

Chorus:
  Then all you gents to the center of the ring.
  And then you come back and balance and swing.
  And when you have swung, remember the call,
  And back to the center and promenade all.
  And promenade, promenade, promenade all,
  And promenade, promenade, promenade all,
  And when you have swung, remember your call,
  And back to the center and promenade all.

Other variants by Louise Aldridge, Quinton, Pittsburg County; Ethel Rose Baird, Bixby, Tulsa County; Wanda Dalton, Curtis, Woodward County, from Childers, Texas; William Lorenzen, El Reno, Canadian County; Elsie Montgomery, Sunset, Beaver County, from Darrouzett, Texas; Mrs. Della I. Young, Cheyenne, Roger Mills County, from Vashti Young.

103
STOLE MY PARTNER
(Florette McNeese, Oklahoma City, Oklahoma County, from her pupils.)

Cf. "Steal Partners," Dudley and Payne (Texas), *PTFS,* 1:25.
1 You stole my partner to my dislike, (*Three times.*)
  And also my dear darling.

2 I'll get her again if it costs me my life, etc.

3 Just reel and reel to your delight, etc.

104
SUSAN JANE
(Beatrice Jennings McMullin, Norman, Cleveland County, brought from Kentucky to Missouri, then to Kay and Grant Counties, on Oklahoma-Kansas border.)

Based on a Negro rhyme. See "Oh, Susan, Quit Your Fooling," Dobie (Texas), *PTFS,* 6:134-135.
For variants of Stanza 1 (close to the OLD JOE CLARK stanza, "Went down to Dinah's house"), cf. "Oh, Ain't I Gone?", Ames (Missouri), *JAFL,* 24:300; "Sally Ann," Perrow (Kentucky), 28:183; "Allie Bell,"

ibid. (Mississippi), p. 188; White (Alabama, North Carolina), pp. 333-334.
Cf. Hamilton (Northeastern Missouri), 27:291-292; Wilson (Ozarks),
pp. 75-76.

See OH, AIN'T I SWEET.

1 I went down to see my Susan,
    She met me at the door;
  She told me that I needn't come
    To see her any more.
  She'd fell in love
    With Rufus Santa Jackson Payne.
  I looked her in the face and said,
    "Good-by, my Susan Jane."

Chorus:
  O, Susan Jane, O Susan Jane,
  O, Susan, quit your fooling,
    And give your heart to me,
  Or give me back my love again,
    And then I'll let you be.

2 Your mouth is like a cellar,
    Your foot is like a ham,
  Your eyes are like the owl's at night,
    Your voice is never calm.
  Your hair is long and curly,
    You look just like a crane.
  I looked her in the face and said,
    "Good-by, my Susan Jane."

3 I once did love you dearly,
    But ne'er can love again.
  I looked her in the face and said,
    "Good-by, my Susan Jane."
  Susan is deceiving.
    She will not do to trust.
  I've trusted all the girls in town
  And leave her now I must.

Variant ("Susie Girl") by Atlee M. Garrett, Loco, Stephens County.

105
SUSIE BROWN

(Florette McNeese, Oklahoma City, Oklahoma County, from her pupils.)

Cf. "Susie Brown," Pound (Nebraska, *Syllabus*), p. 74; "Cuckoo
Waltz," Wolford (Indiana), pp. 36-37 (two texts).

"Susie (Susan) Brown" occurs in "Hogs in the Cornfield," Ames (Missouri), *JAFL,* 24:318; COFFEE GROWS ON A WHITE OAK TREE, OLD JOE CLARK, VIRGINIA.

For Stanza 3, see GOLDEN SLIPPERS.

Played like COFFEE GROWS ON A WHITE OAK TREE.

1 Choose your love as we go round, (*Three times.*)
    My lovely Susie Brown.

2 Three times round the poker whirl, etc.

3 Fare you well, my pretty little miss, (*Three times.*)
    With the golden slippers on. (*Three times.*)
Fare you well, my pretty little miss,
    With the golden slippers on.

106

SWEETHEART A-HUNTING

Cf. "Fooling," Douthitt (Kentucky), pp. 33-34; "We're a true love-a-honey," Heck (Cincinnati), *JAFL,* 40:28; "Long Summer Day," Shearin and Combs (Kentucky), p. 36 (excerpt). Dr. Josiah H. Combs, of Texas Christian University, reports this from Knott County, Kentucky, under the title "Sail Around the Ocean."

Sail around the ocean on a long summer day, (*Three times.*)
Sail around the ocean, and it's buttermilk and whey.

Face your beauty on a long summer day, (*Three times.*)
Face your beauty and it's buttermik and whey.

Kneel to your beauty, etc.

Kiss your beauty, etc.

Rise to your beauty, etc.

(Also Kittredge, *JAFL,* 20:276-277.)

A

(No Title)

(Sung by Professor Kenneth C. Kaufman, Norman, Cleveland County, who played it in Eastern Custer County.)

1 Walk and talk together on a long summer day, (*Three times.*)
Rocky road to Jordan and we'll all roll away.

2 Sweethearts hunting on a long summer day, etc.

3 Swing Miss Liza single on a long summer day, etc.

B

(O. B. Campbell, Medford, Grant County.)

1 Sweetheart a-hunting
    On a long summer day.
Sweetheart a-hunting
    On a long summer day.

2 Oh, where shall I find her
    On a long summer day?
Oh, where shall I find her
    On a long summer day?

3 Hanging on the corner
    On a long summer day.
Hanging on the corner
    On a long summer day.

4 We'll walk and talk together
    On a long summer day.
We'll walk and talk together
    On a long summer day.

5 Daddy killed a nigger
    On a long summer day.
Daddy killed a nigger
    On a long summer day,

6 Killed him with a shovel,
    And we'll all run away.
Killed him with a shovel,
    And we'll all run away.

C

(No Title)

(J. Kyle McIntyre, Ardmore, Carter County, from Montgomery County, East Tennessee.)

1 Lady on the green grass,
    Long summer day.
Lady on the green grass,
    Long summer day.

2 Come in upon the ocean,
    Long summer day.
Come in upon the ocean,
    Long summer day.

3 Choose your lover,
    Long summer day.
Choose your lover,
    Long summer day.

4 Now or never,
    Long summer day.
Now or never,
    Long summer day.

107

'TAIN'T GOIN' TO RAIN NO MORE

Based on Negro dance and minstrel songs, which have also been the source of the popular song by Wendell Hall. See " 'Tain't Gwine Rain No Mo'," Scarborough (Texas), pp. 106-108 (two texts).

For "My old mistress she told me," cf. "Run, Nigger, Run!", Harris (*Uncle Remus and His Friends*), p. 200; "Run, Nigger, Run!", Lomax (*American Ballads and Folk Songs*), p. 230; "Raise a Rukus Tonight," "Gwine to Git a Home By an' By," Odum and Johnson (*Negro Workaday Songs*), pp. 173-175 (three texts), 176; "John Booker," Perrow (Mississippi), *JAFL,* 28:138; "As I was going up a new-cut road," "As I was walkin' 'long the new-cut road," "Fragment from Pore Mournah," "My Ole Mistis," Scarborough (Virginia, Texas, Tennessee), pp. 106, 165, 194, 223-225; "Promises of Freedom," Talley, pp. 25-26; White (Alabama, North Carolina), pp. 134, 151-152 (three texts, with annotations).

Hattie Bell Bethea reports the following from Nellie C. Ellerbe, Librarian, Marion, South Carolina:

> My ole mistis promised me
> When she died she'd set me free.
> My ole mistis dead and gone,
> Left ole Sambo hoin' corn.

For "Some folks say that a nigger won't steal," cf. "Some Folks Say," Bass (South Carolina), *JAFL,* 44:425; Harris, *loc. cit.;* Lomax, *loc. cit.;* "Raise a Rukus Tonight," Odum and Johnson, *op. cit.* p. 174; "Oh, Mourner!," Perrow (Mississippi), *JAFL,* 28:135-136; " 'They Steal' Gossip," Talley, p. 110; White (Alabama), p. 138; "Some Folks Say," *idem* (Alabama, North Carolina), pp. 370-372 (five texts); "Whar Did You Cum From?," *idem,* p. 449. *Addenda:* "Fragment" ("From a college or glee club, song, 'Poor Mourner' "), Pound (Nebraska, *Syllabus*), p. 72: "Way Down Yonder in the Cornfield," Shay (*My Pious Friends and Drunken Companions*), p. 79.

Atlee Margaret Garrett, Loco, Stephens County, reports the following variant of "Down in De Cornfield:"

> Some folks say that a crow won't steal,
>> Way down yonder in de corfiel',
> But I caught one in de cornfiel',
>> Way down yonder in de cornfiel'.
>
> *Chorus:*
>> *Down in Mobile,*
>> *Down in Mobile,*
>> *How I love that pretty yaller girl*
>> *Down in Mobile.*
>
> Set a trap for a big blue jay,
>> Way down yonder in de cornfiel',
> He took my trap an' ran away,
>> Way down yonder in de cornfiel'.

For "Grasshopper settin' on a sweet 'tater vine," cf. Talley, p. 173; Wilson (Ozarks), p. 89.

For "The animals are a-comin' in two by two," cf. Scarborough, p. 181; White (North Carolina, Alabama), pp. 103, 141-143 (two texts).

Cf. "Hurry, Boys, Hurry, *or* 'Tain't Gonna Rain No More," Douthitt (Kentucky), pp. 37-38; "Blackbird," " 'Tain't Goin' to Rain No More," "Rabbit," Dudley and Payne (Texas), *PTFS,* 1:10, 12-13; "Ain't Gonna Rain," Sandburg (Iowa, Nebraska), p. 141.

A

It Ain't Gonna Rain No More

(William Plaster, Meeker, Lincoln County.)

1 Two little sisters form a ring,
>> It ain't gonna rain no more.
> Now you break and now you swing,
>> It ain't gonna rain no more.

2 Two old boys do the same,
>> It ain't gonna rain no more.
> Now you break and now you swing.
>> It ain't gonna rain no more.

3 Rain, hail, sleet, snow,
>> It ain't gonna rain no more.
> It rained last night, and the night before,
>> It ain't gonna rain no more.

4 Aces, diamonds, deuces, spades,
    It ain't gonna rain no more.
It ain't raining now like it was a while ago,
    It ain't gonna rain no more.

(*Repeat for "Three little sisters," "Four little sisters," etc.*)

Extra stanzas:
    Meet your honey with a pretty bouquet,
        It ain't gonna rain no more.
    Flap your wings and fly away.
        It ain't gonna rain no more.

    Hands in your pockets and your head against the wall,
        It ain't gonna rain no more.
    Take a chew of tobacco and promenade all,
        It ain't gonna rain no more.

B

It Ain't Gonna Rain No More

(Bertha Matthews, Norman, Cleveland County, from Chickasha, Grady County.)

1 My old mistress she told me,
    It ain'ta gonna rain no more.
When she died she'd set me free,
    It ain'ta gonna rain no more.
    It ain'ta gonna rain no more.

    She lived so long her head got bald,
        It ain'ta gonna rain no more.
    She give it up, not dyin' at all,
        It ain'ta gonna rain no more.
        It ain'ta gonna rain no more.

2 She had an ol' bonnet all ruffled round the brim,
    It ain'ta gonna rain no more.
Looked like a crow's nest hangin' on a limb,
    It ain'ta gonna rain no more.
    It ain'ta gonna rain no more.
She had another bonnet all ruffled round the crown,
    It ain'ta gonna rain no more.
Looked like poor folks livin' in town,
    It ain'ta gonna rain no more.
    it ain'ta gonna rain no more.

324

C

(No Title)

(Ruby Pfautsch, Norman, Cleveland County, from Texas.)

1 What did the blackbird say to the crow?
    'Tain't gwine rain no mo'.
'Tain't gwine hail an' 'tain't gwine snow,
    'Tain't gwine rain no mo'.

Chorus:
    'Tain't gwine rain, 'tain't gwine snow,
    'Tain't gwine rain no mo'.
    Steal up everybody,
    'Tain't gwine rain no mo'.

2 Gather corn in a beegum hat,
    'Tain't gwine rain no mo'.
Ole Massa grumbles if you eat much of that,
    'Tain't gwine rain no mo'.

3 Two an' two an' round up four,
    'Tain't gwine rain no mo'.
Two an' two an' round up four,
    'Tain't gwine rain no mo'.

4 Six, two, round up four,
    'Tain't gwine rain no mo'.
Six, two, round up four,
    'Tain't gwine rain no mo'.

5 Rabbit skipped the garden gate,
    'Tain't gwine rain no mo'.
Picked a pea an' pulled his freight,
    'Tain't gwine rain no mo'.

6 Oh, ladies, 'tain't gwine rain, 'tain't gwine snow,
    'Tain't gwine rain no mo'.
Rabbit et a turnip top,
    'Tain't gwine rain no mo'.
He went off a-hippety-hop,
    'Tain't gwine rain no mo'.

7 Rabbit hiding behind a pine,
    'Tain't gwine rain no mo'.
Had one eye shut an' another eye blind,
    'Tain't gwine rain no mo'.

8 Bake them biscuits good an' brown,
    'Tain't gwine rain no mo'.
Swing your ladies round an' round,
    'Tain't gwine rain no mo'.

D

(Florette McNeese, Oklahoma City, Oklahoma County, from her pupils.)

1 Down the center and divide the ring,
   'Tain't goin' to rain no more.
Meet in the hall and bow and swing,
   'Tain't goin' to rain no more.
Promenade your corner girl,
   'Tain't goin' to rain no more.
Meet on the corner and do the whirl,
   'Tain't goin' to rain no more.

Chorus:
  Rainin' on the hillside, fare you well,
    'Tain't goin' to rain no more.
  Rained all yesterday and day before,
    'Tain't goin' to rain no more.

Directions: Form a circle. The couple who are to start the game march across the center and divide the ring, the boy going one way and the girl another on the outside of the ring. They 'meet in the hall' at the starting place. As the chorus is sung, all promenade in couples. Then a new boy takes the lead, and the first line of the stanza changes to 'Brand new boy with the same old girl.' At the end of the second round, another boy leads, until all have led. The first line then becomes: 'Brand new boy and brand new girl.' "

Variant and additional stanzas:
See that rabbit behind that pine,
   'Tain't goin' rain no more.
One eye out and the other one blind.
   'Tain't goin' rain no more.

Hey, all ladies,
   'Tain't goin' rain no more.
'Tain't goin' sleet and 'tain't goin' snow,
   And 'tain't goin' rain no more.
    (Winnifred Spencer, Walters, Cotton County.)

Chase the goose, chase the goose,
   It ain't going to rain no more.
Give that girl the double whirl,
   So it ain't going to rain no more.
    (Lavelle McDaniel, Norman, Cleveland County, from Opal Poindexter, Covington, Garfield County.)

Some folks say that a nigger won't steal,
   But I caught two in my cornfield.
One had a basket and the other had a hoe;
If that ain't stealing, well, I don't know.
    (Jane Bowman, Pauls Valley, Garvin County.)

The night was dark and dreary,
  The air was full of sound.
The old man stole the last clean sheet,
  And joined the Ku Klux Klan.

Some folks say that niggers won't steal,
But I caught three in my cornfield.
One had a bushel, and another had a peck,
And the other'n had a cornstalk round his neck.

Had an old hat and it had no crown,
  It ain't goin' to rain no more.
Looked like a terrapin settin' down,
  It ain't goin' to rain no more.
    (Cora Frances Starritt, Ada, Pontotoc County.)

Grasshopper settin' on a sweet 'tater vine,
Wants a chew o' 'backer but he won't get mine.
Hurry, boys, hurry,
It ain't agoin' to rain,
It ain't agoin' to snow,
It ain't agoin' to rain no mo'.
    (C. L. Cowan, Okemah, Okfuskee County.)

Circle four in the middle of the floor,
  It ain't going to rain no more.
The blue jay said to the crow,
  "Hurrow (*sic*), John, hurrow."
It ain't going to rain, it ain't going to snow,
It ain't going to rain no more.
It rained last night and the night before,
But it ain't going to rain no more.
    (Alec Gilbreath, Atoka, Atoka County, who played it near Lehigh, Coal
    County.)

The animals are a-comin' in two by two,
  'Tain't goin' t' rain no more.
The elephant, the lion, an' the kangaroo,
  'Tain't goin' t' rain no more.
    (Mrs. Ora Morris, Oklahoma City, Oklahoma County, who played it at Buena
    Vista, Carroll County, and in Benton County, Arkansas.)

Rained last night in the kitchen door,
  And it ain't agonna rain no more.
Rained last night in the kitchen door,
  And it ain't agonna rain no more.

327

Chorus:
> *Break loose, trail home,*
>> *And it ain't agonna rain no more.*
> *Break loose, trail home,*
>> *And it ain't agonna rain no more.*
> (Professor Kenneth C. Kaufman, Norman, Cleveland County, who played
> it in Eastern Custer County.)

Other variants by Christine Bettis, Norman, Cleveland County; Delphin Delmar Bledsoe, Marlow, Stephens County; Ruth Davis, Fort Worth, Texas; Viola Bernice Harris, Porter, Wagoner County.

108
THREE DUKES
(Mrs. L .D. Sayers, Norman, Cleveland County.)

For British versions, see Broadwood and Fuller-Maitland (*English County Songs*), p. 77; Chambers, p. 139; "Forty Dukes," Dearmer and Shaw (*Song Time*), pp. 72-76; "Here comes three duks a-riding," Douglas, p. 75; "Three Dukes," Gomme, 2:233-255, 455 (31 texts); "Three Knights from Spain," *idem*, 2:257-279, 455-456 (38 texts); "Here Comes a Lusty Wooer," *idem*, 1:202-203; "Here Comes One Virgin," *idem*, 1:203; "Here's a Soldier," *idem*, 1:206; "Jolly Hooper, *idem*, 1:287-289 (two texts); "Jolly Rover," *idem*, 1:293-294; "We are three brethren out of Spain," "Trip, trap over the grass," Halliwell (*The Nursery Rhymes of England*), pp. 107-108, 126-127; "Here come three brethren all out of Spain," etc., Northall, pp. 383-385 (five texts); "The Three Jews from Spain," Kidson and Moffat (*Eighty Singing Games*), p. 11; "The Duke of Rideo (or Riddeo)," Udal, pp. 355-358 (three texts); "Here Come Three Dukes A-Riding," Walter (*Old English Singing Games*), pp. 14-15.

For American versions, see "Here Come Three Dukes A-Riding," Babcock (Washington, D. C.), *American Anthropologist*, 1:258-259; Bolton (Virginia), p. 118 (counting-out rhyme); "Three Dukes A-Riding," Gardner (Michigan), *JAFL*, 33:129-131 (three texts); "There came a Jew (duck, duke) ariding," Heck (Cincinnati), *JAFL*, 40:8-9; "Here Comes a Duke," Newell, pp. 47-50 (three texts); "Raz-Ma-Taz-a-Ma-Tee," Randolph (Ozarks, Missouri), *JAFL*, 42:229-230; "Here Come Two Dukes A-Roving," Shearin and Combs (Kentucky), p. 36 (excerpt); "Here Comes a Young Man Courting," Talley, pp. 85-86; "There Comes Two Dukes A-Roving," Van Doren (Eastern Illinois), *JAFL*, 32:486-487; "Here Come Four Dukes A-Riding," Wolford (Indiana), pp. 52-54.

Dr. Josiah H. Combs, of Texas Christian University, reports the following from Gilmer County, West Virginia, as a variant of "Four Young Ladies" (THREE OLD MAIDS):

Here comes an old lady from Newfoundland,
  Newfoundland, Newfoundland,
Here comes an old lady from Newfoundland.
  So early in the morning.

Oh, what do you come for,
  Come for, come for, etc.

I've come for to get married,
  Married, married, etc.

Who do you think you'll marry,
  Marry, marry, etc.

I think I'll marry —— [*name*], etc.

"Here partners are chosen. They walk side by side singing the remainder of the stanza, then the whole game is repeated."

1 Here come three dukes riding,
    Riding, riding,
  Here come three dukes riding,
    Ransum, tansum, tea.

2 What are you riding here for,
    Here for, here for, etc.

3 We are riding here to get married,
    Married, married, etc.

4 [Why don't you marry us, sir,
    Us, sir, us, sir, etc.]

5 You are all too ragged and dirty,
    Dirty, dirty, etc.

6 We are just as good as you are,
    You are, you are, etc.

  Then one of the group says:
  Through the kitchen, and through the hall,
  Take the fairest one of all.

  Then there are four dukes come riding, etc., until all of those in Group Two are in Group One.

Variants:

You are all too black and greasy,
  Greasy, greasy,
You are all too black and greasy,
  So ransom ma tansom ma tee i o.

329

The fairest one that I can see,
  That I can see, that I can see,
The fairest one that I can see
  Is Mary, come walk with me.
  (Mabel Harryman, Lexington, Cleveland County.)

The fairest one that I can see,
  I can see, I can see,
The fairest one that I can see,
  Will you come and walk with me?
  (Bertha Matthews, Norman, Cleveland County, who played it in Texas.)

You're all too brown and freckled, etc.
  With a ransome a tansome a tee.
  (Mrs. L. T. Monnett, Norman, Cleveland County, who played it in Missouri.)

Then little Jenny come walk with me, etc.
  Rismal, tasmal, tee.
  (Helen A. Cook, Norman, Cleveland County, who played it in Texas County,
  in the Panhandle of Oklahoma.)

The old maid she wouldn't come, etc.
  Rassamatassamatee.

The old maid she had to come, etc.
  (Hazel Black, Higgins, Texas.)

Other variants by Virginia Bartley, Duncan, Stephens County; Louise James, Norman, Cleveland County.

109

THREE OLD MAIDS

Based on the nursery rhyme. See "Three Children Sliding," Dearmer and Shaw (*Song Time*), pp. 56-57 (where it is attributed to John Gay, 1685-1732); "Three Children Sliding on the Ice," Graham (*Traditional Nursery Rhymes*), p. 23; Halliwell (*The Nursery Rhymes of England*), p. 19 (where only two stanzas of a long tale are printed, with the note: "The following was most probably taken from a poetical tale in the 'Choyce Poems,' 12 mo. Lond. 1622. As it is a very popular nursery song, I shall give the tale to which I allude in No. 30." The complete title of the work referred to is *Ovid de Arte Amandi &c. Englished together with Choice Poems, and rare Pieces of Drollery*.); "Three Children Sliding on the Ice," *Mother Goose* (Dent and Dutton), p. 72.

Cf. "Two Young Couples Skating Went," Ball (Idaho), *JAFL*, 44:6-7; "Three Little Girls A-Sliding Went," Gardner (Michigan), *JAFL*, 33:128-

129 (three texts); "Three Old Bums," Hamilton (Northeast Missouri), *JAFL,* 27:301; "Six Little Girls A-Sliding Went," Wolford (Indiana), p. 88.

Dr. Josiah H. Combs, of Texas Christian University, reports "Four Young Ladies" from Gilmer County, West Virginia.

A

(Cora Huddleston, Norman, Cleveland County.)

1 Three old maids skating went,
    Skating went, skating went.
  Three old maids skating went,
    So early in the morning.

2 Ice was thin and they fell in,
    They fell in, they fell in.
  Ice was thin and they fell in,
    So early in the morning.

3 Ask some one to help them out,
    Help them out, help them out.
  Ask some one to help them out,
    So early in the morning.

Directions: "There are three ladies joining hands inside of a large circle of standers-by. While the outside circle of people sing, the three old maids skip around and around. During last stanza they choose a partner, when the singers repeat, 'Ask some one to help them out.' The chosen partners swing the three old maids, and then the three old bachelors remain in center, and song is repeated, changing the word 'maid' to some non-feminine phrase. They proceed to do as the old maids did, skip round, keeping time with the music and doing according to the words of the song.

"This play dance is repeated for hours at play-parties or square dances, each time the girls and boys choosing the one who they liked best—so to speak, had a crush on."

B

THREE OLD MAIDS AT A SKATING RINK

(Gerald Whitlaw, Waynoka, Woods County.)

1 Three old maids at a skating rink,
    At a skating rink, at a skating rink,
  Three old maids at a skating rink,
    So early in the morning.

2 The ice was thin, and they fell in,
   And they fell in, and they fell in,
The ice was thin, and they fell in,
   So early in the morning.

3 Three old bums come to help them out,
   Come to help them out, come to help them out,
Three old bums come to help them out,
   So early in the morning.

C

THREE OLD MAIDS WENT SKATING ON THE ICE

(Viola Harris, Porter, Wagoner County.)

1 Three old maids went skating on the ice,
   Skating on the ice, skating on the ice.
Three old maids went skating on the ice
   On a summerish day.

2 The ice was thin, so they all fell in,
   They all fell in, they all fell in.
The ice was thin, so they all fell in,
   On a summerish day.

3 Choose your partner and swing them in,
   Swing them in, swing them in.
Choose your partner and swing them in,
   On a summerish day.

4 Change again, and they all fell in,
   They all fell in, they all fell in.
Change again, and they all fell in,
   On a summerish day.

5 Change again, and they all fell out,
   They all fell out, they all fell out.
Change again, and they all fell out.
   On a summerish day.

Other variants by Bonnie Mae Close, Oklahoma City, Oklahoma County; Mary Esther Coffman, Geary, Blaine County; Ruby Home, Calumet, Canadian County; William Lorenzen, El Reno, Canadian County; Alvin C. Meixner, Alva, Woods County; Madeline Tarpley, Shamrock, Texas; Doris G. Waters, Ponca City, Kay County, from her pupils.

110

TIDEO

Cf. "Pass One Window," Ames (Missouri), *JAFL,* 24:311; "Toddy O'," Douthitt (Kentucky), p. 31; "Ti-de-o," Hamilton (Northeast Missouri), *JAFL,* 27:294; "Pass One Window Tidy O," Pound (Nebraska, *Syllabus*), p. 76; "Jingle at the Window," Randolph (Ozarks, Missouri), *JAFL,* 27:214-215 (also *The Ozarks,* pp. 156-158); "Dance-Song" ("Lead a man, di-dee-o"), Scarborough (North Carolina), pp. 115-116; "Jingle at the Window," Wilson (Ozarks), pp. 83-84; "Tideo," Wolford (Indiana), pp. 96-97. "Toddy O" is requested by Payne (Texas), *PTFS,* 1:35-38.

For "Jingle at the Window," see DOWN IN ALABAMA.

A

(Sung by Charlie Carr, Noble, Cleveland County.)

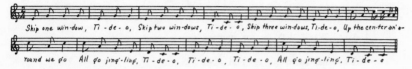

Skip one window, Tideo,
Skip two windows, Tideo,
Skip three windows, Tideo,
Up the center an' around we go.
All go jingling, Tideo,
Tideo, Tideo,
All go jingling, Tideo.

("It's more of a kid's game. I learned it when I was a kid.")

B

(Beatrice Jennings McMullin, Norman, Cleveland County, brought from Kentucky to Missouri, then to Kay and Grant Counties, on Oklahoma-Kansas border.)

1 Skip one window, tideo,
  Skip two windows, tideo,
  Skip three windows, tideo,
  Skip four windows, tideo.

2 Skip to the center
    And choose your beau,
  Then dance around
    With a tideo.

Directions: "Couples form circle holding hands. Raise arms to denote windows. A couple skips windows in opposite direction, meet, promenade."

C

(Willis Goetzinger, Beaver, Beaver County.)

1 Skip one window, tideo,
  Skip two windows, tideo,
  Skip three windows, tideo,
  Jingle at the window, tideo.

2 Swing to the center and bow to your beau.
  Jingle at the window, tideo.
  Jingle, jingle, little Joe,
  Jingle at the window, tideo.

Directions: "All form circle holding hands. When the song gets to the fifth line, the lady and her partner swing with a dance hold during the fifth and sixth lines, and promenade during the last two. The song is then repeated."

D
Tideo-O
(Clifford Chandler, Crescent, Logan County.)

1 Asked her if she'd be my wife,
  Said she wouldn't for a barlow knife.
  Asked her sister and she said, "No."
  Down to the center, bow to your beau,
  All come a-jingle on tideo-o.

2 Tideo-o, here we go,
  All come a-jingle on a tideo-o.
  Tideo-o, here we go,
  All come a-jingle on a tideo-o.

E
(No Title)
(Professor Kenneth C. Kaufman, Norman, Cleveland County, who played it in Eastern Custer County.)

Tingalo, tingalo,
Then we'll all go tingalo.
Skip to the center and balance your beau,
Then we'll all go tingalo.

F
(Ezra Van Horn, Norman, Cleveland County.)

1 Skip one window, Tideo, etc. (*as in B.*)

Chorus:
  I take Jim and you take Joe,
  And all go Ting-a-ling Tideo.

2 Ting-a-ling-ling-ling,
    Ting-a-ling-lo,
  Ting-a-ling-ling-ling,
    Tideo.

Other variants by Ethel Rose Baird, Bixby, Tulsa County; Gladys Mary Bednar, Luther, Oklahoma County; Jessie Lee Bryant, Billings, Noble

County; Leonard C. Dresser, Lahoma, Garfield County, who played it near Vernon, Garfield County; Franklin W. Ewing, Higgins, Texas; Alec Gilbreath, Atoka, Atoka County, who played it at Silverton, Texas; Mary Haxel, Purcell, McClain County, who played it near Noble, Cleveland County, and Washington, McClain County; Frances T. Henderson, Fort Cobb, Caddo County, from New Mexico; Helen Jacobs, Tulsa, Tulsa County; Fanny W. Kelly, Jefferson, Grant County; Mrs. Ora Morris, Oklahoma City, Oklahoma County, who played it at Buena Vista, Carroll County, and in Benton County, Arkansas; Forest Nelson, Duncan, Stephens County; Lucy I. Pitts, Oklahoma City, Oklahoma County, from Middle Tennessee; Audra A. Plumlee, Norman, Cleveland County; Glenn A. Roe, Oklahoma City, Oklahoma County, who played it at Frederick, Tillman County; Dorothy Long, Billings, Noble County, from her pupils; Madeline Tarpley, Shamrock, Texas; Sam West, Duke, Jackson County, from Om Earl Hitt, Jackson County; Mrs. Della I. Young, Cheyenne, Roger Mills County, from J. R. Weatherly, Elk City, Beckham County.

111

TURKEY IN THE STRAW

(Helen Jacobs, Tulsa, Tulsa County; Katherine Harris, Norman, Cleveland County.)

For this "classical American rural tune," see Sandburg, pp. 94-97 (three texts); "Zip Coon," Spaeth (*Read 'Em and Weep*), pp. 17-19 (where the date of the "father of them all" is set at about 1815). Goldberg (*Tin Pan Alley,* p. 37) attributes "Zip Coon" to George Nichols, with its origin, according to Charles H. Day, in a "rough jig dance called 'Natchez Under the Hill.' "

For Stanza 1, cf. "One More Drink," Henry, *JAFL,* 44:83; "Another Little Drink Won't Do No Harm," Shay (*Drawn from the Wood*), pp. 37-38; "Little Red Hen," Talley, pp. 37-38.

For a play-party version, see Van Doren (Eastern Illinois), *JAFL,* 32:489.

> 1 There was an old hen, she had a wooden leg.
> She was the best old hen that ever laid an egg.
> She laid eggs all around the farm.
> Another little drink wouldn't do us any harm.

> 2 Cat had a kitten, the kitten had a pup.
> Say, old lady, is your rhubarb up?
> There's plenty of rhubarb all round the farm,
> And another little drink wouldn't do us any harm.

3 The lightning flashed and the thunder roared.
  The little old pig laid down and snored.
  I picked up a rock and hit 'im in the jaw,
  And knocked out a tune called "Turkey in the Straw."

112

TURN, CINNAMON, TURN

See "Turn, Cheeses, Turn," Gomme, 2:311-312 and "Green cheeses, yellow laces," Halliwell (*The Nursery Rhymes of England*), p. 122, which ends: "Turn, cheeses, turn!"

Cf. "Sugar Lump," Babcock (Washington, D. C.), *American Anthropologist*, 1:256; Douthitt (Kentucky), pp. 32-33; Dudley and Payne (Texas), *PTFS*, 1:22-23; "Florida Song Games," *JAFL*, 15:193; Newell (Florida), p. 231.

A

(No Title)

(Mrs. Ora Morris, Oklahoma City, Oklahoma County, who played it at Buena Vista, Carroll County, and in Benton County, Arkansas.)

1 Somebody's rocking my sugar lump, (*Three times.*)
  Oh, turn, cinnamon, turn.

2 You better give her up, you've rocked her enough, etc.

3 I wouldn't give her up for a box of snuff, etc.

B

(Audra A. Plumlee, Norman, Cleveland County.)

1 Oh, a little more cinnamon, my sugar lump, (*Three times.*)
  Oh, turn, cinnamon, turn.

2 Oh, I'm getting tired, my sugar lump, etc.

Other variants by Jane Bowman, Pauls Valley, Garvin County; J. Kyle McIntyre, Ardmore, Carter County; Winnifred Spencer, Walters, Cotton County, from Jefferson, Marion County, Texas; Sam West, Duke, Jackson County, from L. F. Holm, Jackson County.

113

TWINKLE, TWINKLE, LITTLE STAR

(Sung by Clayton Black, east of Noble, Cleveland County.)

See STAR PROMENADE.

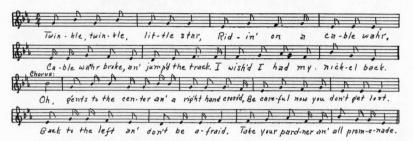

1 Twinkle, twinkle, little star,
   Ridin' on a cable wahr.*
Cable wahr broke, an' jumped the track,
   I wish'd I had my nickel back.

Chorus:
   Oh, gents to the center an' a right hand crossed.
   Be careful now you don't get lost.
   Back to the left an' don't be afraid.
   Take your pardner an' all promenade.

114

TWO LITTLE SISTERS

For ballad versions, see Barry (New England), *JAFL,* 18:130-132 (two texts); Barry, Eckstrom, and Smyth (*British Ballads from Maine*), pp. 40-46 (five texts); Belden (Missouri), *JAFL,* 19:233; Campbell and Sharp (*English Folk Songs from the Southern Appalachians*), p. 16; "The Twa Sisters," Child, No. 10; Cox (West Virginia), pp. 20-22 (three texts); Davis (Virginia), pp. 93-104 (eleven texts); Hudson (Mississippi, *Specimens*), pp. 4-5; Moore (Oklahoma), No. 3; Pound (North Carolina; Missouri, from Kentucky, *American Ballads and Songs*), pp. 11-13 (two texts); "There Was an Old Woman," *idem* (Nebraska, *Syllabus*), p. 11; Taylor, *JAFL,* 42:238-246.

For dance usage, cf. Hudson (*Culture in the South*), p. 524; Pound (*Poetic Origins and the Ballad*), pp. 53-54; Thomas (Kentucky), pp. 3-5, 70-73.

---

* Ridin' on a gable bar.—Charlie Carr, Noble, Cleveland County.

Raine (*The Land of Saddle-Bags,* p. 117) notes: " 'Bowee down!' and 'Bow and balance to me!' are a remnant from an old dance jingle, which was occasionally sung by dancers even after the music was furnished by the fiddle."

As is related to the square dance, "Two Little Sisters."

A

(Audra A. Plumlee, Norman, Cleveland County.)

1 Two little sisters side by side,
  Saying I do, saying I do.

2 Two little sisters side by side,
  The boys are bound for you,
  The boys are bound for you,

3 Two little sisters side by side,
  One of them promised to be my bride,
  I'll be kind to my true love
  If she'll be true to me.

B

BOW-EE DOWN (BOW YE DOWN)

(Mrs. Demma Ray Oldham, Oklahoma City, Oklahoma County, who heard it in Arkansas.)

1 There lived an old lady by the northern sea,
    Bow-ee down!
  There lived an old lady by the northern sea,
    Bow and balance to me!
  There lived an old lady by the northern sea,
  And she had daughters, one, two, three,
    I'll be true to my love,
    If my love'll be true to me.

2 A young man came a-courting there, etc.
  And he made choice of the youngest fair, etc.

3 He bought this youngest a beaver hat,
  And the oldest sister didn't like that.

4 As they walked down the water's brim,
  The oldest pushed the youngest in.

5 O sister, O sister, lend me your hand,
  And you may have my house and land.

6 She floated down the miller's dam,
  The miller drew her safe to land.

338

7 And off her finger took five gold rings,
   Then into the water he plunged her again.

Note: "This is an old dance song, the leader singing alone, all except the last two lines of each stanza. All joined in the chorus on the last two lines."

C

THE OLD WOMAN BY THE SEASHORE

(Mrs. L. T. Monnett, Norman, Cleveland County, who played it in Missouri.)

1 The miller he courted the eldest one,
      Bow down, bow down.
   The miller he courted the eldest one,
      For the bow was bent for me.
   The miller he courted the eldest one,
   Although he loved the youngest one.
      Bow down, tiddle tum tee.

2 He gave to the youngest a beaver hat, etc.
   The eldest she got mad at that, etc.

3 He gave to the eldest a diamond ring,
   Into the water she did fling.

4 O sister, take a walk with me
   To some foreign countree.

5 She threw her over a high stone wall.
   Into the water she did fall.

6 O sister, reach to me your hand,
   And I will give you house and land.

7 O no, I'll not reach to you my hand,
   And I don't want your house and land.

8 Sometime she sank and sometime she swam
   Until she reached the miller's dam.

9 The miller he reached out his hook and line.
   Out of the water she did climb.

115

VIRGINIA

Cf. "Down in Alabama," Piper (Western Nebraska, Western Iowa), *JAFL,* 28:266-267 (two texts).

See COFFEE GROWS ON A WHITE OAK TREE, DOWN IN ALABAMA, SHOO FLY, SKIP TO MY LOU.

A

Virginia

(Raymond Hugh Guthrie, Wakita, Grant County.)

1 Great big white house, nobody living in it,
Nobody living in it, nobody living in it.
Great big house, nobody living in it,
Old Virginia style.

2 Shake a little bit and bear on the shoulder,
Bear on the shoulder, bear on the shoulder,
Shake a little bit and bear on the shoulder,
Old Virginia style.

B

Hello Susan Brown

(May G. Miller, Norman, Cleveland County.)

Big white house and nobody living in it, (*Three times.*)
Hello! Susan Brown.

C

(No Title)

(Fern Tuttle, Norman, Cleveland County, from his grandmother, who played it in Indiana.)

Great big house and nobody living in it,
Nobody living in it, nobody living in it.
Great big house and nobody living in it,
Oh, what a shame.

D

(No Title)

(William Lorenzen, El Reno, Canadian County.)

Way down in Alabam,
Where Jonas stole a ham;
A great big house and nobody living in it.
Way down in Alabam.

Variant by Madeline Tarpley, Shamrock, Texas.

116

WAIT FOR THE WAGON

A sentimental song by R. B. Buckley, organizer of Buckley's minstrels, 1843 (Pound, *Syllabus,* pp. 47-48). See *Good Old-Time Songs,* No. 3, p. 44; *The Negro Forget-Me-Not Songster,* pp. 38-40; Shearin and Combs (Kentucky), p. 23 (described).

Sullivan (*Our Times*), 2:177, notes that the song was known for its chorus. According to Mrs. L. T. Monnett, of Norman, it was used as an advertisement for the Studebaker wagon. Mrs. Edna Muldrow, of Norman, reports a fragment of a Civil War parody. (Cf. Hudson, *JAFL*, 39: 85-86).

For a play-party version, see Wolford (Indiana), pp. 98-99.

A

(Chester Harley Anderson, Guthrie, Logan County; Jane Bowman, Pauls Valley, Garvin County; Mary Virginia Maloy, Norman, Cleveland County; Stewart E. Myers, Oklahoma City, Oklahoma County, from Maynardsville, Union County, Tennessee.)

1 Will you come with me, my Phyllis (dear),
    To yon blue mountains free?
Where (When) (the) blossoms smell the sweetest,
    Come rove along with me.
It's every Sunday morning,
    When I am by your side,
We'll jump into the wagon
    And all take a ride.

Chorus:
    Wait for the wagon, (Three times.)
    And we'll all take a ride.

2 Where the river runs like silver
    And the birds they sing so sweet,
I have a cabin, Phyllis,
    And something good to eat.
Come, listen to my story,
    It will relieve my heart.
So jump into the wagon
    And off we will (we'll) start.

3 Do you believe, my Phyllis dear,
    Old Mike (Red Mike) with all his wealth,
Could (can) make you half so (as) happy
    As I with youth and health?
We'll have a little farm,
    A horse, a pig, (and) a cow,
And you will (shall) mind the dairy
    While I do (go) guide the plough.

4 Your lips are red as poppies,
    Your hair so slick and neat,
All braided up with dahlias
    And hollyhocks so sweet.
It's every Sunday morning,
    When I am by your side,
We'll jump into the wagon
    And all take a ride.

5 Together on life's journey
    We'll travel till we stop,
    And if we have no troubles (trouble),
    We'll reach the happy top.
    Then come with me, sweet Phyllis,
    My dear, my lovely bride,
    We'll jump into the wagon,
    And all take a ride.

B

(John Cunningham, Watonga, Blaine County, from his father William Cunningham,
who brought it from Homestead, Blaine County.)

1 Every Sunday morning,
    Miss Lucy by my side,
    We'll jump into the wagon
    And we'll all take a ride.

Chorus:
    Wait for the wagon, (Three times.)
    And we'll all take a ride.

Other variants by Tephia Folsom, Atoka, Atoka County, from Ed Butler
(colored) Atoka; Agnes Frick, Oklahoma City, Oklahoma County; Lacie
Huff, Norman, Cleveland County; Ruth Revelle, Oklahoma City, from
Haywood County, Tennessee; Lydia Rorem, Oklahoma City, Oklahoma
County; Winnifred Spencer, Walters, Cotton County.

117
WALK ALONG, JOHN

Related to the square dance.

Allen, Ware, and Garrison (*Slave Songs of the United States*), p. 67,
give "Shock Along, John" as the title of a "corn-song, of which only the
burden is remembered"—

    Shock along, John, shock along.
    Shock along, John, shock along.

For A, cf. the minstrel song, "Walk Along, John," by Dan D. Emmett.
Cf. Wolford (Indiana), pp. 100-101.

A

(Sung by Orville Nichols, Mountain Park, Kiowa County, from Cordell, Washita
County.)

342

Shut your mouth, an' hush your talkin',
Join eight hands, an' let's go walkin'.
Walk along, John, with your paper collar on.
Walk along, John, with your paper collar on.

B

(Alec Gilbreath, Atoka, Atoka County.)

1 Shut your mouth, shush your talking.
Join eight hands, let's go walking.
Break loose, started home,
Lady in the lead, all going wrong.

2 First couple out, couple on the right, circle four,
In the middle of the floor.
Lady do-ce-do,
Gent come down with heel and toe.

3 Break loose, walk along, John,
Same place you started from,
Break loose, walk along, John,
Same place you started from.

4 Circle four
In the middle of the floor.
Lady do-ce-do,
Gent come down with heel and toe.

5 Do-ce your corner girl,
Back round your partner girl.
Corner left, partner right,
Right and left all the way round.

6 Go on, boys,
Don't be ashamed,
Looking down the road
Like hogs in the cane.

118
WALKING ON THE GREEN GRASS

For British versions, see "Tripping up the Green Grass," Broadwood and Fuller-Maitland (*English County Songs*), pp. 106-107; Gomme, 1:153-169 (fourteen texts); Northall, pp. 381-382 (five texts).

For American versions, see "Sweet Pinks and Roses," Clarke (Virginia Negroes), *JAFL*, 3:288; Dudley and Payne (Texas), *PTFS*, 1:20; "Walking up the green grass," Heck (Ohio), *JAFL*, 40:29 (two texts); "Tread,

Tread the Green Grass," Newell, pp. 50-51, 226-229 (three texts); "Taking a Walk," Talley, p. 183. *Addendum:* "Florida Song Games," *JAFL,* 15: 193-194.

For "walk the chalk," see OLD JOE CLARK.

See THE OCEAN IS WIDE.

A

(Sung by Leondis Brown, Noble, Cleveland County.)

1 Walkin' on the green grass,
    Dusty, dusty, dust.*
Come all ye handsome ladies
    An' present to me your hand (paw).
Oh, you're not so very handsome,
    But take you if you please.
I'll take you by your lily-white hand,
    An' walk the chalk with me.

Chorus:
    Walk the chalk, the butter an' cheese,
      Oh, walk the chalk, the candy.
    Walk the chalk, the butter an' cheese,
      An' swing those girls so handy.

2 The road is wide an' you can't step it.
  I love you an' you can't he'p it.

---

    * "The 'dust' of the rhyme is a corruption . . . it represents the Scotch (in other words, Old English) *adist,* the opposite of *ayont,* meaning *this way,* come hither."— Newell, pp. 50-51.

3 The rose's red an' violet's blue.
Sugar's sweet an' so are you.

4 Oh, the sea is deep an' full of salt.
If we don't marry, it'll be your fault.

5 The road is long an' full of gravel.
By your side I'm bound to travel.

6 The road is long an' full of crooks.
I hope some day you'll be my cook.

("It doesn't make any difference which one of those comes first. Whenever I
get to singin' 'em at a party, I can think of 'em better.")

B

(Mary Virginia Maloy, Norman, Cleveland County, from her mother, who learned it in
Texas.)

Walking on the green grass, thus — thus,
Come all you pretty fair maids and walk along with us,
And if you are as fair as your mother used to be,
We'll take you by the hand and trip along with thee.

119
WE CAUGHT A YOUNG SQUIRREL

(Mrs. Bertha Downing, Norman, Cleveland County, who played it in Southern Noble,
Northeastern Logan, and Northern Payne Counties.)

We caught a young squirrel
    Right here in the wood.
He tries to get out
    And will if he's good.

120
WEEVILY (WEAVILY) WHEAT

A Virginia reel, related to the Scotch "Weaving Game" (Hofer, p. 38).
Based on a Jacobite song of Bonnie Prince Charles Stuart, the Pretender. See "Come boat me ower, come row me ower," Gummere
(*Scottish Ballads*), 2:399; "O'er the Water to Charlie," Macquoid (*Jacobite Songs and Ballads*), p. 148, and *The Universal Songster*, 2:94; "Over
the water, over the lee," Halliwell (*The Nursery Rhymes of England*), p.
11; the same, with additional stanza, *Mother Goose* (Dent and Dutton), p.
76.

Dr. Josiah H. Combs, of Texas Christian University, reports from Pike
County, Kentucky, the following version of an "old Scotch rallying-song
upon the landing of Charles Stuart, the Young Pretender, at Moidart, in
Inverness-shire, July, 1745":

There's news from Modart came yester e'en,
  Will soon yastermony ferly;
For ships royal have just come in,
  And landed royal Charlie.

Come through the heather and round him gather,
  You're all the welcomer early;
Around him cling with all your kin,
  For who'll be king but Charlie?

Come through the heather and round him gather,
  Come Ronald, come Donald, all together;
And crown your rightful, lawful king;
  For who'll be king but Charlie?

Sandburg (p. 161) traces the American survivals of Jacobite ballads to "Scotch Highlanders who were harassed during Prince Charlie's time, left their homes to take up life in the Alleghanies and to spread westward." (Cf. Miles, p. 121.)

For Stanza 1 of B, cf. the English folk-rhyme (Northall, p. 352):

You find milk and I'll find flour,
And we'll have a pudding in half an hour.

For Stanza 2 of A, see "Fol Dol Sol," Shearin and Combs (Kentucky, p. 36 (excerpt).

For Stanza 5 of A and Stanza 1 of D, see LONDON TOWN; and for the latter, see also OH, AIN'T I SWEET and OLD JOE CLARK.

Cf. Ames (Missouri), *JAFL,* 24:302-303; Ball (Idaho), *JAFL,* 44:16-18; Blair (Kentucky), *JAFL,* 40:98-99; "Mr. Cooler he lub sugar and tea," Davis (South Carolina Negroes), *JAFL,* 27:253-254; Dudley and Payne (Texas), *PTFS,* 1:17-19; Hamilton (Northeast Missouri), *JAFL,* 27:290-291; Hofer (*Children's Singing Games, Old and New*), p. 38; "Trot, Charley," Hogue (Ozarks, *Back Yonder*), pp. 85-87; "Charlie," Hudson (Mississippi), *JAFL,* 39:193-194 (two texts); Lomax (*American Ballads and Folk Songs*), pp. 290-293 (two texts); Mahan and Grahame (Iowa), pp. 48-51; Miles (Tennessee, Kentucky), *Harper's,* 109:121; "Charley over the Water," Newell, (New York), p. 171; "Charlie over the water," Newton (*Graded Games and Rhythmic Exercises*), pp. 14-15; Piper (Nebraska, Western Iowa, Montana), *JAFL,* 28:278-280 (four texts, including "Over the river to Charley" and "Rolly, Rolly"); Randolph (Ozarks, Missouri), *JAFL,* 42:207-209 (also *The Ozarks,* pp. 147-149); "Over the River to Charley," Rourke (*Davy Crockett*), pp. 160-161; Sandburg (Indiana), p. 161; "Charlie's Sweet," Sharp (*Nursery Songs from the Appalachian Mountains*), No. 12; "Dog in the wood," Scarborough (Alabama), pp.

133-134 (with "Charley, will you come out to-night" reported by Kittredge from Massachusetts, note, p. 286); "Charlie," Shearin and Combs (Kentucky), p. 35 (described); "Charley over the Water," *Social Plays, Games,* etc., p. 15; Sullivan (Indiana and North Carolina, *Our Times*), 2:158-160; "He loves sugar and tea," Talley, pp. 84-85; "Prince Charley," Thomas (Kentucky), pp. 6-7, 69; Van Doren (Eastern Illinois), *JAFL*, 32:488; Wolford (Indiana), pp. 102-106.

A

CHARLEY

(Florette McNeese, Oklahoma City, Oklahoma County, from her pupils. Tune from Professor Kenneth C. Kaufman, Norman, Cleveland County, who played it in Eastern Custer County.)

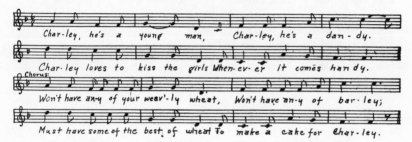

Char-ley, he's a young man, Char-ley, he's a dan-dy.
Char-ley loves to kiss the girls When-ev-er it comes handy.
Chorus:
Won't have an-y of your weav'-ly wheat, Won't have an-y of bar-ley;
Must have some of the best of wheat to make a cake for Char-ley.

1 Charley, he's a young man,
  Charley, he's a dandy,
  Charley loves to kiss the girls
  Whenever it comes handy.

Chorus:
  Won't have any of your weav'ly wheat,
  Won't have any of barley;
  Must have some of the best of wheat
  To make a cake for Charley.

2 If you love me as I love you,
  We'd have no time to tarry,
  We'd have the old folks fixin' round
  For you and I to marry.

3 Daddy went to Shuffletown,
  Mother went to Dover.
  Sister wore her slippers out
  Kicking Charley over.

347

4 My stepdad and mammy too,
    Let us children suffer.
  They fell out and had a bout
    And he went off and left her.

5 Won't you marry me, my pretty little miss?
    Do you think I'd marry my cousin
  When I can get such boys as thou
    For sixteen cents a dozen?

Directions: Played with the grand right and left.

B

Over the River to Charley

(Mrs. Demma Ray Oldham, Oklahoma City, Oklahoma County, who played it in
Arkansas.)

1 I want no more of your weavely wheat,
    I want no more of your barley.
  I want some flour in half an hour
    To bake a cake for Charley.

Chorus:
  Oh, Charley's neat and Charley's sweet,
    And Charley he's a dandy.
  Charley is the very lad
    That sold his coat for candy.

2 I won't marry a flippy flirt,
    And I won't marry a dandy.
  But I will marry Charley boy
    Whenever it is handy.

3 It's over the river to feed my sheep
    And gather up my barley.
  It's over the river to feed my sheep,
    It's over the river to Charley.

C

(Pauline Goodson, Blackwell, Kay County.)

1 Come, little heels, and trip together,
    Monday morning early.
  First go up and then go down.
    It's true I love you dearly.

Chorus:
  And I don't want any your weavily wheat,
    I won't have any your barley.
  I must have the best of wheat
    To make a cake for Charley.

348

2 Oh, Charley, he's a nice young man,
  Charley, he's a dandy.
Charley likes to kiss the girls
  Because they taste like candy.

3 And it's over the river to feed the sheep,
  It's over the river to Charley.
It's over the river to feed the sheep
  And toss them over some barley.

Directions: "It was played by the girls and boys forming in two lines. One couple at an end go up and down the line. The boy then goes toward the center, meeting the girl from the opposite corner. He swings the girl, and this process is continued."

D

CHARLIE IS A NICE YOUNG MAN

(Beatrice Jennings McMullin, Norman, Cleveland County, brought from Kentucky to Missouri, then to Kay and Grant Counties, on Oklahoma-Kansas border.)

1 The higher up the cherry tree,
  The riper grow the cherries.
The sooner the boys court the girls,
  The sooner they will marry.

2 Go choose the girl with the roving eye
  That's got the most money.
Go choose the girl with the roving eye
  And kiss and call her honey.

3 Oh, I won't have any of your weavily wheat,
  I won't have any of your barley,
But I will take some more of the good old rye
  To bake a cake for Charlie.

4 Oh, Charlie is a nice young man,
  Oh, Charlie, he's a dandy.
Charlie, he's the very one
  That treats the girls on candy.

E

TWISTIFICATION

(Lacie and Kaspar Huff, Norman, Cleveland County, from W. T. Huff.)

1 Five times five is twenty-five,
  And five times six is thirty,
Five times seven is thirty-five,
  And five times eight is forty.
Five times nine is forty-five,
  Five times ten is fifty,
Five times eleven is fifty-five,
  And five times twelve is sixty.

349

2 Oh, I won't have none o' your weevily wheat,
    An' I won't have none o' your barley.
But give to me some good old rye,
    To make a cake for Charley.

3 Charley is a handsome lad,
    Charley is a dandy.
Charley is the very one
    Who drank up all my brandy.

F

(Mrs. Jennie Harris Oliver, Fallis, Lincoln County.)

1 Over the river to feed my sheep,
    Over the river to Charlie.
Over the river to feed my sheep
    And gather in some barley.

2 Step or two with your weevily wheat,
    Step or two with your barley.
Step or two with your weevily wheat
    And gather in some barley.

3 I don't want none of your weevily wheat,
    Don't want none of your barley;
Don't want none of your weevily wheat
    To make a cake for Charlie.

4 Scorn-a-man round with your weevily wheat,
    Scorn-a-man round with your barley.
Scorn-a-man round with your weevily wheat
    To make a cake for Charlie.

5 Up and down with your weevily wheat,
    Up and down with your barley.
Up and down with your nice clean wheat
    To make a cake for Charlie.

Directions: "1. Two rows stand facing. The corners lead out crisscross.
           "2. The facing rows step out and back.
           "3. Vigorous shaking of head.
           "4. Couples walk around each other, backs turned.
           "5. Couples in turn join hands and sing up and back."

G

STEALING PARTNERS

(Irene Billups, Oklahoma City, Oklahoma County, from Mississippi.)

Charlie is a nice young man,
    Charlie is a dandy.
Charlie he's a nice young man,
    He buys cake and candy.

Directions: "The circles of couples were formed with one boy in the middle. As the music started, the circles moved around; and when the music stopped, each boy tried to get a girl. There was always one extra boy left, and then it was his turn to take his place in the center. I have only one verse of the song used. It was sung to the tune of 'Yankee Doodle.' The name of the one in the center was substituted for 'Charlie.'" (Played like "Charley over the Water," Newell p. 171.)

Variants:

Charley here and Charley there,
   Charley over the ocean.
Charley will never marry
   Until he takes a notion.
      (Mrs. T. H. Maness, Oswalt, Love County.)

Charlie he's a nice young man,
   Charlie he's a dandy.
Charlie loves to swing the girls
   Because they are so handy.
      (Bertha Matthews, Norman, Cleveland County.)

Charley he's a good old man,
   Charley he's a dandy.
Charley he's a good old man,
   He feeds his girls on candy.
      (Alice Flora Hare, Norman, Cleveland County, from Bernice Taylor, Norman.)

Other variants by Wanda Irene Dalton, Curtis, Woodward County; Ruth Davis, Forth Worth, Texas; Margaret Durkee, Norman, Cleveland County, from Mrs. P. R. Durkee and Mrs. L. B. Durkee; Catherine Harris, Antlers, Pushmataha County, from S. B. Hackett, Norman, who played it in Arkansas; Mary Virginia Maloy, Norman, Cleveland County, from Texas; Mrs. Anne McClure, Oklahoma City, Oklahoma County, who played it in Benton County, Arkansas; Ruby Pfautsch, Norman, Cleveland County; Lynn Scott, Holliday, Texas; C. B. Williams, Elk City, Beckham County.

121
WE'RE MARCHING TO QUEBEC

Based on a war ballad (Belden, *JAFL*, 25:14), it has been variously assigned Revolutionary (Newell, below) and War of 1812 origin (Pound, *The Cambridge History of American Literature*, p. 505; *Poetic Origins*, p. 204).

Cf. "Old Quebec," Ball (Idaho), *JAFL,* 44:19; "Old Quebec," Hamilton (Northeast Missouri), *JAFL,* 27:293; "Quebec Town," Hoke (North-Carolina), *JAFL,* 5:118 (like Newell); "Marching to Quebec," Johnson, (*What They Say in New England*), pp. 229-230; "Marching to Quebec," "Quebec Town," Newell (Pennsylvania, Massachusetts, North Carolina), pp. 125-126, 246; "Old Quebec," Pound (Nebraska, *Syllabus*), p. 75; "We're Marching Down to Old Quebec," Randolph (Ozarks, Missouri), *JAFL,* 42:206-207 (also *The Ozarks,* pp. 146-147); "Old Quebec," Shearin and Combs (Kentucky), p. 37 (excerpt); "Marching to Quebec," Van Doren (Eastern Illinois), *JAFL,* 32:491; "We're Marching Down to Old Quebec," Wedgwood (Southwestern Nebraska, Southern Iowa, from Missouri), *JAFL,* 25:271; "Marching to Quebec," Wolford (Indiana), p. 65-67. *Addendum:* Kittredge (Kentucky), *JAFL,* 20:275.

See PRETTY LITTLE PINK.

A

(Florette McNeese, Oklahoma City, Oklahoma County, from her pupils.)

1 We're marching down to old Quebec,
   The drums are loudly beating.
 The American boys have gained the day,
   And the British are retreating.

2 The war's all over, and we'll return
   Back to the place where we started.
 We'll open the ring and choose another
   To relieve the broken-hearted.

Directions: "Two lines are formed, one of boys and one of girls. One couple marches up and down, another follows, and soon all are marching about the room to a rather dignified dance step. 'We're Marching to Quebec' becomes in some sections 'We're Marching to New Orleans.' The origin of the words may be historical, with the later variation of place."

B

MARCHING DOWN TO OLD BERLIN

(Doris G. Waters, Ponca City, Kay County, from her pupils.)

1 We're marching down to old Berlin,
   Where the drums are loudly beating.
 The American boys have gained the day
   And the Germans are retreating.

2 The war's all over and we will turn back
   To the place where we first started.
 Open up the ring and choose another one in
   To relieve the broken-hearted

Other variants by Chester Harley Anderson, Guthrie, Logan County; John Cunningham, Watonga, Blaine County, from his father, William, who played it at Homestead, Blaine County; Juanita Curtis, Glencoe, Payne County; Leonard C. Dresser, Lahoma, Garfield County, who played it near Vernon, Garfield County; Margaret Hudson, Bartlesville, Washington County; Fanny W. Kelly, Jefferson, Grant County; Virginia R. Nelson, Clinton, Custer County; Dorothy H. Smith, Oklahoma City, Oklahoma County; Madeline Tarpley, Shamrock, Texas.

122

WE WON'T GO HOME TILL MORNING

(Atlee Margaret Garrett, Loco, Stephens County.)

The music and directions for the dance of this name (given as English) are found in Elsom and Trilling (*Social Games and Group Dances*), pp. 172-175.

For the title line, cf. "We'll All Go Down to Rowser's," Randolph (Ozarks, Missouri), *JAFL*, 42:217-218 (also *The Ozarks*, p. 161); "Cincinnati Girls," Wolford (Indiana), p. 32, the last line of which is "And we won't go home till morning."

From Kentucky Dr. Josiah H. Combs, of Texas Christian University, reports the following:

> I won't go home till morning,
>   Till morning, till morning;
> I won't go home till morning,
>   I'll stay with the girls all night.
>
> The chickens they are crowing,
>   Are crowing, are crowing;
> The chickens they are crowing,
>   And says it is daylight.
>
> 1 We won't go home till morning, (*Three times.*)
>   Till daylight doth appear.
>
> 2 So say, all of us, (*Three times.*)
>   We won't go home till morning
>   Till daylight doth appear.

Directions: "A dance similar to the Virginia reel in formation. The lines, however, approach and retreat after the manner of the old English game, 'Here Come Three Dukes a-Roving'; then the boys form bridges by joining hands, under which the girls march."—Florette McNeese, Oklahoma City, Oklahoma County, from her pupils.

"Swing around in a circle. The leader swings each girl in turn, and her partner swings the leader's girl."—Katherine Harris, Norman, Cleveland County.

123

WILSON'S BARROOM

"Wilts in the Ballroom" is requested by Payne (Texas), *PTFS*, 1:35-38. For "fiddler's drunk," cf. "Angelina," Ames (Missouri), *JAFL*, 24: 299; "Josey," Dudley and Payne (Texas), *PTFS*, 1:12; and see COFFEE GROWS ON A WHITE OAK TREE, (LITTLE) BROWN JUG, WINDING UP THE BALLROOM.

A

Wilson Ballroom

(Sung by Levi Wilcox, Noble, Cleveland County.)

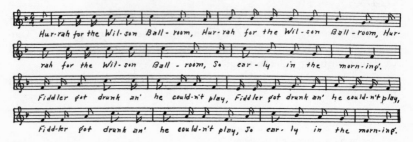

Hur-rah for the Wil-son Ball-room, Hur-rah for the Wil-son Ball-room, Hur-rah for the Wil-son Ball-room, So ear-ly in the morn-ing. Fiddler got drunk an' he could-n't play, Fiddler got drunk an' he could-n't play, Fidd-ler got drunk an' he could-n't play, So ear-ly in the morn-ing.

1 Hurrah for the Wilson Ballroom, (*Three times.*)
So early in the morning.

2 Fiddler got drunk an' he couldn't play, etc.

B

(Mrs. T. H. Maness, Oswalt, Love County.)

1 The fiddler's drunk and he can't play, (*Three times.*)
So early in the morning.

2 Hurrah for Wilson's barroom, etc.

C

Shoo Tang

(Sam West, Duke, Jackson County, from Edd Stockton, Jackson County.)

1 Once and a half, Shoo Tang, Shoo Tang, Shoo Tang.
Turn around, Shoo Tang, Shoo Tang.
Howdy do you do! Shoo Tang, Shoo Tang.

2 They all went down to the Wilson Ball,
   The Wilson Ball, the Wilson Ball.
   All went down to the Wilson Ball,
   So early in the morning.

124

WINDING UP THE BALLROOM

(Sung by Leondis Brown, Noble, Cleveland County.)

See WILSON'S BARROOM.

1 We're windin' up the ballroom,
   The ballroom, the ballroom.
   We're windin' up the ballroom
   So early in the morning.

2 Right an' left in the ballroom, etc.

3 Ladies all dressed 'n' ready for the ball, (*Three times.*)
   So early in the morning.

4 The fiddler got drunk and he couldn't play, etc.

125

WROP CANDY

(Mrs. Anne McClure, Oklahoma City, Oklahoma County, from the North Carolina
mountains.)

Cf. "Rock candy, my ladies," White (North Carolina), p. 162, and
note: " 'Rock candy,' like 'jump Jim Crow' and, later, 'Ball the Jack,' was
a dance step."

See LITTLE GIRL ROCKIN', OLD JOE CLARK.

1 Tuk me to Raleigh, (*Three times.*)
   To learn to wrop candy.

2 Ladies so handy, etc.

3 Rock on to Georgetown, etc.

Note: "Here's one from the North Carolina mountains, learned from a farm-hand on my Uncle's farm, when I was a child. This man was a native of the Carolina mountains, handsome and huge, and he sang without accompaniment and with a charming naïveté. There must have been yards to it. How I wish I could recall more!"

126
YONDER COMES A HEAVENLY CREATURE
(O. B. Campbell, Medford, Grant County.)

A dialogue singing-game, based on the folk-song, "No, John" ("O, No, John," "My Man John," etc.), to be distinguished from the "closely allied" "The Keys of Canterbury" ("The Keys of Heaven," "Paper of Pins," "Madam, I Am Come to Court You," etc.). For a good account of the song and its affiliations, cf. Sharp (*One Hundred English Folksongs*), p. xxxv.

For British versions of "No, John," see "Oh My Man John," Graham (*Traditional Nursery Rhymes*), pp. 28-29; "My Man John," *Journal of the Folk-Song Society*, 1:85; "O No John," Sharp (*Folk-Songs from Somerset*), Set II, pp. 20-22 (also *One Hundred English Folksongs*, pp. 154-155); "My Man John," *idem* (*Folk-Songs from Somerset*), Set V, pp. 20-23 (also *One Hundred English Folksongs*, pp. 150-153).

For American versions of the song, see "Yankee Boys," Carter (North Carolina), *JAFL*, 46:36-37; "The Spanish Lady," Cox (West Virginia), pp. 465-466 (with annotations; "sometimes used as a game-song"); "The Spanish Lady," Moore (Oklahoma), No. 133: "No Sir," "What Care I for Gold and Silver?", Pound (Nebraska, *Syllabus*), pp. 43, 77 (where it is compared to "The Quaker's Courtship," *Syllabus*, p. 44; *American Ballads and Songs*, pp. 223-224; cf. "The Quaker's Wooing," Barry (Massachusetts), *JAFL*, 18:55-56 (two texts); Newell, pp. 94-95); "The Courtin' Cage," Randolph (*The Ozarks*), pp. 216-219: "No, Sir," Tolman and Eddy (Ohio), *JAFL*, 35:405-407 (two texts, with annotations by Kittredge).

For British versions of the game, see "There Stands a Lady on a Mountain," Douglas, p. 85; "Lady on the Mountain" (seven texts), "Lady on Yonder Hill" (two texts), Gomme, 1:320-324; "Here stands a lady on a mountain" (given as a version of "Sally Water"), Northall, p. 376.

For American versions of the game, see "Here She Stands, a Lovely Creature," Babcock (Washington, D. C.), *American Anthropologist*, 1:247; "There she stands, a lovely creature," Newell (New York), pp. 55-56; "No, Sir," Wolford (Indiana), pp. 73-74.

356

Dr. Josiah H. Combs, of Texas Christian University, reports the following from Gilmer County, West Virginia, as the opening stanza of "King William Was King James' Son":

Here stands a lovely creature,
    Who she is I do not know.
I have caught her for her beauty.
    Let her answer yes or no.

The "Lady on the Mountain," otherwise the "Lovely (Charming, Heavenly) Creature" may have become "The Spanish Lady" out of deference to her father, often designated as a "Spanish merchant" or "Spanish captain" (a merchant to Spain?).

1 Yonder comes a heavenly creature,
    Who she be I do not know.
I'll go and court her for her beauty,
    Whether she says yes or no.

"No, no, no, sir, no."
All her answers to me were no.

2 "Madam, I have gold and silver,
    Madam, I have house and land.
Madam, I have a world of pleasures,
    All I want is your right hand.

"No, no, no, sir, no."
All her answers to me were no.

3 "What do I care for your gold and silver?
    What do I care for your house and land?
What do I care for your world of pleasure?
    All I want is a handsome man."

"No, no, no, sir, no."
All her answers to me were no.

127.

YONDER SHE COMES

Cf. "Yonder She Comes," Ames (Missouri), *JAFL*, 24:310; "Lordy, What a Man," Dudley and Payne (Texas), *PTFS*, 1:29-30; "I'll Be the Reaper" (Version II), Gardner (Michigan), *JAFL*, 33:103-104; "Marriage," Newell (Massachusetts), pp. 59-62; "Loving Couple," Piper (Western Nebraska), *JAFL*, 28:275-276; "Roving Bachelor," Tolman and Eddy (Indiana), *JAFL*, 35:431-432; "Getting Married," Wolford (Indiana), pp. 43-44. *Addendum:* "I wonder where Maria's gone," Kittredge (Kentucky), *JAFL*, 20:275-276.

See IT RAINS AND IT HAILS.

A

(Winnifred Spencer, Walters, Cotton County, from Jefferson, Marion County, Texas.)

Yonder she comes,
    And it's how do you do?
And it's how have you been
    Since I last met with you?

B

GETTING MARRIED

(Chester Harley Anderson, Guthrie, Logan County.)

1 Here stands a couple,
    Hand joined in hand.
He wants a wife
    And she wants a man.

2 They can get married
    If they will agree,
So march down together
    In sweet harmony.

3 Now they are married
    And since it is true,
Off to war
    This young man must go.

4 Mourning and mourning;
    And this shall be the cry;
Can't we make them joy
    By raising up our arms.

C

(No Title)

(Dr. S. R. Hadsell, Norman, Cleveland County.)

A couple starts it by marching down the aisles.

1 [*Missing.*]

(*They separate and go in opposite directions.*)
2 Off to the wars, to the wars he must go,
    Weeping and wailing, this shall be the cry:
If I don't see my true love,
    Surely I will die.

(*After they meet again.*)
3 Oh, here comes my true love,
    And how do you do?
How have you been
    Since I parted from you?

(Down the line through raised arms.)
4 Oh, the war's all over,
    And I'm safe from harm.
Won't you give us joy
    By the raising of your arms?

128

YOU'RE FROM VIRGINNY

(Joseph Edward Terral, Oklahoma City, Oklahoma County.)

See SHOOT THE BUFFALO.

1 You're from Virginny
    An' I'm from Arkansaw,
But I've got the Battle-Ax
    An' I know you want a chaw.

Chorus:
    I know you want a chaw,
    I know you want a chaw.
      I've got the Battle-Ax
    An' I know you want a chaw.

2 Bite it off an' chew it,
    Here comes my mother-in-law,
Bite it off an' chew it,
    'Cause I know she wants a chaw.

Chorus:
    I know she wants a chaw, etc.

3 Chew it up an' spit it out,
    Best you ever saw,
You an' me an' mother-in-law,
    We all want a chaw.

Chorus:
    We all want a chaw, etc

359

APPENDIX

Social Status and Customs of the Play-Party

I

(Interview with Katherine L. Harris, Norman, Cleveland County, sophomore in the University of Oklahoma, July 13, 1936)

I started to play when I was fourteen, five years ago. I lived five years at Moore — went through high school there — and have been in Norman two years.

The occasion is a "party," the plays are "games." They're really dances except for the music.

The typical leader is usually some boy that's well-liked in the community — a favorite — loud-mouthed and funny. Every one can hear him. Being in the country, he's red-faced — just a country boy. Not a smart aleck. He must know all the games they play. He goes to all the parties — once a week during the winter. I don't know if they're playing so much now. Things like that are going out. He remembers all the verses that they know, and if it's "Old Joe Clark is a married man," he substitutes some one's name — maybe some one that isn't married — to embarrass them. Some one that's bashful and has his best girl with him — and perhaps hasn't been before. You don't have to know these games to play them. You just get in and do what they tell you to and you get on all right. He changes lines if he's clever enough to do it.

If a boy leads a party one time, they insist that he lead the next. The same boy begins singing while the rest are playing. Most of them join in and help out. He may get tired and some one else will lead out while he's resting. Most of them have religious objections against dancing. There's no drinking at these parties. If any one drinks, they get rid of them. They're just there for clean sport.

The ages range from fourteen to the young married people. They usually clear out the biggest room in the house and all that can fit in play. They just vacate a room. They usually take down the curtains and sit in the window. Some sit out while the others play — just to cool off — and stand in the door or stay in the corner if they aren't afraid of getting their toes stepped on.

There are no invitations and no refreshments. No one expects any. The person that is going to give the party tells his neighbors and they tell their neighbors.

They begin about dark. You can leave any time you want to. They break up about 10:30 or 11. They don't stay late. You get too tired. After

361

you've played half a dozen of them, you're ready to leave. They dress in ordinary clothes. I've seen some in work clothes — boys in overalls and girls in print dresses — house dresses. Young children of school age and older folk may come along to watch. At Denver several of the girls' mothers brought them. They stayed in the other room and watched.

I always get dizzy. At Denver I had to swing around a large circle and nearly fell out of the door when I got through. Nearly always some one does that. There's nearly always some one that's green. I remember a German couple like that. We substituted their names. We didn't rub it in. You've got to be a sport to go to parties. If a lot more people knew these games, they'd have a lot of fun. They're sort of rough. You don't have to play if you don't want to. I went out of curiosity. I don't dance — never did and have no desire to. People who are shy would enjoy them. You're just drug into them and you have to go in or you'll ball up the game.

Many of them will start walking and pick up others as they go. You don't have to have a date to go. Any boy that happens to be loose there is your partner. Every one forgets about dates — most of them — if they do have them. You get to dance with more than one.

There were no resting-games or ice-breakers at the parties I went to. There's usually more couples than can fill the room, and you can alternate. Usually there are more boys than girls. The oldest are in their twenties — not any over thirty. You usually outgrow them before twenty-five.

A lot of times they are given for special occasions — a birthday, New Year's, any time you have any entertainment. A lot of times in the fall or spring we'll have our wienie roasts and play these games. You sing as you go. The way seems long. Usually it's on some creek where there's no brush, sometimes on a hill or hillside. Once in a while they'll get together for an ice cream social for a variation. They have box suppers but not with the party games.

They come any way they can get there — cars, horses. There are refreshments when it's more private.

We tried to play them once in town when I first came here, but it didn't work — because the atmosphere was different. I think it's more what you say backwoods — in the blackjacks. You have to go at least ten miles out to get really good ones. Denver is ten miles out. You can get them in closer but they aren't so good. Out on the river flat, out around Pleasant Valley schoolhouse, they have some good games. Also at Pleasant Hill — Pleasant Hill is next to Grotts, so you see you have to go pretty far out. They usually have them on Friday instead of Saturday night. On Saturday night they get ready for Sunday — come to town.

There are houses I went to where they wouldn't allow them to dance. If they started, they'd get them out of it as soon as they could.

Sometimes in introducing a new game, if a girl knew it, she'd lead it. Maybe she'd been in a different community and they played it differently.

I was just an outsider invited in. Some of them have come to school at the University, but they live out there — away from things. I've gone fifteen miles to a party — a radius of five or ten miles is the average. The other community would have a party the same night. They'd go by school districts, though they don't hold them in schools. A few may come from another district, but they would be considered outsiders.

Mother came from Kentucky, but father was born and raised and went to school here. I don't think I'll ever see the day when they won't be sung, but it won't last for many years. They don't play them like they used to.

There's a certain lilt to the tunes. There's something about them you recognize when you hear it.

The kids wouldn't stand for love-making. They come there to play.

Typically funny verses are "Little red wagon painted blue," "Maw made buttermilk in Paw's old shoe" — things like that are funny.

Three Old Maids isn't so strenuous. Miller Boy isn't so strenuous. Sugar and Tea is awful — just like a square dance. Old Joe Clark and Skip to My Lou are not quite so strenuous. Those three and Way Down in the Holler [Bird in the Cage] are the most popular.

II

(Interview with Lloyd M. Jemison, near Temple, Cotton County, sophomore in the University of Oklahoma, May 18, 1936)

As a general rule, the houses, especially the tenant farmers', aren't large enough to accommodate the crowd that comes. Every one comes, from the old people to the very youngest, so they'll make a procession, carrying torches and lanterns, and string out, and walk to a clearing. On the way they'd sing various songs, each song originating at the head of the column, and it would go weaving down the line so that by the time it reached the end another stanza would be starting at the head.

First they'd build a great fire. Every one scattered out to bring in firewood — trees, brush, limbs, anything they could get. Having built the fire and in order to give it time to burn down to coals, they'd play games and sing songs. I remember Brown Jug, Buffalo Girls. I didn't know any of those. I'd just catch fragments of them and by the time I'd catch on they were on to something else.

They roast wienies and toast marshmallows. There's always pies and cakes that the ladies would bring. At every country party every one brings something to eat. There's a tradition that you should. This was in the fall and spring — about Thanksgiving and Easter time.

One Saturday night one farmer would give a party, another Saturday night another farmer would give one. They had a continuous social circle. A city feller would find it hard to break in. They sort of resented him. But I knew them pretty well, and they always invited me. I played football with many of them. Even at that the last one I went to they were going to gang up on me and whip me. I haven't been back since then. That was in 1933-34. The last one I went to was in 1935.

There are three districts — Red River district, Cache, and Gregg. The Red River bunch are the most resentful. Nearly all of them drink — the younger people. It's considered very sissified if you ever refuse to fight or don't drink. The Cache district is the very opposite — a little reserved, more friendly, and drinking is rarely allowed. Gregg is just a mixture between those two.

Watermelon time is a great time for these things. They all get together in the watermelon patches. At box suppers these songs were not so prevalent or at picnics, but they are sung. Box suppers were in cold weather. They usually picked the schoolhouse or an exceptionally large house for the box supper.

They don't often dance. The older people don't approve of it. Red River dances. They dance the roughest kind of dances. I refer to round dances. They hardly ever dance square dances. They're more prevalent, however, in Cache and Gregg. The Red River is just composed of a bunch of people that think it foolish to get an education and go to college. Of course, most of them have gone to high school. "Sissy" is a fighting word among them. Cache is the most old-fashioned. But more go to school from there. The boys take good care of themselves. Most of them are athletes.

III

(Interview with Mrs. Gladys Wharton, Norman, Cleveland County, August 4, 1936)

I taught at Union Springs School — three miles northeast of Pauls Valley, in Garvin County. It is a small union graded school which serves just that district.

The youngsters of high school age played them. There were about twelve parties in the school year. Each class gave two — one each semester — and other individuals worked in a few. If the youngsters were smart

364

and wanted to give a party, they'd do it as an individual and the authorities couldn't object. There was a country club on a lake — the Pauls Valley Country Club — and they used the yard three times during the spring. They'd use the homes and the schoolhouse — take out all the seats in one or two rooms, put up all the chalk and erasers. Even if they went on a wienie roast and marshmallow roast, they played these games.

They'd usually select one, two, or three youngsters who were good at hollering the songs to lead. The freshmen didn't care much for them. One freshman complained that his party was taken over by the older students who played the games. "Just as bad as a dance," he said. He was just out of the grades and felt awkward when he tried to play them. Maybe later in the year he'd get over that. Mostly the juniors and seniors played them. The students are older than city students. The seniors would average nineteen to twenty-one — the juniors, eighteen. Fifteen or sixteen is a good age for the freshmen.

Refreshments at school parties were quite a problem. I was freshman sponsor and decided to have them. Each girl was to bring a cake, and each boy was to contribute a dime to buy the colored powders for punch. I was to bring the sugar. The youngsters are spoiled out there. They expected the teacher to furnish the refreshments. One boy brought a dime, and one girl brought a cake. But I bought a few colored powders, left over from the seniors, and I brought some sugar, and we had enough punch to go round for the hungry mob. It was the same way with the senior sponsor. At their homes they usually served something.

Soapstick [On to Galilee] gave more chance for group play — not so complicated or individual. Every one got a chance to be the big shot.

The other teachers didn't take part. I was the only one that did. I don't know what they thought of me. Your party wasn't successful unless you had games. The entertainment committee of three would get together and decide what games to play, and make out the list, and I'd check over it. Most of them were new to me, but I'd play and catch on.

IV

(Interview with J. B. Hill, principal of Blue Jacket High School, Craig County, July 15, 1936)

The party is a school function. It's generally late in the fall and in the spring — Friday evening. For three years the seniors have had a closing celebration the last of the season. They always invite the juniors and let the juniors bring a friend. The juniors will also have a celebration and invite the seniors and let them bring a friend. They'll have a huge affair of it. They very often come eight and ten miles to attend. They come in cars — once in a while some one comes on horseback. They come in groups. They don't have to bring a date. The usual party is informal. They generally gather in the winter time at 7:30 and in the spring time at 8 or 8:30. The graduating affair is quite a dress affair; they wear real nice clothes.

The party would be given in the house of one of the children — in the largest room. There would be about thirty-five present. There would be no adults except the friends or relatives of the family. I was present as sponsor and to dismiss them. They'd always beg for one more. It's hard to get them to break up before 11:30. In the spring they're apt to stay till 12:30. They start later and get out and mill around. The leader is generally some one with a strong personality and good voice — generally one of the outstanding intellects. He is never appointed but automatically takes the leadership — some one who can size up the situation and go ahead. The ages range from sixteen to eighteen. They have a policy of obligation refreshments. In winter time they generally serve hot chocolate, sandwiches or cookies, and in spring generally home-made ice-cream and cake. The spirit is carefree — no partiality one to the other.

They had one girl. She went with a fellow named Seymour, and they found they could affect her by calling her Seymour. I tried to stop it and couldn't without making it worse. I had one fellow who was a comedian. Some one would play a French harp and he'd do a little dance — burlesque.

Among the games played were Buffalo Girls, Captain Jinks, The Girl I Left Behind Me, Gents to the Center, Skip to My Lou, and Do-Se-Do. At first it kind of bored me. Then I saw how they enjoyed themselves and I played some of them with them. I almost had to. They insisted. I tried to throw those tunes off my mind. I didn't want them haunting me.

V

(Interview with Lonnie D. Huddleston, Librarian, University High School, Norman, Cleveland County, July 24, 1936)

In the Adair School District, Cleveland County, in 1926, most of the parties were conducted at homes where there were children anywhere from ten to twelve, fourteen, and sixteen years old on up. Both the children and the grown people attended the party. They usually had some stringed band to furnish the music. That's where the play-party after the games were played was turned into the dance. But if they were real play-parties they usually had one swinging game going in one room, another in another room, and some card game like pitch in another. There were some families that didn't allow dancing, so it didn't do any good for the fiddlers to be there, though they wanted to be there, as they got paid for playing at dances.

It was the same thing over and over, but they would round up four, six, eight, etc., until they filled their set out. They usually had some one responsible for carrying on the song — usually a boy in the neighborhood who knew the tune and could sing the song well. However, I have been to parties where girls led. The players would chime in, especially on the chorus or the refrain.

Refreshments weren't always common. When I was a kid, I went to ice-cream socials. Now the refreshments have developed into the sandwich style, cookies, etc. Take back in 1916 to '20, sometimes they made candy — pulled candy after the games.

Some one would go around the neighborhood and make up a party. They'd have it different places. They were usually held on week-ends, depending upon the community. Some communities had dances on the week-ends, so they'd have the play-party earlier in the week. They'd have them out-of-doors. More of the play-parties were held out-of-doors than the dances, because they had to have floors for the dances. Lanterns were put up outside on wires between the trees. Some of the dances they had, the younger children who did not dance would be playing their swinging games outside. A number of these parents who do not care for dancing would usually stop the swinging games before they turned into a dance. I've known many parents who kept the fiddlers out because they knew the dance would turn to drinking.

Games collected at Adair School in 1926: In the Wilderness [On to Galilee], Jew-Tang-Jew, Cream and Peaches [Consolation Flowing Free], Joe Clark, Rouser, Brown Jug, Pig in the Parlor, John Brown [John Brown Had a Little Indian], Sandy Land, [Circle Left], Miller Boy, Dan Tucker, Hello Susan Brown, Sugar Candy [Coffee Grows on a White Oak Tree].

VI

(Interview with Frances Lillie, Guthrie, Logan County, July 26, 1936)

A friend of mine taught school in the country and some of the kids out there had a watermelon party or an ice-cream sociable. They came from miles around — as many as thirty miles. We'd have just loads of home-made ice cream. All the young folks gathered in the field or the yard. Most of the elderly men would play, but the women would cut the watermelon and get the ice cream ready. The old men would get a kick out of playing and jollying up the young girls.

No instruments — just clapping of hands. It's been about three years ago.

Also barn dances, pie suppers, box suppers.

They'll always have one Virginia reel or square dance. Sometimes some one will have a banjo and he'll play it. There are some people there who don't believe in instruments in church, but at the dances they don't mind.

They played running games — Drop the Handkerchief, Brick Yard, Flying Dutchman, Run, Sheepie, Run.

Stanzas of some of the games:

> Moses had an overcoat,
> Hung it on the wall.
> Some one stole that overcoat,
> And Moses had to bawl.

> Down the river, oh, down the river,
> Down the river we go.
> Down the river, oh, down the river,
> Down the O-hi-o.

A chorus of one game:

> Nickety, nackety, hey, John daffety,
> Wallity, wallity, rustical quality,
> Nickety, nackety, now, now, now.

VII

(Interview with Reford Helms, near Denver, Cleveland County, August 7, 1936)

Last Monday my girl was going to Texas and she wanted me to give her a party. Everybody came — people from Oklahoma City. Somebody's told them — somebody's friend. There were a hundred people. Nine cars and two wagons, not counting the footbackers. It lasted till morning. Our clock was out of order, and I couldn't tell what time it was.

I've heard of people who never saw it rain, but I've never heard of people who never saw a party.

I'd rather go to a dance. More pep. You can shuffle your feet. They don't have fights and drinking at parties. They do at dances.

Some of the songs are Round Up Four in Jutang, Five Old Maids Went Skating on the Ice, Rat's in the Bush, Coffee Grows, Jingo Tideo, Hands Up Round the Wilderness, In Somebody's Little White House, Miller Boy, One More Time in Sandy Land.

VIII

(Interview with Edgar "Peck" McCarley, near Denver, Cleveland County, August 7, 1936)

We just get somebody to give them. Somebody just takes a notion to give a party. Mostly indoors. Mostly winter. It's a whole lot cooler. Front parlor and bed room — move the beds out — what furniture they got in it. Begin just when they get there. Just come from around here mostly — five or six miles. From eight years on up to thirty. The little ones that play play with the big ones. Some of them wears everyday clothes — some of them dress. Mostly gingham dresses. Very few of them serves refreshments. Lemonade and cake — something like that — sometimes ice cream. I don't know nothing about the going home afterwards. Well-behaved.

In leading I just sing. I play the games while I sing them. I don't call dances. I go to them once in a while. The young folks just naturally like to go to parties.

There are three or four guys that sings round here. Some of the songs are Jingle Tideo, Coffee Grows on a White Oak Tree, Four Hands Down to Rowser, Gents to the Center, I Sent My Brown Jug Down to Town, Pig in the Parlor, Old Joe Clark.

I hardly ever make up new verses. I just learned them by going to parties where other boys sing them. The young Indians go to some of them. They play just like everybody.

King William Was King James's Son, Little Fight in Mexico — I've seen them played but I don't know them. Shoot the Buffalo — I know part of it.

I believe they're just as popular now as they ever were. They have quite a few of them out here in the winter time, when it isn't so hot. In the summer you can't play them. You'll smother to death.

IX

(Interview with Minnie Stapp, of the Shawnee tribe, Newalla, Cleveland County, August 10, 1936, at Big Jim Mission)

The place: The Big Jim Country and Little Ax — two miles west and a mile north. Also around Pink, in Pottawatomie County, and Knoles, in Cleveland County — four and a half miles north of here.

The time: About twelve years ago to the present.

In the seventh grade at Knoles we played the swinging games, which were Bushwelder (Round the Wilderness — Bushwelder must be the latest name they give it, and they sing it that way; I could hardly sing it),

Shoot the Buffalo, Skip to My Lou My Darling, Tag, Upset the Waste-basket, Spin the Pan, Wink, Pleased or Displeased, Taking Out Life Insurance, Gossip, Postoffice, Ain't Gonna Rain No More, Lize Jane, Old Joe Clark, Old Dan Tucker, Sugar and Tea, Sandy Land, Turkey in the Straw. I watched Baltimore played.

In the homes of the different school children. From twelve to twenty-four. There were older people who were chaperons — they took part and played as much as the youngsters did. Everyone in the neighborhood six miles around. From about October until the first of May. Sometimes they have them in May and in the summer, though usually it is too hot to play swinging games.

The harmonica plays in between the games. They had the round dances in between the games. Sometimes they announced the parties as being social parties and turned them off into square dances. When they do that, they call in the buddies and not outsiders. They'd have fiddle and git-tar. Sometimes they would serve refreshments and sometimes they wouldn't. Ice cream and cake, lemonade and cake, candy alone.

Any night — when the children could get the consent of their parents. About 8:30 in the winter time, and break up about 12. We had them on Saturday night to a minute before 12. The dances would last between 2 and 4.

Dress clothes and party frocks. Not very many fights. Any drinking, smoking, chewing? A little bit of everything — outside. Some go horse-back, some go in cars and buggies and wagons and on foot. There would be babies.

In the front room. Sometimes they'd move the beds out of the bedroom and have two-room parties.

We have pound suppers with play-party games.

The Indians would take part in them freely. Full bloods, mixed bloods. I went there and played with all my might until it was over.

There's quite a change. They don't seem to be so interested in the games. When they do give a party, they hardly want to play. All the youngsters have grown up to older people, and the other generation doesn't play. They have parties occasionally and they play games. The crowd is getting where they like the liquor more. I don't know hardly what to think of it. All the parties I go to I play as much as I used to, but I do notice the change.

This is what they do. They draw the interest of the young people, and in that way they gather together, and they get acquainted much quicker. That is, if the people like to go to parties.

Very few radios out here. They have cars. Indians and whites mix equally. Sometimes they would and sometimes they wouldn't have escorts. They'd trade dates after the parties.

I've led in the games. My girl friend would give these parties and want me to lead them. To be a leader you have to know the games and know how to direct the players. He has to be ready to talk, to meet the strangers and introduce them and make them feel at home — to see that they have partners if they seem to stand in the back against the wall. If the strangers have a game they would like to have the crowd play, the leader would see that the crowd have their attention and play their games. He didn't change the verses. A good leader should be able to tell jokes and tease the people without hurting their feelings. He had to be able to take a teasing himself in a good humor. Sometimes if a leader has to go in and entertain the older people or see if other things are in order, such as setting up the table and making the lemonade, he'd turn it over to another. There'd be as many as four leaders besides him. He was master of ceremonies. Just a few times the boys were leaders. However, the boys were just as good leaders. Whenever a boy leads, he has a boy help him.

In playing some games such as Barnyard Fowl, it was a very embarrassing game. It's the way they take it. For instance, there was a one-eyed boy. We brought him into the room and told him to sit in a seat. He did. A girl told him to bray like a donkey. He did. She told him to take three steps forward and quack like a duck. Which he did. Take another step forward and cackle like a hen. Then turn around and cackle at his nest. The whole group was laughing at him because he did cackle at his nest. But he didn't know what they were laughing about until he got back to his seat. When he got back he found the egg sitting on the seat, and he knew the reason and was embarrassed. He didn't see the egg.

X

(Interview with James Spybuck, care of Henry Mack, Tecumseh, Pottawa-tomie County, at Shawnee Stomp Dance, Big Jim's Crossing, August 10, 1936)

I live at Tulsa. I was raised between Tulsa and Sperry. I played them around here about six months ago. I've been living here about five years. I played them before and quit. I've played them about five years. I sung some for the kids. I got tired singing. A lot of others knew them, so I quit. I quit going to dances.

Old Joe Clark, Sugar and Tea, Cross Right Over to the Opposite Lady, Make My Livin' in Sandy Land.

371

They held them in the homes. They give it out about a week ahead. All different ages. I'm half Cherokee and half Shawnee. Just a few of us kids went. Sometimes I might be the only Indian at parties. Generally cleaned up — white and blue shirt. Went alone the biggest part of the time. A few of them served refreshments — cocoa, cake, ice cream. Summer time. Winter time too cold. Out and indoors. No fights. A few would drink — not much.

I enjoy them. A lot of fun in singing. Just to help the rest out. Sometimes they'd be no one there who knew them and I'd start them till some one else came. Just to show them I'm a sport.

I don't want to say that I won't play them again. I may.

Granger went:

> I'd rather be a drunkard,
>   And with the drunkards stand,
> With a fruit-jar on my shoulder
>   And a bottle in my hand.

Then farmers and soldiers.

I made some up.

Little Brown Jug, Standing on a Platform, Coffee Grows were some others.

XI

(Interview with Rev. and Mrs. E. S. Hobson, Big Jim Mission, near Denver, Cleveland County, August 2, 1936)

[Mr. Hobson, at Mount Gilead, north of Columbus, Ohio, played Skip to My Lou and Old Dan Tucker, forty years ago. Mrs. Hobson went to parties at Sturgeon Bay, Wisconsin, ten or fifteen years ago.]

Here they are called parties and party games — given on birthdays, etc. Parties have stood the competition of the movies but not of commercial dances. The log place where dances are held is a rendezvous for bootleggers.

People go and take their families here. With us it was usually young people. At church groups they played the same games, and young and old both were invited.

Most of them do not serve refreshments around here. Back in Wisconsin they wouldn't think of having a party without refreshments. Here they occasionally have ice cream or a watermelon feast.

The older ones who are acquainted with the games and used to playing them will play with the young folks. The older people will mostly visit. In the summer time the older people fill the house, though sometimes they play in- and outdoors both. In cool weather when they can't have it outdoors they clear out one room.

This is their main form of amusement. A few of the Indians meet with the white people. They go to school together.

XII

*(Interview with Mrs. Arden Brown, Idabel, McCurtain County, July 18,
1936)*

As a girl I observed them in Arkansas, Little River County, Ashdown, between 1908 and 1913, and since 1913 in McCurtain County.

I guess maybe they are dying out. I don't believe they're playing those games in the rural districts. The towns and the good roads are drawing people to the picture shows and the cheap dance halls in the small towns. More of the religious people would permit a play-party than they would a dance.

The parties would be held on Friday and Saturday evenings in some one's home. The things that were carried on in the public halls were frowned on. General oral invitations — never heard of a written one. All of the young people of the community and some of the older people who still felt young. They'd even bring the children with them and put them in bed — in the bedroom — pallets around. They moved all the furniture out and lined the chairs around the walls. Sometimes they wouldn't have enough chairs; they'd put a board across two chairs. There'd usually be more than would want to take part in one particular game. They wouldn't know that one or something. The time: after dark till about 12 o'clock. Where I lived was a little town. I think you'd find they'd go long distances. The refreshments: cake and fruit and great freezers of homemade ice cream — coffee in the winter time. I wouldn't say the parties were large — the communities were small and the towns were small — under forty.

The games: Old Joe Clark, Weevily Wheat, Going Down to Rowser, The Girl I Left Behind Me, Slap-in Slap-Out, Buffalo Girls, Coffee Grows on White Oak Trees, Skip to My Lou. No kissing games.

My mother was very religious, and I didn't get to go very often.

XIII

*(Interview with Dr. and Mrs. Howard P. Doole, University of Nebraska)
April 26, 1931)*

In town (Adams, Gage County, Nebraska). Each set had its own parties — two years apart. At a "party" or "evening party," people were asked to go. The play party was free for all.

Run, Sheep, Run and Late for Supper were played. School games were choosing games. The kissing games would be kids' sport — the boy-conscious stage — ten or twelve years old. The youngsters would be too shy to kiss. The little children played Old Witch and Lubin, Green Gravel and Mulberry Bush.

In North Central Kentucky (Sturgis, near Owensboro) the old folks danced the square dances and the young folks watched. These were indoor parties. They met at one of the homes and gradually the young folks went out of doors, and the old folks danced the Virginia reel, with one piano. Those who were strait-laced didn't come. Doughnuts, cider, and apples were served. The girls wear organdie. In the grand right and left they pick you up and whirl you round and literally pitch you to the next partner.

The very youngest would come earlier and play King James and Go In and Out the Window (playing over at the other side) and go home early.

In 1920 the parties were dying out in Kentucky on account of the automobile.

XIV

(Interview with Lee M. Nuzum, Oklahoma City, Oklahoma County, August 3, 1936)

Fifteen years ago, between Tucumcari and Melrose, around Jordan, in Quay County, New Mexico, they played old-fashioned games — swinging games, they called them — Granger, Shoot the Buffalo, The Girl I Left Behind Me, Jutang, Little Liza Jane, Skip to My Lou, Little Red Wagon. At my home, Taiban, about thirty-five miles from the other place, in 1920, they didn't play these games at all, on account of religious objections. There was a Union Church and Sunday School composed of North and South Methodist, Baptist, and Presbyterian — one Sunday for each.

The parties were given for the young people at people's homes. The ages ran from fifteen to twenty-eight. Usually they were on Friday or Saturday night. If you heard about it, you were invited. Common refreshments were ice cream and cake in the summer. They were held both out-of-doors and indoors. They were just considered a pastime.

XV

(Interview with Walter R. Smith, Saint Louis Public Schools, Pottawatomie County, July 15, 1936)

This was in the Cheyenne-Arapaho country, around Vici, in Northwest Dewey County, and near the corner of three counties, Dewey, Ellis, and Woodward.

My father was a preacher and opposed to those things. So I lost out entirely on the dances and almost entirely on the play-parties. Of course, I had some contact, but the thing died out there. I saw it die — pretty definitely. It was the shift of interest about 1911 or '12 due to the coming of the railroad and the opening up of the section to outside influences. We were thirty-five miles from the railroad and left pretty much to ourselves.

In the early day the big entertainment was to get together and have a big feed, on almost any provocation. A birthday was a good time. The people would haul all they could eat and more. I think that it then gave way in popularity to ice-cream suppers, and those were almost always accompanied by party games. I understand that out there the time previous, before the real settlement, among the nesters and cattlemen — the later ranch days — the dance was the big entertainment. The country was opened in '92. Up to around 1900 the dances were the big entertainment, and with the coming of the settlers we have about what I have shown. There were some dances held all along there. But I was quite young then and may not have the right picture there.

I remember instances of difficulties in school because certain teachers allowed children to play party games. Certain patrons just raised cane particularly if the children were allowed to play kissing games — Oats, Peas, Beans, and Barley Grows, King William Was King James' Son.

I don't know when, but it is a long time since I heard of those party games being played there. I suppose they are.

Now as to the exact details of those games, I'm almost at a loss. I remember the songs they sang at various games were given to a lot of variations. Some fellow would come in from another community with new words and variations on it. I knew one youngster who had a habit of that. He was pretty good at improvising stanzas. I don't think I could call to mind any of his productions. He was something of a comic — as we referred to him then, a monkey — given to telling funny stories, cracking jokes, getting gags on people, never serious. I don't believe they'd be too much significance in the jingles that he made. He would substitute a line or two or shift. I don't know about this youngster's originality either — a lot of that may have been copied or borrowed. He was almost a total failure in school — never serious enough — didn't finish the eighth grade.

Any one came — it was a general invitation. In most cases no one would have felt honored if he received a special invitation. Nothing elaborate was planned. Just the word got around, by grapevine almost, that there'd be a party at a certain time and place. Almost always refreshments were served — cake, coffee, sandwiches, usually beef — it was cow country. Or in summer time ice-cream. That wasn't any small task either when ice had to be hauled thirty-five miles from the railroad, over horrible roads.

In the parties I know about, they would come eight or ten miles. When we came there in 1900, there were people who had lived there twelve years — nesters — just a few. They reported that the young folks rode horseback to dances twenty-five miles. But I never saw any one going that far.

Whole families would come in wagons. Especially this is true for summer. In the winter time they didn't come that distance or in such great numbers. Small children came along with the family. There was no one to leave them with. When the children got sleepy, they were put to bed on the beds of the wagons, on quilts.

The favorite time of the week was Saturday night — Friday probably a close second. Then there were no towns to go to on Saturday night. I think that did shift to Friday night after the railroad. The usual time of gathering was about dark or shortly after. The party might last till nearly midnight.

It was confined to the young and younger folks — the unmarried. Once in a while the young married people and the mothers and fathers would get in and play — just to show that they were still young, and they enjoyed it — generally for a short time, and they got out. I remember one woman — gray-haired — past fifty, but that's the exception. Sometimes the younger children, ten to twelve or younger, would get off and play by themselves — more nearly school games. London Bridge, etc., was not very popular at the parties except among the younger children.

These summer-time outdoor parties — one reason they were so much more popular was the limited space in the house — dugouts, sod houses — they didn't give room for playing those games — that is, for any number.

There was not a lot of dressing up. However, as I recall it, the predominant thing among the boys was white shirt and blue serge trousers, cut on the full peg pattern, with more or less a preponderance of fancy belt loops — long, made to order — diagonals cut out. The buttons on the tabs of pockets were very frequently square buttons or diamond-shaped — sometimes loud blue or white. One thing that seems remarkable was that the cowboy stuff wasn't popular then. The hats worn were large. Sun and wind makes it advisable. But none of the young men wore sombreros. They didn't wear chaps. In exceptional cases they dress up that way now — the effect of the moving pictures.

Pretty generally the women's dress was rather conservative — simple, inexpensive stuff. Silks and satins were unheard of. Ginghams and prints. A woman wanted to be dressed neatly, and wear a new dress, but didn't go in for expensive dress. The older men would come very frequently in new overalls. A few people wore boots — those who wore them habitually. You could see bandanas worn, but they were not predominant.

The harmonica was the most common instrument — played by some youngster who wanted to show off a bit — entirely separate from the general proceedings. A lot of the people had scruples against dancing, and music would have made it a dance. They'd tell you that the only difference was vocal instead of instrumental music. One of their objections to the play-party was that it led to the dance.

There were fights occasionally. Drunkenness was almost unknown. A person who came to a party drinking was regarded as pretty crude. Fights grew out of jealousy over certain girls — sometimes more or less the natural spirit of contest — the question of who's the better man. I've heard of parties being broken up, but I never knew of such a case. It might be due to dislike for some one connected with the party or giving the party. It would have taken some force because it would be healthily resisted. As late as 1926 at Supply as superintendent of schools I gave a Hallowe'en party to the senior class, and I was told by the students that I couldn't give one because it would be broken up. But I had no trouble. It's done in the spirit of a lark. They felt they were licensed to do it at that time.

In the latter part of 1914 I spent some time out in Beaver County. I was just working around through the country — a work tramp, I guess you'd call it. And I found conditions there just about like what they were five years before in my county — just the same thing done over again. That led me to believe that the conditions were typical of a new country. I didn't attend play-parties, but I would hear about them being given as I went around. That seemed to be the chief pastime there. I was in Texas County and the Panhandle of Texas as far south as Old Ochitree. An ice-cream supper would be announced. The usual procedure was a coöperative enterprise. They'd all chip in on bringing the ice out. Everybody would bring milk, sugar, eggs, flavoring, extract — generally more than could be used. They didn't seem to be stingy. Generally more ice cream was frozen than could be used. There was a surprising number of five-gallon freezers out there. During the summer it was a weekly affair — particularly in the latter part — July, late August and early September. The crops were more nearly laid by.

Just last week I was back home, and my mother invited in all my brothers and sisters and all the in-laws. A great big assemblage came in there, and we went through with this ice-cream procedure. I suppose this would show that this was her idea of having a good time still.

At Saint Louis I don't see much interest in the play-party. Nothing like what we had out there. They have parties and play some of those party games. Parties are among the younger and young set. Fewer older persons attend, and fewer of them know what goes on there. There are so many other things now to take their place. One of the favorite pastimes among the school students (down even to the sixth grade) is the wienie roast. We don't like the things — they are rather hard to chaperon. But we never saw fit to draw a deadline. We sponsor them. Less of the kissing games and of the old-time party games. Mostly chasing games — tag — healthy fun — Three Deep, Drop the Handkerchief.

Down there there's a tendency to the old dances, due to the radio. That was my best guess. The farming class — tenants largely — more nearly so. Employees of oil companies. The Phillips camp is a half mile from my schoolhouse. The Fourth of July, the Crosby Camp on the Blue, south of Ada, put on a square dance.

In Dewey County the games included Buffalo Gals, Cheat 'er Swing, The Girl I Left Behind Me, Going Down to Rowser, John Brown Had a Little Indian, Little Brown Jug, Liza Jane, London Town, Old Dan Tucker, Pawpaw Land (they called it Pawpaw Bend), Pig in the Parlor, Sandy Land, Shoot the Buffalo, Skip to My Lou.

XVI

(Interview with R. F. Albers, Bartlesville Public Schools, Washington County, August 4, 1936)

It was in Canadian County, about twelve miles west of Minco, in 1911 or '12. I was just a farm boy, working around home, going to country school in the winter time. I was about eleven or twelve, and I wasn't old enough to play them. The group that played those were the young eligibles. Sometimes young married men, young matrons, would play them. Usually they'd carry on their neighborhood gossip.

They had a real social significance. They were clean, wholesome, entertaining. They afforded the social intercourse. The singing took the place of music. They gave expression to romance — gave opportunity for it to begin. The walk home afterward was, I suspect, the initial phase of many a romance. The country dance was frequented by an element that sometimes was objectionable. These games were the social life of the religious

378

— those that preferred not to have the rough stuff that went with the dance, about their homes.

Most of them would play them the year round. But the Lutherans would except Lent. I suspect the Catholics would have too, but there were none.

It was at any one of the farm homes, most likely where there were young people who wanted entertainment. Even young married people who had no family of their own would open up their house to them in memory of old times when they went the rounds.

The invitation — by word of mouth, never written — was passed around to any one that wanted to come. That might reach over a school district — a radius of three or four miles — in the early days, ten miles. Any evening, I suspect, excepting Sunday. Word would be sent out that the play-party would be held at a certain place. The farm boys would quit work a little earlier, get shaved and dressed. If they had time, they might go to town to get some chewing gum to give to their best girl. They'd wear their Sunday clothes — the best they had. Anything was acceptable. Then blue shirts weren't stylish — they were everyday. White was stylish. But they would come even in a blue shirt, and blue serge pants. In cold weather, blue serge suits. The girls wore the dresses of the time, all the way from prints to woolens. If a girl had a print trimmed in organdie, that was a mark of distinction, especially laundered for the occasion. Black cotton hose — that was before rayon came in.

About 8 they'd begin to arrive. They were ushered into the parlor. If there was an organ, some one would play. There might be a violin, guitar, accordion, or French harp. Any of those might be found, and sometimes there might be none of them. They would sing, make conversation, tell stories, make jokes, and make puns. They usually waited for one person who was considered the life of the party. They waited until he arrived.

He'd usually be a person of pleasing personality — not necessarily good-looking — usually witty — and must be especially willing to take a joke on himself. His stock-in-trade was jokes, wit, but he had to be a fellow who could take it as well as give it. Never a smart aleck. He never became a leader; he just didn't fit into the psychology of the group. There had to be something substantial and real to any person who was respected in those communities. A smart aleck could start something but he couldn't always finish it. He didn't have the intelligence, like the life of the party.

The life of the party was usually a person that was infinitely considerate of the happiness of his hostess. The party might run late on Saturday night. When midnight came, the next hour was Sunday, and things had to stop. Frequently several of the others might want to go on playing after twelve o'clock, but the life of the party would quit and call things off at that time. He'd refuse to have anything further to do with it.

If there was quite an element of married people, there'd usually be refreshments. If most of them were young people, they wouldn't think so much of refreshments. Especially if there were older women with marriageable daughters, they'd prepare the refreshments and make it seem as if the daughters had done it, to tempt the young swains with the dainties as well as with the daughters.

Then there was an element that always went — ten to fifteen years old — too bashful to go on the floor and play. They'd sit around, but frequently they'd stay outdoors until dark, then go home. But if they professed culture, they'd sit inside and maybe be called upon if a partner was needed, especially if dressed up. Frequently that element went just in their work clothes, with no intention of playing. They appeared more frequently where the older people appeared also. They brought their babies too.

Then when they had played and perhaps had refreshments and time came to go home, most of them would have made contacts — perhaps a quickly whispered contact made during a game — and the girls would have their escorts. The bolder ones would wait and ask a girl in the presence of others, but they'd rather not.

Once they got outside, the means of conveyance didn't matter. A few of them had buggies. Some came on horseback. Some walked. If a girl had come without an escort and the boy had a horse, he'd lead his horse. They would consider the walk home as the real part of the evening. The play-party was just the preliminary.

Human nature showed itself there like anywhere else. There'd be little tragedies. There might be a wallflower now and then. There might be two swains interested in the same girl, and it would have to be settled then or the next day — at any rate before the next party, because it would have to be decided who was going to take her. Fights were rare. One of the interesting parts of it was that boys and girls might pick cotton all day — if it was in the fall, and fall was the favorite time; in the summer there weren't many — they'd go home and clean up, as they'd say, and get ready to go to the party. Back in the cotton patch the next day they'd yawn and talk about it and feel sophisticated because they'd been up late the night before.

It was very rare that any one drank. The boys would go outside to smoke, and if they did they'd chew gum when they came in so that their

380

breath wouldn't be offensive. Altogether a more cleanly and wholesome social life than the Student Union dance.

I know a life of the party who could tell you much more about what went on — Dr. W. A. Franklin, director of curriculum at Ponca City. If you could get him to reminisce about play-parties, you could get a true picture. The life of the party — if he had black curly hair, his social success was assured. He is just typical of what the life of the party should be, physically and mentally — a good solid character. He was a native of Texas, while I came in from the North, Nebraska, and just got a glimpse of that before I left the community and went to school.

The games were incidental. They were just something to pass away the time — to take the awkwardness off waiting. They were meant to bring the sexes together.

Educational opportunities were so limited, I withdrew myself and read the few papers and books I could find instead of going the rounds of the parties. That was just the time when the buggy went out and the automobile came in. I didn't see very much of that, but I think I got a true picture.

BIBLIOGRAPHY

ABBREVIATIONS

JAFL   *The Journal of American Folk-Lore.*
PTFS *Publications of the Texas Folk-Lore Society.*

I. THE PLAY-PARTY

AMES, MRS. L. D. "The Missouri Play-Party." *JAFL*, 24 (1911): 295-318.
BALL, LEONA NESSLY. "The Play Party in Idaho." *JAFL*, 44 (1931): 1-26.
BLAIR, KATHRYN. "Swing Your Partner." *JAFL*, 40 (1927): 96-99. (Kentucky.)
BOTKIN, B. A. "The Play-Party in Oklahoma." *PTFS*, 7 (1928): 7-24.
COMBS, JOSIAH H. "Songs, Rhymes, and Fragments from Kentucky and West Virginia, 1910-1924" (in MS.).
DOUTHITT, S. W. "Play-Parties in Kentucky." *Letters* (The University of **Kentucky), 3** (1930): 30-38.
DUDLEY, R. E., and PAYNE, L. W., JR. "Some Texas Play-Party Songs." *PTFS*, 1 (1916): 7-34.
GARDNER, EMELYN E. "Some Play-Party Games in Michigan." *JAFL*, 33 (1920): 91-133.
HAMILTON, GOLDY M. "The Play-Party in Northeast Missouri." *JAFL*, 27 (1914): 289-303.
HUDSON, ARTHUR PALMER. *Specimens of Mississippi Folk-Lore* (q.v.), pp. 123-131.
JACOBS, ADAM. "Party Plays." *Theatre Arts Monthly*, 15 (1931): 247-250.
J. B. S. "The Gin-Around." *Godey's Lady's Book and Magazine*, 89 (1874): 61-64.
MAHAN, BRUCE E. and GRAHAME, PAULINE. "Play-Party Games." *The Palimpsest* (The State Historical Society of Iowa), 10 (1929): 33-67.
McNEESE, FLORETTE. "Dance Games of the Frontier" (in MS.). (Including Oklahoma.)
MILLER, G. M. "The Dramatic Element in the Popular Ballad" (q.v.), pp. 30-31.
OWENS, WILLIAM A. "The Play-Party in Texas." *Southwest Review*, 18 (1932-33): 169-178.
———— *Swing and Turn: Texas Play-Party Games.* Dallas: Tardy Publishing Co., 1936. [*Too late to collate.*]
PAYNE, L. W., JR. "Finding List for Texas Play-Party Songs." *PTFS*, 1 (1916): 35-38.
PIPER, EDWIN FORD. "Some Play-Party Games of the Middle West." *JAFL*, 28 (1915): 262-289. (Illinois, Iowa, Kansas, Michigan, Montana, Nebraska.)
RANDOLPH, VANCE. "The Ozark Play-Party." *JAFL*, 42 (1929): 201-232 (also *The Ozarks: An American Survival of Primitive Society* (q.v). Chapter VI).
VAN DOREN, CARL. "Some Play-Party Songs from Eastern Illinois." *JAFL*, 32 (1919): (169) 486-496.
WEDGWOOD, HARRIET L. "The Play-Party." *JAFL*, 25 (1912): 268-273. (Iowa, Nebraska.)
WILSON, CHARLES MORROW. *Backwoods America* (q.v.), Chapter VIII.
WOLFORD, LEAH JACKSON. *The Play-Party in Indiana. Indiana Historical Collections.* Indianapolis: Indiana Historical Commission, 1916.

II. TRADITIONAL GAMES AND NURSERY RHYMES

BABCOCK, W. H. "Games of Washington Children." *American Anthropologist*, 1 (1888): 243-284.
BACKUS, EMMA M. "Song Games from Connecticut." *JAFL*, 14 (1901): 295-299.
BARING-GOULD, S. *A Book of Nursery Songs and Rhymes.* London: Methuen and Co., 1895.
BURCHENAL, ELIZABETH. *Folk Dances and Singing Games.* New York: G. Schirmer, 1909.
CHAMPLIN, JOHN DENISON, and BOSTWICK, ARTHUR E. *The Young Folks' Cyclopaedia of Games and Sports.* New York: Henry Holt and Co., 1890.

CLARKE, MARY OLMSTED. "Song-Games of Negro Children in Virginia." *JAFL*, 3 (1890): 288-290.

CRAMPTON, C. WARD. *The Folk Dance Book.* New York and Chicago: The A. S. Barnes Co., 1909.

CULIN, STEWART. "Street Games of Boys in Brooklyn, N. Y." *JAFL*, 4 (1891): 221-237.

DARBY, LORAINE. "Ring-Games from Georgia." *JAFL*, 30 (1917): 218-221.

DEARMER, PERCY, and SHAW, MARTIN. *Song Time.* London: J. Curwen & Sons, Ltd., 1915.

DOUGLAS, NORMAN. *London Street Games.* London: The St. Catherine Press, 1916.

ELSOM, J. C., and TRILLING, BLANCHE M. *Social Games and Group Dances.* Philadelphia and London: J. B. Lippincott Co., 1919.

"Florida Song Games." *JAFL*, 15 (1902): 193-195.

GOMME, ALICE BERTHA. *The Traditional Games of England, Scotland, and Ireland.* 2 vols. London: David Nutt, 1894-98.

GRAHAM, JOHN. *Traditional Nursery Rhymes.* London: J. Curwen & Sons, Ltd., 1911.

GRAHAME, PAULINE. "School-Day Games." *The Palimpsest* (The State Historical Society of Iowa), 10 (1919): 68-81.

HALLIWELL [—PHILLIPS], JAMES ORCHARD. *The Nursery Rhymes of England. Percy Society Publications, IV.* London: T. Richards, 1842.

—— *Popular Rhymes and Nursery Tales.* London: J. R. Smith, 1849.

HECK, JEAN OLIVE. "Folk Poetry and Folk Criticism, as Illustrated by Cincinnati Children in Their Singing Games and in Their Thought about These Games." *JAFL*, 40 (1927): 1-77.

HENRY, MELLINGER E. "Nursery Rhymes and Game-Songs from Georgia." *JAFL*, 47 (1934): 334-340.

HOFER, MARI RUEF. *Children's Singing Games, Old and New.* Chicago: A. Flanagan & Co., 1901.

HORNBY, JOHN. *The Joyous Book of Singing Games.* New York: The Macmillan Co., 1914.

ISHAM, CADDIE S. "Games of Danville, Va." *JAFL*, 34 (1921): 116-120.

KIDSON, FRANK, and MOFFAT, ALFRED. *Eighty Singing-Games.* London and Glasgow: Bayley & Ferguson, 1907.

MASON, M. H. *Nursery Rhymes and Country Songs.* London: Metzler & Co., Ltd., 1878, 1908.

Mother Goose. London: J. M. Dent & Sons, Ltd.; New York: E. P. Dutton & Co. [n.d.]

NEWELL, WILLIAM WELLS. *Games and Songs of American Children.* New York: Harper & Bros., 1883, 1903.

NEWTON, MARION BROMLEY. *Graded Games and Rhythmic Exercises for Primary Schools.* New York: A. S. Barnes & Co., 1908.

RIMBAULT, EDWARD F. *Nursery Rhymes.* London: Cramer, Wood & Co. [n.d.]

SHARP, CECIL J. *Nursery Songs from the Appalachian Mountains.* 2 vols. London: Novello & Co. [cop. 1921-23]

Social Plays, Games, Marches, Old Folk Dances, and Rhythmic Movements for Use in Indian Schools. Washington: Government Printing Office, 1911.

SPENNEY, SUSAN DIX. "Riddles and Ring-Games from Raleigh, N. C." *JAFL*, 34 (1921): 110-115.

WALTER, L. E. *Old English Singing Games.* London: A. & C. Black, Ltd., 1926.

WIER, ALBERT E. *Songs the Children Love to Sing.* New York and London: D. Appleton & Co., 1916.

III. BALLAD, FOLK-SONG, AND FOLKLORE

ALLEN, WILLIAM FRANCIS, WARE, CHARLES PICKARD, and GARRISON, LUCY McKIM. *Slave Songs of the United States.* New York: A. Simpson & Co., 1867.

ASHTON, JOHN. *Modern Street Ballads.* London: Chatto & Windus, 1888.

Bibliography

BALES, MARY VIRGINIA. "Some Negro Folk-Songs of Texas." *PTFS*, 7 (1928): 85-112.

BARING-GOULD, S., and SHEPPARD, H. FLEETWOOD. *A Garland of Country Song.* London: Methuen & Co., 1895.

BARRY, PHILLIPS. "Some Traditional Songs." *JAFL*, 18 (1905): 49-59.

———— "Traditional Ballads in New England." *JAFL*, 18 (1905): 123-138, 191-214, 291-304.

———— "The Transmission of Folk-Song." *JAFL*, 27 (1914): 67-76.

BARRY, PHILLIPS, ECKSTROM, FANNY HARDY, and SMYTH, MARY WINSLOW. *British Ballads from Maine.* New Haven: Yale University Press, 1929.

BASS, ROBERT DUNCAN. "Negro Songs from the Pedee Country." *JAFL*, 44 (1931): 418-436.

BECKWITH, MARTHA WARREN. "The English Ballad in Jamaica." *Publications of the Modern Language Association of America*, 39 (1924): 455-483.

BELDEN, HENRY MARVIN. "Balladry in America." *JAFL*, 25 (1912): 1-23.

———— *A Partial List of Song Ballads and Other Popular Poetry Known in Missouri.* Columbia: Missouri Folk-Lore Society, 1907, 1910.

BOHME, FRANZ M. *Geschichte des Tanzes in Deutschland.* Leipzig: Breitkopf & Härtel, 1886.

BOLTON, HENRY CARRINGTON. *The Counting-Out Rhymes of Children.* London: Elliot Stock; New York: D. Appleton & Co., 1888.

———— "More Counting-Out Rhymes." *JAFL*, 10 (1897), 313-321.

BOTKIN, B. A., *editor. Folk-Say, A Regional Miscellany: 1930.* Norman: University of Oklahoma Press, 1930.

BRADLEY, WILLIAM ASPENWALL. "Song-Ballets and Devil's Ditties." *Harper's Monthly Magazine*, 130 (1914-15): 901-914.

BRAND, JOHN. *Popular Antiquities of Great Britain.* Edited by W. Carew Hazlitt. London: J. R. Smith, 1870.

BROADWOOD, LUCY E., and FULLER-MAITLAND, J. A. *English County Songs.* London: The Leadenhall Press, Ltd., New York: Charles Scribner's Sons, 1893.

BRYANT, WILLIAM CULLEN. *The Family Library of Poetry and Song.* New York: Fords, Howard, & Hulbert, 1886.

BURCHENAL, ELIZABETH. *American Country-Dances.* New York: G. Schirmer, 1918.

CAMPBELL, OLIVE DAME, and SHARP, CECIL J. *English Folk Songs from the Southern Appalachians.* New York and London: G. P. Putnam's Sons, 1917.

CARTER, ISABEL GORDON. "Some Songs and Ballads from Tennessee and North Carolina." *JAFL*, 46 (1933): 22-50.

CHAMBERS, ROBERT. *Popular Rhymes of Scotland.* Edinburgh: W. & R. Chambers. [1847?]

CHAPPELL, WILLIAM. *Popular Music of the Olden Time.* 2 vols. London: Cramer, Beale, & Chappell, 1859.

CHAPPLE, JOSEPH MITCHELL. *Heart Songs.* Boston: The Chapple Publishing Co., Ltd., 1909.

CHILD, F. J. *The English and Scottish Popular Ballads.* 5 vols. Boston and New York: Houghton Mifflin Co., 1882-1898.

COLCORD, JOANNA C. *Roll and Go, Songs of American Sailormen.* Indianapolis: Bobbs-Merrill Co., 1924.

COMBS, JOSIAH H. "'Cornstalk Fiddle and a Buckeye Bow.'" *Folk-Say, A Regional Miscellany: 1930*, pp. 239-250. Norman: University of Oklahoma Press, 1930.

———— "Dialect of the Folk-Song." *Dialect Notes*, 4 (1916): 311-318.

———— *Folk-Songs du Midi des États-Unis.* Paris: Les Presses Universitaires de France, 1925.

COUCH, W. T., *editor. Culture in the South.* Chapel Hill: The University of North Carolina Press, 1934.

COX, JOHN HARRINGTON. *Folk-Songs of the South.* Cambridge: Harvard University Press. 1925.

CRADDOCK, JOHN R. "The Cowboy Dance." *PTFS*, 2 (1923): 31-37.

DAVIS, ARTHUR KYLE, JR. *Traditional Ballads of Virginia*. Cambridge: Harvard University Press, 1929.

DAVIS, FREDERICK J., and TOZER, FERRIS. *Sailors' Songs or "Chanties."* London and New York: Boosey & Co. [n.d.]

DAVIS, HENRY C. "Negro Folk-Lore in South Carolina." *JAFL*, 27 (1914): 241-254.

DOBIE, J. FRANK. "Ballads and Songs of the Frontier Folk." *PTFS*, 6 (1927): 121-183.

DUNCAN, LELAND L. "Further Notes from County Leitrim." *Folk-Lore*, 5 (1894): 176-210.

EDMANDS, LILA W. "Songs from the Mountains of North Carolina." *JAFL*, 6 (1893): 131-134.

EGGLESTON, EDWARD. *The Circuit Rider*. New York: Charles Scribner's Sons, 1901. [cop. 1878]

FAUSET, ARTHUR HUFF. "Negro Folk Tales from the South (Alabama, Mississippi, Louisiana)." *JAFL*, 40 (1927): 213-303.

———— "Tales and Riddles Collected in Philadelphia." *JAFL*, 41 (1928): 529-557.

FINGER, CHARLES J. *Frontier Ballads*. Garden City: Doubleday, Page & Co., 1927.

FORD, MR. and MRS. HENRY, assisted by MR. and MRS. BENJAMIN B. LOVETT. *"Good Morning."* Dearborn: The Dearborn Publishing Co., 1926.

FORD, ROBERT. *Vagabond Songs and Ballads of Scotland*. Paisley and London: Alexander Gardner, 1904.

GAINES, FRANCIS PENDLETON. *The Southern Plantation*. New York: Columbia University Press, 1925.

GAINES, NEWTON. "Some Characteristics of Cowboy Songs." *PTFS*, 7 (1928): 145-154.

GILCHRIST, ANNIE G. "Note on the 'Lady Drest in Green' and Other Fragments of Tragic Ballads and Folk-Tales Preserved amongst Children." *Journal of the Folk-Song Society*, 6: 80-90.

GOLDBERG, ISAAC. *Tin Pan Alley*. New York: The John Day Co., 1930.

Good Old-Time Songs. See Wehman Bros.' *Good Old-Time Songs*.

HARRIS, JOEL CHANDLER. *Uncle Remus and His Friends*. New York: McKinlay, Stone, and Mackenzie. [c. 1920]

———— *Uncle Remus: His Songs and His Sayings*. New York: D. Appleton and Co., 1921.

HENRY, MELLINGER E. "More Songs from the Southern Highlands." *JAFL*, 44 (1931): 61-115.

HERD, DAVID. *Ancient and Modern Scottish Songs, Heroic Ballads, etc*. Glasgow: Kerr & Richardson, 1869 [reprinted].

HOGUE, WAYMAN. *Back Yonder*. New York: Minton, Balch & Co., 1932.

———— "Ozark People." *Scribner's*, 89 (1931): 509-520.

HOKE, N. C. "Folk-Custom and Folk-Belief in North Carolina." *JAFL*, 5 (1892): 113-120.

HUDSON, ARTHUR PALMER. "Ballads and Songs from Mississippi." *JAFL*, 39 (1936): 93-194.

———— *Folksongs of Mississippi and Their Background*. Chapel Hill: The University of North Carolina Press, 1926. [*Too late to collate.*]

———— "Folk-Songs of the Whites." *Culture in the South*, pp. 519-546. Chapel Hill: The University of North Carolina Press, 1934.

———— *Specimens of Mississippi Folk-Lore*. Ann Arbor: Edwards Bros., 1928 [mimeographed].

The Ideal Home Music Library. Compiled and edited by Albert E. Wier. 10 vols. New York: Charles Scribner's Sons, 1913.

Bibliography

JACKSON, GEORGE PULLEN. *White Spirituals in the Southern Uplands*. Chapel Hill: The University of North Carolina Press, 1933.

JACOBS, JOSEPH. *More English Fairy Tales*. London: D. Nutt, 1894.

JEKYLL, WALTER. *Jamaican Song and Story. Publications of the Folk-Lore Society*, LV. London: David Nutt, 1907.

JOHNSON, CLIFTON. *What They Say in New England*. Boston: Lee and Shepard, 1896.

JOHNSON, GUY B. "Negro Folk-Songs." *Culture in the South*, pp. 547-569. Chapel Hill: The University of North Carolina Press, 1934.

KENNEDY, R. EMMET. Black Cameos. New York: Albert & Charles Boni, 1924.

KEPHART, HORACE. *Our Southern Highlanders*. New York: Outing Publishing Co., 1913.

KITTREDGE, G. L. "Ballads and Rhymes from Kentucky." *JAFL*, 20 (1907): 251-277.

——— "Ballads and Songs." *JAFL*, 30 (1917): 283-369.

LELAND, CHARLES GODFREY. "Children's Rhymes and Incantations." *JAFL*, 2 (1889): 113-116.

LOMAX, JOHN A. *Cowboy Songs, and Other Frontier Ballads*. New York: Sturgis & Walton, 1916; The Macmillan Co., 1918.

LOMAX, JOHN A., and LOMAX, ALAN. *American Ballads and Folk Songs*. New York: The Macmillan Co., 1934.

MACQUOID, G. S. *Jacobite Songs and Ballads*. London: Walter Scott. [1887?]

Marsh's Selection, or Singing for the Million. Three volumes in one. New York: Richard Marsh, 1854.

MILES, EMMA BELL. "Some Real American Music." *Harper's Monthly Magazine*, 109 (1904): 118-123.

MILLER, G. M. "The Dramatic Element in the Popular Ballad." *University of Cincinnati Studies*, Series II, I, 1905.

Minstrel Songs Old and New. Boston: Oliver Ditson & Co. [1882?]

MOONEY, JAMES. "Folk-Lore of the Carolina Mountains." *JAFL*, 2(1889): 95-104.

MOORE, ETHEL PERRY. *An Experiment in Collecting and Classifying the Folk-Songs Sung in Oklahoma* (in MS.). 1926. University of Oklahoma Library.

The Negro Forget-Me-Not Songster. Philadelphia, Baltimore, New York, Boston: Fisher & Brother. [18—?]

NORTHALL, G. F. *English Folk-Rhymes*. London: Kegan Paul, Trench, Trübner & Co., Ltd., 1892.

ODUM, HOWARD W., and JOHNSON, GUY B. *The Negro and His Songs*. Chapel Hill: The University of North Carolina Press, 1925.

——— *Negro Workaday Songs*. Chapel Hill: The University of North Carolina Press, 1926.

OSBORN, MARY ELIZABETH. "Country Dance Calls from the Catskill Mountains." *American Speech*, 3 (1927): 142-145.

PARKER, HAYWOOD. "Folk-Lore of the North Carolina Mountaineers." *JAFL*, 20 (1907): 241-250.

PARSONS, ELSIE CLEWS. "Folk-Lore from Aiken, S. C." *JAFL*, 34 (1921): 1-39.

——— *The Folk-Tales of Andros Island, Bahamas*. Memoirs of the American Folk-Lore Society, XIII. New York: The American Folk-Lore Society, 1918.

——— "Notes on Folk-Lore of Guilford County, North Carolina." *JAFL*, 30 (1917): 201-208.

PASKMAN, DAILY, and SPAETH, SIGMUND. *"Gentlemen, Be Seated!"* Garden City: Doubleday, Doran & Co., Inc., 1928.

PAYNE, L. W., JR. "Some Texas Versions of 'The Frog's Courting.'" *PTFS*, 5 (1926): 5-48.

PERROW, E. C. "Songs and Rhymes from the South." *JAFL*, 25 (1912): 137-155; 26 (1913): 123-173; 28 (1915): 129-190.

PIPER, EDWIN FORD. "Quadrille Calls." *American Speech*, 1 (1926): 391-395.

POUND, LOUISE. *American Ballads and Songs*. New York: Charles Scribner's Sons, 1922.

———— *Folk-Song of Nebraska and the Central West: A Syllabus. Nebraska Academy of Sciences Publications,* IX, 3, 1913.

———— "Oral Literature." *The Cambridge History of American Literature,* IV, pp. 502-516. New York: G. P. Putnam's Sons, 1921.

———— *Poetic Origins and the Ballad.* New York: The Macmillan Co., 1921.

———— "A Recent Theory of Ballad-Making." *Publications of the Modern Language Association of America,* 44 (1929): 622-630.

———— "The Term 'Communal.' " *Publications of the Modern Language Association of America,* 39 (1924): 440-454.

———— "Traditional Ballads in Nebraska." *JAFL,* 26 (1913): 351-366.

RAINE, JAMES WATT. *The Land of Saddle-Bags.* New York: The Council of Women for Home Missions and Missionary Education Movement of the United States and Canada. [cop. 1924]

RANDOLPH, VANCE. *The Ozarks: An American Survival of Primitive Society.* New York: The Vanguard Press, 1931.

RICHARDSON, ETHEL PARK, and SPAETH, SIGMUND. *American Mountain Songs.* New York: Greenberg, Publisher, 1927.

RIGGS, LYNN. *Big Lake.* New York: Samuel French, 1927.

RORIE, DAVID. "Stray Notes on the Folk-Lore of Aberdeenshire and the North-East of Scotland." *Folk-Lore,* 25 (1914): 342-363.

ROURKE, CONSTANCE. *American* Humor. New York: Harcourt, Brace and Co., 1931.

———— *Davy Crockett.* New York: Harcourt, Brace & Co., 1934.

SANDBURG, CARL. *The American Songbag.* New York: Harcourt, Brace & Co., 1927.

SARGENT, HELEN CHILD, and KITTREDGE, G. L. *English and Scottish Popular Ballads,* Boston and New York: Houghton, Mifflin Co., 1914.

SCARBOROUGH, DOROTHY. *On the Trail of Negro Folk-Songs.* Cambridge: Harvard University Press, 1925.

SCHELE DE VERE, M. *Americanisms; The English of the New World.* New York: Charles Scribner & Co., 1872.

SCOTT, ROY S. "The Cowboy Dance of the Northwest." *PTFS,* 4 (1925): 53-58.

SHARP, CECIL J. *English Folk-Chanteys.* London: Simpkin, Marshall, Hamilton, Kent & Co., Ltd., 1914.

———— *English Folk Songs.* 2 vols. London: Novello & Co., 1920.

———— *Folk-Songs from Somerset.* London: Novello & Co., Ltd.; New York: The H. W. Gray Co., 1908.

———— *One Hundred English Folksongs.* Boston: Oliver Ditson Co., 1916.

———— *The Sword Dances of Northern England.* London: Novello & Co., Ltd., New York: The H. W. Gray Co. [1912-13]

SHAY, FRANK. *Drawn from the Wood.* New York: The Macaulay Co., 1929.

———— *My Pious Friends and Drunken Companions.* New York: The Macaulay Co., 1927.

SHEARIN, HUBERT G., and COMBS, JOSIAH H. *A Syllabus of Kentucky Folk-Songs. Transylvania University Studies in English,* II. Lexington: Transylvania Printing Co., 1911.

SHOEMAKER, HENRY W. *North Pennsylvania Minstrelsy.* Altoona: Altoona Tribune Co., 1919.

SMILEY, PORTIA. "Folk-Lore from Virginia, South Carolina, Georgia, Alabama, and Florida." *JAFL,* 32 (1919): 357-383.

SMITH, L. L. *Old Time Dance Calls.* Northboro, Ia. [n.d.]

SMITH, REED. *South Carolina Ballads.* Cambridge: Harvard University Press, 1928.

———— "The Traditional Ballad in the South." *JAFL,* 27 (1914): 55-66.

SPAETH, SIGMUND. *Read 'Em and Weep.* Garden City: Doubleday, Page & Co., 1927.

———— *Weep Some More, My Lady.* Garden City: Doubleday, Page & Co., 1927.

STANARD, MARY NEWTON. *Colonial Virginia, Its People and Customs.* Philadelphia and London: J. B. Lippincott Co., 1917.

Bibliography

SULLIVAN, MARK. *Our Times*, II. New York: Charles Scribner's Sons, 1927.

TALLEY, THOMAS W. *Negro Folk Rhymes*. New York: The Macmillan Co., 1922.

TAYLOR, ARCHER. "The English, Scottish, and American Versions of the 'Twa Sisters.'" *JAFL*, 42 (1929): 238-246.

TERRY, RICHARD RUNCIMAN. *The Shanty Book*. Part I. London: J. Curwen & Sons, Ltd., 1921.

THOMAS, GATES. "South Texas Negro Work-Songs: Collected and Uncollected." *PTFS*, 5 (1926): 154-180.

THOMAS, JEAN. *Devil's Ditties*. Chicago: W. Wilbur Hatfield, 1931.

THORNTON, RICHARD H. *An American Glossary*. 2 vols. Philadelphia and London: J. B. Lippincott Co., 1912.

TOLMAN, ALBERT H., and EDDY, MARY O. "Traditional Texts and Tunes." *JAFL*, 36 (1922): 335-432.

TRUITT, FLORENCE. "Songs from Kentucky." *JAFL*, 36 (1923): 376-379.

UDAL, JOHN SYMONDS. *Dorsetshire Folk-Lore*. Hertford: Stephen Austin & Sons, Ltd., 1922.

The Universal Songster; or, Museum of Mirth. 3 vols. London: Jones & Co. [1825-27]

WEBB, W. PRESCOTT. "Notes on Folk-Lore of Texas." *JAFL*, 28 (1914): 290-299.

Wehman Bros.' Good Old-Time Songs. Nos. 1, 2, 3. New York: Wehman Bros. [cop. 1910, 19—?, 1914]

WHITE, NEWMAN I. *American Negro Folk-Songs*. Cambridge: Harvard University Press, 1928.

WILSON, CHARLES MORROW. *Backwoods America*. Chapel Hill: The University of North Carolina Press, 1935.

YOUNG, DELLA I. "The Pioneer Dance." *Folk-Say, A Regional Miscellany: 1930*, pp. 253-265. Norman: University of Oklahoma Press, 1930.

INDEX TO PART ONE

1. AUTHORITIES

(Not including citations of texts)

2. SUBJECTS

3. TITLES

(Including citations of words, lines, stanzas, and other mention)

INDEX TO PART TWO

1. TITLES

(Not including variants)

2. TUNES

3. FIRST LINES

(Not including variants)

Index

399